TRAVEL✦SMART®
PACIFIC NORTHWEST

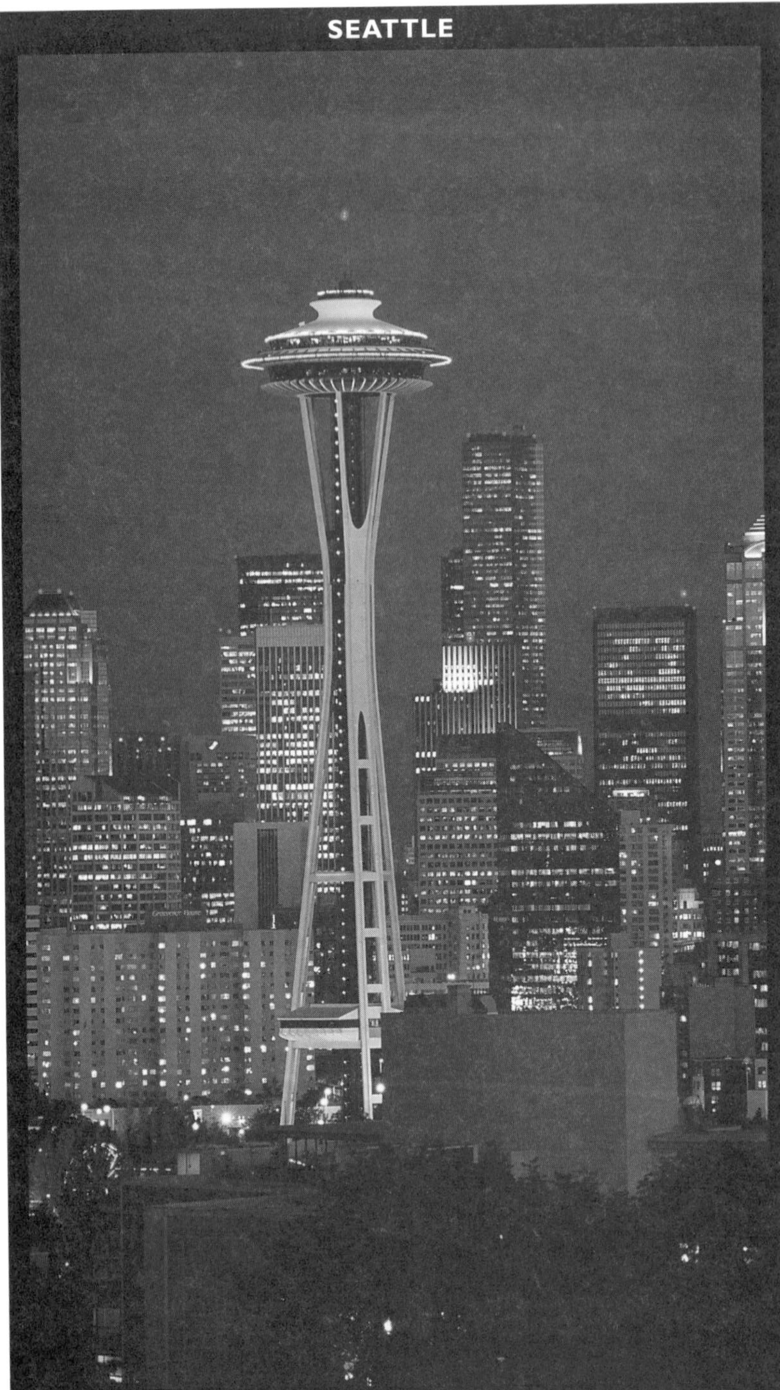

John Elk III

Karlee Kraehn Drake
&
David Drake
7/2001

TRAVEL SMART®

PACIFIC NORTHWEST

Third Edition

Jena MacPherson

TRAVEL✦SMART: PACIFIC NORTHWEST

3rd EDITION

Jena MacPherson

Published by
Avalon Travel Publishing
5855 Beaudry St.
Emeryville, CA 94608, USA
Printing History
3rd edition— January 2001
5 4 3 2 1

Please send all comments, corrections, additions, amendments, and critiques to:

TRAVEL✦SMART
PACIFIC NORTHWEST
AVALON TRAVEL PUBLISHING
5855 BEAUDRY ST.
EMERYVILLE, CA 94608, USA
e-mail: info@travelmatters.com
www.travelmatters.com

ISBN: 1-56691-248-2
ISSN: Pending

Editors: Gregor Krause, Suzanne Samuel
Index: Grace Fujimoto
Graphics Coordinator: Erika Howsare
Production: Marie J.T. Vigil, Darren Alessi
Design: Marie J.T. Vigil
Cover Design: Janine Lehmann
Cartography: Kathy Sparkes, Mike Morgenfeld
Map Editor: Mike Ferguson

Front cover photos: large—© John Elk III (Bend)
small—© John Elk III (Seattle)
Back cover photo: © John Elk III (covered bridge, Applegate Valley)

Distributed in the United States and Canada by Publishers Group West
Printed in the United States by R.R. Donnelley

TRAVEL SMART: PACIFIC NORTHWEST A GUIDE THAT GUIDES

Most guidebooks are primarily directories, providing information but very little help in making choices—you have to guess how to make the most of your time and money. *Travel Smart: Pacific Northwest* is different: By highlighting the very best of the region and offering various planning features, it acts like a personal tour guide rather than a directory.

TAKE THE STRESS OUT OF TRAVEL

Sometimes traveling causes more stress than it relieves. Sorting through information, figuring out the best routes, determining what to see and where to eat and stay, scheduling each day—all of this can make a vacation feel daunting rather than fun. Relax. We've done a lot of the legwork for you. This book will help you plan a trip that suits you—whatever your time frame, budget, and interests.

SEE THE BEST OF THE REGION

Author Jena MacPherson is a born and bred Northwesterner. She has handpicked every listing in this book, and she gives you an insider's perspective on what makes each one worthwhile. So while you will find many of the big tourist attractions listed here, you'll also find lots of smaller, lesser-known treasures, such as the inspiring Mt. Angel Abbey south of Portland or the funky Nutcracker Museum in Leavenworth, Washington. And each sight is described so you'll know what's most—and sometimes least—interesting about it.

In selecting the restaurants and accommodations for this book, the author sought out unusual spots with local flavor. While in some areas of the region chains are unavoidable, wherever possible the author directs you to one-of-a-kind places. We also know that you want a range of options: one day you may crave oysters on the half shell, while the next day you would be just as happy (as would your wallet) with Chinese dim sum. Most of the restaurants and accommodations listed here are moderately priced, but the author also includes budget and splurge options, depending on the destination.

CREATE THE TRIP YOU WANT

We all have different travel styles. Some people like spontaneous weekend jaunts, while others plan longer, more leisurely trips. You may want to cover as much ground as possible, no matter how much time you have. Or maybe you prefer to focus your trip on one part of the region or on some special interest, such as history, nature, or the outdoors. We've taken these differences into account.

Though the individual chapters stand on their own, they are organized in a geographically logical sequence, so that you could conceivably fly into Portland or Seattle, drive chapter by chapter to each destination in the book, and end up close to where you started. Of course, you don't have to follow that sequence, but it's there if you want a complete picture of the region.

Each destination chapter offers ways of prioritizing when time is limited: In the Perfect Day section, the author suggests what to do if you have only one day to spend in the area. Also, every Sightseeing Highlight is rated, from one to four stars:

★★★★ must see
★★★ highly recommended
★★ worthwhile
★ see if you have time

At the end of each sight listing is a time recommendation in parentheses. User-friendly maps help you locate the sights, restaurants, and lodging of your choice.

And if you're in it for the ride, so to speak, you'll want to check out the Scenic Routes described at the end of several chapters. They take you through some of the most scenic parts of the region.

In addition to these special features, the appendix has other useful travel tools:

- The Mileage Chart and Planning Map help you determine your own route and calculate travel time.
- The Special Interest Tours show you how to design your trip around any of six favorite interests.
- The Calendar of Events provides an at-a-glance view of when and where major events occur throughout the state.
- The Resources tell you where to go for more information about national and state parks, individual cities and counties, bed-and-breakfasts, and more.

HAPPY TRAVELS

With this book in hand, you have many reliable recommendations and travel tools at your fingertips. Use it to make the most of your trip. And have a great time!

WHY VISIT THE PACIFIC NORTHWEST?

The Pacific Northwest is home to Microsoft and Starbucks, Boeing and Nike, the Dawgs and the Ducks, the venerated Oregon Shakespeare Festival, Seattle's amazing new Experience Music Project—and much, much more.

Whether you come in summer to cruise the San Juan Islands, hike the West Coast Trail, or golf the plethora of courses around Bend; or in winter to cross-country ski around the Bavarian-style village of Leavenworth, snowboard the slopes of Mt. Hood, or spend a Dickensian Christmas eating plum pudding and sipping tea in Victoria, you'll find a richly complex region with diverse arts, ethnic groups, landscapes, and options that excite the imagination. This is, after all, where cultures as ancient as the legend-rich native peoples, and as forward-looking as Bill Gates's software universe, merge.

Yes, it rains here. That's why much of the region is a delicious, emerald green. And why storm-watching is a favorite wintertime sport. Yes, you might face congested roads or long ferry lines to reach the gem destinations dotting the thousands of miles of saltwater coastline. That's what keeps those spots quiet and delightfully low-key much of the year.

These few drawbacks are simple reminders that here Nature rules. Strictures of weather and terrain are part of the trade-off for a vast, masterful blueprint that melds forests, waters, mountains, deserts, volcanoes, and creatures—from eagles to orcas—in a vital, awe-inspiring way. Bona fide Northwesterners, be they transplants or natives, happily adjust. Besides, if it gets too

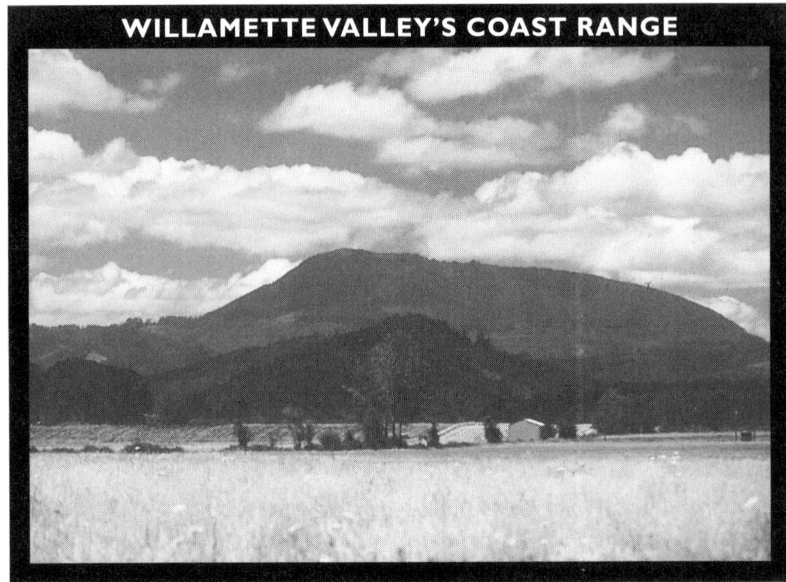
WILLAMETTE VALLEY'S COAST RANGE

Corvallis CVB

wet or crowded on the coastal side of the region, you can always head east to the dry, less populated side. And if you really don't want to wait in a ferry line, you can hop a floatplane to your waterfront destination and arrive in minutes rather than hours. There are choices.

Oregon, Washington, and British Columbia have plenty of them. They also have more in common than their coastal connection and the watery swath of the mighty Columbia River. Erase the international boundary and you'll find a cohesive region where breathtaking mountains, crisscrossed with trails, rise high in the Cascade and Coast Ranges. You'll find a region where fishing villages lie on saltwater bays and elaborate wineries perfume fertile, produce-rich valleys. The bounty of all this inspires the work of talented chefs and provides succulent menu choices in the grandest restaurants or the simplest cafés.

And last, but perhaps most important, you'll find people, born here or drawn here from many other parts of the world, who love this place passionately.

So, naturally, come visit. But be forewarned. There's so much to see that even those of us who've been here all our lives—and try to see and experience everything we can—can't see it all. The following chapters and special interest tours in the appendix will help you plan your trip and choose the best from all that's here.

LAY OF THE LAND

Surprise. A preponderance of mountains and evergreens is what you'll notice most about the Northwest, especially if you fly into Portland past Mt. Hood, into Seattle by Mt. Rainier, or into Vancouver with Mt. Baker and Grouse Mountain in sight. Two ranges, the Coast Range in British Columbia and the Cascades (divided into the North and South Cascades) in Washington and Oregon, dominate. Other ranges include the impressive Olympic Mountains and Oregon Coast Range and the Blue Mountains.

The Puget/Willamette Trough separates the two major coastal mountain chains. It's made up of the Hecate Strait and the Strait of Georgia in British Columbia; Puget Sound in Washington; the Chehalis and Cowlitz River valleys in Washington; and the Willamette River in Oregon. Coastline and waterways dominate our way of life in this part of the Northwest. Lush temperate rain forests cloak the western side of the region. By contrast, the interior is a desert plateau, a basin of sometimes harsh and haunting landscape. And yet here, too, water—especially the Columbia River—has its impact.

With one side of the region very wet and one very dry, the yin and yang quality of the Northwest is underscored. Despite its extreme differences, or perhaps because of them, there is harmony, there is balance here.

FLORA AND FAUNA

From sea kelp and tidepool critters to high mountain wildflowers and eagles, the nature lover has plenty to see. There are rain forests draped with moss and wetlands crowded with birds, verdant sedge-rich deltas and sagebrush-dotted high deserts. The mix of climate and soils here makes this the best place in the world for conifers to grow. And fortunes as well as houses have been built with Douglas fir, cedar, and pine. So many, in fact, that there are few old-growth trees left, and certain ones, like those in Campbell Grove near Lake Quinault Lodge on the Olympic Peninsula, have become tourist destinations in themselves. In spring, showy rhododendrons fill home and public gardens alike. In fall, decidious maple trees and blueberry bushes turn the dark green forests brilliant red and gold, and the highways near spots like Tumwater Canyon outside Leavenworth in Washington's Cascades become thick with leaf-lookers.

HISTORY AND CULTURES

The first people to come to the Northwest walked across a bridge of land from Siberia when the continents were connected north of the Bering Strait. And that was thousands and thousands of years ago. They survived the Ice Age and the volcanic turmoil of the region. They thrived on fish, berries, and roots, made utensils of shells, wove baskets of bark and reeds, and built shelters and canoes of wood. They worshipped the mountains, the creatures, and the bounty of the land and passed on their history and values in their legends. While there were many tribes, there were basically two groups: those who lived in relatively stable communities along the rivers and shores west of the Cascade Mountains and were a fishing people; and those of the interior plateau, who adopted use of the horse and were more nomadic like the Plains tribes. The largest group in the region lived along the coast.

Signs of the native peoples—now commonly referred to as Native Americans in the States and First Peoples or First Nation in Canada—are visible all over the Northwest. You'll see totem poles of the Northwest coast peoples pointing toward the heavens in wilderness areas and cities of the coastal regions, particularly of British Columbia. The whole town of Duncan, on Vancouver Island, is an outdoor museum to the totem pole; at the excellent Cowichan Native Village, you can often see totem carvers at work, as well as knitters making the prized Cowichan sweaters. British settlers taught the Cowichans to knit their fisherman-style sweater in one piece, and over time the knitters added designs, like animals or snowflakes, to individualize the natural, rustic, and very warm garments. You'll see teepees, signs of the lifestyle of the interior plateau peoples, at the Yakama and Warm Springs Reservations. Visitors can camp in these native-style dwellings on both reservations.

There are noted collections of art and artifacts not to be missed by the serious student, especially at the Museum at Warm Springs Reservation in Oregon, the University of British Columbia's Museum of Anthropology in Vancouver, and the Royal B.C. Museum in Victoria. There are also outstanding tribal heritage centers on reservations, like those of the Makah at the northwest tip of the Olympic Peninsula and the Yakama in eastern Washington. And there are many other displays, exhibits, galleries, and events around the region, some of which are mentioned in upcoming pages. You'll also see the modern gaming casinos of the tribes, which range from modest structures to very elaborate complexes with restaurants and art stores.

While the native peoples revere traditions, they are very much of the modern world. Examples of this are the brightly colored lithographs, artwork, and innovative glass work you will see. One of the most stunning examples of modern native art is the Spirit of Haida Gwaii, by the late Canadian artist Bill Reid. The sculpture of a large canoe is filled with legendary creatures of Haida mythology more often found on totems—Raven, Eagle, Grizzly, Mouse Woman, Beaver, Frog, and Wolf. It is located in the new Vancouver International Airport, and it's worth a trip whether you are flying or not. Books of all sorts have been

CASCADIA—A BORDERLESS REGION

"Cascadia" is used to describe the areas covered within this book of Oregon, Washington, and southwestern British Columbia, areas spanned by the Cascade mountain range, a verdant expanse of forests and water. Seismologists use the term to identify the portion of North America that lies between Cape Mendocino, in northwestern California, and the southernmost tip of the Queen Charlotte Islands just off Canada's west coast.

However, the word was first found in the 1823 to 1827 journals of botanist David Douglas, who is thought to have used it because of the waterfalls found in the Columbia River Gorge, especially impressive Multnomah Falls. This first use seems most fitting, for magnificant falls dot the region—Silver Falls in the Willamette Valley, Salish Falls near Seattle, and Shannon Falls on the road to Whistler—all easily accessed and well worth a stop.

written about the history of the Northwest's native peoples and their totems, masks, basketry, fishing, customs, and legends. See "Recommended Reading" on page 16.

While the native people's heritage goes back centuries, white settlement came recently—in the last few hundred years. In 1778 British captain James Cook explored the coast of what is now Oregon, Washington, and British Columbia. Captain George Vancouver charted Puget Sound in 1792, and that same year the American captain Robert Gray arrived at the mouth of the Columbia River and named the river after his ship. In 1803 Lewis and Clark charted the way west, opening it for thousands to follow along the Oregon Trail. Then gold had its impact on many communities. The Fraser Canyon Gold Rush brought droves of miners north from the fields of California in the 1850s as well as from other parts of the globe, and the Klondike Gold Rush of the late 1890s made wealthy merchants out of Seattle provisioners and set the community on a road of future growth and prosperity.

The Chinese who labored on the railroads and in the fishing industry established residential and commerical districts in Vancouver, Victoria, Seattle, and Portland; most still thrive. You can still see the homes of wealthy English sea captains and merchants built in the oldest Oregon and Washington seaports

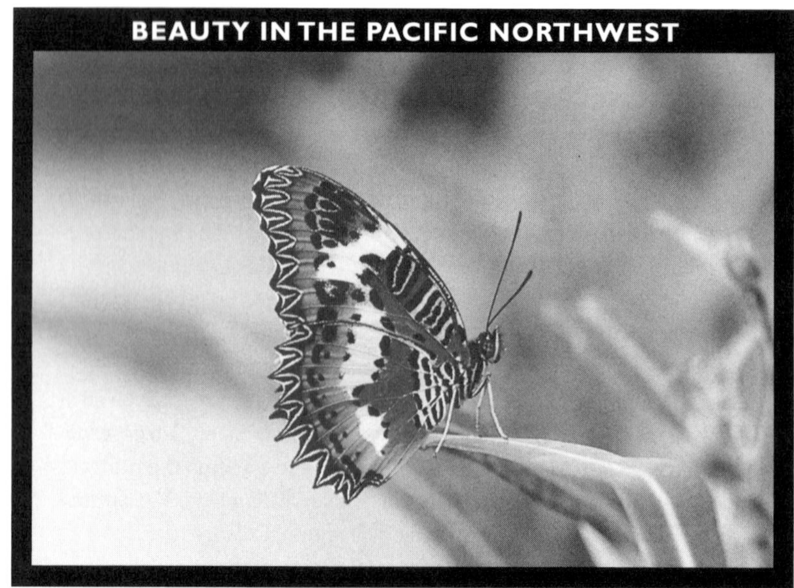

Crystal Garden

of Astoria and Coupeville; and the influences of Scandinavians who settled the fishing village of Poulsbo on the Kitsap Peninsula west of Seattle. Dutch dairy farmers settled Ferndale and Lynden in northwest Washington; Scots came to farm the Willamette Valley, bringing names like Dundee to their new settlements; the Basques brought sheep and their cuisine to eastern Oregon. All imprinted their cultures on the region. There are the more recent migrations—the Japanese who brought their horticulture techniques, the Hispanics who arrived in the 1930s and '40s and worked the newly irrigated fields of the interior, and prosperous Chinese from Hong Kong into Vancouver and other parts of British Columbia. These examples don't encompass everyone, but they certainly show the rich ethnic diversity here.

And then there's the modern-day culture creature produced by the region itself: the quintessential Northwesterner. Here's a thumbnail sketch. He or she has at least one pair of hiking boots and a knapsack (from REI), fishing gear in the closet, well-worn gardening gloves, a favorite neighborhood restaurant hangout (too many to list), stacks of books around the house from a favorite bookstore (Powell's in Portland, Elliott Bay in Seattle, Munro's in Victoria, or Duthie's in Vancouver), and a four-wheel-drive vehicle. He or she owns or is friends with someone who owns a sail- or motorboat. And despite all this outdoorsy stuff, there could be formal wear in the closet for arts and philanthropic functions. The best kind of Northwesterner is a renaissance person making the most of this renaissance region.

THE ARTS

Music, dance, theater, and the visual arts thrive in this environment of natural beauty. Special museums—the Seattle Art Museum, designed by Robert Venturi; the Vancouver Art Gallery with its collection of Emily Carr paintings; unique Maryhill Museum, overlooking the Columbia River with its unexpected Auguste Rodin sculptures; and the Northwest Museum in LaConner, Washington, focusing on Northwest School artists Mark Tobey, Morris Graves, and others—all contribute to the rich fabric of the region. Notable Northwest artists include glass artist Dale Chihuly of Tacoma, whose work is exhibited all over the world, including the Louvre. The new International Glass Museum, opened in 2000 in his hometown, showcases his art.

Besides glass, a lesser known specialty of the region is the work of Northwest woodcrafters. It is considered some of the finest in the world. In woodworking galleries in Portland, Seattle, and smaller towns, you will see one-of-a-kind pieces crafted primarily from maple, walnut, and cherry. Styles spring from classics like Shaker, Craftsman, Asian, and Scandinavian furniture, or are a product of the artist's vision, like sculpted figures or organically designed shapes. The Northwest Gallery of Fine Woodworking, a Seattle area cooperative, is considered to be the most successful cooperative in the country, exhibiting such artisans as David Gray, Judith Ames, Hank Holzer, Michael Peterson, and Thomas Stangeland, to name a few of the hundred or so Northwest craftsmen who exhibit here and elsewhere.

There are also excellent painters, potters, and artisans. Many gravitate to small towns along the Oregon coast, to central Oregon around Bend, or to Puget Sound, the San Juans, and the Gulf Islands. You will find galleries and evidence of the artists' work (and open houses or art tours at different times of the year) when you visit these areas. Granville Island is unique in that it is a whole community of top craftsmen and artisans' studios, along with the prestigious Emily Carr Institute of Art and Design, in the midst of urban Vancouver, British Columbia. Another surprise is the eastern Oregon town of Joseph, where three foundries make bronze and other metal sculptures for patrons around the world.

Live theater is also dynamic—perhaps in Seattle most of all, but also in Vancouver, Tacoma, Portland, and Ashland (home to the Oregon Shakespeare Festival). And there are many community theaters. There are dance companies here—like the Pacific Northwest Ballet in Seattle—and music of all kinds.

CUISINE

So much food, too little time. You won't believe all the wonderful food experiences to be had in the Northwest! You'll just have to taste-test for yourself. Food folks debate the issue of whether or not there is a "Northwest Cuisine." There is. In my view, it's based on bountiful seafood, fresh (often organic) produce, simplicity, and preparations that include specialties of the region—like salmon, Dungeness crab, mushrooms, and Walla Walla sweet onions. Asian overtones are common. For years running, the Wild Ginger restaurant, near Pike Place Market in Seattle, with its satay bar and creative Pan-Asian menu, has topped the list of favorites for locals and visitors alike. And Vancouver's food scene, recently enriched with an infusion of talented chefs from Hong Kong, makes Chinese food a must-have on any visit. In Northwest cities and increasingly in rural areas there's a rich pool of culinary talent and a growing variety of restaurants. Your only problem will be deciding what kind of food you want to experience.

To get the best the region has to offer, here are some hints. Be prepared to indulge yourself in seafood. The salmon, prepared simply for centuries over outdoor fires, is still best grilled, although most restaurants offer it poached or baked as well. Dungeness crab is sweet and succulent and with a little butter, heavenly; Penn Cove mussels in a simple garlic wine broth (for dipping crusty bread) can often be found in haute cuisine restaurants and on modest bar menus. Then there's the mysterious and strange-looking geoduck (pronounced "gooey duck")—if you see it on the menu, try it. Do you like its surprising sweetness? Ditto on the elusive razor clams, which are usually breaded and lightly sautéed. Their season is random and short so try them when you can. And finally, oysters—dozens of varieties ranging from sweet tiny Olympias to earthy European Flats—are all raised in waters that are cool and remarkably clean. There are plenty of oyster bars (you'll find the most in Seattle) where they are shucked fresh and served with regional microbrews (Portland is the capital of brews) and wines (see the Wine Regions Tour on page 280). Note, too, that seafood vendors will often ship their product around the country; Pike Place Market fishmongers are known for this.

Then consider menu choices that include other regional classics. The cheeses: Oregon blue, Bandon's cheddar, Tillamook Vintage Reserve (white and gold cheddars), Cougar Gold—that scrumptious, nutty white cheddar–like cheese produced by Washington State University's creamery—and the handcrafted goat or sheep cheese made by artisans like Sally Jackson in Washington and David Wood of Saltspring Island. The specialty produce: hazelnuts from the Willamette Valley, lamb from Ellensburg in central Washington, and salmon candy and farmed venison in British Columbia.

The fruit? Washington apples, Rainier cherries, pears from the Hood River Valley, peaches from British Columbia's Okanagan Valley, grapes from the Yakima and Columbia Valleys, cranberries from coastal bogs, and other berries from lush growing areas all over, abound. To get the best of the region, ask your server, "What's fresh? What's in season?"

OUTDOOR ACTIVITIES

If you don't bring your hiking boots to hit a trail, or plan to paddle a boat, or explore the backcountry of the region, you're missing the true personality of the Northwest. Skiing, snowboarding, and windsurfing—particularly on the Columbia Gorge and Howe Sound in British Columbia—are more vigorous options that offer devotees some peak experiences. Kayaking the Cascadia Marine Trail (a 150-plus-mile route from South Puget Sound to Canada), is growing in popularity as more camping sites are established along the way. Bicycling (or mopeding in the San Juans) is a perfect way to explore the islands here. A visit to the Kite Flying Museum at Long Beach, Washington, may draw you into a sport that attracts thousands to the Kite Flying Festival there each summer. Or you may opt for a ride in a rainbow-colored hot air balloon over the vineyards of the Northwest.

Government facilities throughout the region—state and provincial park offices, National Park Service and Forest Service offices—provide maps and valuable tips and information. If the outdoors is a new world for you, Recreational Equipment, Inc. (REI), a cooperative with stores around the country, has long been the place to get outdoor information and gear and to connect with knowledgeable people. Their impressive flagship store in Seattle, with biking trails and an indoor rock climbing facility, is an easy, one-stop way to explore outdoor options and learn of classes, programs, or tours.

And, finally, there's gardening. It may be the most common outdoor activity in the Northwest. Public gardens, seed and bulb growers, and terrific nurseries are scattered around the region. Victoria's Butchart Garden and the International Rose Test Garden in Portland may be the most famous, but there are many others, including estate gardens, like Lakewold in Tacoma and the Bloedell Reserve on Bainbridge Island, that are open to the public. Large bulb-growing areas lie near Salem, Oregon, for iris, dahlia, and tulip bulbs, and near Mt. Vernon and LaConner, Washington, for tulip and daffodil bulbs. Each year in February, thousands of garden fanciers descend upon the impressive Pacific Northwest Flower and Garden Show at Seattle's Washington State Convention Center.

PLANNING YOUR TRIP

Before you set out on your trip, you'll need to do some planning. Use this chapter in conjunction with the tools in the appendix to answer some basic questions. First of all, when are you going? You may already have specific dates in mind; if not, various factors will probably influence your timing. Either way, you'll want to know about local events, the weather, and other seasonal considerations. This chapter discusses all of that.

How much should you expect to spend on your trip? This chapter addresses various regional factors you'll want to consider in estimating your travel expenses. How will you get around? Check out the section on local transportation. If you decide to travel by car, the Planning Map and Mileage Chart in the appendix can help you figure out exact routes and driving times, while the Special Interest Tours provide several focused itineraries. The chapter concludes with some reading recommendations to give you various perspectives on the region. If you want specific information about individual cities or counties, use the Resource Guide in the appendix.

HOW MUCH WILL IT COST?

Nice hotel rooms in Portland, Seattle, and Vancouver average around $150 per night. Luxury hotels cost more, as do fancy B&Bs. Many B&Bs offer less expensive rooms (often with a shared bath) and of course include breakfast. Choosing hotel packages or off-season times to visit can considerably reduce costs. Many chain or budget choices are well located in all three areas. Your dollar may stretch further in British Columbia as the exchange rate at publication time is about $1.40 Canadian for $1 U.S. However, in British Columbia expect to pay goods and services tax (GST), which will be reimbursed at border offices. There is no sales tax in Oregon. In Washington it's about 8.6 percent but varies by county.

Summer camping cuts costs, and there are hostels as well, or you can choose to stay in suburban areas with chain lodging, rather than in pricier urban areas. You can also save by coming off season. Vancouver has its Entertainment Season from October to April, when hotels offer better rates, and Seattle has its Super Saver season about the same time. Many fine city and resort hotels have weekend packages that offer extra value. Food is available in a wide range of prices. Thai, Mexican, Japanese, and Chinese restaurants offer good value for families. Inexpensive quick meals can be had at food fairs in city shopping malls.

A LOOK AT LODGING

Remember I mentioned that the Northwest is full of choices? Well, when it comes to sleeping and eating, that goes double, and it's worth extra comment. My favorites are the special places that have unique qualities all their own while reflecting the region as well. When it comes to "best sleeps" they range from mountaintop camps, where your mattress is heather and your fellow travelers may be marmots and eagles, to posh grand hotels with turndown service, chocolates, and a down pillow to sink into at the end of the day.

For generations, the Benson in Portland, the Olympic Four Seasons in Seattle, the Hotel Vancouver, and the Empress in Victoria have hosted the world's traveling elite and provided meeting spots for their communities' memorable moments. Thankfully, these grand hotels have been carefully updated or renovated so that much of their original glory is intact. Some of their restaurants and watering holes are legendary—the London Grill (Benson), the Georgian Room (Olympic), the Bengal Room (Empress)—and lend a sense of "occasion" to simply meeting a friend for drinks. Although new in 1989, the scale and presence of the Chateau Whistler will soon put it in this category. There are also individualized inns and properties that have a "grand" reputation. Sooke Harbor House, west of Victoria, has been called one of the world's best B&Bs. And Salishan Lodge on the Oregon Coast wins awards and the affection of a legion of guests. I also have a great fondness for the region's genteel "secret" hotels—those stalwarts that may have dated furnishings but are always booked because generations of families return again and again appreciating the location, value, and convenience: the Mallory in Portland, the Camlin in Seattle, the Sylvia overlooking English Bay in Vancouver.

Camping options abound. There are many beautiful and amenity-rich state, national, and provincial parks with a variety of options ranging from drive-in, numbered sites with RV hookups, showers, bathrooms, and picnic tables nearby, to more spartan sites for backpackers. Some of the prettiest spots are along the Oregon, Washington, and British Columbia coastlines and in the Cascade Mountains. Costs average $10 per night; reservations are often required, and trail passes are required for hikers. Then, in Washington, there are the more primitive Department of Natural Resources (DNR) sites where you must pack in your water, pack out your garbage, and leave the site as if you had never been there. These sites offer unique remote wilderness experiences at no cost. New yurt tent camps offered in Oregon and Washington by reservation—many at beach sites—let you camp without taking along a lot of gear.

A very special type of camping is offered along the the Cascadia Marine Trail, an award-winning water route for kayaks, canoes, and other beachable wind- or human-powered craft. It runs from the south end of Puget Sound to the Canadian border (with plans to extend into Canada). There are more than 40 sites along the current 140-mile route, and many are quite primitive.

CLIMATE

We've agreed that it rains here. But that's only half true. In the Northwest, it rains most on the coastal, temperate side of the region, particularly in winter. Summer temperatures on the coastal side average in the 70s; very hot weather is a rarity. The interior, eastern side of the region is dry, with extremes of temperature, and most of the precipitation comes in the form of snow. Winter temperatures slip into the teens, and summer highs can top 100 degrees Fahrenheit. All the mountains and valleys combine to produce weather patterns and result in sometimes quirky and unexpected climate differences. The Hoh Rain Forest on the Olympic Peninsula is the wettest place in Washington; nearby Sequim, a popular and growing area for retirees, is the driest spot west of the mountains. It rains more in Vancouver than in Seattle and Portland.

WHEN TO GO

What's your pleasure? Summer or winter activities? The Northwest is a year-round destination. July is the busiest month for the ferry system, and with the odds high for good weather you can encounter hordes of summer travelers in the most popular haunts. July and August are the hottest months in the region's interior; consistent temperatures in the 90s are not uncommon. These are favorite months for boat charters, and the busiest in the American San Juans and Canadian Gulf Islands. It's always a good idea to check for special regional events that draw thousands of visitors to an area, like Portland's Rose Festival and Vancouver's Jazz Festival in June, and Seattle's Seafair in July and early August.

April, May, September, and October can have surprisingly good weather in many parts of the region and fewer crowds. These are particularly good times to visit the wine regions, with spring barrel tastings in April and harvest festivals in September or October.

ORIENTATION AND TRANSPORTATION

There are three major international airports—Sea-Tac (halfway between Seattle and Tacoma in Washington), Portland, and Vancouver. Depending upon your objectives, there are many ways to plan your trip. Visiting just major cities? Then you can easily get around without a car, as long as you like walking and are willing to adapt to the transit systems. Amtrak's route offers a scenic tour from Portland to Vancouver, B.C. Portland has a light rail system (you ride free downtown), and Vancouver B.C. has an equivalent Sky Train. It's free to ride Seattle's bus system (Metro) downtown, and the Monorail takes you from downtown to Seattle Center. To do a city tour without a car you can fly into the Sea-Tac (Seattle-Tacoma), Portland, or Vancouver airport, then take a shuttle into the city. You can also ferry or fly (floatplane, helijet, or small plane) to Victoria.

Interstate 5 offers the quickest (though straight-as-an-arrow at times) route from the California border to the Canadian border. U.S. Highway 101 is the two-lane route along the coastline of Washington, Oregon, and British Columbia (the Sunshine Coast). It is scenic and slow as it meanders through small towns, dead-ending—or, you could say, beginning—at the tiny, picturesque village of Lund, a jumping-off point to the wilds of Desolation Sound.

FERRIES AND FLOATPLANES

The ferry and floatplane systems of Washington and British Columbia are unique in North America—both are a way to travel and a pleasurable experience in themselves. While the Washington State Ferries and the B.C. Ferries are North America's biggest ferry fleets, there are private ferry systems (best known is the *Victoria Clipper,* with regular service between Seattle and Victoria) that offer tour services as well as transportation; they may charge more, but they also offer more conveniences—advance booking, lodging packages, connections with sight-seeing cruises (like whale-watching trips), special seasonal trips, and ground transportation between ports.

You'll find that ferries come in all sizes: tiny foot ferries on Victoria Harbour and Vancouver's waterways; their somewhat larger siblings that carry 15 or so cars back and forth on short hops between small islands of the American San Juans and the Canadian Gulf Islands; and the jumbo and super ferries of the B.C. Ferry System that ply the waters of the Georgia Strait and have dining rooms, gift stores, and computer stations. Ferries are a culture in themselves.

Using the ferry systems in the Northwest can make you a bit frantic, particularly if you aren't used to it. It demands you plan ahead, hurry up, then wait. And, finally, once you are aboard you must relax, whether you want to or not. It's best to develop a special mindset for taking the ferries. While July is the busiest season on all runs, you can encounter a long ferry line at any time of year—on popular weekend runs, when there's a special event, or on the last run of the day. Missing a ferry after you've cut short your visit somewhere, pushed the speed limit, and gotten cranky with your kids can only double your frustration. Don't let it make you crazy. Always, always carefully check the ferry schedule (available from toll takers and at terminals). Weekday and weekend schedules often differ. Don't assume anything about the schedule, unless you are very familiar with it. Plan to make reservations for B.C. Ferries trips to the Southern Gulf Islands, up the Inside Passage, on the new Discovery Coast passage to Bella Coola, and for cars boarding Washington State Ferries from the San Juan Islands to Sidney, British Columbia.

On the larger vessels, on all but the stormiest days, the ride is so smooth that the sound of the engines could lull you to sleep. However, if it's a gorgeous sunny day, the eye-popping scenery will keep you glued to the windows or lead you on deck into the hair-ruffling breezes. Foot passengers and cyclists load first and have the advantage over motorists, who can get left behind at the dock when the ferry is full. Whenever possible avoid commuter runs—the busiest are between Vancouver and Swartz Bay (Vancouver Island), Seattle and Bainbridge, and Edmonds and Kingston north of Seattle, and Mutilteo and Clinton (on Whidbey Island). Friday evening and Saturday morning traffic is heaviest westbound, and Sunday afternoon traffic is heaviest eastbound. Food service aboard varies according to the size of ship and length of run; usually shorter and faster runs have the basics—sandwiches, fruits, yogurts, and beverages. Longer runs often have full-service restaurants. If you bring pets, plan to keep them in the car, on a leash, or in carriers in outside cabin areas of Washington State Ferries. On B.C. Ferries vessels, pets must remain on the car deck.

Commuting by floatplane is one way Northwesterners get around the long ferry lines and time-consuming border crossings between Washington and British Columbia. Long a favorite way for sportsmen to reach landlocked lakes for fishing, this mode of travel has become increasingly popular in recent years. Like riding a ferry, the journey is an adventure in itself. Kenmore Air has two air harbors in Seattle, at the north end of Lake Washington and its busiest terminal at the southwest end of Lake Union. It runs daily scheduled flights to Victoria and the San Juan Islands. Harbour Air, in British Columbia, runs scheduled flights between Victoria and Vancouver. Sound Flight, whose terminal is at the south end of Lake Washington, offers specialty trips all over the Northwest. While it costs more to take a floatplane, it's like riding a magic carpet and can translate into an extra day's worth of time you won't spend in ferry lines.

WHAT TO BRING

Remember that Eddie Bauer, REI, and Nordstrom dress the Northwest. Business meetings aside, nice casual—i.e., khaki slacks, shirt, or blouse and/or sweater—will be just fine in all but the most elegant restaurants and private clubs or events, such as fancy theater, ballet, or symphony performances—although you'll see casually dressed folks even then. Here, as most places, jeans (or shorts) and casual shirts or T-shirts are typical knocking-around garb for most daytime activities.

A lightweight turtleneck or T-shirt, with blouse or shirt, sweater, and light jacket can handle most changes in temperature on the coastal side of the region. If you are planning a hike or a high altitude visit (i.e. to Mt. Rainier, Whistler, or Mt. Hood), the classic travel approach to layering is important. Never assume that because it's sunny and beautiful when you start out that you shouldn't take extra clothing. The reverse is true as well. Summer days can begin overcast and by midday be blistering, so don't forget your sunglasses and sunscreen. Also important is appropriate footwear—hiking boots for the serious stuff and walking shoes or flat boots with ankle support to tour gardens, parks, and sometimes uneven city streets. Knapsacks or fanny packs are a good idea if you are comfortable wearing them.

Now, a word about umbrellas. If you have a small packable one, by all means bring it. However, a rain hat or a raincoat with a hood is preferable to an umbrella if you're not used to carrying one. And if there's a real downpour, you may want to head for some shelter. If you especially want to walk in the rain—and yes, lots of us do want to—that's different. Even then, many public gardens and some hotels have umbrellas available to use during your visit.

CROSSING THE BORDER INTO CANADA

There are about a dozen border crossings into Canada from Washington state. The most active—open 24 hours—are at Blaine (Peach Arch and Pacific Highway crossings) and Sumas in western Washington and Osoyoos in eastern Washington. If you plan to visit Canada, keep a few things in mind before you leave home: Each adult needs proof of U.S. citizenship, (a passport or a voter's registration card and a driver's license). Children should have picture ID or a birth certificate, and if not traveling with their legal guardians, a written authorization letter and contact number. Cats and dogs need a valid certificate indicating they've received a rabies shot within the last three years. Handguns and weapons are not allowed. Call Canada Customs' public information line (in Winnepeg) with questions 204/983-3500 or visit www.ccra-adrc.gc.ca.

You'll find duty-free stores at border crossings and on the *Victoria Clipper* and *Princess Marguerite* runs between Seattle and Victoria. These shops offer travelers staying longer than 48 hours savings on perfumes, liquor, and tobacco. Washington State Ferries takes U.S. cash and personal checks drawn on Washington banks; no credit cards. B.C. Ferries accepts travelers checks, U.S. and Canadian cash, Mastercard, and VISA. Keep individual receipts over $50 for items purchased in Canada; when you return to the United States you can submit these at border crossings/duty-free shops to get a rebate of GST—a tax on most goods and services purchased during your 48-hour-plus visit. Keep in mind that food and lodging are not included.

RECOMMENDED READING

When Sir Bulwar Lytton wrote, "It was a dark and stormy night," he could very well have had winters in the Pacific Northwest in mind. And what better way to spend the time than to curl up with a good book. The Northwest is home to many best-selling authors, such as mystery writer J.A. Jance, fantasy writer Terry Brooks, and romance writer Jayne Ann Krentz (aka Amanda Quick), and the home of passionate readers. Bookstores are everywhere, ranging from small specialty stores such as Flora & Fauna Books, a nature and garden book shop in Seattle's Pioneer Square, to renowned one-of-a-kind book worlds like Powell's in Portland, to the large chain stores. Many have areas for reading and relaxing, and often coffee bars—visit any one of these and you'll find plenty of books about the Northwest. Here are some suggestions on various perspectives.

Ice and volcanoes created our landscape. *Cataclysms on the Columbia,* by John Eliot Allen, Marjorie Burns, and Sam C. Sargent (Timber Press, 1986), is a layman's guide to the features produced by the catastrophic Bretz Floods in the Pacific Northwest. And *Northwest Passage: The Great Columbia River,* by

William Dietrich (Simon & Schuster, 1995), offers a grand tour of the many sides and forces of the Columbia River. *The Natural History of Puget Sound Country*, by Arthur R. Kruckeberg (University of Washington Press, 1991 and 1995), provides an understanding of the complexity of western Washington. *The Good Rain: Across Time and Terrain in the Pacific Northwest,* by Timothy Egan (Vintage Books, 1991), is a personal and political look at the environmental bounty of the Northwest. *A Sierra Club Guide to the Natural Areas of Oregon & Washington,* by John Perry and Jane Greverus Perry (Sierra Club Books, 1983–1997), provides a practical guide for visitors.

The University of Washington Press in Seattle has published many books on the Northwest including histories and colorful pictorials, often of exhibits on Northwest native peoples (call 800/441-4115 for a catalog or to order books). Oregon State University Press, 541/737-3166, and Washington State University, 509/335-3564, also publish books on the Northwest.

A particularly impressive pictorial book that gives readers a look at a magnificent collection of art made by the Kwakiutl Indians of northern Vancouver Island is *Chiefly Feasts: The Enduring Kwakiutl Potlatch,* edited by Aldona Jonaitis (American Museum of Natural History, 1991). *Native Peoples of the Northwest: A Traveler's Guide to Land, Art, and Culture,* by Jan Halliday and Gail Chehak in cooperation with the affiliated tribes of Northwest Indians (Sasquatch Books, 1996; www.sasquatchbooks.com), is a useful and informative guide to learning about the native peoples as you travel the region. *Totem Poles,* by Canadian author Pat Kramer (Altitude Publishing Canada Ltd., 1995), is a 112-page handbook that looks at the origin, history, and symbols of totem poles.

Undaunted Courage: Meriwether Lewis, Thomas Jefferson, and the Opening of the American West, by Stephen E. Ambrose (Simon & Schuster, 1996), is a reconstruction of the journey from Meriwether Lewis's viewpoint. *Sons of the Profits,* by William C. Speidel (Nettle Creek Publishing Company, 1967), is an entertaining look at Seattle's not-always-upstanding founding fathers. *Puget's Sound,* by Murray Morgan (University of Washington Press, 1979), looks at the development of the southern sound and Tacoma. And a very different and more recent pioneering journey of a different sort is told in *Dorothy Stimson Bullitt: An Uncommon Life,* by Delphine Haley (Sasquatch Books, 1995), the story of Seattle's legendary businesswoman who built and managed the King Broadcasting Company. She was dubbed "the Queen of King" was born in 1892 and died in1989, a vigorous influence on the city till the end.

Good books to carry along to enrich your travel knowledge include *Garden Touring in the Pacific Northwest: A Guide to Gardens and Specialty Nurseries in Oregon, Washington and British Columbia,* by Jan Kowalczewski Whitner (Alaska Northwest Books, 1993).

Walking guides are helpful: Try *Hiking the Great Northwest* or *100 Classic Hikes in Washington,* both by Ira Spring and Harvey Manning (Mountaineers Books, 1998) or *Pacific Northwest Hiking* by Ron Judd (Foghorn Press, 1999). Locals have made popular *Winter Hikes in Puget Sound and the Olympic Foothills* by Robert Mooers (Sasquatch Books, 1998). Or, try *A Waterfall Lover's Guide to the Pacific Northwest* by Greg Plumb (Mountaineers Books, 1998). *Walking Portland,* by Sybilla Avery Cook (Falcon, 1998), is a new book that looks at 30 walks that show off the historic neighborhoods and forested paths of Portland.

Golfers should check out the most recent edition of *Golf Courses of the Pacific Northwest* by Jeff Shelley (Fairgreens Media, 1997) and *Northwest Golfer: A Guide to every Gold Course Where the Public is Welcome in Oregon and Washington* by Kiki Canniff (K12 Enterprises, 1996). For fans of rustic architecture a new pictorial, *Great Lodges of the West,* by Christine Barnes (W. W. West, Inc., 1997), includes large photo sections on Paradise Lodge, Timberline Lodge, and Crater Lake Lodge.

The Wine Project: Washington State's Winemaking History, by Ronald Irvine with Walter J. Clore (Sketch Publications, 1997), explores the history and founding of the Washington wine industry. More practical pocket guides on wines and food, such as *Northwest Wines: A Pocket Guide to the Wines of Washington, Oregon & Idaho,* by Paul Gregutt and Jeff Prather (Sasquatch Books, 1994) help with dining choices. The ever helpful *Zagat Surveys: Pacific Northwest Restaurants* and *Vancouver Restaurants* (the latest version you can get your hands on) are opinion polls by readers.

Traveling with your pet? Several books will make your trip more fun: A popular book with local pet lovers, *The Seattle Dog Lover's Companion* by Steve Giordano (Foghorn Press, 1996), gives suggestions of things to do with your pet in the city. *Doin' the Northwest with Your Pooch* by Eileen Barish (SCB Distributors, 1998), *Traveling with Your Pet 1999,* and *On the Road Again With Man's Best Friend: A Selective Guide to the West Coast and British Columbia's Bed and Breakfasts, Inn, Hotels and Resorts that Welcome You and Your Dog* by Dawn Habgood (Dawbert Press, 1997) will all help you find pet-friendly accommodations. Although the U.S.-Canada border is an open one, there are certain restrictions to bringing pets across with you. At a minimum, plan to bring your pet's recent immunization records.

1 SEATTLE

Snowcapped mountain views, tangy salt air, and water, water everywhere. Add rain to the equation and you have the few things about this virile northwestern city that have remained constant over the last 150 years. When Seattle's forefathers arrived here in 1851, they were reminded of another grand seaport in the east; they settled their townsite and called it New York-Alki (adding a word that means "by-and-by" in the native Chinook language). The name didn't stick, but today, Seattle's Fifth Avenue shops have the gloss and chic of that other Fifth Avenue. And the city skyline is an impressive forest of skyscrapers—such as the 76-story Bank of America Tower (called the Columbia Tower by many locals), which dwarfs the 42-story Smith Tower, the fourth-tallest building in the world when it was built in 1914.

Seattle is beginning to live like modern-day Manhattan, too. Pricey condominiums web downtown. Dining out is a way of life for city dwellers, restaurants are lively and varied, and new ones are cropping up all the time. Richly diverse neighborhoods make up the fabric of the city. Live theater abounds.

In the 1970s, Seattle architect Victor Steinbrueck and a group called Allied Arts launched a vigorous effort to save historic Seattle. Pike Place Market became the group's most visible cause. Since then, what almost crumbled beneath a wrecking ball has become the heart and pulse of the city. For if ever there was a poem to Seattle—to the whole Northwest—it's here in the living and breath-

SEATTLE

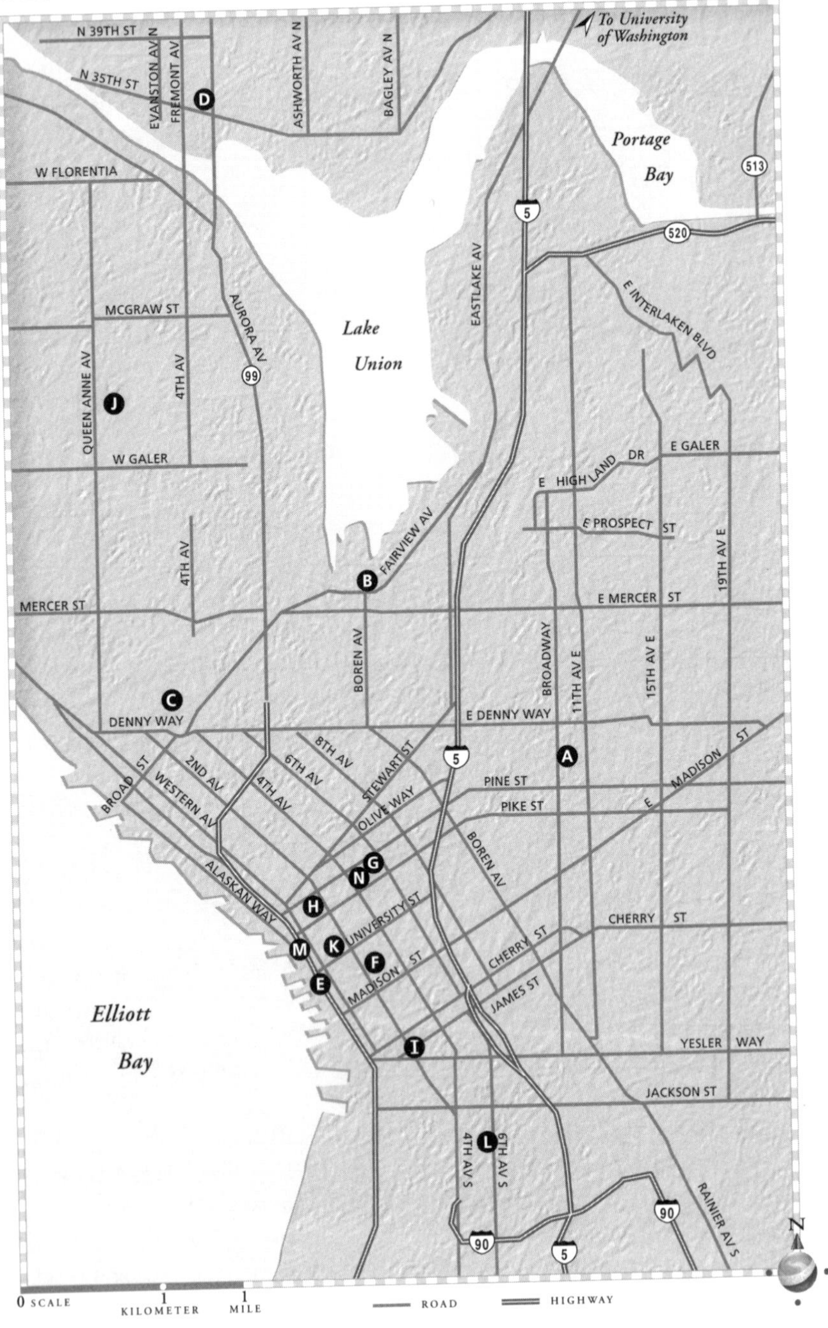

To University of Washington
N 39TH ST
N 35TH ST
EVANSTON AV N
FREMONT AV
ASHWORTH AV N
BAGLEY AV N
Portage Bay
W FLORENTIA
Lake Union
EASTLAKE AV
E INTERLAKEN BLVD
MCGRAW ST
AURORA AV
QUEEN ANNE AV
4TH AV
W GALER
E GALER
E HIGHLAND DR
E PROSPECT ST
FAIRVIEW AV
19TH AV E
MERCER ST
E MERCER ST
BOREN AV
BROADWAY
11TH AV E
15TH AV E
DENNY WAY
E DENNY WAY
8TH AV
6TH AV
STEWART ST
2ND AV
4TH AV
BROAD ST
WESTERN AV
OLIVE WAY
PINE ST
PIKE ST
E MADISON ST
ALASKAN WAY
UNIVERSITY ST
CHERRY ST
MADISON ST
JAMES ST
Elliott Bay
YESLER WAY
JACKSON ST
4TH AV S
6TH AV S
RAINIER AV S
N
0 SCALE
1 KILOMETER
1 MILE
ROAD
HIGHWAY

ing daily life of Pike Place Market, a haiku to the rich bounty of the land, the people, and the sea that define this region.

A PERFECT DAY IN SEATTLE

Any day the sun shines is a perfect day in Seattle. Yet, rain or shine, the perfect way to begin your day in this bracing and bustling town is to start early, on foot, and head to Pike Place Market for breakfast. Soak up the action at this historic community within a city, then walk south along First Avenue to take in the Seattle Art Museum and the interesting shops and galleries nearby. From here, amble down the Harbor Steps to the waterfront and explore. Catch the trolley to Pioneer Square for a look at the historic business district, go on to the International District for Asian foods, goods, and herbalists. Take a Metro bus through the bus tunnel back to the center of town and get off at Westlake Center. Shop your way up the mall's four levels to the food fair and the Seattle Center Monorail. You can take this elevated train a mile north to the Seattle Center, home of the Space Needle and the Key Arena, where Seattle's Supersonics play.

If it's a wonderfully sunny day, cut your serious sight-seeing in half and head to the waterfront—downtown, Lake Union, Green Lake, the Ballard Locks, or the beaches at either Alki or Golden Gardens. (Or hop a ferry to Bainbridge Island and sample the prettiest commute in the Northwest.) Laze in the sun or find a waterfront restaurant for something cold to drink, then plot your dinner destination. A half dozen restaurants along the Ship Canal from Fremont to Shilshole have outdoor view seating where you can watch the boat traffic as the sun sets.

ORIENTATION

Seattle is a port city of 500,000-plus. Its business district is bordered on the west by saltwater Elliott Bay and Puget Sound. Pike Place Market District, along

SIGHTS

- Ⓐ Capitol Hill
- Ⓑ Center for Wooden Boats and Northwest Seaport
- Ⓒ Experience Music Project (EMP)
- Ⓓ Fremont Neighorhood
- Ⓔ Harbor Steps and SOMA
- Ⓕ Metro Transit Tunnel ("Bus Tunnel")
- Ⓖ Nordstrom
- Ⓗ Pike Place Market
- Ⓘ Pioneer Square
- Ⓙ Queen Anne Hill
- Ⓚ Seattle Art Museum
- Ⓒ Seattle Center
- Ⓛ Uwajimaya/ International District
- Ⓜ Waterfront & Streetcar
- Ⓝ Westlake Center

Note: Items with the same letter are located in the same area.

First Avenue, overlooks the waterfront and Highway 99 traffic on the raised Alaskan Way Viaduct. Ferries leave Seattle's waterfront (Washington State Ferries terminal, Colman Dock, Pier 52, 800/843-3779 in state or www.wsdot.wa.gov/ferries/) to carry commuters west to Bainbridge Island and Bremerton on the Kitsap Peninsula; and to Victoria B.C.

Interstate 5 (running north and south) marks the east edge of downtown proper, separating it from Capitol Hill, First Hill, and the neighborhoods of Madison Park, Washington Park, and Leschi, which border Lake Washington. Seattle is connected to "the Eastside"—the largely upscale communities of Bellevue, Kirkland, Redmond, and Mercer Island—via two bridges: the Evergreen Point Floating Bridge (SR520) and the Mercer Island Floating Bridge (I-90). Traffic backs up on both bridges during commute times, 7 to 9 a.m. and 4 to 6 p.m., or when there's an accident.

Lake Union and Queen Anne Hill lie to the north of downtown; the neighborhood of Magnolia is west of Queen Anne Hill. The waterway from Lake Washington to Puget Sound—along Montlake Cut, Portage Bay, Lake Union, and the Lake Washington Ship Canal—divides the city from the North End, which runs to the city limits.

At the south edge of the city are Pioneer Square, the International district, and the beginning of the industrial area of town, which gets crowded during Mariners games at Safeco Stadium. Along the waterfront, south of downtown, is the Port of Seattle.

Parking downtown is expensive, though prices vary widely; some garages and lots charge outrageous rates. Those lots with good locations and more reasonable rates include the parking garage in Pacific Place (between Sixth and Seventh Avenues off Olive) and the Public Market Parking Garage, 1531 Western Avenue.

Although plans are moving ahead for a rapid transit system in Seattle, at present commuters who choose public transportation rely primarily on Metro (Metropolitan Transit System) buses, 206/553-3000, to get around the city and to outlying areas.

Some good bus or boat tours offer quick and fun orientations to the city. Complete city tours are offered by Grayline Tours, 206/624-6349, and Seattle Tours (smaller coach, fewer pickup stops), 206/660-TOUR. Argosy Tours, 206/623-4252, offers tours in boats (including speedboats) of the harbor, Ballard Locks, and Lake Washington; their new dinner cruise ship, the *Royal Argosy,* offers delicious gourmet food as you explore waterways of the city. A highly unusual and whimsical way to see the city is with Ride the Ducks, 206/441-3825 or 800/817-1116. These highly visible amphibious craft (WWII vintage) tour you around the city and onto Lake Union; reservations suggested.

Visitors can get more information from the Seattle King County Convention and Visitors Bureau, 800 Convention Place (on the Galleria level of the Washington State Convention and Trade Center at Pike Street and Eighth Avenue) 206/461-5840, www.seeseattle.org.

SIGHTSEEING HIGHLIGHTS

★★★★ HIRAM M. CHITTENDEN LOCKS

Shilshole, 206/783-7059

www.nws.usace.army.mil/opdiv/lwsc

Also called the Ballard Locks, this is a don't-miss slice of Seattle life—especially in summer, when a constant parade of pleasure boats leaves the freshwater of Lake Washington, Lake Union, and Salmon Bay to ply the Lake Washington Ship Canal into Puget Sound. Underwater viewing windows on the south side of the locks let you watch salmon migration. Note the huge sequoia trees in the Carl English Jr. Botanical Garden on the north (entry) side of the locks. There is a visitors center here with displays on the locks. On some summer Sundays, bands perform outdoor concerts.

Details: *West of the Ballard business district, take Market Street west (it turns into 54th, then watch for signs to the locks). The grounds are open daily 7 to 9; the visitors center is open daily, 10 to 6 mid-May to mid-September; otherwise Thursday through Monday 10 to 4. Admission is free. (1–2 hours)*

★★★★ EXPERIENCE MUSIC PROJECT (EMP)

Seattle Center (at Fifth Avenue N. and Broad St.)

www.emplive.com

A monument to American pop music, this high-tech interactive multimedia museum opened in the summer of 2000. The $240 million, Frank Gehry–designed structure, funded by billionaire Paul Allen, on the grounds of the Seattle Center, is hard to miss. Just look for the massive red, bronze, and silver undulating steel. You wear headphones to explore the interactive exhibits and hear a wide selection of music. Over 80,000 items are on show—including one of the first electric guitars and those used by Bob Dylan, Muddy Watters, and Kurt Cobain. Costumes, handwritten lyrics, and an extensive sound archive are also found here.

Details: *Located at the southeast edge of the Seattle Center, sum-*

mer hours (from Memorial Day to Labor Day) are 9 a.m. to 11 p.m.; winter hours vary. Admission: $19.95 adults; $15.95 seniors and students; $14.95 ages 7 to 12; free for ages 6 and under. (1 hour)

★★★★ MUSEUM OF FLIGHT

9404 E. Marginal Way South, 206/764-5720
www.museumofflight.org

Home to the first jet-powered *Air Force One* (a Boeing VC-137B) and many other planes, this is a visual delight and a must for anyone who loves flying. Historical exhibits are in the Red Barn, the original Boeing factory. Kids love sitting in the cockpit of an airplane; adults gravitate to the flight simulator used to train pilots. And there's a great gift shop.

Details: *Located at the southwest corner of Boeing Field. Take exit 158 from Interstate 5. Open daily 10 to 5, Thursday 10 to 9. Two free tours. Admission: $9.50 adults; $4 ages 5 to 17. (2 hours)*

★★★★ PIKE PLACE MARKET

First Avenue and Pike Street, 206/682-7453
www.pikeplacemarket.org

Founded in 1907 as an experiment to bring farmers and consumers together without the middleman, Pike Place Market is one of the oldest continuously operating farmer's markets in the United States. It's home to hundreds of businesses, a hundred farmers, several hundred artists (it was a favorite subject of artist Mark Tobey), and over 500 residents. Breathe deeply of the heady stew—the scent of bakeries, fresh fish, saltwater, and coffee. In midsummer, go before 10 a.m. (crowds pack the place after that). Tour the market's four levels. Look down at the names imprinted in the market's tiles for a sense of the people who have supported the renovation. You could spend a lot of time here; however, a few hours will give you a sampling. The farmers' tables are in the North Arcade. Don't miss the Economy Arcade, with DeLaurenti's Italian Market, Post Alley's Perennial Tea Room, and restaurants such as the Pink Door. The very first Starbuck's coffee shop is also here.

Details: *Open Monday through Saturday 9 to 6, Sunday 11 to 5, but individual shop openings vary. Check with the Pike Place Market PDA for information. You can pick up a copy of their fine dining and restaurant guides at the main entrance information booth. Park on Western Avenue in the Public Market parking garage, and take the elevator to the North Arcade. (1–2 hours)*

PIKE PLACE MARKET

Pike Place Market PDA

★★★★ PIONEER SQUARE

Underground Tour, 206/682-4646; reservations strongly recommended

www.undergroundtour.com

This is the historic business district of Seattle, which lies south of present-day downtown between the waterfront and the International District. There are restaurants, galleries, and shops, but the don't-miss destinations here include the **Northwest Gallery of Fine Woodworking, Elliott Bay Books,** and the **Klondike Gold Rush National Park** facility at 117 South Main. The much photographed landmark **pergola** is at First Avenue and Yesler Way in Pioneer Park Place near the entrance to Doc Maynard's Public House and **Bill Speidel's Underground Tour,** a fun and unique look at the city's history .

Details: *(2 hours for the square, 2 hours for the Underground Tour)*

★★★★ SEATTLE ART MUSEUM

100 University Street, 206/625-8900

www.seattleartmuseum.org

Architect Robert Venturi designed this uplifting space. The large stone camels on the steps of the gallery were longtime guardians outside the entrance to the original Seattle Art Museum, now the Seattle Asian Art Museum on Capitol Hill (see page 33). There are changing special exhibits and a wonderful Northwest native arts collection. You can join in an authentic tea ceremony in an authentic Japanese teahouse.

Details: *between First and Second Avenues. The museum store offers a huge collection of art books (specialties) and gifts. The café offers light meals. Admission is $7 for adults (the ticket is good for admission to the Seattle Asian Art Museum if used within a week). (1–3 hours)*

★★★★ SEATTLE CENTER

206/684-7200 for upcoming events
206/684-8582 (recorded information), www.seattlecenter.com

The site of the 1962 World's Fair. Seattle Center is now home to the **Space Needle, Pacific Science Center,** Paul Allen's **Experience Music Project** (see page 23)**, Key Arena, Pacific Northwest Ballet, Seattle Repertory Theater, Intiman Theater, Seattle Children's Theater,** and **Children's Museum.** The grounds here offer a pleasant stroll, and you can take the elevator to the top of the Space Needle for incredible views. The **Fun Forest Amusement Park** draws kids of all ages. The center celebrates the beginning of summer with the Northwest Folklife Festival over Memorial Day weekend and marks the end with the Bumbershoot Arts Festival during Labor Day weekend.

Details: *A mile north of downtown Seattle, the center is open year-round. (3 hours)*

★★★ BAINBRIDGE ISLAND

Bloedel Reserve, 206/842-7631
www.bloedelreserve.org

Frequent ferry runs make a visit to this island suburb a snap. Leave your car behind, and you can explore antiques shops, galleries, and eateries along Winslow Way and Madison Street. You'll need to take your car to visit the **Bloedel Reserve,** a beautiful estate-turned-public-garden on the northwest part of the island.

Details: *A 35 minute ride from Seattle's Pier 52 (Colman Dock) puts you on the island. Reservations are required to visit Bloedel Reserve. Admission is about $6. (5 hours)*

★★★ BALLARD

Northwest Seattle, 206/784-9705 (chamber of commerce)

The Ballard area northwest of downtown is the heart of the Scandinavian community, strongly involved in the fishing industry. West of the Ballard Bridge is Fisherman's Terminal, home to Puget Sound's fishing fleet. Historic **Ballard Avenue** is experiencing a revival with arts and home furnishings and accessories shops. It's fun to explore; also here are pubs that draw national jazz, blues, rock, and zydeco acts. **Market Street,** Ballard's main street, has Scandinavian specialty shops. **Shilshole Marina** and **Golden Gardens,** a stretch of beach with walking paths, picnic areas, and wetlands, are well worth exploring. The **Nordic Heritage Museum** has displays showing the Scandinavian influence on Northwest life, as well as contemporary exhibits of art.

Details: *Take 15th Avenue West northwest from downtown (off 15th Avenue west at the Emerson/Nickerson exit); continue north across Ballard Bridge and turn left at Market Street. Follow it to the Ballard Locks. The museum is north of the locks at 3014 N.W. 67th Street, 206/789-5707. Open Tuesday through Saturday 10 to 4 and Sunday noon to 4. Admission $4. (4–6 hours for the whole area, 1–2 hours for the museum)*

★★★ BLAKE ISLAND

Tours from Seattle Waterfront piers 55 and 56
206/443-1244, www.tillicumvillage.com

This whole island is a marine park featuring **Tillicum Village Northwest Coast Indian Cultural Center.** They serve alder-smoked salmon dinners and showcase a native dance exhibition. A scenic boat crossing makes this a special day trip from Seattle's waterfront. Go in the morning, take a picnic, hike the three-mile trail around the island, and catch a late afternoon or evening boat back.

Details: *Tours daily May 1 through mid-October and weekends throughout the year. Cost is about $50, including boat ride and meal; $24 per person boat ride only. (4–6 hours)*

★★★ FREMONT NEIGHBORHOOD

Crossing the bridge into Fremont from downtown, you pass a welcome sign: "The Center of the Universe, set your watch back five minutes." This is your first clue that Fremont is a very quirky place. Your next may be the rocket poised for takeoff at the corner of 35th Street and Evanston Avenue. Stroll and check out the fun galleries, below-street hideaways, and retro shops, and soak up the sense of creative

A TASTE OF WOODINVILLE

Woodinville, a community a half-hour's drive northeast of Seattle that has mushroomed in size, is becoming more and more an entertainment destination. For years, Chateau Ste. Michelle, 14111 N.E. 145th, 425/488-3300 or www.ste-michelle.com, the largest winery in the state, has been the draw. Tours are offered from 10 to 4:30 daily and summer outdoor concerts on the lovely grounds feature a schedule of well-known performers.

Nearby is Redhook Ale's largest brew facility and pub, 24300 N.E. 145th, 425/483-3232, tours daily. Next door is Columbia Winery, 14030 N.E. 145th, 425/488-2776, the destination of the Spirit of Washington, 800/876-7245, a vintage dinner train that leaves from Renton, at the southeast end of Lake Washington. Plans are also in the works for the well-known Herbfarm restaurant to have a new home nearby.

independence that is rampant here. Check out Frank & Dunya's creative furniture, Fritzi Ritzi's retro clothing, and Tribes' native art. The Empty Space Theater is here, as is Redhook Ale's Trolleyman Pub. The district is thick with small, innovative eateries—some pricey but most not. Don't look for white linen and china but for all kinds of fun or quick meals.

Details: *At the northwest end of Lake Union. A #26 bus from Fourth Avenue downtown goes to Fremont. (2 hours)*

★★★ GREEN LAKE

Seattle's Green Lake has a 2.8-mile paved path around the lake, where Seattleites routinely walk, jog, in-line skate, and bicycle. During warm months, paddle boats and canoes can be rented at the recreation center, and there are swimming beaches. There are eateries and coffee shops, particularly around the north end of the lake.

Details: *Go north on Aurora Avenue and watch for signs to Green Lake at about 50th Street. You can rent bicycles and in-line skates at Gregg's Green Lake Cycle, east of the lake, 206/523-1822. (1 hour to "walk the lake")*

★★★ HENRY ART GALLERY

NE 41st and NE 15th, 206/543-2280 (recorded message) or 543-2281, www.henryart.org

This gallery on the University of Washington campus, noted for its contemporary art collection, was recently expanded to almost three times its original size, and the new facility includes a café. It's a block from "the Ave," the University district's eclectic main business street.

Details: *Open 11 to 5 Tuesday through Sunday, until 8 on Thursday. Admission is $5. (1 hour)*

★★★ HARBOR STEPS AND SOMA

Downtown Seattle

Seattle's newest downtown neighborhood, SOMA (South of Market Area) has sprung up south of Pike Place Market along First and Western Avenues. At First Avenue and University Street, the Harbor Steps—with water features, plantings, and an outdoor sculpture tucked between modern high-rise apartment buildings—descend west to Western Avenue, a block from Seattle's waterfront. This is a favorite sunny-day lunch spot for downtown office workers. Wolfgang Puck's Cafe, 1225 First, 206/621-9653, is at the top of the steps. The Inn at Harbor Steps, 1221 First, 206/748-0973 or 888/728-8910, is an elegant, well-located hideaway lodging next door.

Details: *Harbor Steps is across from the Seattle Art Museum at First Avenue and University Street. (1 to 2 hours)*

★★★ QUEEN ANNE HILL

North of downtown Seattle

Queen Anne Hill, one of Seattle's oldest neighborhoods, just five minutes from downtown, rises to about 460 feet and is the highest spot in Seattle, offering expansive vistas. It's divided into two shopping districts: Lower Queen Anne, around busy Seattle Center, and Upper Queen Anne, on top of the hill, which feels like a small town's main street with coffee shops, bistros, and a wide variety of restaurants. For a mini morning or afternoon getaway, spend a few hours and get to the top of Queen Anne. Check out Homing Instincts, a home and accessories shop with a hidden courtyard, Ravenna Gardens accessories and garden shop, and Nelly Stallion and Annie Cruz for high-style clothing. Pasta & Co. is a fun stop for food fans and gourmets. And the Queen Anne Thriftway started the city's trend of grocery shopping as entertainment.

Details: *Seattle Center is at the heart of Lower Queen Anne; Upper Queen Anne is a six-block stretch of Queen Anne Avenue North from Galer to McGraw. (2 hours)*

★★★ UWAJIMAYA/INTERNATIONAL DISTRICT

519 Sixth Avenue S., 206/624-6248

www.uwajimaya.com.

This large Asian market with its shiny blue-tile roof, shopping (giftwares are upstairs), and busy parking lot, draws people in to see and shop the kalidescope of amazing seafoods and specialty foods. The cafeteria and Japanese deli offer tasty options for refueling.

Details: *a block from the Bus Tunnel's south terminal; No admission fee. (1 hour)*

★★★ WATERFRONT & STREETCAR

Downtown Seattle

Seattle's waterfront experienced a revitalization in the 1990s, and it bustles. Here the Seattle Aquarium and Omnidome Film Experience are fun family destinations. There are plenty of restaurants—try Ivar's Acres of Clams, a tradition for fish and chips, or the more upscale Elliott's for oysters on the half shell (Argosy tours, including their dinner cruise, leave from next door). There are also luxury condominiums, an international trade center, the terminus for Washington State Ferries (regular ferries to Bainbridge Island and Bremerton on the Kitsap Peninsula leave from here), and the terminal for the *Victoria Clipper.* Explore by foot or take the Waterfront Streetcar, which runs from Myrtle Edwards Park at the north end to the south end of the waterfront and continues to Pioneer Square and the International District, ending at Fifth Avenue and Jackson Street.

Details: *Fares and schedules are posted at trolley stops. Seattle's only waterfront hotel, the Edgewater, is located here. (3 hours)*

★★★ WASHINGTON PARK ABORETUM

Lake Washington Blvd. E., 206/543-8800; Japanese Garden, 206/684-4725

http://depts.washington.edu/wpa

This was Seattle's first park. Though it's beautiful year-round, spring is especially nice in this 200-acre park with cherry trees, rhododendrons, and azaleas in their glory. The arboretum is south of the University of Washington, adjacent to the neighborhood of Washington Park. A walled Japanese garden has a teahouse and monthly tea ceremony demonstrations.

Details: *Located off Madison Street. Free tours are offered on weekends from the Graham Visitor Center, 1502 Lake Washington Blvd., E. Open daily 10 to 4. The Japanese Garden is open March through November. Admission is $2.50 for adults. Park open daily 8 to sunset. (2 hours)*

★★★ WEST SEATTLE

Seattle's founders landed on Alki Beach in West Seattle. Visit the Log House Museum for exhibits and displays on the history of Seattle and the Duwamish people who first lived here. Alki beach is a popular destination for summer sunbathers, volleyball fans, and in-line skaters. The Mediterranean-style Phoenecia at Alki restaurant views the action.

Details: *The museum is at 3003 61st Avenue S.W. just off Alki Avenue; 206/938-5293. Phoenecia, 206/935-6550. (1 hour)*

★★★ WOODLAND PARK ZOO

50th and Fremont Avenues; 206/684-4800
www.zoo.org

North of downtown, near Green Lake, the zoo features natural settings with few barriers for the animals residing here. Exhibits on 92 acres include an elephant forest, a butterfly exhibit, a tropical rain forest, and the Northern Trail that covers six acres of dramatic landscape and focuses on animals who live in the cold regions of the far North—brown bears, river otters, bald eagles, and the snowy owl. There's also a food court (bring cash or traveler's checks if you want to eat here).

Details: *From I-5 take NE 50th Exit (#169), go west on 50th Avenue about a mile to Fremont Avenue and the zoo's south gate. Open daily, including holidays, March 15 through October 14, 9:30 to 6; 9:30 to 4 the remainder of the year. Admission is $9 for adults, $8.25 for seniors and students with ID. (2–3 hours)*

★★ CENTER FOR WOODEN BOATS AND NORTHWEST SEAPORT

1002 Valley and 1010 Valley, 206/382-2628
www.cwb.org

GREATER SEATTLE

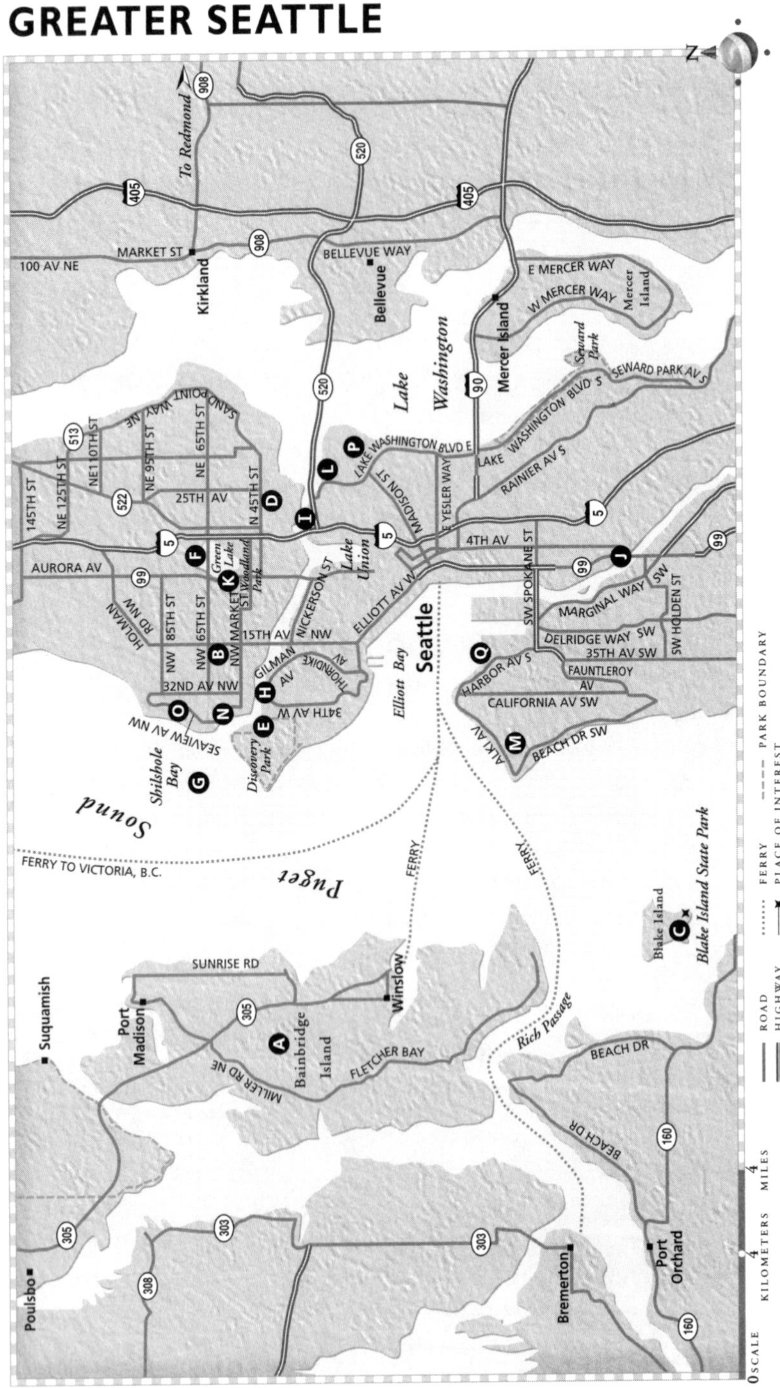

These two stops make up the three-acre Maritime Heritage Center park on Lake Union. The center displays wooden vessels, and you can rent a classic wooden rowboat or a sailboat here (or take a course in building a boat). At Northwest Seaport you can tour the schooner *Wawona* and the tugboat *Arthur Foss.*

Details: *At the south end of the lake near the Burger King. Docks are open for viewing boats from 11 to 5 daily except Tuesday. Rentals from 11 to 7; costs vary depending on size, but start with $12.50 for a rowboat. Admission to the center is free, to the seaport by donation. (1–2 hours)*

★★ BURKE MUSEUM OF NATURAL HISTORY AND CULTURE

17th Avenue NE, 206/543-5590; for recorded information 206/543-7907, www.washington.edu/burkemuseum

This museum on the University of Washington campus is known for its Native American art collection. There's also an expanding dinosaur collection.

Details: *At the north entrance to the UW campus. Open daily 10 to 5, until 8 on Thursday. Admission is $5.50. (1–2 hours)*

★★ CAPITOL HILL

A widely diverse neighborhood, east of downtown. The northwestern crest of the hill is home to some of the city's most beautiful old homes and mansions. The main shopping district lies along Broadway Avenue, a lively shopping and gathering place for counterculture

---

SIGHTS

- Ⓐ Bainbridge Island
- Ⓑ Ballard
- Ⓒ Blake Island
- Ⓓ Burke Museum of Natural History and Culture
- Ⓔ Discovery Park
- Ⓕ Green Lake
- Ⓖ Henry Art Gallery

SIGHTS *(continued)*

- Ⓗ Hiram M. Chittenden Locks
- Ⓘ Museum of History and Industry
- Ⓙ Museum of Flight
- Ⓚ Woodland Park Zoo
- Ⓛ Washington Park Arboretum
- Ⓜ West Seattle

FOOD

- Ⓕ Duke's Green Lake Chowder House
- Ⓝ Hiram's
- Ⓞ Ray's Boathouse
- Ⓟ Rover's
- Ⓠ Salty's on Alki
- Ⓕ Six Degrees

Note: Items with the same letter are located in the same area.

groups and conservatives alike. Volunteer Park, home of the Seattle Asian Art Museum, is at the north end of the hill.

Details: *From downtown follow Pike Street to E. Pike and Broadway and go north. The entrance to Volunteer Park is on 14th E. and Prospect between Broadway and 15th Avenue E. The museum is open Tuesday through Sunday 10 to 5 and Thursday 10 to 9; closed Monday; 206/654-3100. Admission: $3 suggested donation. (1 hour)*

★★ DISCOVERY PARK

This 500-plus-acre park features the Daybreak Star Indian Cultural Center, a lighthouse, and plenty of trails and a beach that looks west over Puget Sound.

Details: *Northwest of downtown in the Magnolia neighborhood; 206/386-4236. (2 hours)*

★★ METRO TRANSIT TUNNEL ("BUS TUNNEL")

206/553-3000

Completed in 1990, this is a 1.3-mile underground bus-only roadway beneath downtown Seattle, linking Westlake Center with the International District. Access to the tunnel, at the south end, is a half block from Uwajimaya, an Asian market, and next to Union Station.

Details: *No fares are charged in the 7- by 20-block downtown Ride Free Zone. (15 minutes)*

★★ MUSEUM OF HISTORY AND INDUSTRY

2700 24th Avenue East, 206/324-1125

www.seattlehistory.org

The exhibits on early Seattle history include historic rooms, an exhibit on the Great Seattle Fire, a cable car, and a miniatures collection. There's a new exhibit on the salmon industry. Combine a visit here with a stroll; the Washington Park Arboretum's Foster Island walking trail starts east of the museum's parking lot.

Details: *South of Husky Stadium; open daily 10 to 5. Admission: $5.50 suggested donation, $1 for kids. (1 hour)*

★ NORDSTROM

500 Pine Street, 206/628-2111

www.nordstrom.com

Most shoppers in the United States know of Seattle-based Nordstrom as the gem of a department store whose service philosophy

BELLTOWN—
A HIP, HAPPENING FOOD LOVER'S HANGOUT

If there's a restaurant district in Seattle—it's Belltown. This growing high-rise residential area north of the downtown business district is filled with dozens and dozens of great and good eateries that fit every budget. Tom Douglas's Dahlia Cafe and Palace Kitchen (see page 37) are favorites here. So is Queen City Grill, 2201 First Avenue, 206/443-0975, especially for a reliable Caesar salad. Flying Fish, 2234 First Avenue, 206/728-8595, is chef Christine Keff's popular (if noisy) seafood eatery; she's opened a new, lower-key restaurant, Fandango, nearby at 2313 First Avenue, 206/441-1188. Also in Belltown is chef Kerry Sear's elegant Cascadia, 2328 First Avenue, 206/448-8884, serving pricey but terrific regional food. The Icon Grill, 1933 Fifth Avenue, 206/441-6330, is a fun, upscale spot filled with pink glass and quirky art. A budget-wise choice is the Noodle Ranch, 2228 Second Avenue, 728-0463, a personal favorite. The coconut soup is sinfully good.

These are just a few of the many choices you'll find in this part of town.

brings shoppers back time after time. The Nordstrom brothers started their shoe store on Seattle's First Avenue in 1901. Their flagship store in downtown Seattle, between two shopping malls, Westlake Center and the ritzy Pacific Place, has two restaurants, a whole floor of shoes, and a fish aquarium in the kids department.

Details: *Between Fifth and Sixth Avenues. (½ hour—or all day)*

FITNESS AND RECREATION

Walk, jog, or bicycle along the waterfront at Myrtle Edwards Park, which begins at the north terminal of the Waterfront Trolley. North of the park is Seattle's newest golf facility, a nine-hole executive course at Interbay. It has a two-level driving range and putting facility. Kite flying at Gasworks Park north of Lake Union is fun to do or fun to watch. The Burke-Gilman Trail runs through Gasworks Park from Ballard in Northwest Seattle—you can bike or walk part of the 30-plus-mile trail from North Seattle to the east side of Lake Washington. Drive north about a half hour to Everett and you can take an all-day whale-watching tour with the Mosquito Fleet, 1724 W. Marine View Drive, 800/325-6722.

There are three classic Seattle viewpoints: from Kerry Park on Queen Anne Hill (West Highland Drive and Third Avenue West), perhaps the most photographed view of Seattle's skyline; from Volunteer Park in front of the Seattle Asian Art Museum; and from West Seattle's Admiral District Park.

SPECTATOR SPORTS

"The wave" was born in Seattle, and this is a city that definitely loves its sports. Professional teams are the Mariners (baseball), 206/346-4001 or www.mariners.org; the Seahawks (football) 425/827-9777 or www.seahawks.com; the Supersonics (men's basketball) 206/217-9622 or www.supersonics.com; Seattle Storm (women's basketball) 206/217-9622 or www.wnba.com; the Thunderbirds (hockey) 206/448-7825, and the Sounders (soccer) 800/796-7425. The Mariners play in the ritzy—new in 1999—Safeco Field with its retracting roof. The Seahawks will play in Husky Stadium (after the King Dome was imploded in 2000) until their new home is built. Individual tickets can be purchased through Ticketmaster (206/622-4487). The hottest ticket in town (unless a professional team makes the play-offs) is a football game at the University of Washington Husky Stadium, with the excitement of 70,000-plus fans doing the wave to cheer on the Huskies, views of Lake Washington and the Cascades, and tailgating in automobiles and in boats. That's right. A whole contingent of fans arrive by boat (some families have done so for decades) to moor behind the stadium. And you can arrive by boat, too! Brunch-and-boat packages are available through several restaurants. Call Argosy Cruises, 206/623-1445, or Power Tours, 206/682-8864, for boat schedules and departure spots. Power Tours has packages that include tickets (pricey, but good to know if you're keen to go and don't have game tickets). Also, other UW Huskies teams serve up many men's and women's spectator events and are always in the hunt for one championship or another. Call 206/543-8463 (recorded message) or 206/543-2210 for events, schedules, and ticket information.

FOOD

Coffee bars—Starbucks, Tully's, Seattle's Best Coffee, and many more—are almost as thick as rain, and many offer cozy chairs for relaxing. Oyster bars (which do serve other seafood as well) are Seattle specialties—popular downtown area haunts are **Anthony's Bell Street Diner,** 206/448-6688, on the waterfront at the foot of Bell Street; the **Brooklyn Seafood-Steak & Oyster House,** 1212 Second Avenue, 206/224-7000; **Elliott's Oyster House,** on pier 56, 206/623-4340; **McCormick's,** 722 Fourth Avenue, 206/682-3900; and Shuckers, (in the Four Seasons Hotel), 206/621-1984. **Emmet Watson's Oyster Bar,** 206/448-7721, in Pike Place Market, is the most casual of the lot.

The "best" when it comes to restaurants is a crowded list. At the top of the favorites list is **Rover's,** 206/325-7442, tucked away in the Madison Park neighborhood east of downtown. Known for consistent, beautifully prepared food, especially seafood, they offer fairly pricey five-course meals. Another favorite, **Wild Ginger,** 1401 Third Avenue, 206/623-4450, offers a la carte Pan-Asian meals for a competitive Seattle-restaurant price. And yes, the food at both restaurants is wonderful. Tom Douglas's restaurants—**Dahlia Lounge,** 2001 Fourth Avenue, 206/682-4143; **Etta's Seafood,** 2020 Western Avenue, 206/443-6000; and the **Palace Kitchen,** 2030 Fifth Avenue, 206/448-2001—in the Belltown and Pike Place Market areas—also get high marks. Check out Douglas's website: www.tomdouglas.com.

There are notable hotel restaurants, too. For a special occasion or splurge, dress up to go to **Fullers,** in the Sheraton, 206/447-5544; the **Georgian Room,** in the Four Seasons, 206/621-7889; and the **Hunt Club,** 900 Madison Street, in the Sorrento Hotel, 206/343-6156. Expect fine food, top service, soothingly elegant settings (and a tab to match). A little more relaxed, **Tulio's,** in the Hotel Vintage Park, 1100 Fifth Avenue, 206/624-5500, specializes in Italian food and **Andaluca,** in the Mayflower Park Hotel, 206/382-6999, is a romantic, gem-toned hideaway with tapas-style dishes.

The **Canlis Restaurant,** 206/283-3313, north of downtown on Aurora Avenue, a Seattle tradition for generations, still has the cachet of being a "luxe" place to go to have a Canlis salad (like a Caesar) and grilled steak or scampi for that special-event dinner. Updated in recent years (by Bill Gates's architect, Jim Cutler), it still offers its signature piano bar and a breathtaking view of Lake Union.

The **El Gaucho,** 2505 First Avenue, 206/728-1337—a longtime favorite Seattle steak house, gone for a while and resurrected in recent years—is known for its cigar room. **Oliver's,** 206/382-6995, in the Mayflower Hotel, makes award-winning martinis.

Food stalls for quick take-away meals and many wonderful eateries are hidden away in Pike Place Market (request their restaurant guide and map and their fine dining guide brochure by calling 206/682-7453). Lunch on the outdoor terrace of the **Pink Door,** 206/443-3241, with its romantic arbor and view of Elliott Bay, is a real treat. **Campagne,** 206/728-2800, across from the

SEATTLE

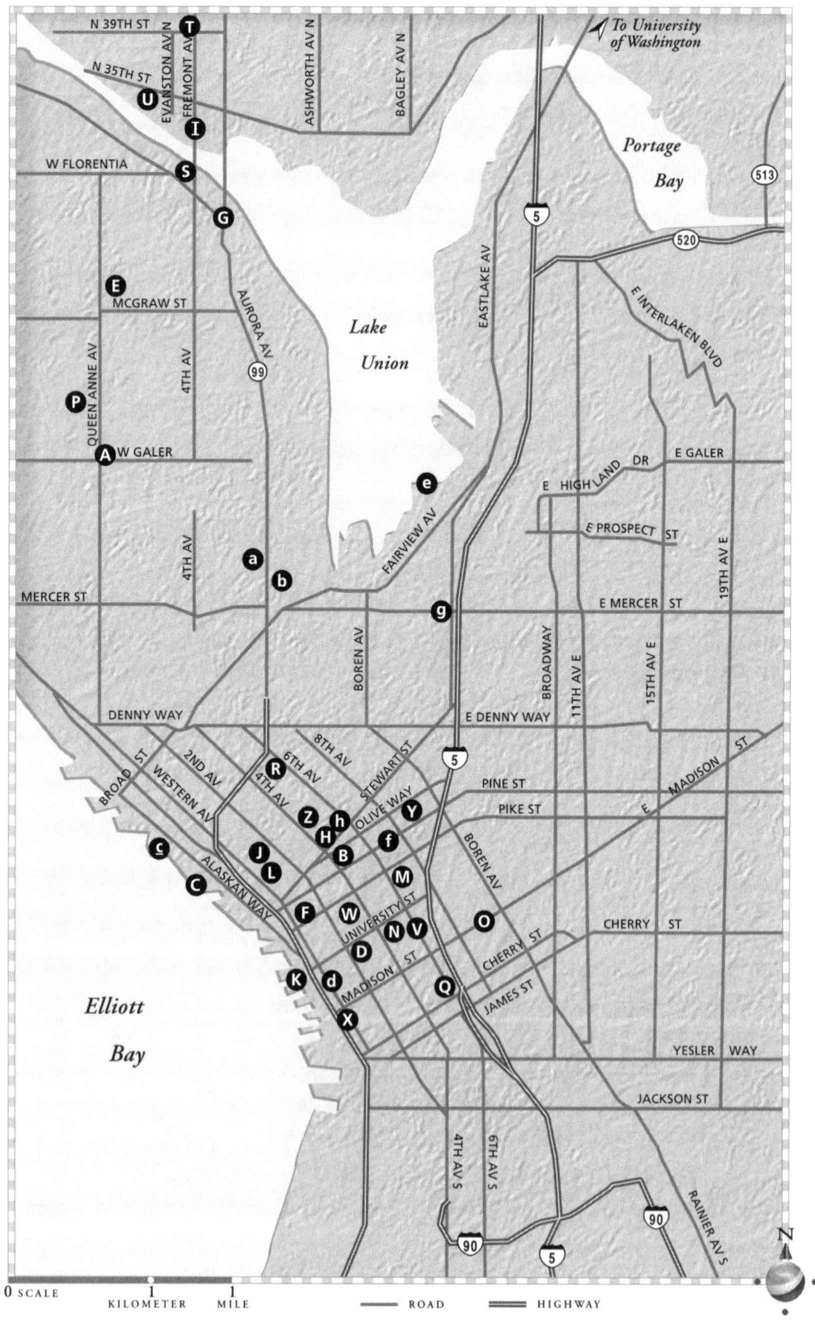

To University of Washington
Portage Bay
Lake Union
Elliott Bay
N 39TH ST
N 35TH ST
EVANSTON AV N
FREMONT AV N
ASHWORTH AV N
BAGLEY AV N
W FLORENTIA
MCGRAW ST
AURORA AV
QUEEN ANNE AV
4TH AV
W GALER
EASTLAKE AV
E INTERLAKEN BLVD
E HIGHLAND DR
E GALER
E PROSPECT ST
FAIRVIEW AV
MERCER ST
E MERCER ST
BOREN AV
BROADWAY
11TH AV E
15TH AV E
19TH AV E
DENNY WAY
E DENNY WAY
BROAD ST
WESTERN AV
2ND AV
6TH AV
8TH AV
STEWART ST
OLIVE WAY
PINE ST
PIKE ST
E MADISON ST
ALASKAN WAY
UNIVERSITY ST
MADISON ST
CHERRY ST
JAMES ST
YESLER WAY
JACKSON ST
4TH AV S
6TH AV S
RAINIER AV S
0 SCALE
1 KILOMETER
1 MILE
ROAD
HIGHWAY
N

Inn at the Market, is another at the top of the "bests" lists (its bistro on the lower level is the place for a chic and tasty breakfast—try a French-style omelet). **El Puerco Lloron,** 206/624-0541, serves budget Mexican food in a lively setting behind the market off Western Avenue.

On Queen Anne Hill the fun diner-style **5 Spot,** 1502 Queen Anne Avenue North, 206/285-SPOT, is always packed for weekend breakfasts. **Buongusto,** 2232 Queen Anne Aveue, 206/284-9040, serves Italian food. Also on Queen Anne Avenue North, the **Hilltop Ale House,** 206/285-3877, and **Paragon Bar & Grill,** 206/283-4548, with entertainment—jazz, blues, reggae—are lively night spots. **Kaspar's,** 19 West Harrison, 206/298-0123, on Lower Queen Anne Hill, is an elegant spot with European-style food.

In Fremont you'll find fun and funky neighborhood hangouts. At the **Fremont Noodle House,** 3411 Fremont Avenue North, 206/547-1550, try the roast duck and noodle soup with a bottle of Bangkok Beer—and finish with a bowl of coconut ice cream. Redhook Ale's **Trolleyman's Pub,** 3400 Phinney North, 206/548-8000, offers microbrews, sandwiches, and soups. Though the

---

FOOD

- A 5 Spot
- B Andaluca
- C Anthony's Bell Street Diner
- D Brooklyn Seafood-Steak & Oyster House
- E Buongusto
- F Campagne
- G Canlis Restaurant
- H Dahlia Lounge
- I El Camino
- J El Gaucho
- F El Puerco Lloron
- K Elliott's Oyster House
- F Emmet Watson's Oyster Bar
- F Etta's Seafood
- L Flying Fish
- I Fremont Noodle House
- M Fullers
- N Georgian Room (Four Seasons Olympic)

FOOD *(continued)*

- O The Hunt Club
- P Longshoreman's Daughter
- Q McCormick's
- B Oliver's
- R The Palace Kitchen
- F Pike Place Market
- F The Pink Door
- S Ponti Seafood Grill
- N Shuckers
- T Swingside Cafe
- U Trolleyman's Pub
- V Tulio's
- W Wild Ginger

LODGING

- X Alexis
- Y Camlin Hotel
- Z Claremont
- N Four Seasons Olympic
- a Hampton Inn/Seattle Center

LODGING *(continued)*

- b Holiday Inn Express/Seattle Center
- C Hotel Edgewater
- d Hotel Monaco
- W Hotel Vintage Park
- d Inn at Harbor Steps
- F Inn at the Market
- F International Hostel
- F Pensione Nichols
- e M.V. *Challenger*
- B Mayflower Park
- f Paramount Hotel
- g Residence Inn by Marriott/Lake Union
- M Sheraton Seattle
- O Sorrento
- h Westin Hotel

Note: Items with the same letter are located in the same area.

SNOHOMISH ANTIQUES

Antiques buffs can combine a day of exploring with their favorite puttering in the small riverfront community of Snohomish, 35 miles and a half hour north of Seattle. Snohomish was settled in the gold rush days of the mid-1800s and thrived as a pioneering logging town in the 1880s. For decades, though, it's been known less for timber and more for antique furniture and accessories; it's home to more than 350 antiques dealers and considered the antiques capital of the Northwest.

To reach Snohomish, take Interstate 5 north from Seattle; at Everett take Highway 2 east (Exit 194) and follow the signs. Star Center Mall, 829 Second Street, houses 165 dealers. Park in the large lot, then explore three packed levels of antiques that include everything from Civil War memorabilia to antique comic books. Stroll south to the four-block stretch of First Street, where smaller enclaves such as River City Antiques and Victoria Village are packed with Victorian furniture. Avenues A through E, west of the business district, comprise the historic part of town. The area is dotted with old Victorian homes, many accented with gingerbread trim. The Blackman House, 118 Avenue B, built by pioneer logger Hyrcanus Blackman in 1878, is now a museum operated by the Snohomish Historical Society. Stop by their office, next door, for a self-guided walking map of historic homes. Snohomish has a number of restaurants, coffee shops, saloons, and bakeries. For an old-time lodging experience, check out the 1914 Grand Hotel, a comfortably updated inn on First Street with antique-filled rooms; some share a bath. For more information, call the Snohomish Chamber of Commerce at 360/568-2526.

walls are pale pink at **El Camino,** 607 North 35th Street, 206/632-7303, the weekend atmosphere in this Mexican-style restaurant is as boisterous as the riotously colorful tablecloths. Try the **Longshoreman's Daughter,** 3508 Fremont Place North, 206/633-5169, for breakfast or lunch, for classics with a twist. The **Swingside Cafe,** 4212 Fremont North, 206/633-4057, offers "downtown" food at a better price in a more modest setting.

If you want to play hooky from sight-seeing on a beautiful, sunny afternoon, visit the restaurants along the Lake Washington Ship Canal: **Ponti Seafood Grill,** 3014 Third Avenue North, 206/284-3000, across the bridge from Fremont, and **Hiram's,** 5300 34th Avenue NW, 206/784-1733, overlooking the Ballard locks. At Shilshole Bay, **Ray's Boathouse,** 6049 Seaview Avenue North, 206/789-3770, another Seattle institution; and **Anthony's** next door, 6135 Seaview Avenue North, 206/783-0780, offer decks or terraces with great views of the boat traffic. At Green Lake you'll have water views from **Six Degrees,** 7900 East Green Lake Drive, 206/523-1600, and **Duke's Green Lake Chowder House,** 7850 North Green Lake Drive, 206/ 522-4908. And in West Seattle, **Salty's on Alki,** 1936 Harbor Avenue SW, 206/937-1600, offers a panorama of the water and Seattle's skyline along with seafood.

LODGING

There's a wide range of lodging types and prices in Seattle. To get the most out of your visit, plan to stay in or near downtown.

You have several quite different choices in or near Pike Place Market. At the high end there's the charming English country–style hideaway, **Inn at the Market,** 86 Pine Street, 206/443-3600, with Campagne Restaurant across the courtyard. The **Pensione Nichols,** 1923 First Avenue, 206/441-7125 or 800/440-7125, with a wide range of room rates, offers a continental breakfast, comfortably updated rooms—some with a shared bath—and views. A little more expensive is the **Claremont,** 2000 Fourth Avenue, 206/448-8600 or 800/448-8601, with a gracious lobby and updated units in an older hotel building.

At the very basic and thrifty end of the spectrum is the **Hostel International of Seattle,** 84 Union Street, 206/622-5443, at the south end of the market off Western Avenue. Also at the south edge of the market, but much harder on the wallet, is the **Inn at Harbor Steps,** 1211 First Avenue, 206/748-0973 or 888/728-8910, a sophisticated hideaway, kitty-corner from the Seattle Art Museum. **Hotel Edgewater,** 2411 Alaskan Way, 206/728-7000 or 800/624-0670, is Seattle's only waterfront hotel.

The city's grande dame is the **Four Seasons Olympic,** 411 University Street, 206/621-1700 or 800/821-8106. Smaller luxury hotels include the **Alexis,** 1007 First Avenue, 206/624-4844 or 800/426-7033, not far from the Seattle Art Museum, **Hotel Vintage Park,** 1100 Fifth Avenue, 206/624-8000 or 800/624-4433; and the **Hotel Monaco,** 1011 Fourth Avenue, 206/621-1770 or 800/945-2240, in downtown. **The Sorrento,** 900 Madison Street, 206/622-6400 or 800/426-1265, with palm trees out front, is one of the town's most romantic hotels. **Mayflower Park Hotel,** 405 Olive Way, 206/623-8700

SIDE TRIP: THE SNOQUALMIE VALLEY

In 1998, one hundred miles of Interstate 90, from Seattle east to Thorpe, was designated a National Scenic Byway. Following the Mountain to Sound Greenway, the route starts in West Seattle at historic Alki Beach, goes east over Lake Washington's floating bridge, and past Lake Sammamish and Issaquah. Roughly tracing the South Fork of the Snoqualmie River into the Cascade foothills, it cuts through the verdant Snoqualmie Valley and fir-thick hillsides like a wide and dignified boulevard on its way to eastern Washington.

Enroute are many historic and recreational attractions. To sample a few, take exit 22, detouring north and east of the interstate. You'll pass Preston, a small turn-of-the-century Scandinavian mill town. At Fall City, the final upstream landing for early steamboats, turn right. In a few miles you'll reach dramatic 270-foot **Snoqualmie Falls.** *The falls were a gathering place for native peoples from both sides of the Cascades. Take the hike down to the base of the falls and follow the boardwalk to view them, and you'll understand the impressive, mystical quality the falls possess. Overlooking the falls is the luxury* **Salish Lodge & Spa** *(6501 Railroad Avenue, 425/888-2556 or 800/ 826-6124 or www.coastalhotel.com/washington/snoqualmie/salish). The excellent restaurant here is a perfect destination, especially on weekends when their hearty special breakfast may be the only meal you'll need all day. Or you can stay overnight and sample the soothing effects of a massage or a spa soaking pool.*

Visit the town of Snoqualmie with its historic train cars and railroad museum; and the town of North Bend, where the rocky face of Mt. Si rises to the north. Here you can meet up with I-90 at exit 32 and loop back to Seattle.

If you continue east on the interstate over Snoqualmie Pass, the route passes Cle Elum and the nearby mining town of Roslyn and ends at Thorpe, in the dry cattle country of Kittitas County (Interstate 90, of course, continues on). A map of outings and activities along the route can be viewed on The Mountains to Sound Greenway Trust website: www.mtsgreenway.org.

or 800/426-5100, is a small European-style hotel that offers a central downtown location and access directly into Westlake Center. All of these hotels have delightful restaurants on site.

The **Paramount Hotel,** 724 Pine Street, 206/292-9500, new in 1997, is within a block or so of the Washington Convention Center and competitively priced, given that Seattle is an expensive city. The slightly less expensive **Camlin Hotel,** 1619 Ninth Avenue, 206/682-0100, a longtime favorite older hotel, is also near the Washington Convention Cente, as is the **Sheraton Seattle,** 1400 Sixth Avenue, 206/621-9000 or 800/204-6100, with a terrific glass collection in Fuller's Restaurant. The **Westin Hotel,** 1900 Sixth Avenue, 206/728-1000 or 800/228-3000, is at the north end of the business district (Seattle is its international headquarters).

Unique and affordable lodging (some accomadations are roomy with great views, others are tight quarters) can be had on Lake Union aboard the M.V. *Challenger* tugboat, 206/340-1201, or in yachts moored nearby.

There are several chain accommodations around Seattle Center and the south end of Lake Union that are good choices for families. There's a new **Hampton Inn,** 700 Fifth Avenue North, 206/282-7700 or 800/426-7866, and a Holiday Inn, 226 Aurora Avenue North, 206/441-7222 or 800/465-4329, near Seattle Center. At the southwest end of Lake Union is a **Residence Inn by Marriott,** 800 Fairview Avenue North, 206/624-6000 or 800/331-3131.

Seattle's Super Saver program, with downtown hotel savings up to 50 percent, runs November 7 through March 31; reservation lines open October 31. A Hotel Hotline operates from April to October offering peak-season travelers the lowest room rates at hotels in downtown Seattle, the Sea-Tac Airport area, the University district or Bellevue. Call 206/461-5882 or 800/535-7071 (U.S. only).

SHOPPING

There are plenty of shopping options, particularly in downtown Seattle along Pine Street. Don't miss the sparkling Pacific Place (at Sixth and Pine) with Tiffany's, Cartier, Williams-Sonoma, Cutter & Buck et. al, and lots of eateries. Pacific Place connects west to the Nordstrom flagship store (at 500 Pine Street) via a sky bridge. In the next block west is Westlake Center, a four-story vertical mall containing over 80 shops, including Neiman-Marcus, and eateries. The plaza in front of the center, on Pine Street, is a lively gathering spot. The Bon Marché department store is next door. Fifth Avenue stores include Eddie Bauer, 206/622-2766; and Coldwater Creek, 206/903-0830. Other attractive downtown shopping areas include Seattle City Centre at Fifth Avenue and Pike Street and Rainier Square on Fifth between Union and University Streets. Nike Town, at Sixth and Pike, 206/447-6543, and Old Navy, at Sixth and Pine, 206/264-9341, are high-energy places that appeal to teens.

Fun and funky shopping can be had in Pike Place Market and in the Fremont district. And when it comes to fun and funky it's hard to beat two Seattle specialty destination shops—Ruby Montana's Pinto Pony, at 1623 Second Avenue downtown, 206/443-9363 or www.rubymontana.com, with Western doodads large and small and plenty more; and Archie McPhee & Co., Outfitters of Popular Culture, 2428 N.W. Market Street in Ballard, 425/745-0711, www.archiemcphee.com, where you can buy those hard-to-find items such as a "Professor Bones" skeleton, a rubber chicken, and much, much more.

Also away from downtown, east of the University district, is University Village. You'll find many upscale shops such as Abercrombie & Fitch, Sundance, Eddie Bauer, and Fran's Chocolates, and some good restaurants. An even longer drive from downtown, Northgate and Southcenter Malls and Bellevue Square are popular shopping destinations.

NIGHTLIFE

Seattle is one of the biggest theater towns in the country, with diverse offerings to please every taste. Check schedules for the Seattle Repertory Theater, 155 Mercer Street, 206/443-2210; ACT, 700 Union Street, 206/292-7676; and Intiman, Seattle Center, 206/269-1901; or Empty Space, 3509 Fremont N., 206/547-7633. The Paramount, 911 Pine Street, 206/682-1414; and the Fifth Avenue, 1308 Fifth Avenue, 206/625-1418, are two visually fabulous restored theaters that book popular shows and entertainment. For symphony music and special musical events get tickets at the stunning new Benaroya Hall, 200 University Street, 206/215-4800.

Dimitrou's Jazz Alley, 2033 Sixth Avenue, 206/443-8247, in the Denny Regrade area not far from the Westin Hotel, is one of the best jazz venues on the coast. And nearby, the offbeat Crocodile Cafe, 2200 Second Avenue, 206/441-5611, packs in Gen-X crowds. For lively late night jazz and blues in bars and coffee hangouts, try Pioneer Square, south of downtown, or Ballard Avenue in the Ballard neighborhood northwest of downtown. Broadway Avenue on Capitol Hill is also a lively evening gathering spot. There are several downtown movie theaters and entertainment complexes, including Pacific Place, 600 Pine Street, 206/652-2404, and City Centre, 1420 Fifth Avenue, 206/622-6465.

Scenic Route: Whidbey and Fidalgo Islands

Whidbey Island has been called paradise and the Garden of Eden. In 1792, Joseph Whidbey charted the 40-mile-long island—the longest in the contiguous United States—at the entrance to Puget Sound. Today it is home to some of the oldest farms in Washington, the nation's first historical reserve, beachfront parks, a thriving arts community, and a naval station. At its north end, Whidbey is connected to Fidalgo Island and the mainland by Deception Pass Bridge, one of the state's most photographed attractions, and then onward to the Skagit Delta. This route takes you to picturesque waterfront villages. Though the loop is an easy day trip from Seattle, it's much better to make it an overnight or longer.

The Mukilteo ferry terminal is 30 minutes north of downtown Seattle via Interstate 5; watch for exit signs south of Everett. A 20-minute ferry ride puts you at Clinton on the south end of the island. From here Highway 525 goes up the island.

Take South Langley Road to the Whidbey Island Winery, 5237 S. Langley Road, 360/221-2040, where you can sample wines made from Siegerrebe and Madeleine Angevine grapes. Continue north to Langley, a waterfront village of galleries, restaurants, antiques shops, and a performing arts center. An arts and crafts festival held here

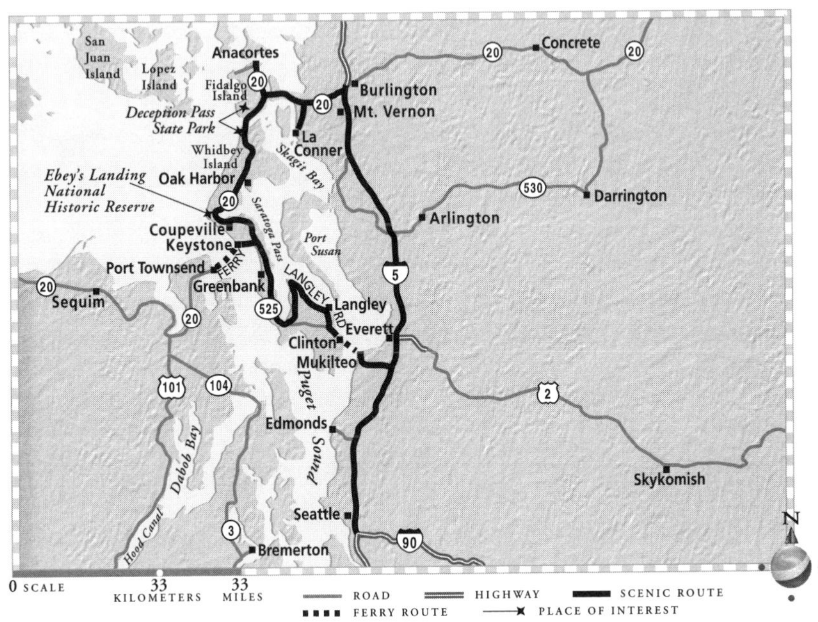

in July and a county fair in August draw crowds. On First, the stylish and contemporary Inn at Langley, 360/221-3033, offers views of Saratoga Passage from jetted tubs in each room and is renowned for its five-course dinners on weekends (by reservation). Get back on 525 and continue north to Greenbank. The picturesque red and white barn at Greenbank Farm, on Wonn Road off Highway 525, was once a dairy. Now it houses a tasting room for Ste. Michelle Winery, open daily from 10 a.m. to 5 p.m., 360/678-7700.

SR 525 becomes SR 20 at the road heading west, to the Keystone Ferry. This ferry takes you to Port Townsend and the Olympic Peninsula, and offers an extension to the loop.

As you approach Coupeville, on Highway 20, you're driving through Ebey's Landing National Historical Reserve, a 17,400-acre national park that encompasses prairies, woodlands, and uplands, a western coastal strip along Admiralty Inlet, Penn Cove, and Coupeville, the state's second oldest town. Here the Coupeville Arts Center draws artists and instructors from all over the world to participate in workshops on needlework, photography, and painting. With its wharf, clapboard storefronts, and Victorian-style homes—many built by sea captains—the town looks much as it did in the 1800s. Stop by the Island County Historical Museum at the west end of Front Street for a self-guided walking tour map of the historical buildings in town. Later take winding Madrona Way west of Coupeville. You'll spot the rafts of Penn Cove mussel farm, famous for the succulent shellfish grown there. Toby's Tavern in Coupeville sells the most Penn Cove mussels on the island, yet having steamed mussels in the cozy old bar at the Captain Whidbey Inn, overlooking Penn Cove, is a real treat. The inn is a separate annex of rooms and several cottages spread on 12 acres, 360/678-4097 or 800/366-4097.

Continuing north on 20 you'll reach Oak Harbor, the island's largest community. A marina, motels, and other services are here. North of here is the Whidbey Island Naval Air Station; you'll likely see and hear planes soaring overhead. As you near Deception Pass watch for signs for Dugwalla Bay Farms' roadside stand. During summer berry season fresh sauces are made daily, and you can buy an ice-cream cone topped with warm berry sauce. You'll soon see signs for Deception Pass State Park, 4,128 acres that flank the northern tip of Whidbey Island and the southern tip of Fidalgo Island. You'll find camping, picnic spots, and lakes and shoreline to explore. Parking areas on either side of the bridge let you stop and walk across.

Once you cross the bridge, you're on Fidalgo Island. The Washington State Ferry terminal, at the outskirts of Anacortes, is the jumping-off spot to the San Juan Islands. Old Town Anacortes has a maritime heritage that goes back more than a hundred years.

Take Commercial Street through the dozen blocks of historic downtown, and you'll see signs of revitalization—spruced-up shops, eateries, a brewpub, art galleries. Don't miss Marine Supply and Hardware—the oldest marine hardware store on the West Coast (on the National Register of Historic Places). Its interior is packed with wooden ships' wheels, portholes, oil lamps, and Greek fishermen's hats, for starters. Drive north a few blocks to the viewpoint at the top of Cap Sante for ringside views of the pleasure boat traffic in the Port of Anacortes Marina. Along the marina, visit the 1919 dry-docked sternwheeler the W.T. Preston, open weekends, 11 to 5. Children love the Anacortes Railway train and can get tickets and board here. The grand old Majestic Hotel, 800-588-4780, on Commercial, is worth a stop. Guest rooms are decorated with antiques; there's a garden, and a restaurant and pub serve up plenty of seafood.

The Skagit Delta, a gorgeous green wedge of alluvial plain, lies between Fidalgo Island and the freeway. In spring it is blanketed with blooming tulips and droves of visitors there to see the flowers. The delta is also an artistic home, for here is where the painters who became known as the Northwest School thrived. The storefronts along this picturesque fishing, farming, and arts village of La Conner look much as they did in the late 1800s. It's the crowds of people who look different, and the gift shops and restaurants that diverge from fishing and farming activities that dominated the town years ago. Don't miss the Museum of Northwest Art, Gaches Mansion, the Tillinghast Seed Company, the Quilt Museum, and the shops and galleries on First Street. The Channel Lodge, La Conner, 360/466-1500, is a 40-unit Craftsman-style inn that clings to the Swinomish Channel offering views of the boat traffic. Viking Cruises 360/466-2639, offers whale-watching trips and tours of Deception Pass from here.

Continue along Highway 20 toward Mt. Vernon and watch for signs for Padilla Bay. A National Estuarine Research Reserve and Interpretive Center is here, and you can learn about the hawks and waterfowl, such as trumpeter swans, that make stopovers on the delta.

2
TACOMA

In the past, Tacoma was thought of as Seattle's rowdy sibling—a mill town, a port town, and a railroad town on south Puget Sound. But this city is through with that image. A steady revitalization is drawing more and more visitors to what is increasingly becoming an international arts and cultural destination. The Broadway Center for the Performing Arts, including the restored 1918 Pantages and Rialto Theaters and the modern and colorful Theater on the Square, form the heart of a performing arts district that draws people from all over. The renovated Union Station and its neighbor, the impressive new Washington State History Museum, also draw visitors.

Hometown of internationally known glass artist Dale Chihuly, the city is slated to open a new Museum of Glass—with working furnaces and resident artists—in the summer of 2002. The Glass Bridge, a walkway connecting the museum to the waterfront, will open at the same time. A year later, the new home of the Tacoma Art Museum will open nearby, with more glass exhibits. More than a hundred years ago, Tacoma was dubbed the "City of Destiny," because it was the railroad terminus on the Puget Sound. Then the tracks moved to Seattle, and at times Tacoma's destiny has been hazy. Now it's as clear as glass.

The city has plentiful scenic attractions, too. Point Defiance Park, with its zoo and aquarium, offers wraparound views of both the freighter traffic on Commencement Bay and ferry and pleasure boaters on south Puget Sound.

Tacoma has also been the city most closely connected to Mt. Rainier. The historic Mountain Highway leads from the city to Paradise Lodge atop the mountain.

A PERFECT DAY IN TACOMA

For a perfect day in Tacoma, visit Point Defiance Park and see the gardens and aquarium. Enjoy a leisurely lunch in the park at the new Anthony's Home Port and get great water views with your steaming bowl of clam chowder. Spend time in the Washington State History Museum. Then move on to Union Station to marvel at the play of light through the pieces of Chihuly glass on exhibit there; the Tacoma Art Museum also displays Chihuly. Have dinner at a restaurant with a view, such as Altezzo or Stanley & Seaforts, and plan your next day—a trip to Mt. Rainier.

ORIENTATION

A hilly port city of about 300,000 on the southeastern shores of Puget Sound, Tacoma lies 18 miles south of Sea-Tac International Airport and 36 miles south of Seattle, off Interstate 5. The large blue Tacoma Dome marks the exit from I-5 to the city center. Tacoma fronts on Commencement Bay, overlooking the busy port district. Downtown is a draw for its theaters, museums, and Antique Row, however it's not a shopping mecca. Attractions are spread out, so it's a city best explored by car. For a visitor information packet, contact the **Tacoma-Pierce County Visitor & Convention Bureau,** 906 Broadway, 800/272-2662; www.tpctourism.org. Shuttle Express offers service between Tacoma and Sea-Tac Airport, 425/981-7070 or 800/487-7433, www.shuttleexpress.com.

SIGHTSEEING HIGHLIGHTS

★★★★ POINT DEFIANCE PARK AND POINT DEFIANCE ZOO AND AQUARIUM

253/591-5335 (recorded message—hours and directions) or 253/591-5337

Within this nearly 700-acre park surrounded on three sides by Puget Sound are an excellent zoo and aquarium, a replica of Fort Nisqually, a Hudson's Bay Company fur trading post (circa 1855), a logging museum, and Never Never Land—a children's fantasy world filled with sculpted storybook characters. There are seven different gardens, in-

TACOMA

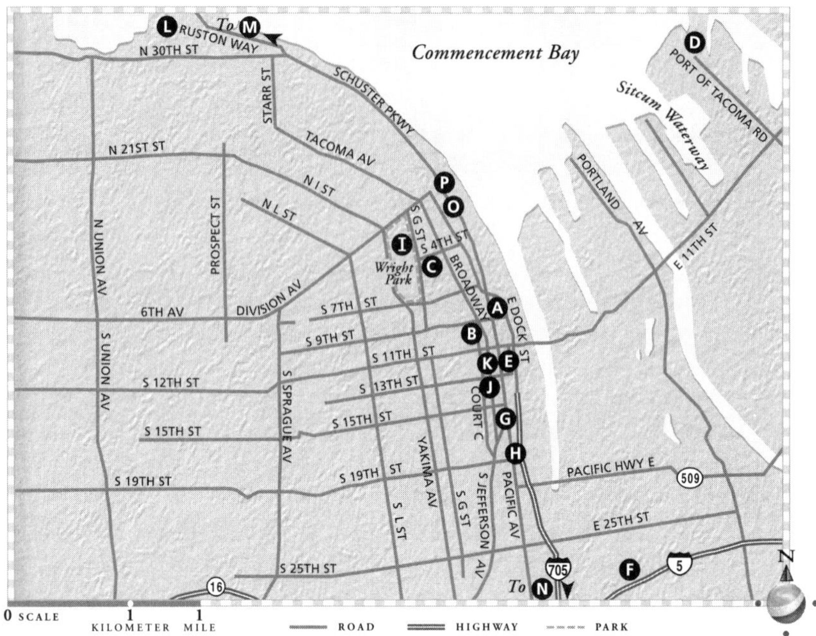

SIGHTS

- A Broadway Center for the Performing Arts
- B Children's Museum of Tacoma
- C Karpeles Manuscript Museum
- D Port of Tacoma
- E Tacoma Art Museum
- F Tacoma Dome

SIGHTS *(continued)*

- G Union Station
- H Washington State History Museum
- I W. W. Seymour Botanical Conservatory

FOOD

- J Altezzo
- K Fujiya

FOOD *(continued)*

- L Harbor Lights
- M Lobster Shop
- N Stanley & Seafort's

LODGING

- O Chinaberry B&B
- J Sheraton Tacoma Hotel
- P The Villa B&B

Note: Items with the same letter are located in the same area.

---

cluding Japanese, rhododendron, dahlia, trial, and herb gardens. In addition, 14 miles of hiking trails offer dramatic views over the water to the Olympic Mountains. Take the ferry to Vashon Island.

Details: *From I-5, take Exit 132 to Highway 16 and take the Sixth*

Avenue Exit and turn left. Take the next right onto Pearl Street and follow signs to Point Defiance Park; signs will direct you to the zoo. Point Defiance Zoo and Aquarium open year-round, 10 to 7 during summer. Admission is $7, seniors $6.55, kids 4 to 13 $5.30, ages 3 and under free. (2–3 hours)

★★★★ WASHINGTON STATE HISTORY MUSEUM

1911 Pacific Avenue, Tacoma, 888/238-4373

This impressive building echoes the design of its neighbor, Union Station; walk in and you feel like you're entering a train station—explore and feel as if you're on a journey into Washington's past. The 106,000-square-foot facility cost $40.8 million to build in 1996. There are permanent exhibits on the fishing, fruit, timber, and wheat industries of Washington. Their geological display gives a visual overview of the formation of the Northwest. The gift shop here sells Washington wines.

Details: *Open Tuesday through Saturday 10 to 5, Thursday until 8, Sunday 11 to 5. Admission is $7, seniors $6, students $5, ages 6 to 12 $4. (2–3 hours)*

★★★ BROADWAY CENTER FOR THE PERFORMING ARTS

901 Broadway (ticket office), 253/591-5894

The renovation of the Pantages Theater is at the heart of the cultural arts center along Broadway. Built as a vaudeville house in 1918 by Alexander Pantages, it is a striking example of early 20th-century Greco-Roman design. The Rialto, also built in 1918, has Beaux Arts decor. These historic venues, as well as Theatre on the Square, showcase regular live theater and musical performances.

Details: *Ticket office open Monday through Friday from 11:30 to 5:30. (1/2 hour to view; performances vary)*

★★★ KARPELES MANUSCRIPT MUSEUM

407 South G St., Tacoma, 253/383-2575

A surprise of a museum showcases original handwritten drafts, letters, and documents of famous people including Napoleon and Thomas Jefferson. The museum hosts special exhibits, too. Across the street from the W. W. Seymour Botanical Conservatory.

Details: *Open 10 to 4 Tuesday through Sunday. Admission is free. (1 hour)*

★★★ LAKEWOLD GARDENS

12317 Gravelly Lake Drive SW, Lakewood, 253/584-3360

SIDE TRIP: MT. RAINIER

Mt. Rainier, "the mountain" of the Northwest, is about a 90-minute drive from Tacoma along the Mountain Highway. En route, you'll pass the visitors center at Longmire, near the National Park Inn (past the western entrance to the park). Stop here or at the Jackson Visitors Center at Paradise to peruse maps, books, videos, and wildflower and wildlife exhibits. A good book on wildflowers will enrich your visit.

Summer afternoon temperatures at Paradise average in the mid-60s with nighttime temperatures in the lower 40s. Hikers should carry extra clothing, rain gear, maps and a compass, and extra food. Keep altitude in mind (Mt. Rainier peaks at 14,411 feet), taking rest breaks as needed; hiking boots are recommended. Hiking staffs and bear bells are available for sale in the gift shops at Paradise Inn, at the visitors center, and at Longmire. Check with the ranger on snow conditions before venturing on the high trails. Peak bloom time with the greatest flower variety and abundance, is July. To reach Mt. Rainier from Interstate 5, take Exit 134, just south of Tacoma. This is Highway 7 (and connects to State Route 706), the most direct route, and is also the route known as the Mountain Highway. For park information and maps, contact Mt. Rainier National Park, 360/569-2211. Park admission is $10. Gray Line of Seattle offers daily escorted bus tours to the mountain; call 800/426-7532.

www.lakewoldgardens.org
These beautiful former private gardens, designed by noted landscape architect Thomas Church, mix Northwest and classic styles with one of the largest Japanese maple and rhododendron collections in the Northwest. This 10-acre estate is considered one of the best gardens in America. A treat for gardeners and non-gardeners alike.

Details: *Open Thursdays through Mondays 9 to 4. Admission $6, seniors and kids under 12, $5. (2 hours)*

★★★ NISQUALLY NATIONAL WILDLIFE REFUGE

One of the few remaining untouched river deltas in the United States, the refuge covers nearly 3,000 acres of salt marsh, forested swamp, and wetland meadows. Boaters, canoers, and kayakers can explore by

It's easy to combine a trip to Mt. Rainier with an overnight visit, and there are some terrific options, like a stay at ***Paradise Inn.*** *While not luxurious, the old lodge is cozy, and it's on a spectacular site. The original guest rooms on the second floor of the main building are not soundproof, so expect creaking floors and thin walls. In keeping with the original building, there are no telephones or televisions. If you want to be awakened early, alert the desk and you'll receive a wake-up knock on the door. There is no elevator; some rooms are handicapped accessible.* ***National Park Inn*** *(Longmire) has 25 rooms; two on the ground floor are handicapped accessible. Built in 1989—similar to the log inn James Longmire built here in 1884—this lodge has an older feel and modern amenities. Rooms are light and cheery, decorated with twig furniture; all have forest views. Rooms fronting the lodge and road have mountain views. For reservations at Paradise Inn and Longmire's National Park Inn, contact Mount Rainier Guest Services, P.O. Box 108, Ashford, WA 98304; 360/569-2275, fax 360/569-2770.* ***Alexander's Country Inn,*** *800/654-7615, one mile west of the Nisqually entrance (on State Route 706) in the small town of Ashford, is another historic lodging. Built in 1912 and renovated over time, it is a comfortable blend of old and new. There are no elevators, phones, televisions, or air-conditioning; and no smoking.*

water. Walking loops up to 5.6 miles take you through wildlife viewing areas. And it's a scenic drive past the refuge on I-5.

Details: *On the Pierce-Thurston county line west of I-5, take Exit 114. Open daily during daylight hours, information office open 7:30 to 4. Admission $2 per family. (1–2 hours)*

★★★ NORTHWEST TREK WILDLIFE PARK
Eatonville, 360/832-6117
www.nwtrek.org

You can take an hour-long tram tour of this 625-acre sanctuary with its herds of free-roaming bison, caribou, and bighorn sheep. And you'll see wolves and grizzly bears and birds of prey in contained natural habitats. There are five miles of walking trails.

Details: *The park lies about 17 miles east of Tacoma off SR 161*

TACOMA AND MT. RAINIER REGION

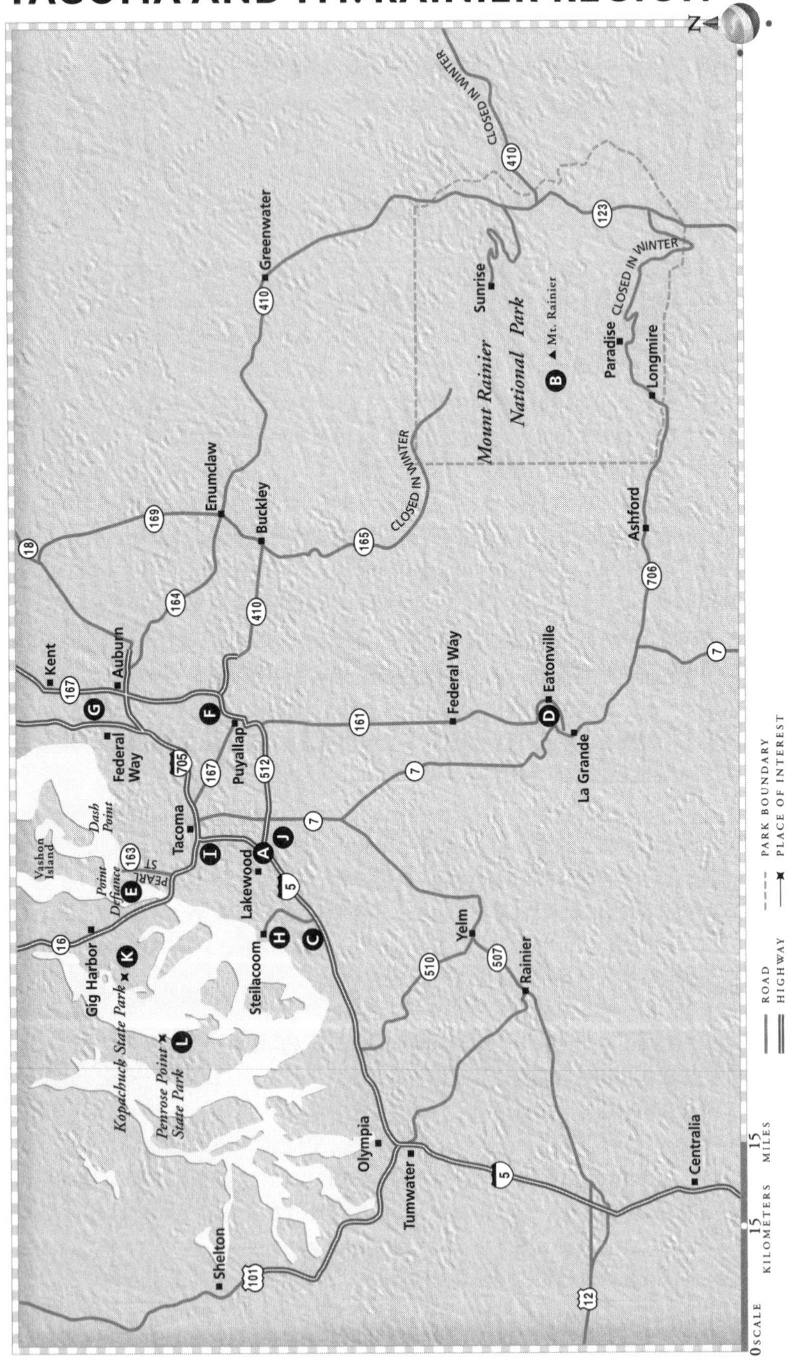

near Eatonville; call for directions. Open at 9:30 daily. Admission is $8.25 for adults, $7.75 for seniors, $5.75 for kids 5 to 17, $3.75 for kids 3 and 4, free for ages 2 and under. (2–3 hours)

★★★ STEILACOOM

Washington's oldest incorporated town lies west of Tacoma. The whole town of Steilacoom is on the National Register of Historic Places and includes the oldest standing church in the state. Bair Drug & Hardware Museum, with a delightful 1906 soda fountain, is a café as well and serves up old-fashioned ice-cream sodas, sasparilla, and sundaes.

Details: *Maps of a self-guided walking tour are available at Steilacoom Historical Museum at 112 Main Street in the lower level of the town hall. Bair Drug, 1617 Lafayette Street, serves breakfast and lunch; open daily year-round, 9 to 4. (1–2 hours)*

★★★ UNION STATION

1717 Pacific Avenue, Tacoma, 253/931-7884

Built in 1911 by the Northern Pacific Railroad, this landmark domed brick building was a railway station until 1983. Now it's a federal courthouse with a public rotunda that exhibits Chihuly glass. It's well worth a quick look before you head into the Washington State History Museum next door.

Details: *(15 minutes)*

SIGHTS

- **A** Lakewold Gardens
- **B** Mt. Rainier National Park
- **C** Nisqually National Wildlife Refuge
- **D** Northwest Trek Wildlife Park
- **E** Point Defiance Park and Point Defiance Zoo and Aquarium
- **F** Puyallup

SIGHTS *(continued)*

- **G** Rhododendron Species Botanical Garden
- **H** Steilacoom

FOOD

- **E** Anthony's Home Port
- **H** E. R. Rogers Restaurant
- **I** Mama Stortini's

LODGING

- **J** DeVoe Mansion B&B

CAMPING

- **K** Kopachuck State Park
- **L** Penrose Point State Park

Note: Items with the same letter are located in the same area.

★★ CHILDREN'S MUSEUM OF TACOMA

936 Broadway, Tacoma, 253/627-6031

Hands-on arts and science exhibits, a play village, lots of colorful fish, activities, and much more keep children entertained.

Details: *Open Tuesday through Saturday 10 to 5, Sunday noon to 5. Admission is $4.25 per person, seniors $3.25, under 2 free. Every Friday night is free from 5 to 9.*

★★ PORT OF TACOMA

One Sitcum Plaza, Tacoma 253/383-5481

The sixth-largest container port in North America, the Port of Tacoma lies north of the city. A 24-hour observation tower, with interpretive information, overlooks Sitcum Waterway and the port activities.

Details: *From I-5 take the City Center Exit (#133), follow signs for 705 north to the A Street Exit. From A Street take a right onto 11th street and follow it to SeaLand Drive. Free admission. Open 24 hours. (1 hour)*

★★ PUYALLUP

Since 1900 Puyallup (pronounced "pew-AL-up") has hosted the Western Washington State Fair, which now draws 1.5 million visitors annually. It is also known for its spring fields of daffodils and other bulb flowers. Seventeen-room Ezra Meeker Mansion, built by Puyallup's founder in 1890, is open for touring

Details: *Meeker Mansion, 253/848-1770; www.meekermansion.com; open mid-March through mid-December, Wednesday through Sunday afternoons. Admission is $4 adults, $3 students and seniors. (45 minutes)*

★★ RHODODENDRON SPECIES BOTANICAL GARDEN

33660 Weyerhaeuser Way S., Federal Way, 253/661-9377

One of the largest collections of rhododendrons in the world, this garden includes 24 acres of rhododendrons, from one-inch Chinese dwarfs to 100-foot Himalayan giants. It's on the Weyerhaeuser Company campus in Federal Way, north of Tacoma.

Details: *Open March to May daily 10 to 4, closed Thursday. Call for additional hours information. Admission $3.50. (2 hours)*

★★ TACOMA ART MUSEUM

12th Street and Pacific Avenue, Tacoma, 253/272-4258

You'll find sculptured glass by Dale Chihuly and the works of other

Northwest artists, as well as classics by Renoir, Chagall, and Dali at this museum.

Details: *Open 10 to 5 Tuesday through Saturday, noon to 5 Sunday. Admission charged. (1 hour)*

★ W. W. SEYMOUR BOTANICAL CONSERVATORY

316 South G Street, Tacoma, 253/591-5330

Built in 1908, this Victorian-style conservatory, in Wright Park contains over 200 species of exotic and tropical plants, including ornamental figs, bird-of-paradise, and bromeliads. It's on the state and National Historic Registers and is located across from the Karpeles Museum.

Details: *From I-5 take Exit 133 to City Center, follow signs for 705 North, take the Stadium Way Exit, turn right on Stadium Way, turn left on Fourth Street to G Street. Open daily 10 to 4:30. Admission free. (1/2 hour)*

FITNESS AND RECREATION

Jogging or walking Ruston Way's two-mile waterfront promenade offers great views of Commencement Bay; more views can be had exploring Point Defiance Park and Zoo.

The Tacoma Dome, the largest wooden dome in the nation, is the venue for sports, entertainment, and trade shows. The city's hockey team, the Tacoma Sabercats, plays here as well. For event information and tickets, call 253/272-6817. Tacoma has a professional baseball team, the Tacoma Rainiers, that plays class-AAA Pacific Coast League baseball at Cheney Stadium; 800/281-3834.

FOOD

Ruston Way is known as Restaurant Row. You'll find **Harbor Lights,** 2761 Ruston Way, 253/752-8600, with waterfront views of Commencement Bay. For decades it's offered delightful classics like steamed clams. Two **Lobster Shop** restaurants offer nice dining options with simply prepared seafood and great views of Commencement Bay. The newer location is at 4013 Ruston Way, 253/759-2165, in a modern setting. The original, 253/927-1513, is across the bay at 6912 Sound View Drive NE off Dash Point Road. The 15-minute drive from downtown Tacoma is worth it if you prefer the ambience and charm of a restaurant in an old house. **Fujiya** at 1125 Court C, 253/627-5319, near the Broadway Theater district and the Sheraton Hotel, has great sushi and Japanese food at reasonable prices. Go to **Stanley & Seaforts,** 115 East 34th Street, 253/473-7300, for a seafood and salad lunch and a great view of Commencement Bay. Also, an incredible view can be had from **Altezzo,** 253/572-3200, at the top of the Sheraton Tacoma Hotel, along with the Northern Italian–style food. **Mama Stortini's** at 3715 Bridgeport Way, 253/566-1976, serves up family-style Italian food. The orders are big; request a full order of spaghetti and you'll probably take half home.

A great family stop for lunch or dinner is the new **Anthony's Home Port,** 5910 N. Waterfront Drive, 253/752-9700, located on pilings over the water next to the Vashon ferry terminal at the base of the Point Defiance Zoo and Aquarium. **E.R. Rogers Restaurant,** 1702 Commercial Street, 253/582-0280, in Steilacoom south of Tacoma offers views of the Tacoma Narrows Bridge, along with salmon dishes and other classics (Sunday brunch and dinners only), in a historic 1891 mansion that's been decorated in the Victorian style.

Or take a day trip and plan to eat at one of the lodges in Mt. Rainier National Park. **Paradise Inn** has a rustic, open-beamed dining room that seats 200. Sunday brunch ($15 per person) is a special event with gourmet touches like crepes and omelets made to order. In Longmire, on the approach to Paradise, the **National Park Inn**'s restaurant offers soups, sandwiches, daily specials, and yummy desserts.

LODGING

Located in the heart of downtown and visible from I-5 is the **Sheraton Tacoma Hotel,** 1320 Broadway, 206/572-3200. There are several popular B&Bs, including **Chinaberry Hill,** a beautifully restored historic Victorian near downtown at 302 Tacoma Avenue N.; 253/272-1282 or www.chinaberryhill.com; and **The Villa,** an impressive Mediterranean-style home nearby at 705 N. Fifth Street, 253/572-1157 or 888/572-1157, www.villabb.com.

South of the city is DeVoe Mansion, 208 East 133rd Street, 253/539-3991 or www.devoemansion.com, which feels like a touch of the Old South. For more B&B listings, contact the Greater Tacoma B&B reservation service, 253/759-4088 and 800/406-4088 or www.tacoma-inns.org; or the B&B Association of Tacoma and Mt. Rainier, 253/593-6098 or 888/593-6098.

There are also plentiful motel lodgings off I-5 south of Tacoma and along the Mountain Highway, just east of the city; contact the visitors bureau, 800/272-2662.

CAMPING

Kopachuck State Park, 360/265-3606, is on Henderson Bay, north of Tacoma, with over 40 campsites for tents and self-contained motor homes up to 35 feet. There's a beach area for exploring; no reservations. **Penrose Point**

State Park, also northwest of Tacoma, overlooks Carr Inlet on Puget Sound, 253/884-2514; no reservations. Mt. Rainier National Park offers five campgrounds (including the popular area of Ohanapecosh at the park's southeastern edge) with tent sites; none have RV hookups. Most sites are open from Memorial Day to mid-October. For details call 360/569-2211.

NIGHTLIFE

Sometimes you'll have to stand in line to get into **Drakes,** 734 Pacific Avenue, 253/572-4144, a popular downtown hot spot. **Jillian's,** 1114 Broadway, 253/572-0300, offers billiards and entertainment. There's evening entertainment at the **Harmon Brewery,** 1948 Pacific Avenue, 253/383-2739, across from the museum. At **The Swiss,** 1904 South Jefferson, 253/572-2821, the entertainment includes a Sunday Polka Dance. Evenings are lively at the **Spar Tavern,** 2121 North 30th, 253/627-8215, a fixture in Tacoma for over a century and a fun place to peruse the walls covered with turn-of-the-century photos. For an evening at the theater, tickets for **Tacoma Actors Guild** (TAG) performances are available at the ticket office at 915 Broadway, near the Theatre on the Square Broadway Street entrance, or by calling 253/272-2145.

Scenic Route: Kitsap Peninsula

This "back door" route to Tacoma takes you on several ferries and gives you a flavor of Bainbridge Island, the Kitsap Peninsula, and Vashon Island. You'll have expansive views of the Cascade and Olympic Mountains on the ferry from Seattle's waterfront to Bainbridge Island (a 35-minute crossing). The ferry landing is north of the town of Bainbridge (formerly called Winslow), which has antiques shops, galleries, and restaurants. If you stay on Highway 305, you'll pass Bainbridge Island Winery, 682 State Highway 305, 206/842-WINE, which has a tasting room.

Continue northwest to the Scandinavian town of Poulsbo, reminiscent of a Scandinavian fishing village—with its boat-filled marina, skyline capped by the First Lutheran Church steeple, and historic district fit snugly along fjordlike Liberty Bay. Known as Little Norway, the town was settled in 1892 by farmers, fishers, and loggers from Norway who saw similarities to their native land; the Nordic character of the community has remained strong. Plan to spend time strolling Front Street's variety of arts and crafts shops, bakeries, and antiques stores. In Verksted Gallery, 1882 Front Street, 360/697-4470, an artists' cooperative that showcases Nordic crafts, you'll see dolls dressed in bunads *(folk costumes) reflecting authentic designs from different villages and districts*

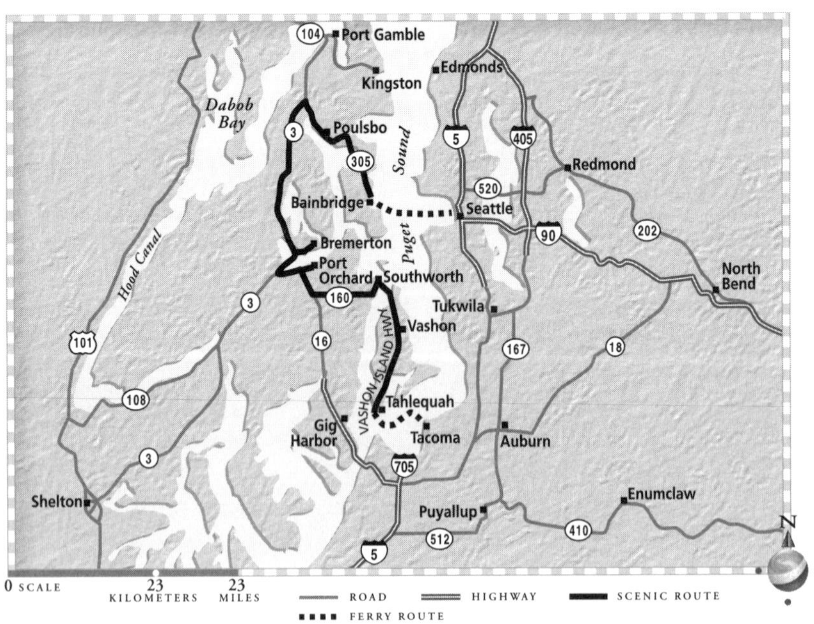

of Scandinavia. The Marine Science Center, 18743 Front Street NE, 360/779-5549, is a great place for kids to get the feel of touch tanks and to see educational exhibits.

From Poulsbo, take Highway 3 south to the city of Bremerton. This is the largest city on the peninsula and home to the Bremerton Naval Museum, 360/479-7447, and Puget Sound Naval Shipyard. You can take a harbor tour of the Navy's mothball fleet for $8.50 (Kitsap Harbor Tours, 360/377-8924) and visit the most decorated ship in World War II, the USS Turner Joy *(Bremerton Historic Ships Association, 360/792-2457).*

From Bremerton, take the 10-mile loop around the west end of Sinclair Inlet to Port Orchard, where antique shopping awaits, and continue east on Highway 166 to Southworth. Take the ferry to Vashon Island, which in recent years has become a bedroom community to Seattle and Tacoma. It is a quiet place that is best explored on bicycle. So if you plan to spend time here, bring your bikes and dress accordingly. Roads are bike-friendly, and you can get a pretty good workout exploring them.

Travel south on Vashon Island to the town of Tahlequah and take the ferry to the Point Defiance Zoo in Tacoma.

3 OLYMPIC PENINSULA

Mists, mystery, moss, and music—that's what comes to mind when I think of the Olympic Peninsula. Mists are easy to explain. You'll find them on beaches, in the mermaid-green rain forest, and curling around the tips of the majestic Olympic Mountains. The mystery aspect is more complex and has at its heart the Native American culture, the legends of the settlers, and the moody atmosphere created by the towering ancient cedar and fir trees.

In the center of Olympic National Park is 7,965-foot Mt. Olympus, snow-capped year-round. Its base is the wettest spot in the lower 48 states, receiving 200 inches of precipitation a year; the three rain forest valleys—the Quinault, Queets, and Hoh—each receive between 141 and 161 inches per year. The moss hangs in curtains from tree limbs in the forest, especially along the Hall of Mosses Trail in the Hoh Valley. You'll likely hear the legend of the Iron Man of the Hoh, John Huelsdonk, an early settler who carried an iron stove on his back for miles through the rain forest.

You can sit on a hay bale or sprawl on a blanket in a meadow and listen to the Chamber Musicians play Mozart and Bach at the Olympic Music Festival's Concerts in the Barn, performed each summer near Port Ludlow. For blues and fiddle music, Fort Worden's summer festival near Port Townsend provides that and more. And, of course, there's the rhythm of the rain, drip, drip, dripping in the rain forest.

A PERFECT DAY ON THE OLYMPIC PENINSULA

The eastern portion of the peninsula is easily reached on a day trip, but it's more fun to overnight. A perfect day would begin early with breakfast at an inn or B&B around Port Ludlow (for golfers), Port Townsend (for history fans), or Sequim (to guarantee your best weather); it would include a meander along Port Townsend's waterfront, a picnic lunch listening to classical music (Concerts in the Barn), and a splurge on dinner at Heron Beach Inn.

A perfect day on the west side of the peninsula includes a thoughtfully reflective walk in the rain forest or along a primitive beach—such as Cape Alava—and ends after dinner at a classic old lodge like Lake Quinault or Kalaloch.

ORIENTATION

The Olympic Peninsula lies to the west of Seattle, Puget Sound, and Hood Canal. Highway 101 almost circles the region (and Olympic National Park and Olympic National Forest), and any visit to the peninsula puts you on this road. Unlike its route along Oregon's coastline, Highway 101 in Washington skirts very few of the state's Pacific beaches, with the exception of a beautiful 13-mile stretch north of Queets that includes Kalaloch and Ruby Beach. You'll find the west side of the Olympic Peninsula wild and undeveloped compared to southwestern washington. The most densely populated areas—Port Angeles, Port Townsend, and Port Ludlow—are on the northeastern peninsula.

Highway 101 to the peninsula can be accessed four major ways: 1) West from Interstate-5 at Olympia, following it north along Hood Canal; 2) From Seattle's waterfront by taking the ferry (**Washington State Ferries,** 800/843-3779 in state or www.wsdot. wa.gov/ferries/) to Bainbridge Island or Bremerton (or from the Edmonds waterfront north of Seattle, by ferrying to Kingston) and driving north and west; 3) From the Oregon Coast by following 101 north; and 4) From Vancouver Island via **Black Ball Transport** ferry (360/457-4491, www.north olympic.com/coho), with two sailings a day to Port Angeles.

The website for the **Olympic Peninsula Visitor's Association** is www.northolympic.com. For extensive B&B options, contact the **Olympic Peninsula Bed & Breakfast Association,** 360/374-6806.

SIGHTSEEING HIGHLIGHTS

★★★★ CAPE FLATTERY

Cape Flattery is at the far northwestern tip of the peninsula. Be pre-

OLYMPIC PENINSULA

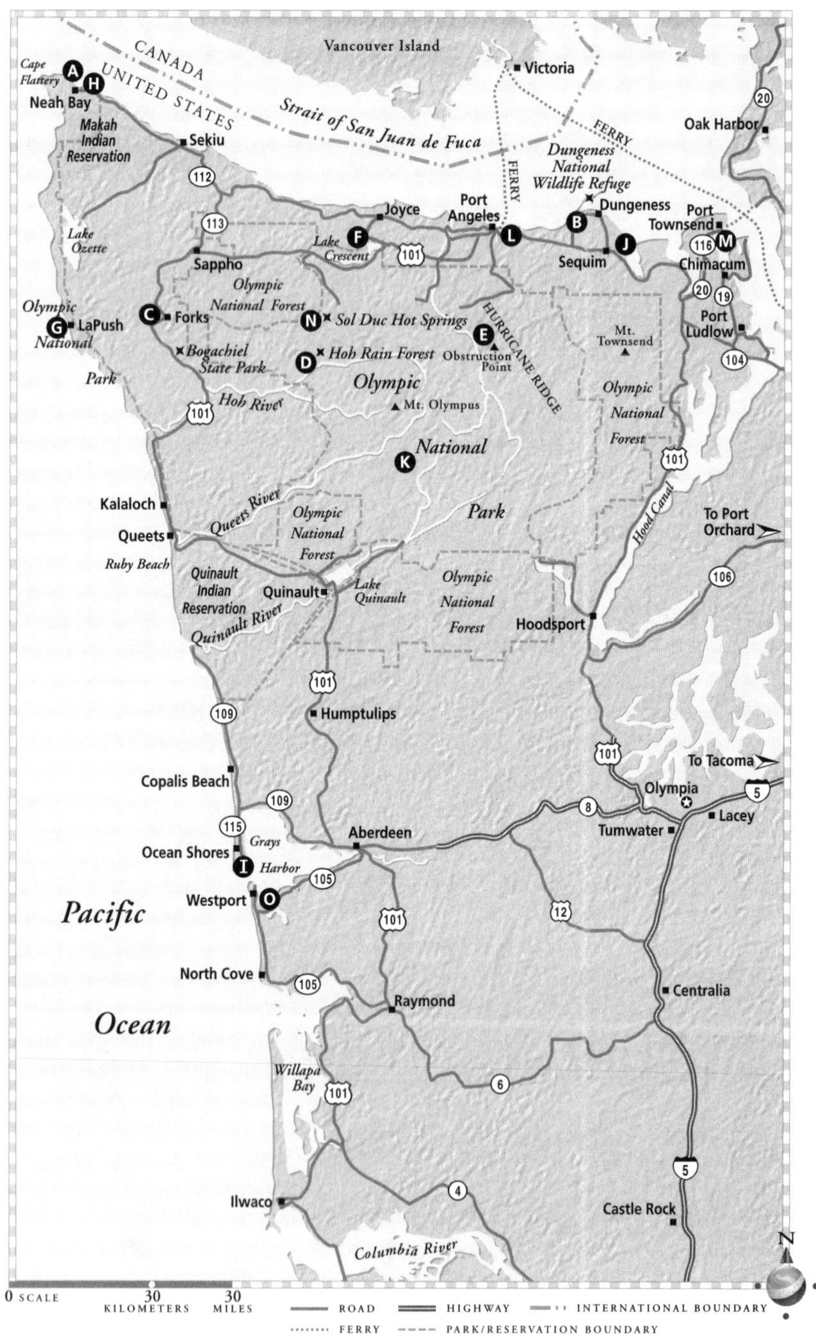

Vancouver Island
CANADA
UNITED STATES
Victoria
Strait of San Juan de Fuca
FERRY
Cape Flattery
Neah Bay
Makah Indian Reservation
Sekiu
Oak Harbor
Dungeness National Wildlife Refuge
Dungeness
Port Angeles
Joyce
Port Townsend
Lake Ozette
Sappho
Lake Crescent
Sequim
Chimacum
Olympic National Forest
Olympic National Park
LaPush
Forks
Sol Duc Hot Springs
HURRICANE RIDGE
Port Ludlow
Bogachiel State Park
Hoh Rain Forest
Obstruction Point
Mt. Townsend
Hoh River
Olympic
Mt. Olympus
National
Park
Kalaloch
Queets
Queets River
Hood Canal
To Port Orchard
Ruby Beach
Quinault Indian Reservation
Quinault
Quinault River
Lake Quinault
Hoodsport
Humptulips
To Tacoma
Olympia
Copalis Beach
Tumwater
Lacey
Grays Harbor
Ocean Shores
Aberdeen
Westport
Pacific
Ocean
North Cove
Centralia
Raymond
Willapa Bay
Ilwaco
Castle Rock
Columbia River
0 SCALE
30 KILOMETERS
30 MILES
ROAD
HIGHWAY
INTERNATIONAL BOUNDARY
FERRY
PARK/RESERVATION BOUNDARY

pared for primitive rutted roads and slow going, but once at the cape you'll find a trail to Cape Flattery Lighthouse. There's a spectacular view of Tatoosh Island and its lighthouse from the cliffs here, where the Pacific Ocean meets the Strait of Juan de Fuca. Little known is that it's the site of a Civil War naval battle between the CSS *Shenandoah* and the USS *Abigail*.

Details: *Going west from Neah Bay, follow the Cape Loop Road. (half day)*

★★★★ HURRICANE RIDGE

Park Visitor Center, 360/452-0330
www.nps.gov/olym/hom.htm

A 17-mile drive along a steep winding road from Port Angeles brings you to over 5,200 feet above sea level, with magnificent views of the glacier-covered peaks, subalpine tundra, and deeply carved river valleys of the Olympic Mountains. You can downhill and cross-country ski and snowshoe the trails in winter. During the summer, park naturalists lead meadow walks.

Details: *From U.S. 101 in Port Angeles, take the Race Street Exit . Obstruction Point Road, a steep 8.4-mile road east of the ridge, offers the best views of Mt. Olympus; open mid-summer to early fall. For general road conditions call the park visitors center. (3 hours)*

★★★★ MAKAH CULTURAL AND RESEARCH CENTER

On SR 112 at Neah Bay, 360/645-2711
www.mcrc.com

This impressive $3 million facility in Neah Bay at the tip of the peninsula contains the artifacts from the Ozette Village ruins, a 2,000-year-old site at Cape Alava. Buried about 500 years ago in a mud slide, the

---

SIGHTS

- Ⓐ Cape Flattery
- Ⓑ Dungeness Spit
- Ⓒ Forks
- Ⓓ Hoh Rain Forest
- Ⓔ Hurricane Ridge
- Ⓕ Lake Crescent
- Ⓖ LaPush
- Ⓗ Makah Cultural and Research Center
- Ⓘ Ocean Shores
- Ⓙ Olympic Game Farm
- Ⓚ Olympic National Park
- Ⓛ Port Angeles
- Ⓜ Port Townsend
- Ⓙ Sequim
- Ⓝ Sol Duc Hot Springs
- Ⓞ Westport

Note: Items with the same letter are located in the same area.

site was excavated in the 1970s. It is sealed, but the artifacts—including harpoons, an old fishing net, carved figures, and household items—are on display at the center. Combine a stop here with a hike at Cape Flattery.

Details: *Summer hours 10 to 5 daily; Wednesday to Sunday remainder of year. Admission about $4. (2 hours)*

★★★★ OLYMPIC NATIONAL PARK

Visitors Center, Port Angeles, 360/452-0330.

Presidents Theodore and Franklin Roosevelt both were instrumental in setting aside over a million acres of wilderness that constitute Olympic National Park, one of the nation's most beautiful parks. You'll find a rare rain forest, wildlife—it's home to the country's largest herd of Roosevelt elk—and 600 miles of hiking trails. There are 57 miles of primitive coastline. The park is surrounded by the reservations of several Native American tribes including the Chehalis, Hoh, Quileute, Quinault, and Makah.

Details: *(full day minimum)*

★★★★ PORT TOWNSEND

Visitor Center, 2437 East Sims Way, 360/385-2722
www.ptguide.com

Seventy buildings in this Victorian-style seaport town of 7,000 are on the National Register of Historic Places; many of the historic homes are B&Bs, and the town itself is a National Historic Landmark. Nearby Fort Worden guarded Admiralty Inlet during World War II and is the site of a popular arts and music festival. The Keystone Ferry leaves from here to Whidbey Island.

Details: *Contact the Port Townsend Chamber of Commerce Visitor Center for tour information. (3 hours)*

★★★ DUNGENESS SPIT

Sequim, 360/457-8451
www.fws.gov

This is a narrow, nearly six-mile-long finger of land that hooks out into the Strait of Juan de Fuca, near Sequim. It's thought to be the longest natural sand spit in the world. The spit is a wildlife refuge, and its inner shores are rich with grasses and shorebirds. A lighthouse is located at its tip.

Details: *About seven miles northwest of Sequim on U.S. 101. Turn*

THE ANN STARRETT MANSION

The 1889 Ann Starrett Mansion that businessman George Starrett built for his bride, Ann, sits on a hill above Port Townsend. Constructed in Victorian Stick style, it is one of Port Townsend's most renowned historic homes and B&Bs. Its turret, gables, gingerbread trim, and pastel colors are a snapshot taker's dream. Inside there are period furnishings, frescoed ceilings, and a unique free-hung three-level staircase. Starrett had a New York artist, George Chapman, create a solar calendar for the rare, eight-sided dome tower that tops the staircase, using the likeness of his wife for the four seasons and four virtues. On the first day of each season (solstice), when the sun shines through the ruby-colored glass installed in the tower's small dormer windows, a beam of light is projected onto that season's figure. Scheduled tours are available. The house is at 744 Clay Street; 360/385-3205 or 800/321-0644 or www.starettmansion.com.

north on Kitchen Dick Road. Open dawn to dusk daily. Admission $2 per family. (2–4 hours)

★★★ FORKS

Chamber of Commerce, 360/374-2531 or 800/443-6757
www.forkswa.com

A town of 5,000, Forks is synonymous with the logging industry and the spotted owl controversy. Here you'll find the Forks Timber Museum and Loggers Memorial. The area is also known for fast-running rivers with steelhead and salmon.

Details: *(1 hour)*

★★★ HOH RAIN FOREST

South of Forks, 360/374-6925

The magical heart of the forest is in the moss-draped trees. The Hall of Mosses Trail is less than a mile long and offers a close-up look at the flora of the rain forest ecosystem.

Details: *Exit U.S. 101 about 13 miles south of Forks and follow the*

SIDE TRIP: THE SHORES OF HOOD CANAL

Captain George Vancouver and his crew sailed into Hood Canal in the spring of 1792. The shores of the 62-mile-long forested fjord were abloom with dogwood and wild rhododendron, its waters filled with oysters, spot prawns, and fish. To the west lay the snowcapped Olympic Mountains. What's beautiful about this canal hasn't changed. Visit in spring or fall for quiet exploring; come in summer and parks and shorefront communities buzz with activity.

This drive is about 135 miles all the way around—starting and ending at the Hood Canal Floating Bridge.

This tour starts from the north (take the Bainbridge Island Ferry from Seattle or the Kingston Ferry from Edmonds) and begins by visiting two very different ports flanking the mouth of the canal.

***Port Gamble** historic site lies seven miles from Kingston, on State Highway 104. A lumber mill built here in 1853 operated until the mid-1990s, and the town housed mill workers and their families. A church, fire station, and many fine old clapboard homes give it the air of a New England village. From the overlook you may see a Trident submarine pass through the waters from the nearby base at Bangor. Before you leave town, pick up a map and ferry schedule at the visitors center.*

*About a mile beyond Port Gamble, go right at Hood Canal Bridge (still State 104), crossing the north end of the canal. On a clear day you'll have close-up views of the Olympic Mountains. Just beyond the bridge, take the Paradise Bay Road exit (the first right). About four miles from the exit you'll see signs to **Port Ludlow Resort,** a residential and vacation community for boaters and golfers. Nearby is the **Heron Beach Inn** (see page 73). Back on State 104, continue west and take the turn-off to **Quilcine** and drive south through forested hills. You'll soon be on U.S. 101.*

*The clean waters of Hood Canal make it a perfect home for oysters. Many bivalves take their names from the rivers that start in the Olympics and feed into the canal, such as Quilcine. The marina and estuary of the Quilcine River is two miles from the highway, on Linger Longer Road. Here, too, is the area's largest oyster seed farm. For oysters, crabs, clams, and other seafood drop by **Hood Canal Seafood Marketplace** in Quilcine (294963 Highway 101; 360/765-4880; open 10 to 7 daily).*

Eleven miles south at **Whitney Gardens and Nursery** *in Brinnon, 306264 Highway 101, 360/796-4411, you'll find a seven-acre display garden, including native rhododendrons, and plants for sale; open daily.* **Dosewallips State Park** *just beyond Brinnon has grassy campsites and beach access. Continuing south 13 miles, you'll find the* **Eldon Schoolhouse B&B,** *N. 36840 Highway 101 at Eldon, 360/631-5109. It's set back from the road and offers three units with baths and water views. The* **Hungry Bear Restaurant** *(next to the Eldon Schoolhouse B&B), 360/877-5527, is a classic café with booths.*

It's fun to buy oysters and other seafood direct from the growers and hard to beat the selection at the **Hama Hama Company,** *N. 35959 Highway 101, 360/877-5890, south of Eldon.*

Hoodsport, *12 miles south of Eldon, is the largest community along the west side, with a marina, motels, and eateries. You can taste a local vintage made from Island Belle grapes at the* **Hoodsport Winery,** *N. 23501 Highway 101, 360/877-9894; open daily 10 to 6.*

Potlatch State Park *has waterfront picnic sites near the* **Skokomish Indian Reservation.** *Watch for* **Joan's Smoked Salmon,** *20031 N. Highway 101, 360/877-6737, for vacuum-packed smoked steelhead, salmon, and oysters—frequently samples are available for tasting.*

Take State Highway 106, as the canal sharply hooks east, and you'll follow the Hood Canal's gold coast—a mix of modest and grand vacation homes along the south shore. **Victoria's Restaurant,** *E. 6790 Highway 106, 360/898-4400, is a good reason to stop in Union for fried oysters from nearby Skokomish Bay, local fresh berries, and hearty country breakfasts on Sunday mornings. Reservations suggested.*

Alderbrook Inn/CRISTA Conference Center, *E. 7101 Highway 106, 800/622-9370, was once best known for its 18-hole golf course. However, the lodge complex has been refurbished in recent years and is a good family destination. There are 78 lodge rooms and 22 two-bedroom cottages dotting the forested grounds. Kayaks, paddleboats and motorboats are available for rent. A restaurant fronts the water. No alcohol is served.*

road 19 miles to the visitors center. Open summers 9 to 6:30, remainder of the year 9 to 5. (1–2 hours)

★★★ LAKE CRESCENT

This is an impressive 12-mile-long, glacier-carved freshwater fishing lake west of Port Angeles. Its known for its Beardslee trout and gemlike setting. The lodge on its shores (see page 76) was visited by Franklin Roosevelt. A mile-long trail leads to 90-foot Marymere Falls.

Details: *17 miles west of Port Angeles on U.S. 101. (2 hours)*

★★★ OCEAN SHORES

Chamber of Commerce, 360/289-2451 or 800/76-BEACH

There's plenty of action at this sprawling fifties-style beach community on the southwestern edge of the Olympic Peninsula. On a beautiful day the six miles of flat sandy beach turn into a highway for horseback riders, mopeds, cars, kite flyers, and strollers. Away from the beach there's plenty of activity, too—bicycling, bumper cars, boating, gambling, golf—enough to keep all family members happy. Ocean Shores Reservations Bureau offers information on lodging and a central booking service, 800/562-8612 or 360/289-2430 or www.oceanshoresreservation.com.

Details: *Ocean Shores is about 120 miles south of Forks, 70 miles west of Olympia. (half day or longer)*

★★★ WESTPORT

800/345-6223

www.westportwa.com

You can fish from boats or from shore in this town on Washington's southwestern coast. Deep-sea fishing charters run year-round. There's surf fishing here (the surf is so good you'll even see surfers—in wetsuits, of course), a breakwater area, and jetties to fish from as well. You can go crabbing in season in the inner harbor off any of the floats or docks. Whale-watching season is March through May; you can join a charter boat excursion or view whales from the city viewing tower. The Westport Maritime Museum has whaling exhibits.

Details: *22 miles southwest of Aberdeen. Crab rings and bait are available at the Hungry Whale Grocery on Montesano Avenue, 360/268-0136, the town's main street, and at Neptune Charters, 360/268-0124, across from Float 14. (half day or overnight)*

★★ LAPUSH

This coastal community is home to the Quileute Indian Nation, whose square-mile reservation is located at the mouth of the Quileute River. Beach hiking and osprey- and seal-watching are tops here. Try First Beach, a mile-long crescent beach with resident ospreys at the south end.

Details: *Watch for the exit onto SR 110, two miles north of Forks. (half day)*

★★ OLYMPIC GAME FARM

1423 Ward Road, Sequim, 800/778-4295
www.olympicgamefarm.com

You can drive or take guided walks through buffalo, elk, and zebra habitats, where many other wild animals roam. Predators like lions, tigers, leopards, wolves, and cougars are in enclosures. There's a petting zoo for smaller children. A fishing pond is open during the summer.

Details: *Open daily at 9 a.m, closing times vary. Admission about $6 adults, free for kids 4 and under. (1 hour)*

★★ SEQUIM

Sequim Visitors Information Center, 360/683-6197 or 800/737-8462, www.cityofsequim.com

The town of Sequim (pronounced "squim"), population about 4,000, is the driest spot in western Washington, with an annual rainfall of approximately 16 inches (a perfect example of how Northwest weather can differ dramatically over short distances). Growing numbers of active retirees who play golf, boat, and like easy access to Victoria from nearby Port Angeles are locating here. Sequim hosts the oldest festival in the state, the Irrigation Festival; a Lavender and Jazz Festival; and a Salmon Bake in August. Saturday mornings from April to October you can visit the Open Aire Market downtown for local produce, flowers, and entertainment. The Olympic Game Farm, wineries, a flower farm, and Dungeness Golf Club are nearby.

Details: *To reach the visitors center, take the Washington Street exit (the first exit as you approach from the east) from U.S. 101 and go two miles; it's on the right. (1 hour)*

★★ SOL DUC HOT SPRINGS

West of Port Angeles, 360/327-3583
www.northolympic.com/solduc

These hot mineral springs, with hot and cool pool facilities, sit amid the moss-draped forest. This is a popular spot and can be uncomfortably crowded in summer. There is some cabin-style lodging and a campground.

Details: *Drive 30 miles west of Port Angeles on U.S. 101 to the turnoff to the hot springs, then another 12 miles or so. (2 hours or longer)*

★ **PORT ANGELES**
Visitor Information Center, 121 East Railroad Avenue
360/452-2363, www.cityofpa.com

The bustling commercial hub and largest town of the northern peninsula, Port Angeles has a population of about 18,000. It has a five-mile waterfront trail and the Arthur D. Feiro Marine Lab, which offers hands-on encounters with sea creatures. The Black Ball ferry to Victoria leaves from here. The Olympic National Park visitors center is here. Hurricane Ridge is a 40-minute drive south.

Details: *(1–2 hours)*

FITNESS AND RECREATION

Fishing, hiking, river rafting, bird-watching, horseback or llama trekking—these are just some of the activities to pursue on the Olympic Peninsula. Hundreds of trails in the Olympic National Park include rugged beaches, rain forest, and mountain terrain. The Concerts in the Barn run June through September, in an old dairy barn on a 40-acre farm, 10 miles west of the Hood Canal Bridge. For performance and ticket information, contact the Philadelphia String Quartet, P.O. Box 45776, Seattle, WA 98145-0776; 206/527-8839.

Sea kayaking is a favorite of water hounds. Sailors and would-be sailors can try *The Adventuress,* a 101-foot gaff-rigged tall ship, often moored in Port Townsend. Mates teach about the marine environment, navigation, and history. You can sign aboard for day sails (about $35 per person) or longer cruises. Be prepared to hoist or lower sails and to join in singing rousing sea shanties. No experience necessary. Sailings run April through October. For schedule and reservations, call Sound Experience, 360/379-0438, www.soundexp.org.

The Dungeness Golf & Country Club, 1965 Woodcock Road, outside Sequim, has a crab-shaped sand trap. The course is open to the public, and year-round golf packages are available; call 800/447-6826. Boaters will want to check out the John Wayne Marina in Sequim. East of town is 7 Cedars Casino, with a native arts store, operated by the Jamestown S'Klallam tribe. Also around Sequim are several wineries to tour, including Lost Mountain and Neuharth.

Ruby and Kalaloch Beaches are two of the most accessible beach areas. A half dozen short paths off U.S. 101 lead to these driftwood-rich spots. Ruby Beach is a wilderness beach with sea arches and tiny islands. Kalaloch, to the south, has a campground. Tidepool walks are offered by the National Park Service (listed in the park's newspaper).

The Olympic Park Institute offers a wide variety of field-oriented classes covering the arts and the natural and cultural history of the peninsula, from its historic Lake Crescent site. Elderhostel and school programs are also offered. Call 800/775-3720 for a free catalog; or visit www.wni.org/opi.

Half a dozen state park facilities offer camping and/or picnicking close to the canal and include Dosewallips State Park, Potlatch State Park, Twanoh State Park, and Belfair State Park; for information call 800/233-0321; for reservations 800/452-5687; or visit www.parks.wa.gov.

For hiking information and maps on the national forest land on the canal's west shore stop at the U.S. Forest Service office on at the south end of Quilcene on U.S. 101, 360/765-2200. In Hoodsport, the Forest Service office at N. 150 Lake Cushman Road (State 119), 360/877-5254, provides information on the Lake Cushman recreation area. There's an Olympic National Park information office here as well.

Kitsap Peninsula Visitor and Convention Bureau, 2 Rainier Avenue, Port Gamble, is open 9 to 5 daily; 800/416-5615. In Belfair, stop at the North Mason Visitors Information Center, Mary Theler Community Center, E. 22871 Highway 3, open 7:30 to 4 Monday through-Friday; 360/275-5548. For ferry information, call 800/843-3779 in Washington, or 206/464-6400 from out of state.

FOOD

Try the stylish and romantic dining room at the **Heron Beach Inn,** 360/437-0411, in Port Ludlow, for fine Northwest cuisine—especially seafood dishes. Go to Port Townsend's **Lonny's Restaurant,** 360/385-0700, at the Boat Haven for a special dinner. The menu offers rich and delicious seafood dishes among other interesting items. **Khu Larb Thai,** 360/385-5023, in Port Townsend, makes a good stop if you're in the mood for curries and spicy Thai food. For a sandwich, a cup of chowder, and bay views, go to **Cheeks Bistro & Cafe,** 360/379-5244, on Water Street in downtown Port Townsend.

In Port Angeles, it's **C'est Si Bon,** 360/452-8888, for French food and fine dining. Crab is what you come for at the **Three Crabs Restaurant,** 360/683-4264, an un-fancy café and local hangout overlooking the beach in Dungeness, near Sequim (their pies are worth stopping for, too). You'll sometimes see the crab pots steaming outside, and a crab shack offers retail seafood.

OLYMPIC PENINSULA

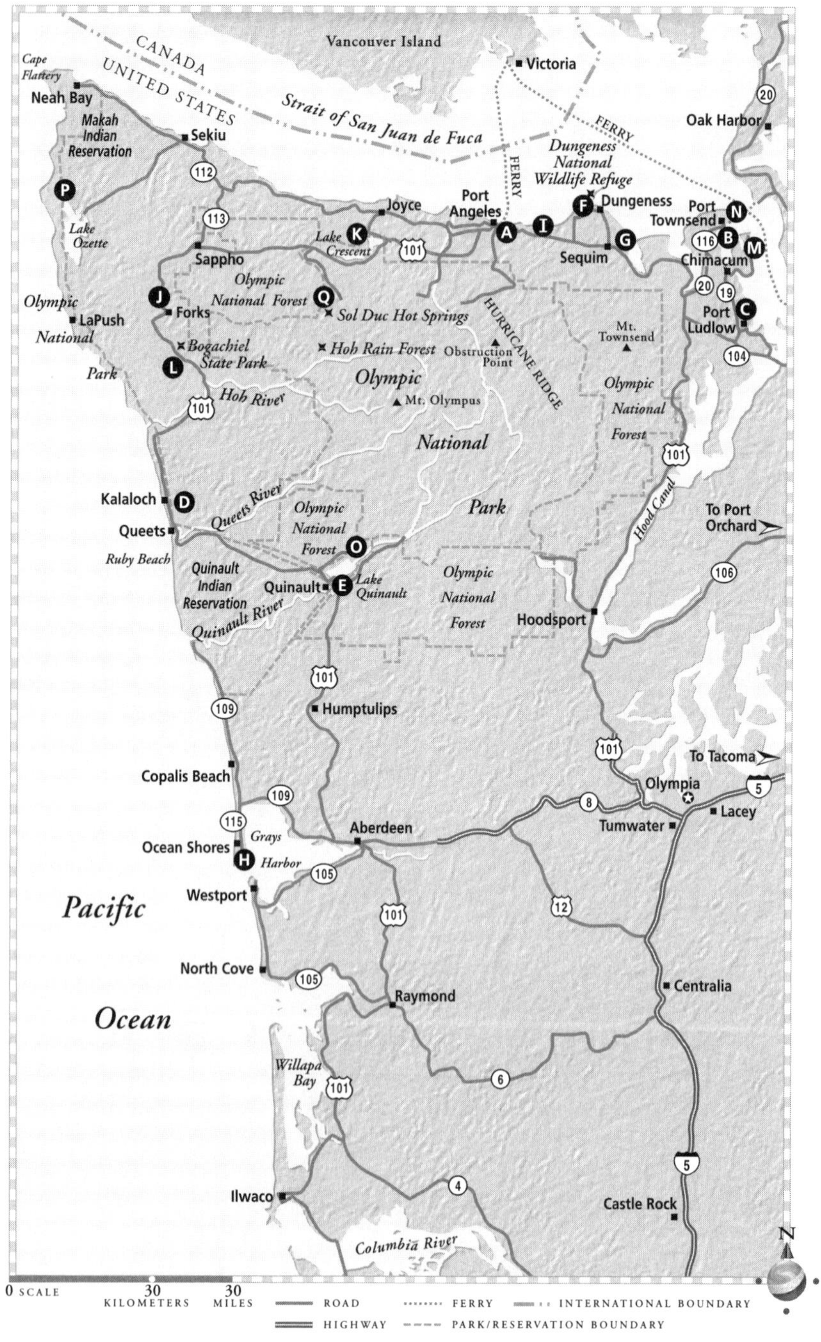

Vancouver Island
CANADA
UNITED STATES
Victoria
Strait of San Juan de Fuca
Cape Flattery
Neah Bay
Makah Indian Reservation
Sekiu
FERRY
FERRY
Oak Harbor
Dungeness National Wildlife Refuge
Dungeness
Joyce
Port Angeles
Port Townsend
Lake Ozette
Lake Crescent
Sappho
Sequim
Chimacum
Olympic National Forest
Sol Duc Hot Springs
HURRICANE RIDGE
Port Ludlow
Olympic National Park
LaPush
Forks
Bogachiel State Park
Hoh Rain Forest
Obstruction Point
Mt. Townsend
Hoh River
Olympic
Mt. Olympus
Olympic National Forest
National
Park
Kalaloch
Queets River
Hood Canal
To Port Orchard
Queets
Olympic National Forest
Ruby Beach
Quinault Indian Reservation
Quinault
Lake Quinault
Quinault River
Olympic National Forest
Hoodsport
Humptulips
To Tacoma
Copalis Beach
Olympia
Lacey
Tumwater
Aberdeen
Ocean Shores
Grays Harbor
Westport
Pacific
Ocean
North Cove
Raymond
Centralia
Willapa Bay
Ilwaco
Castle Rock
Columbia River
N
0 SCALE
30 KILOMETERS
30 MILES
ROAD
HIGHWAY
FERRY
PARK/RESERVATION BOUNDARY
INTERNATIONAL BOUNDARY

The dining rooms at **Kalaloch Lodge** and **Lake Quinault Lodge** make good evening meal destinations, with traditional American food and Northwest seafood offerings.

LODGING

Two posh eastern peninsula lodgings are located a few miles north of the Hood Canal Bridge (see the Scenic Drive on page 68). **Heron Beach Inn,** 1 Heron Road, 360/437-0411, www.heron beachinn.com, is located on its own peninsula on Port Ludlow Bay. It's a romantic destination that mixes ease and elegance in an overgrown cottage by the sea. There are 30 rooms, all with fireplaces and water views. Nearby is **Port Ludlow Resort,** 200 Olympic Place, 800/732-1239, www.portludlowresort.com, a residential and vacation community for boaters and golfers. It's also a good family destination, with boat, kayak, and bicycle rentals, a 300-slip marina, and condominium rentals. The restaurant features area seafood and water views.

Port Townsend's many historic B&Bs are popular destinations for couples; some favorites are the **James House,** 1238 Washington Street, 360/385-1238 or 800/385-1238, www.jameshouse.com, and the **Ann Starrett Mansion,** 744 Clay Street, 360/385-3205 or 800/321-0644, www.starrettmansion.com. The **Old Consulate Inn,** 313 Walter Street, 360/385-6753 or 800/300-6753, www.oldconsulateinn.com, is a dramatic red Queen Anne–style house built in

---

FOOD

- A C'est Si Bon
- B Cheeks Bistro & Cafe
- C Heron Beach Inn
- D Kalaloch Lodge
- B Khu Larb Thai
- E Lake Quinault Lodge
- B Lonny's Restaurant
- F Three Crabs Restaurant

LODGING

- B Ann Starrett Mansion
- G Best Western
- H Best Western Lighthouse Suites Inn
- I Domaine Madeleine
- J Eagle Point Inn
- F Groveland Cottage
- C Heron Beach Inn
- B James House
- D Kalaloch Lodge
- K Lake Crescent Lodge
- E Lake Quinault Lodge
- J Miller Tree Inn B&B
- F Red Ranch Inn
- H Shilo Inn

CAMPING

- L Bogachiel State Park
- M Fort Flagler State Park
- N Fort Worden State Park
- O July Creek
- P Lake Ozette Trails Triangle
- Q Sol Duc

Note: Items with the same letter are located in the same area.

1889 that sits on a bluff viewing Puget Sound, Mount Rainier, and the Olympic Mountains.

With a swimming pool and a pet policy (pets accepted with some restrictions), the **Best Western,** 360/683-0691 or 800/622-0691, on Sequim Bay makes a good stopover for families; ask for family rates. **Red Ranch Inn,** 830 West Washington Street, Sequim, 800/777-4195, www.redranch@holipin.com, is a motel on the main thoroughfare of Sequim that's good for families and golfers. (They often have golf packages with the Dungeness Golf Club.) Some units have kitchens. **Groveland Cottage,** 360/683-3565, www.northolympic.com/groveland, is a turn-of-the-century clapboard home in the village of Dungeness. **Domaine Madeleine,** 360/457-4174, a B&B between Sequim and Port Angeles, has dramatic views overlooking the Strait of Juan de Fuca toward Vancouver Island. **Miller Tree Inn B&B,** 654 East Division Street, 360/374-6806, www.millertreeinn.com, is a rambling and comfortable two-story house on a spacious lot in Forks that's a favorite with fishermen. There are two rooms that accommodate up to four people. **Eagle Point Inn** is a spacious log lodge tucked away in the woods by a river near Forks, 360/327-3236, built by owner-hosts Dan and Chris Christiansen.

There are several classic old lodge-style destinations. **Lake Crescent Lodge,** 21 miles west of Port Angeles, 360/928-3211, www.olypen.com/lake-crescent lodge, has five rooms with a shared bath in the 1916 main lodge, 30 modern guest rooms, and 17 cottages—four built in the 1930s. These are rustic, with fireplaces. Open April through late October. There's a dining room, rowboat rental, and gift shop. For generations, beach lovers have found their way to **Kalaloch Lodge,** about 35 miles south of Forks on U.S. Highway 101, 360/962-2271, www.visitkalaloch.com, to hole up in a rustic cabin above the beach and hope for a storm. There are wide driftwood beaches to explore. Well-known Ruby Beach is six miles north. Kalaloch Lodge has 40 cabins, including 8 original bluff cabins (these have views), a restaurant, and motel rooms. **Lake Quinault Lodge,** 360/288-2900 or 800/562-6672, www.visitlakequinault.com, a rustic and beloved timber structure on the south shore of Lake Quinault, has been enchanting visitors since 1926. A spacious lobby with a fireplace has a gift shop with Native American art. More than 70 rooms include guest rooms, lakeside rooms, and rooms with fireplaces.

Most of the fifties-style motels in Ocean Shores have been upgraded over the years, and you'll find newer beachfront lodging such as the affordable **Best Western Lighthouse Suites Inn,** 800/757-7873, www.bwlighthouse.com, at the north end of town. The $14 million **Shilo Inn,** with its huge saltwater fish tank, 800/222-2244, is also a good value. For a lodging and activities list, call the Ocean Shores Chamber of Commerce, 360/289-2451 or 800/76-BEACH.

BEACHCOMBING

Winter storms churn up the ocean and often deposit interesting finds on the coastline. March is typically the best month to go treasure hunting on the beaches of Washington—particularly more remote spots when you might find a rare glass Japanese float (no longer used by fishermen), interesting driftwood, or items that have fallen off cargo ships.

CAMPING

There are almost 1,000 campsites within **Olympic National Park,** 360/452-0330, including a wide variety of camping options for hikers and car and RV campers; be sure to pack waterproof gear and rain clothes. **Sol Duc** campground, 27 miles west of Port Angeles, then 12 miles into the camp, is a popular campground close to the Sol Duc Hot Springs facility. It also has facilities for the handicapped. **July Creek** is a walk-in campground for hikers on the north shore of Lake Quinault. Its 29 tent sites are situated where the creek empties into the lake. Turn off Highway 101 two miles north of the community of Amanda Park. No reservations are accepted. For information, call Olympic National Park, 360/452-0330.

Another walk-in experience is beach camping at **Lake Ozette Trails Triangle.** It's a bit of a hike, but for a beautiful wilderness beach experience, this Olympic Peninsula gem is the best. From SR 112 near Seikiu, take the well-marked Road 21 turnoff to the ranger station, where the road dead-ends. It's a little over three miles along a boardwalk to Cape Alava (the most westerly point in the continental United States), three miles south on a beautiful sandy beach, and three miles back to the ranger station via another boardwalk. The loop takes about six hours or you can camp overnight. Deer are common, and raccoons especially like this beach. If you camp, hang your food high in the trees so you don't lose it. Make reservations (there's a quota system), 360/452-0300, up to 30 days in advance of your trip.

State parks on the peninsula include **Fort Flagler State Park** on Marrowstone Island, eight miles northeast of Port Hadlock; **Fort Worden State Park** in Port Townsend; and **Bogachiel State Park,** six miles south of Forks. For reservations call 800/452-5687, www.parks.wa.gov.

4 VICTORIA

Rudyard Kipling came to Victoria in 1908 as a journalist covering the opening of the Empress Hotel. He described the city this way:

> To realize Victoria, you must take all the eye admires in Bournemouth, Torquay, The Isle of Wight, the happy valley at Hong Kong, the Doon, Sorrento, and Camp's Bay—add reminiscences of the Thousand Islands and arrange the whole around the Bay of Naples with some Himalayas in the background.

Got that picture? Add another observation that it was "San Francisco on the Solent," and you'll get a complete sense of this elegant but lusty, civilized but exciting, Western frontier boomtown at the turn of the last century.

The Hudson's Bay Company built Fort Victoria on the Inner Harbour in 1843, and the town was a thoroughfare for boats bringing miners from all over the world. Victoria provisioners outfitted these dream-seekers heading to the goldfields of the Frasier and Cariboo. Fortunes were made and society was splendid. The architecture of the homes and public buildings—especially those designed in the 1890s by Victoria's renowned architect Francis M. Rattenbury—proclaims the wealth of the city's forefathers. One of Canada's best known artists, Emily Carr, was born here in 1871 and raised in an elegant home in the historic James Bay neighborhood. A talented and eccentric woman, she painted totems and the wilderness of the Northwest with a genius that is arresting to this day.

A PERFECT DAY IN VICTORIA

A perfect day in Victoria includes tea, history, gardens, and shopping—a which abound. Start with a quick "cuppa" at Murchie's Tea & Coffee, Ltd. on Government Street or a more leisurely repast at Kipling's in the Empress. Walk off your breakfast exploring Victoria's Inner Harbour. Small wooden foot ferries ply the waters. Catch a ride on one to spots on the harbor and walk back along the promenade. Spend time in the Royal British Columbia Museum and strolling Government Street. Have afternoon tea at the Empress or Butchart Gardens, and if at all possible, manage to be in the gardens on a summer Saturday evening for the exciting fireworks show.

ORIENTATION

While Greater Victoria now encompasses a busy city of nearly 400,000 at the south end of the Saanich Peninsula, downtown Victoria is a village at its soul, made for walkers and accented with gardens and the lush hanging flower baskets for which the city is renowned. Travelers making the 2½-hour trip from Seattle on the *Victoria Clipper* arrive in Victoria's Inner Harbour within walking distance of many don't-miss sights, with plenty of food and lodging choices.

Getting to Vancouver Island depends on your travel plans and preferences, and whether you're on foot, have a car, are pressed for time, or have all the time in the world. Foot passengers can reach Victoria from Seattle by taking the ***Victoria Clipper,*** operated by **Clipper Navigation,** from Seattle's Pier 69; call 206/448-5000 in Seattle, 250/382-8100 in Victoria, or 800/888-2535 outside Seattle and Victoria, or check the web at www.victoriaclipper.com. Travelers going by car have other options. **Black Ball Transport,** 360/457-4491, www.northolympic.com/coho, offers two sailings a day (four during summer months) from Port Angeles on the Olympic Peninsula on a first come, first served basis. **Washington State Ferries,** 206/464-6400 or 800/843-3779 (in Washington only), www.wsdot.wa.gov/ferries/, has two daily sailings from Anacortes (87 miles northwest of Seattle) to Sidney, at the northeast end of Vancouver Island's Saanich Peninsula, 17 miles north of Victoria; vehicle reservations (for international travel only) may be made at least 48 hours prior to sailing and confirmed with a credit card. The most frequent ferry service is aboard **B.C. Ferries,** 250/386-3431 or www.bcferries.bc.ca/ferries, from their Tsawwassen terminal (about a half hour south of Vancouver) on large superferries. If you're driving to Victoria via Tsawwassen terminal from Washington, give yourself an extra hour for the border crossing.

Going by air saves time, and there are plenty of regularly scheduled flights. **Kenmore Air,** 206/364-6990 or 800/543-9595 or www.kenmoreair.com, has

VICTORIA

To B
TO OAK BAY AV
TO BEACH DR
CADBORO BAY RD
BEGBIE ST
ROCKLAND AV
RICHARDSON ST
ST. CHARLES ST
FAIRFIELD RD
DALLAS RD
JOAN CRESCENT
FERNWOOD RD
PANDORA AV
JOHNSON ST
YATES ST
RICHARDSON ST
MOSS ST
BAY ST
PRINCESS AV
COOK ST
VANCOUVER ST
QUADRA ST
BLANSHARD ST
COOK ST
QUADRA ST
HUMBOLDT ST
FORT ST
PRINCESS AV
DISCOVERY ST
HERALD ST
FISGARD ST
DOUGLAS ST
GOVERNMENT ST
STORE ST
Bastion Square
WHARF ST
DOUGLAS ST
GOVERNMENT ST
Beacon Hill Park
BELLEVILLE ST
MENZIES ST
Upper Harbor
SUPERIOR ST
NIAGARA ST
SONGHEES RD
ESQUIMALT RD
KIMTA RD
OSWEGO ST
SIMCOE ST
ERIE ST
DALLAS RD
CRAIGFLOWER RD
CATHERINE ST
Harbor
Victoria
FERRY TO SEATTLE, WA
FERRY TO PORT ANGELES, WA
OLD ESQUIMALT RD
LAMPSON ST
ESQUIMALT RD
BEWDLEY AV
PARK TERRACE
FRASER ST

ROAD
PARK BOUNDARY
FERRY
PLACE OF INTEREST

SCALE 0 1 KILOMETER 1 MILE

eight floatplane flights a day from its Lake Union air harbor in Seattle. **Harbour Air,** 250/385-2203, www.harbourair.com, has 10 flights a day, high season, from Vancouver; **West Coast Air,** 800/347-2222 or www.westcoastair.com, has 12 flights daily. Also, **Helijet Airways,** 250/382-6222 or 800/665-4354 or www.helijet.com, offers flights to Victoria from Seattle's Boeing Field (south of downtown) and from Vancouver. **Horizon Air,** 800/547-9308 or www.horizonair.com, provides service between Seattle and Victoria airports.

Tourism Victoria provides a wide variety of information; 250/953-2033, travel.victoria.bc.ca. Also, Tourism Vancouver Island's website, www.islands.bc.ca, provides information on Victoria and other destinations on the island.

SIGHTSEEING HIGHLIGHTS

★★★★ BUTCHART GARDENS

800 Benvenuto Drive, 250/652-5256 (recorded)
www.butchartgardens. bc.ca/butchart/

Each season offers a new kind of beauty in 50-acre Butchart Gardens. The famous Sunken Garden (an old limestone quarry) is filled with thousands of bulbs in spring; the Rose and Italian Gardens are in romantic bloom in summer; and firework displays enchant visitors on summer Saturday evenings. In autumn, dahlias and chrysanthemums offer vibrant contrast to the garnet leaves of maples in the Japanese Garden. In winter, the holly, heathers, Christmas lights, and decorations transform the gardens.

Details: *about 13 miles north of downtown Victoria; Wheelchair accessible. Gardens open daily (including holidays) at 9 a.m.; closing time varies according to time of year. Tea is served in the dining room from noon to 4; reservations recommended; 250/652-8222. There are several*

SIGHTS

- Ⓐ Art Gallery of Greater Victoria
- Ⓑ Butchart Gardens
- Ⓒ Chinatown
- Ⓓ Craigdarroch Castle
- Ⓔ Crystal Garden
- Ⓕ Empress Hotel
- Ⓖ Government House Gardens
- Ⓗ Inner Harbour
- Ⓘ James Bay and Beacon Hill Park
- Ⓙ Legislative Buildings
- Ⓚ Maritime Museum of B.C.
- Ⓛ Royal British Columbia Museum
- Ⓜ Victoria Eaton Centre

ENGLISH COUNTRY WEEKEND

English country weekends have been in style for centuries for good reason. You can experience just such a getaway at Markham House B&B in Sooke, just 40 minutes southwest of Victoria. The Tudor-style home on wide lawns with flowers and small ponds seems carved out of the English countryside. You may be greeted at the lynchgate (a pitch-roofed entry gate that shields you from the weather) by Lyall Markham or Virgil the black Lab. And it's likely that once you're inside, Sally Markham will offer up "a nice cup of tea." Upstairs you'll find your soothing, non-fussy country-style room with luxurious down and feather beds. Nearby is 17-Mile House, an ivy-covered historical pub. Go there and you'll find the "local" with requisite dartboard and separate areas for dining or drinking. On Sundays, a special offering is the seafood platter of succulent prawns, oysters, and crab. (Markham House, 1853 Connie Road, 250/642-7542 or 888/256-6888, www.sookenet.com/ markham)

other restaurants on site. Admission to the gardens is seasonal, about $6–$12 (U.S.). (2–3 hours)

★★★★ EMPRESS HOTEL

721 Government Street, 250/384-8111 or 800/441-1414
www.fairmont.com

A grand stone chateau whose image defines the city, the Empress was named for Queen Victoria, the empress of India. It's one of the most beloved institutions in North America. The guest list here includes luminaries of the last century: Rudyard Kipling, Charles Lindbergh, Shirley Temple, Rita Hayworth, the King and Queen of Siam, John Travolta, Barbra Streisand, and Mel Gibson are but a few. The British royal family are frequent visitors. The Empress was designed by Francis M. Rattenbury and opened in 1908. Its stately Edwardian charm had aged and faded by the mid-1960s when "Operation Teacup" was launched. Since then, Canadian Pacific Hotels has invested more than $50 million to return the grand lady to her former glory. Stay here if you can afford it, or come to view, shop, or eat. The Canadian Pacific store has

BOXING DAY SALES

In Canada, the day after Christmas is Boxing Day, a national holiday. An English tradition, it goes back centuries to when the 'Lord of the Manor' would deliver boxes of leftover food from his Christmas celebration to his serfs. Today, as one Victoria native put it, "the tradition probably refers to the boxes used to pack home everyone's purchases!" Stores on Government Street (and elsewhere in the city) celebrate the holiday by dramatically marking down their stock. You'll find enticing bargains on china, Scottish sweaters, English tweeds, Irish linens, and more.

archival art-quality posters for around $20 (U.S. funds) that make great souvenirs. And a dinner in the rich, wood-paneled Empress Room, with its massive château fireplace, Tudor arches, and stained- glass window panels (not to mention the food), is a mental souvenir you won't soon forget.

Details: *The dress codes for tea at the Empress are less stringent than in years past. For instance, jeans are now allowed. (1 to 1½ hours for tea)*

★★★★ INNER HARBOUR

Visitor Information Centre, 812 Wharf Street; 250/953-2033

www.tourismvictoria.com

The site of Fort Victoria, built by the Hudson's Bay Company in 1843, this is a gathering spot for street artists and musicians, sailing vessels, and visitors. Foot ferries take you all over the harbor. Fishing and sightseeing cruises leave from here. Stop by the information office at the north edge of the harbor for maps, brochures, and other information, including tips for fishing and whale-watching.

Details: *(1½–2 hours)*

★★★★ ROYAL BRITISH COLUMBIA MUSEUM

675 Belleville Street, 250/387-3701 or 800/661-5411. For ecotour information, 250/387-5745

www.rbcm1.rbcm.gov.bc.ca

A fixture in Victoria for over a hundred years, this is a very special museum. Exhibits on the fishing industry and whaling history of British Columbia are fascinating, but it's the displays on aboriginal culture that the museum is known for. Outside the museum in Thunderbird Park are huge totem poles and ceremonial houses. Inside are more totems and extensive displays. April through October the museum runs nearly 50 ecotours in British Columbia, ranging from guided field trips to sailing excursions. Check out their new National Geographic IMAX Theater, which offers films featuring the museum's exhibits.

Details: South of the Empress. Open daily 9 to 5. Admission is $5 adults, $2.50 seniors, $1.50 children (U.S.). Wheelchair accessible. (2 hours or more)

★★★ ART GALLERY OF GREATER VICTORIA

1040 Moss Street, Victoria; 250/384-4101

You'll find the work of Emily Carr here, as well as a permanent collection of Canada's finest Japanese art that includes 10,000 works. In the garden is the only Shinto shrine outside Japan. It's located in Victoria's historic Rockland district near Craigdarroch Castle and the Government House.

Details: *Open Monday through Saturday 10 to 5, Thursday 10 to 9, and Sunday 1 to 5. Admission is $5; free general admission on Monday. (2 hours)*

★★★ CHINATOWN

Before World War I, when Victoria was a major port of entry on the West Coast, this was the largest Chinatown in Canada. It is marked by the colorful Gate of Harmonious Interest. Don't miss mysterious Fan Tan Alley, a narrow interior street and the legendary location of gambling dens and opium houses.

Details: *The gates mark the main entry on Government and Fisgard Streets. (1 hour)*

★★★ CRAIGDARROCH CASTLE

1050 Joan Crescent, 250/592-5323.

Robert Dunsmuir, a prosperous British Columbia Coal baron, died months before this majestic mansion was completed in 1889. His wife, Joan, lived there for the next 18 years, managing the business left to her. Their fortune is reflected in the unique architecture, the sweeping staircases, the exquisite woodwork, and the stained glass throughout.

Rooms and furnishings have been restored to their Victorian-era beauty.

Details: *Off Fort Street; open daily; admission about $5 (U.S.) (1 hour)*

★★★ JAMES BAY AND BEACON HILL PARK

The historic James Bay neighborhood is the oldest residential district in the city. Take a walking, bicycling, or carriage tour to best explore it. You can visit Emily Carr's birthplace, a Victorian gingerbread heritage house at 207 Government Street.

Details: *Horse-drawn carriages are found near the Empress and Parliament Buildings; bicycle tours can be arranged through Pacific Rim Bicycle Tours, 250/881-0585. (2 hours)*

★★★ LEGISLATIVE BUILDINGS

250/387-3046 (tour and special event information)

Designed in the 1890s by Victoria's renowned architect Francis Rattenbury, these grand buildings (also called the Parliament Buildings) are the second structures you notice when sailing into the harbor (the Empress is the first). The grounds are always beautifully planted with flowers. Enjoy them as you stroll the harbor. Don't miss the Legislative Buildings at night, outlined in sparkling white lights and looking like a fairyland.

Details: *Free guided tours are offered Monday through Friday. (½ to 1 hour)*

★★★ MARITIME MUSEUM OF B.C.

Bastion Square, Victoria, 250/385-4222

Explore historic Bastion Square, then take in maritime history through a vast collection of models and sailing ship displays. You can imagine "Rumpole of the Bailey" in the newly refurbished Vice-Admiralty Courtroom on the third floor, which can be reached via a large open-cage elevator. The museum underwent a renovation in 1998 that added 12 new galleries.

Details: *Open daily 9:30 to 5:30. Wheelchair accessible. Adults $5, seniors $4. (1–2 hours)*

★★ CRYSTAL GARDEN

713 Douglas Street, 250/381-1213

This historic glass-roofed building behind the Empress, designed by

CRAIGDARROCH CASTLE

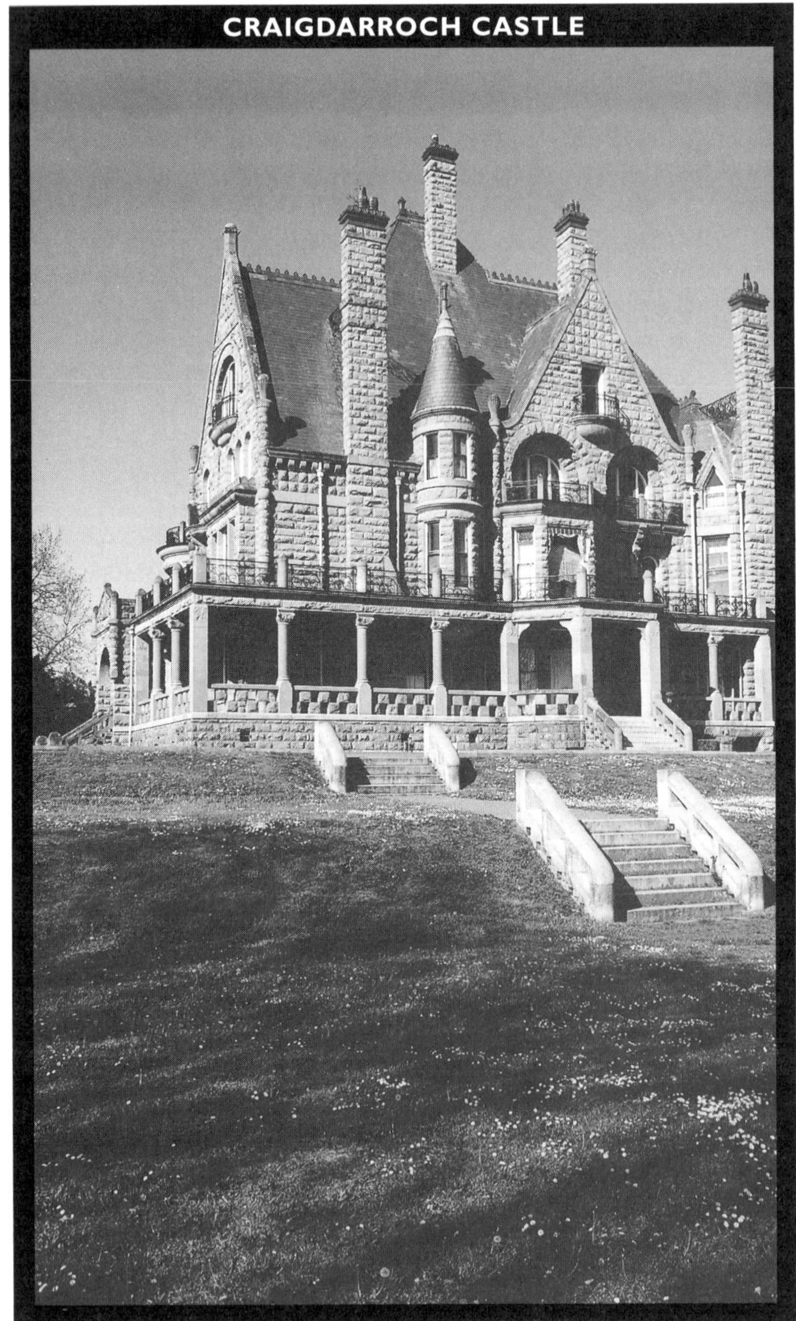

Jeff Barber / Craigdarroch Castle

Francis Rattenbury and P. L. James, once housed the largest indoor saltwater swimming pool in the British Empire. Now it contains thousands of exotic plants, tropical birds, and tiny monkeys.

Details: *Open daily. Admission is $7 adults, $6 seniors, $4 children (Canadian). (1 hour)*

★★ GOVERNMENT HOUSE GARDENS

1401 Rockland Avenue, Victoria

Queen Elizabeth visited these lovely restored gardens on the grounds of the lieutenant governor's residence. You can take a self-guided tour of the nearly 15-acre grounds.

Details: *Open from sunrise to sunset. Admission is free. (1 hour)*

★★ VICTORIA EATON CENTRE

Corner of Government and Fort Streets, Victoria 250/389-2228.

This vertical mall's 100-plus shops include Purdy's Chocolates, and Eaton's department store. It's worth a visit to see the massive British Empire clock that hangs from the ceiling of the 85-foot atrium. The food circus on the fourth floor is a good place for a fast-food stop.

Details: *(1 hour)*

FITNESS AND RECREATION

The Galloping Goose Trail—or simply "The Goose"—is a favorite of locals and visitors alike for walking, biking, and horseback riding. More than 40 miles long, it leads from downtown—you can access it at the west end of the Johnson Street Bridge, on the Inner Harbor—to Sooke, with a spur north into the Central Sanich Peninsula. Along the way the trail goes through forest and past canyons, lakes, and streams. For maps and details visit the regional parks website at www.crd.bc.ca/parks/parkgse.htm.

Salmon fishing and whale-watching are close at hand and fun for all members of the family. You can leave from the Inner Harbour, Sooke Harbour, or Oak Bay. I caught my first chinook salmon (a thrilling experience) on an outing with Gordy's Guides, 250/642-4998, one of a number of services that operate out of Sooke Harbour. From the Oak Bay Beach Hotel, you are close to the departure point for whale-watching cruises on the **M.V. *Pride of Victoria,*** a 45-foot catamaran. Cruising to see orcas (killer whales) is a popular event; call 250/592-3474 or 800/668-7758. Victoria's 150-acre **Beacon Hill Park** is only a five-minute walk south from downtown along Douglas Street and contains a rose garden, wild bird sanctuary, a century-old cricket pitch, and a children's petting zoo.

FOOD

Afternoon tea in Victoria is a classic experience. Two of the best, albeit most expensive, tea services are at the Palm Court in the Tea Lobby of the **Empress Hotel,** 250/384-8111. The dining room of the historic main house at **Butchart Gardens,** 250/652-8222, also serves a wonderful tea. Reservations are a must for either of these in high season. Other options are the **Oak Bay Beach Hotel,** 1175 Beach Drive, 250/598-4556, and the **Windsor House Tea Room & Restaurant** in Oak Bay, 250/595-3135. For fine dining in elegant settings, try the **Empress Dining Room** (see above) or the **Victorian Restaurant** at the Ocean Pointe Resort, 250/360-2999. Excellent food can be found in more casual eateries. The **Herald Street Cafe,** 546 Herald Street, 250/381-1444, is famous for its lighter-than-air crab cakes in cilantro-lime pesto. The real fantasy builder is the Shaker lemon pie. **Cafe Brio,** 944 Forte Street, 250/383-0009, opened in the late 90s by the creator of the Herald Street Cafe, has a menu featuring organic vegetables grown from special seeds. It's a chic destination along Antiques Row on Fort Street, with a mini-courtyard, terra-cotta-colored exterior, and lively paintings on the walls. Crowded, noisy, and fun, **Pagliacci's,** 1011 Broad Street, 250/386-1662, serves Italian food reasonably priced in a high-energy atmosphere near Eaton Centre. You'll find Italian specialties in a quieter setting at **Il Terrazo,** 555 Johnson Street, 250/361-0028. It's hidden away off Waddington Alley and has outside dining in a walled courtyard where umbrellas ward off the sun and outdoor heaters warm the evening, making for cozy, romantic dining. The un-fancy **Wonton Noodle House** on Fort Street, 250/383-0680, is known for its yummy noodle dishes and good prices. **Re-Bar Modern Food,** 50 Bastion Square, 250/361-9223, offers healthy vegetarian cuisine and a juice bar that serves up refreshing fruit smoothies. The Re-Bar is popular for weekend brunch, and you'll often see the line of people waiting to be seated extending out the door. **Spinnakers Brew Pub Restaurant,** 308 Catherine Street, 250/386-2739, on the Inner Harbour waterfront, is Canada's oldest brewpub. It offers great waterfront views and a wide variety of traditional ales and lagers brewed on the premises. **Sooke Harbor House Restaurant,** 250/642-3421, a 40-minute drive west of Victoria, is the place for connoisseurs seeking Canadian regional cuisine.

Christmas is a wonderful time to visit this city for food. There are British feasts and celebrations at Craigdarroch Castle, the Empress, and the Oak Bay

VICTORIA

ROAD — PARK BOUNDARY — FERRY — PLACE OF INTEREST

SCALE 0 — 1 KILOMETER — 1 MILE

Hotel. In February the **Victoria Symphony Society's Pacific Northwest Wine Festival,** 250/385-9771 or www.victoriasymphony.bc.ca, featuring wines of the Northwest in seminars and tastings and highlighting the cuisine of Victoria, is reason enough to visit..

LODGING

It doesn't matter where the traveler is from, the Northwest or New York, if you bring up Victoria, two very different lodgings, each reflecting the essence and culture of the region, are usually mentioned: the Empress and Sooke Harbor House. The Beaconsfield Inn is a third name that also comes up. **The Empress Hotel,** 250/384-8111 or 800/441-1414, www.com/empress, is one of the most beloved of the vast and impressive chain of château-style hotels that Canadian Pacific runs across Canada. Afternoon tea here is legendary. If you're going to splurge on a grand hotel stay, this is it. Surprisingly, it's a kid-friendly place with a welcoming bag of playtime goodies for young folks. There are 475 rooms, a pool and spa, and an Entrée Gold option with breakfast included. **Sooke Harbor House,** 1528 Whiffen Spit Road, 250/642-3421, www.sookenet.com/shh, has a well-deserved reputation for excellence—for its location, artful rooms, food, and vigorous attention to detail by owners Sinclair and Frederica Philip. The romantic clapboard inn overlooking Sooke Harbor is a 40-minute drive west of Victoria. The on-site restaurant is known for seafood cui-

---

FOOD

- A Butchart Gardens
- B Cafe Brio
- C Empress Dining Room
- D Herald Street Caffe
- E Il Terrazo
- F Oak Bay Beach Hotel
- G Pagliacci's
- C Palm Court
- H Re-Bar Modern Food
- I Sooke Harbor House Restaurant
- J Spinnakers Brew Pub Restaurant
- C Tea Lobby
- J Victorian Restaurant

FOOD *(continued)*

- F Windsor House Tea Room & Restaurant
- L Wonton Noodle House

LODGING

- M Beaconsfield Inn
- N Best Western
- O Days Inn
- C Empress Hotel
- P Holland House Inn
- Q Magnolia Hotel & Suites
- F Oak Bay Beach Hotel

LODGING *(continued)*

- K Ocean Pointe Resort Hotel & Spa
- R Quality Inn
- I Sooke Harbor House
- J Spinnakers Guest House

CAMPING

- S Goldstream Provincial Park
- T Island View Beach RV/Tent Park
- U Thetis Lake Campground

Note: Items with the same letter are located in the same area.

sine with regional, fresh, and organic ingredients (many grown on the premises). The food is pricey but worth it. A new addition brings the room count to more than 20. The **Beaconsfield Inn,** 998 Humboldt Street, 250/384-4044, www.islandnet.com/beaconsfield/, is tucked away in a residential community about four blocks southeast of the Empress. Named after a luxurious hotel in London frequented by King Edward VII, it has an English country house atmosphere; nine rooms are individually decorated with antiques. The inn does not allow smoking and is not suitable for children under 18. **Holland House Inn,** 595 Michigan Street 250/384-6644, 800/335-3466, www.islandnet.com/~holndhus, is a cheery and elegant 14-room retreat two blocks south of the Empress. Rooms range from small and cozy to spacious antiques-filled hideaways. High tea is served every afternoon. The two-year-old **Magnolia Hotel & Suites,** 623 Courtney Street, 250/381-0999, 877/624-6654 or www.magnoliahotel.com, is a 66-room boutique-style luxury hotel—with a lobby fireplace and lots of mahogany—within easy walking distance of the Inner Harbor and only a block from the Empress.

The **Oak Bay Beach Hotel,** 1175 Beach Drive, 250/592-3474 or 250/598-4556, is located "behind the tweed curtain" in the thoroughly English village of Oak Bay, a 10-minute drive from downtown; it's on the water and adjacent to a marina. You can take a whale-watching cruise nearby or enjoy lazing in the hotel's waterfront garden. The **Ocean Pointe Resort Hotel & Spa,** 45 Songhees Road, 800/667-4677, www.oprhotel.com, is a modern and elegant châteaulike hotel with 250 rooms at the entry to the harbor; a full-service spa and excellent waterfront restaurant make this a sybaritic choice. **Spinnakers Guest Houses,** 308 Catherine Street, 250/386-2739, includes a historic Victorian-style house with five rooms (queen beds), adjacent to Spinnakers Brew Pub, on the Inner Harbour. Two more guest houses are nearby. These are ideal adult getaways. Breakfast included at the pub.

There are also numerous international chain hotels on the Inner Harbour. The **Best Western,** 800/528-1234; **Days Inn,** 800/329-7466; and **Quality Inn,** 800/228-5151, are near the *Victoria Clipper* terminal.

Call Tourism Victoria's reservation line, 800/663-3883, to make reservations at any hotel in the city.

CAMPING

Though tent camping wouldn't be my first choice for accommodations when visiting Victoria (I camped here in the rain as an impoverished student), there are over a dozen campgrounds and RV parks in the Greater Victoria area. Good bets are **Island View Beach RV/Tent Park,** 250/652-0548, close to

SALTSPRING ISLAND

A visit to Saltspring Island, north of the Saanich Peninsula, is an easy way to sample B.C.'s Gulf Islands (the Canadian version of Washington's San Juan Islands) spread along the Strait of Georgia. Saltspring is perhaps the best known, especially as an enclave of artists. While the island is delightfully quiet, it's home to some high-quality sleeps. Waterfront Hastings House, 160 Upper Ganges Road, 250/5372362 or www.hastingshouse.com, is a Relais and Chateau property and, though well worth it, the priciest spot on Saltspring

Also delightful and stylish, with plenty of white wood, pine, and floral accents, is the Old Farmhouse, 1077 North End Road 250/537-4113. The Saturday market held in the island's main village, Ganges, is a don't-miss for the real flavor of Saltspring. The ferry terminal to the island is north of Victoria, near the Schwartz Bay Ferry terminal.

Butchart Gardens; **Goldstream Provincial Park,** 250/391-2300, in the heart of old growth forest, 12 miles north of Victoria, and **Thetis Lake Campground,** 250/478-3845, six miles north of the city center.

SHOPPING

Shoppers can get plenty of exercise walking historic Government Street, with its wide array of china, woolens, and Irish and Scottish clothing shops. Long-time favorite specialty shops here include **Rogers Chocolates,** 913 Government Street, 250/384-7021 or 800/663-2220, www.rogerschocolates.com, a fixture in Victoria since 1885, and a must-stop for at least one pink-wrapped chocolate creme candy. **Murchie's Tea & Coffee,** 1110 Government Street, 250/383-3112 or www.murchies.com, offers a wide array of loose and packaged teas, gift packs, and accessories, as well as a beverage bar. **Old Morris Tobacconist,** 1116 Government, 250/382-4811, is worth a browse even for nonsmokers. **Munro's Books,** 250/382-2464, is also a favorite must-stop.

Check out Cowichan sweaters (a thick fisherman-style garment), mittens, and more at **Cowichan Trading Co.,** 1328 Government, 250/383-0321; and **Sasquatch Trading, Ltd.,** 1233 Government Street, 250/386 9033. You will also see quality masks, drums, carvings, and more aboriginal art in places throughout the city. **Alcheringa Gallery,** 665 Fort Street, 250/383-8224 or www.alcheringa-gallery.com, is tops in the city for native art of the Northwest and other regions.

On **Bastion Square,** across from the Maritime Museum, you'll find **Dig This,** 45 Bastion Square, 250/385-3212, a gardening store that carries a video on how to create Victoria's hanging baskets. If you love fabrics and interior furnishings, head to **Chintz & Company,** 1720 Store Street, 250/381-2404, in a large two-level brick building somewhat off the beaten path.

The entrance to **Chinatown,** at Government and Fisgard Streets, is marked by the red and ornate Gate of Harmonious Interest. You'll see signs to historic and narrow **Fan Tan Alley,** a hidden retreat for the Chinese in times long past. Nearby is **Market Square,** a colorful two-level shopping area in restored buildings that are the heart of Victoria's Old Town. **Antique Row** (along Fort Street east of Douglas) is a favorite destination for those who crave vintage English-style furniture and accessories.

ACTIVITIES FOR KIDS

Kids love the **Royal British Columbia Museum,** the monkeys at the **Crystal Palace,** riding on the foot ferries, and carriage rides in the horse-drawn buggies that queue up near the Legislative Buildings. The Butterfly Gardens near Butchart Gardens (20 minutes from Victoria) are also a hit.

And what can beat cuddling a cockroach at the **Bug Zoo** at 1107 Wharf Street, 250/384-2847, or seeing iguanas or boa constrictors at the **Reptile Zoo,** 1420 Quadra Street, 250/885-9451? **Willows Beach** in Oak Bay offers calm waters for swimming and plenty of sand for castle building.

NIGHTLIFE

There's plenty of music and nightlife in Victoria's pubs and clubs. **Millenium Jazz Club,** 1605 Store Street, 250/360-9098, is an elegant spot beneath **Swans Hotel & Brewpub,** 506 Pandora. The **Sticky Wickett Pub,** 919 Douglas Street, 250/383-7137, is a city tradition, and its four floors offer plenty of options, from quieter eating rooms to lively pool and darts rooms. **Legends,** 250/383 7137 (entrance adjacent to the Sticky Wicket), is the largest nightclub in town and has a state-of-the-art sound system where all ages come to dance to rock and roll, rhythm and blues, and jazz. You can also listen to jazz in the Empress's **Bengal Lounge** on Thursday and Friday nights.

Pacific Opera Victoria opens its season each fall in the **McPherson Playhouse,** and there are summer plays here as well.

5 COWICHAN VALLEY AND UP-ISLAND

The Cowichan Valley, 45 minutes northwest of Victoria by car, is known for its dairies, logging, and increasingly for its wines and arts. It's also known for Cowichan sweaters—rustic fisherman-style sweaters made from the wool of local sheep and crafted in distinctive patterns of cream, brown, and gray tones by Cowichan native peoples who learned how to knit from British settlers in the mid-1800s. A sweater-knitting demonstration is among many excellent exhibits at the Cowichan Native Village in Duncan. Chemainus, at the north end of the valley, was once a dismal mill town on the skids. Now it's a vibrant mural town rich in the history of the area and a center for the arts. Attractions around South Cowichan Valley communities such as Cobble Hill, Cowichan Bay, and Shawnigan Lake, include provincial parks and small wineries to explore.

Further up-island, the city of Nanaimo is one of the fastest growing in Canada. One look at the harbor and coastline tells you why. You can take a ferry from here to explore Gabriola, one of the Gulf Islands. Parksville and Qualicum Beach north of Nanaimo offer a playground for sunseekers, and since a new stretch of Highway 1 has circled around these communities, they have become off-the-beaten-path destinations. Rathtrevor Provincial Park is a beautiful spot claiming wide stretches of sandy beach that have more in common with the Oregon coast than the rocky shores that dominate Washington's coast.

COWICHAN VALLEY AND UP-ISLAND

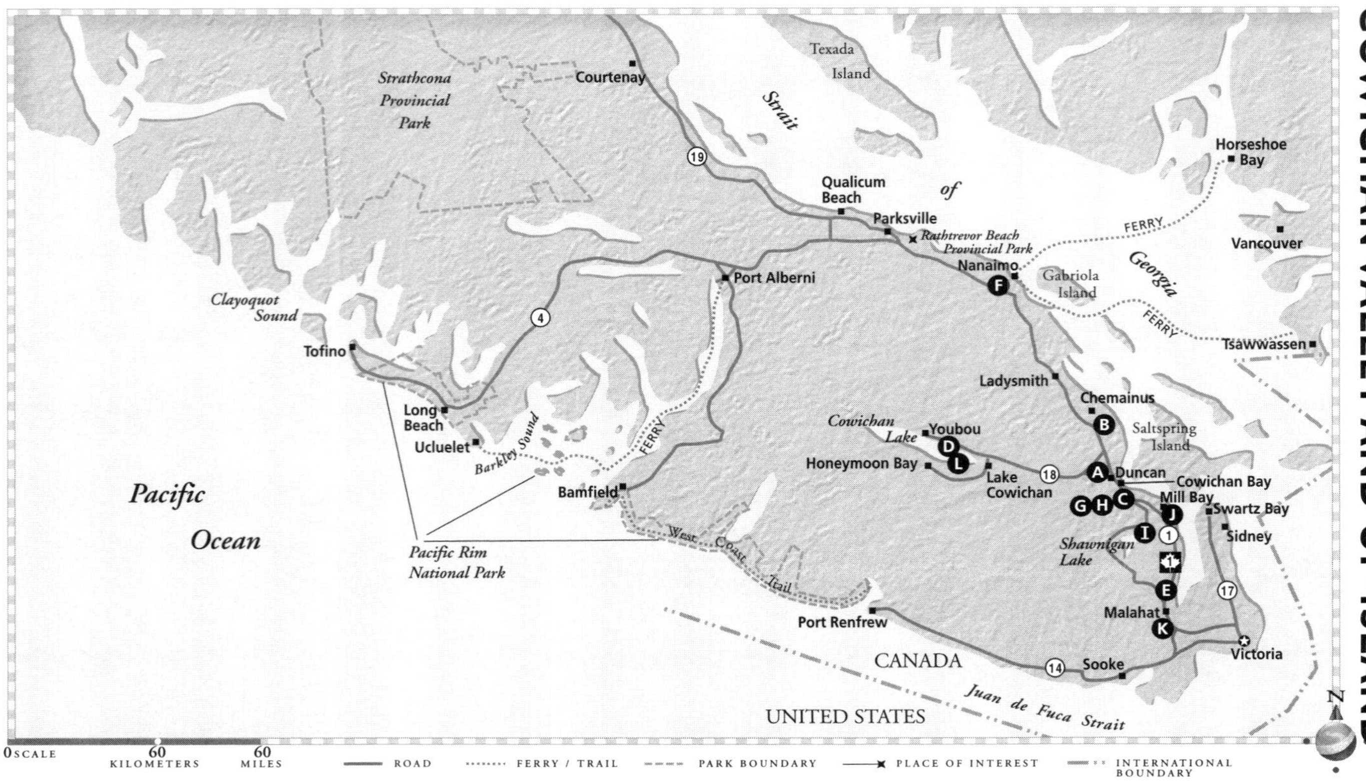

A PERFECT DAY IN THE COWICHAN VALLEY

Drive up-island on a clear day and stop at the lookout at Malahat Pass. Visit a winery or two around Cobble Hill. Stop in Duncan to spend time in the Cowichan Native Village and take a look at the town's totems. The mural town of Chemainus provides a rich cultural experience and has plenty to explore. Then check into Fairburn Farm; plan dinner at Sahtlam Lodge and enjoy river, bird, and night sounds—the perfect romantic way to end the day.

ORIENTATION

The Trans-Canada Highway (Highway 1) leads northwest from Victoria to the Cowichan Valley and can be accessed from Victoria by following Douglas Street north (watch for signs). It takes about an hour to reach Duncan by car.

You can also travel to the valley by train on **VIA Rail's E&N (Esquimalt and Nanaimo) Line,** which has a once-daily trip from Victoria (the station is at 450 Pandora Avenue, Victoria; 250/383-4324 or 800/561-3949 from the U.S.) to Courtenay, near Campbell River. It leaves Victoria early in the morning and returns about dinnertime. It stops at Chemainus about 10 a.m. on the way up-island and again about 4 p.m. on its return, making for a convenient and fun day trip. It also stops at Duncan.

From mainland British Columbia, you can catch a ferry to Nanaimo from Tsawassen terminal (south of Vancouver) or the Horseshoe Bay terminals

---

SIGHTS

- A B.C. Forest Museum
- B Chemainus
- C Cowichan Bay
- A Cowichan Native Village
- A Duncan Totems
- D Lake Cowichan
- E Malahat Summit
- F Nanaimo

FOOD

- E The Aerie
- G The Bistro
- H Cobble Hill
- A Starbucks

FOOD *(continued)*

- A Sahtlam Lodge
- H Venturi-Schulze

LODGING

- E The Aerie
- A Best Western Cowichan Valley Inn
- B Bird Song Cottage B&B
- A Fairburn Farm
- C Old Farm Bed & Breakfast
- A Sahtlam Lodge
- I Whistlestop B&B

CAMPING

- J Bamberton Provincial Park
- K Goldstream Provincial Park
- L Gordon Bay Provincial Park
- F Newcastle Island Provincial Park

Note: Items with the same letter are located in the same area.

SIDE TRIP: PACIFIC RIM NATIONAL PARK

There are three parts to this park, which was established in 1970: Long Beach (the Tofino area), the West Coast Trail, and the Broken Group Islands. The easiest to access is Long Beach, about 16 miles of surf and sandy beach. The West Coast Trail, 48 miles long, goes through dense coastal rain forest of cedar, hemlock, spruce, and fir. You must make reservations to hike part or all of the trail; call 800/663-6000.

This route takes you from north of Nanaimo into Pacific Rim National Park, along Provincial Highway 4. **Port Alberni,** *at the northern end of Alberni Inlet, is the jumping-off spot for boat connections into Barkley Sound.*

Eagle Nook Ocean Wilderness Resort, *800/760-2777 or 604/723-9842 (open May to October), is located on Barkley Sound a short cruise away from the Broken Group Islands. Only reached by boat or floatplane, this hideaway offers hiking, sea kayaking, whalewatching, and sport fishing in a comfortable, unexpectedly civilized setting on its own 70-acre peninsula.*

Another easy way to access the Broken Group Islands is from the quaint waterfront village of Ucluelet. ***Tauca Lea by the Sea,*** *800/979-9303, is a new condominium resort blending elegance and rustic grace that sits on a small peninsula of land here. There's a restaurant on premises with great food and harbor views. Scuba diving, kayaking, hiking, fishing, guided nature tours—including whale-watching trips to the Broken Islands—and more are offered through the resort.*

You can drive to the Long Beach area. Just north of Nanaimo, go west on

(northwest of Vancouver). Once in Nanaimo you drive south to reach the Cowichan Valley.

Information and trip planning assistance is available from **Tourism Vancouver Island,** 250/382-3551, fax 250/382-3523; email: tavi@islands.bc.ca; and website: www.islands.bc.ca. Or, for lodging reservations, call West Coast Trail reservations, 800/663-6000. To receive a travel kit, call **Super Natural British Columbia** at 800/663-6000.

SIGHTSEEING HIGHLIGHTS

★★★★ CHEMAINUS

Arts and Business Council, 250/246-4701

Highway 4 from the Island Highway. While the roads are generous and well maintained from Port Alberni, the route beyond narrows and has more twists and turns. Persevere—this journey puts you in the heart of the national park, with lakes, inlets, mountains, and beaches all around. The 46-room ***Wickaninnish Inn,*** *800/333-4604, www.island.net/~wick, is on Chesterman Beach near Tofino. A stone fireplace, hand-adzed cedar posts, and Northwest art grace the lobby of the $8.5 million structure. This world-class resort was built to be the best place in North America to watch storms. There are fireplaces, soaker tubs, balconies, and views of the ocean from the rooms. It's pricey, but well worth it; packages are available. The* ***Pointe Restaurant*** *at the inn features a signature potlatch stew—a succulent combination that includes salmon, prawns, and scallops—served in a copper pot.*

Tofino *is home to a longhouse gallery that holds carvings and modern art of well-known native artist Roy Henry Vickers. Storm-watching season lasts from November through very early March. Note: It is about five degrees warmer here than in the rest of the province. April through October you can fly from Vancouver or Victoria to Tofino, 800/228-6608, and also floatplane from Vancouver via Harbour Air in peak season, 250/278-3478.*

The park is 200 miles northwest of Victoria on Highway 4; contact Pacific Rim National Park Reserve, Box 280, Ucluelet, B.C. V0R 3A0; 250/726-7721. Long Beach Park is open year-round, the West Coast Trail is open April to October, and the Broken Group Islands are open May through September.

More than 30 outdoor murals depict the early settlement and history of this waterfront lumber-town-turned-arts-community. Learn from educational and interpretive programs and walking tours, horse-drawn carriage tours, live theater, artists, and crafts shops (including a fall artist's open house).

Details: *North of Duncan. (2 hours)*

★★★★ COWICHAN NATIVE VILLAGE

200 Cowichan Way, Duncan, 250/746-8119

Features a traditional Big House and a gallery of West Coast art and carvings, a display of Cowichan sweaters, and demonstrations on knitting, beading moccasins, and other crafts. You'll also find a restaurant, coffee shop, gift shop, and bookshop.

Details: *Open mid-May to mid-September 9:30 to 5, otherwise 10 to 4:30. Wheelchair accessible; plenty of parking. Admission $8. (2 hours)*

★★★★ NANAIMO

Tourism Nanaimo, 2290 Bowen Road, 250/756-0106 or 800/663-7337

A Hudson's Bay Company fort was built here in 1850 to protect coal miners brought from England and Scotland. Now the logging industry, a deep-sea harbor, and a pleasant climate are among the reasons this is one of the fastest growing cities in Canada. It is the up-island terminus for Tsawwassen and Horseshoe Bay on the mainland; the new B.C. Ferry terminal at Duke Point is about two miles south of town. A small ferry from downtown Nanaimo goes to Gabriola Island. South of town in Petroglyph Provincial Park are prehistoric rock carvings that represent humans, birds, wolves, lizards, and sea monsters. Each July, the town hosts the International Bathtub Race, in which powered bathtubs and other bizarre craft navigate the Strait of Georgia.

Details: *The city can be reached by car from Victoria or by ferry from the Tsawwassen or Horseshoe Bay terminals near Vancouver. (4–6 hours)*

★★★ B.C. FOREST MUSEUM

2892 Drinkwater Road, Duncan, 250/715-1113

Steam locomotives, a sawmill, a smithy, handcars, logging industry exhibits, and more commemorate the 100-plus years of British Columbia's logging history. A steam train carries passengers over the museum's 100 acres.

Details: *Open daily May through September 9:30 to 6. Admission $7, over 65 and ages 13 to 18 $6. (2 hours)*

★★★ COWICHAN BAY

Cowichan Tourism, 250/715-0709

Europeans settled here in 1862 to farm and fish, and by the turn of the century it was a tourist destination. This waterfront town offers fishing and sight-seeing charters on sailing boats from the harbor, restaurants, and galleries to explore.

Details: *Southeast of Duncan. (2–4 hours)*

★★★ DUNCAN TOTEMS

Chamber Travel Infocentre, 250/746-4636

Duncan has over 30 totem poles that represent a blending of tradi-

The Gourmet Trail

Tucked away in remote spots on Vancouver Island—yet in the midst of farmed and natural island bounty and beauty—are four inns with world-class reputations for cuisine. They include Wickaninnish Inn & Pointe Restaurant, a prime storm-watching destination on the wild west coast at Tofino; the Aerie Resort, a fantasylike retreat high on Malahat Pass with stunning water views; Hastings House, a waterfront English manor house and garden estate on Saltspring Island, and Sooke Harbour House, a stunning white clapboard inn set on a bluff overlooking Whiffen Spit east of Victoria. The inns, the Empress Hotel, their chefs, and island food leaders and producers have come together, identifying a route to these culinary gems called "The Gourmet Trail." The focus is on the bounty of the island—perhaps Dungeness crab, unusual seafoods such as acorn and gooseneck barnacles, and Saltspring Island Lamb or Royal Provisioner, David Woods's cheeses. You could go on foraging expeditions for mushrooms, sip wine and watch the chef at work, or be a "sous chef for a day." You can visit these properties independently; ask for the Gourmet Trail program.

You can also join a tour with third-generation islander Pat Hatchman. "There's no better way to get to know an area than to discover it with locals," says Hatchman, who leads year-round six-day tours to the five lodgings with side trips to island food producers. "It's better in the off-season," she says, "the producers have more time, the hotels have more time, the chefs have more time." Winter offers the best prices of the year—added value for stateside visitors (through April 15, independent tours cost from about $480 for two; guided tours cost $2,700 per person, all inclusive, U.S. funds). This may sound pricey, but most of these properties are Relais & Chateaux properties, some of the most well-run and prestigious inns in the world; and of course the Empress is . . . well, *the Empress.*

To contact individual lodgings: The Empress Hotel, 250/384-8111; Sooke Harbour House , 250/642-3421 Hastings House 250/537-2362, The Aerie Resort 250/743-7115. The Wickaninnish Inn & Pointe Restaurant 250/725-3100 or 800/333-4604. To reach Hatchman call 800/970-7722 or 250/658-5367 or e-mail: hatchman@islandnet.com.

tions of native cultures of the Northwest coast, but most are the carvings of the Cowichan band, who, beginning in 1985, worked with the city to celebrate the renaissance of the art form. You can see carvers at work at the Cowichan Native Village (see page 99).

Details: *Stop by the infocentre for a self-guided tour map. (1 hour)*

★★ LAKE COWICHAN

West of Duncan, Lake Cowichan is a year-round source of giant cutthroat and rainbow trout. The most dense stands of fir on Vancouver Island are in Gordon Bay Provincial Park on the south shore of the lake. Back roads lead from here to the wild west coast and Bamfield in the Pacific Rim National Park.

Details: *About 20 miles west of Duncan on Highway 18. (45 minutes)*

★★ MALAHAT SUMMIT

The Trans-Canada Highway leads northwest from Victoria via Malahat Pass. A stop at the overlook gives you a panoramic view over Saanich Inlet northwest up the Strait of Georgia.

Details: *About 30 miles northwest of Victoria on the Trans-Canada Highway. (15 minutes)*

FITNESS AND RECREATION

Hike the Cowichan River Trail. Ride on a sailboat out of Cowichan Bay with Great Northwestern Adventure Company, Ltd., 800/665-7374. The Cowichan Bay Regatta, the second largest on Canada's west coast, is held here the first weekend in August. Or explore the beaches at Parksville and at Rathtrevor Park.

Golf courses to watch for are the Arbutus Ridge Golf & Country Club, 250/743-5000, in Cobble Hill; the Cowichan Golf and Country Club, 250/746-5333, south of Duncan; and Duncan Meadows Golf Course, 250/746-8993, west of Duncan off Highway 18.

FOOD

The dining room at **Sahtlam Lodge,** 5720 Riverbottom Road, 250/748-7738, is a gourmet experience in a romantic country-woods-by-the-river setting west of Duncan. You can make reservations to stay in one of the cabins at the lodge, but dinner alone is worth the drive (you'll need directions). **The Bistro** at Vigneti Zanatta Vineyard is a special countryside experience; call 250/748-2338 for reservations. There's a **Starbucks** in Duncan, 15-350 Trunk Road, 250/746-9394, for easy breakfasts and quick snacks.

LODGING

Whistlestop B&B, 250/743-4896, is a small waterfront lodge with luxuriously appointed rooms or suites on Shawnigan Lake. Near Duncan is **Fairburn Farm,** 250/746-4637, a working farm on several hundred acres. Reminiscent of the English countryside, it has walking trails through the fields. Also near Duncan, along the Cowichan River, is **Sahtlam Lodge,** 250/748-7738, sahtlam@islandnet.com, with cabins to rent and a wonderful restaurant (see Food, above). **Best Western Cowichan Valley Inn,** north of Duncan on the Trans-Canada Highway, 250/748-2722 or 800/528-1234, has a swimming pool and restaurant and is a good family stop. In Chemainus, try **Bird Song Cottage B&B,** 250/246-9910, within walking distance of the beach and restaurants. In Cowichan Bay, **Old Farm Bed & Breakfast,** 888/240-1482 or 250/748-6410, is a heritage home on an estuary.

CAMPING

Several provincial parks along Highway 1 as you travel up-island offer camping facilities. Most are on a first-come, first-served basis. However, reservations are permitted at some campsites; contact the B.C. Parks district office, 250/391-2300. There is a fee for camping that is sometimes paid through a self-registration system, so it's a good idea to carry money in small denominations. Mid-June through early September is the busiest time. **Goldstream Provincial Park,** on the Goldstream River near Victoria as you head up-island, has beautiful hiking trails that meander through 600-year-old Douglas fir and western red cedar forests. There are numerous special events—nature hikes, bald eagle viewing, and programs for children that can be arranged through the visitors center; call 250/478-9414. **Bamberton Provincial Park,** near Mill Bay, fronts on the Saanich Inlet with views of the water, Saanich Peninsula, the Gulf Islands, and Mt. Baker. **Gordon Bay Provincial Park** is on the south shore of Cowichan Lake, where you can fish for Dolly Varden trout or swim in warm lake waters. **Newcastle Island Provincial Park,** situated in Nanaimo Harbour and reached by passenger ferry, offers camping, swimming, boating, and picnicking.

Scenic Route: Strait of Georgia

The Strait of Georgia separates Vancouver Island from mainland British Columbia. Like Puget Sound, it is dotted with forested islands and rich with mountain scenery. It's a favorite destination of boaters and the first leg of the water journey for cruise ships leaving Vancouver and heading up the Inside Passage to Alaska. Ferries crisscross the strait. In the height of summer, at least 16 sailings a day carry travelers each way between Tsawwassen and Swartz Bay on Vancouver Island. It's the system's most popular run and a good starting point for exploring the Strait of Georgia's coastal communities by car. Buy a Sunshine Coast CirclePac ticket (good for six months) at your first ferry stop and save 15 percent off your fare to circle the strait (contact B.C. Ferries for details, 250/386-3431 or www.bcferries.bc.ca). You'll have spectacular scenery and a variety of ferry, touring, and recreation options, and you'll get a crash course in British Columbia's history and culture.

You can start from Tsawwassen. Large super-ferries ply the waters of the strait through the gemlike southern Gulf Islands—Galiano, Mayne, Pender, and Saltspring—to Swartz Bay. From here a half-hour drive down the Saanich Peninsula takes you to Victoria. Or catch the small ferry from Brentwood Bay that carries you up-island to Mill

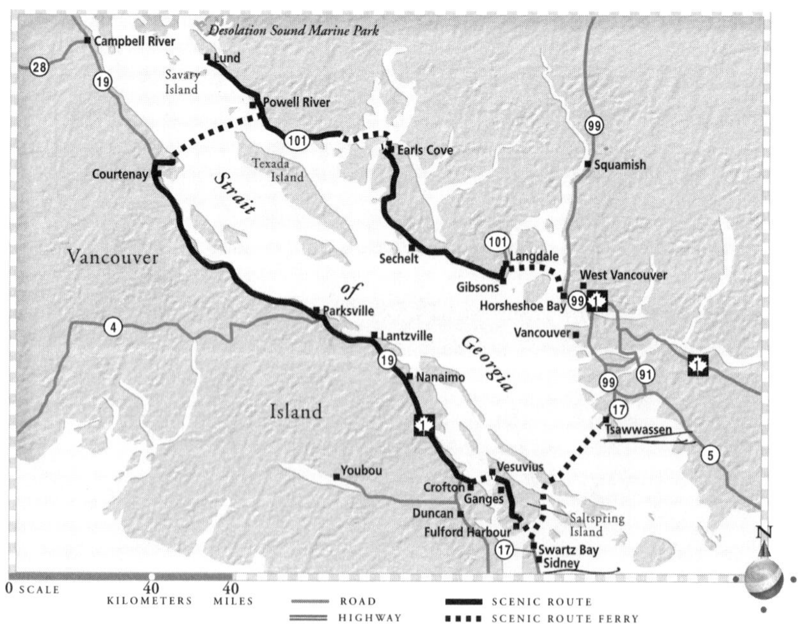

Bay in the Cowichan Valley. You can explore here (see the Cowichan Valley chapter) or drive up-island. Nanaimo is the up-island terminus for travel from Tsawwassen (a two-hour ferry ride) and Horseshoe Bay. Ferries from Tsawwassen land at Duke Point, about two miles south of town. Ferries from Horseshoe Bay land at Departure Bay, north of downtown. North of Nanaimo, the creamy sand shoreline of Rathtrevor Beach Provincial Park and the beach communities of Parksville and Qualicum Beach draw crowds. Summer sun fans also love Denman and Hornby Islands, secluded spots favored by '60s-style dropouts.

Continue northwest along Highway 1 to Comox and Campbell River, renowned as a salmon fishing destination. From Comox, a ferry crosses the strait to Powell River on B.C.'s "Sunshine Coast"—the warmest and driest area in the province. The impressive, snowy Coast Mountains rise up before you on a clear day. They isolate the coast from interior communities, creating a low-key feeling that pervades the area. Crossing takes 1.25 hours.

There's plenty of fishing, camping, and boating along the coast and on Powell Lake. Lund, the small town north of Powell River, at the end of Highway 101, is a jumping-off spot for trips to Desolation Sound. Meander south and two more ferries—Saltery Bay to Earls Cove, Langdale to Horseshoe Bay—put you in West Vancouver, completing your circle.

6 WHISTLER

Princes Charles, William, and Harry skied here in 1998 and drew the international spotlight on Whistler. For years, though, ski magazines have rated it the top ski resort in North America, an amazing achievement considering Whistler Village was built in 1980 and the ski facility had only been operating since the mid-1960s. But more amazing still is that Whistler isn't just a downhill skier's paradise. This two-mountain complex—Whistler and Blackcomb Mountains—and the village areas at their bases offer an all-season recreational cornucopia. You can have great fun here without ever snapping on a ski. Hike, bike, play tennis, and golf top courses. Shop designer stores, galleries, and boutiques. Have a full-service spa getaway, or throw moderation out the window, eat wonderful food, and kick up your heels. If you love a snow-laden landscape, the exhilaration of crisp mountain air, and the feeling that you've stumbled upon a chic alpine hamlet filled with endless possibilities, Whistler is the place to be.

Almost as good as time spent at Whistler is the time spent getting there along Highway 99. The route from West Vancouver offers expansive views of glacially sculpted Howe Sound and the Coast Mountain range. Squamish is a logging town at the north end of the sound in the heart of hiking, climbing, and rafting country. The main entrance to Garibaldi Provincial Park is nearby, as is the village of Brackendale, known for the amazing number of eagles that gather here each January.

A PERFECT DAY AROUND WHISTLER

A perfect summer day starts with breakfast at Durlocher Hof B&B (if you're a guest at the inn), then a ride up the Whistler Mountain gondola, watching the mountain bikers come down the mountain roads as the gondola goes up. Stop at the Roundhouse Lodge to pick up a sandwich and to take in the view from the outside deck. Then hike to Harmony Lake, stopping beside the trail to eat the sandwich and enjoy the views. Go back down the mountain for some shopping and dinner at Bear Foot Bistro while a torchy lounge singer performs. In winter, if you're a skier, a perfect day in Whistler offers sunshine and is spent on the slopes. A perfect evening ends at one of the lively restaurant or nightclub hot spots.

ORIENTATION

Whistler is tucked into the Coast Mountain range about 75 miles north of Vancouver on the Sea to Sky Highway (99 North). The posted speed limit is 80 kilometers per hour (50 mph), and the road is frequently two-lane, so the trip will take about two hours. The scenery is so splendid, though, you'll want to plan extra time for stops if it's your first visit.

The community of Whistler has grown in leaps and bounds in recent years and is spread out along Highway 99. You'll see Whistler signs several miles before you actually reach the village, so have patience. Whistler Village lies at the base between Whistler and Blackcomb Mountains.

Perimeter transportation offers bus service from Vancouver International Airport (about $20 U.S. one way); call 800/663-4265 24 hours in advance for reservations. **B.C. Rail** also provides service from the North Vancouver terminal (see Sightseeing Highlights).

Through **Whistler Resort Association,** 800/944-7853 (in the United States or Canada) or www.tourismwhistler.com, you can arrange for a variety of lodging and ski packages; or get seasonal vacation planners, brochures, reservations, and information. Call the Whistler Activity and Information Centre, 604/932-2394, for recreation and sports information.

SIGHTSEEING HIGHLIGHTS

★★★★ B.C. RAIL'S CARIBOO PROSPECTOR

For reservations, 800/663-8238

B.C. Rail's scheduled train from North Vancouver station meanders through shorefront communities along Burrard Inlet and Howe Sound,

WHISTLER REGION

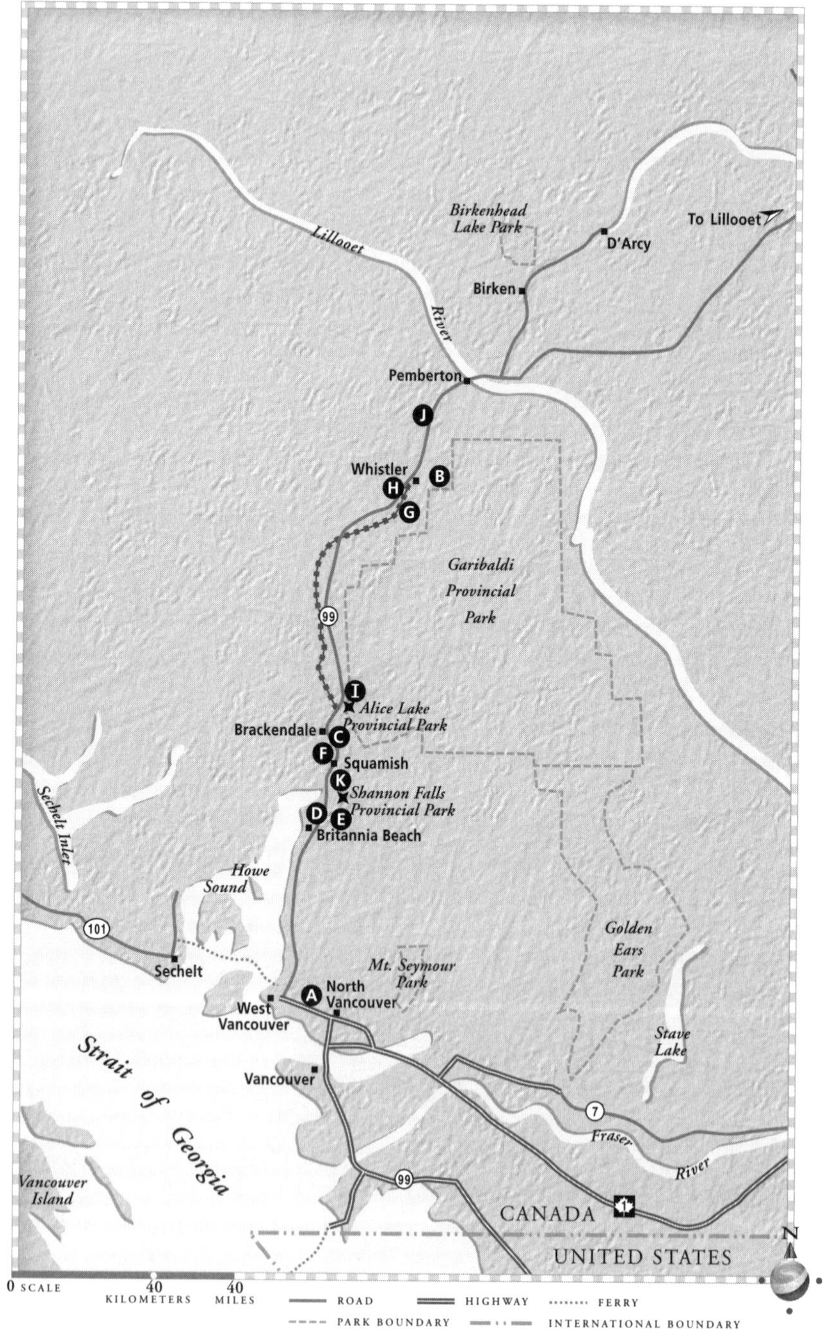

Birkenhead Lake Park
To Lillooet
D'Arcy
Lillooet River
Birken
Pemberton
J
Whistler
B
H
G
Garibaldi Provincial Park
99
I
Alice Lake Provincial Park
Brackendale
C
F
Squamish
K
Shannon Falls Provincial Park
D
E
Britannia Beach
Sechelt Inlet
Howe Sound
101
Sechelt
Mt. Seymour Park
Golden Ears Park
A
North Vancouver
West Vancouver
Stave Lake
Strait of Georgia
Vancouver
7
Fraser River
99
Vancouver Island
CANADA
UNITED STATES
N
0 SCALE
40 KILOMETERS
40 MILES
ROAD
HIGHWAY
FERRY
PARK BOUNDARY
INTERNATIONAL BOUNDARY

hugging the coastline as it goes and offering ever more spectacular water and mountain views. Then it leaves the water and continues north through Cheakamus Canyon to Whistler. You can do it as a day trip or combine it with the full route, which continues on to Pemberton, Lillooet, and points north as far as Prince George on its 463-mile run through B.C.'s Cariboo gold country.

Details: *One round-trip daily between North Vancouver and Whistler leaves North Vancouver at 7 a.m. and returns at 6:40 p.m. (arriving at 9:15 p.m.). Round-trip package rate about $50 U.S., includes breakfast and dinner. Departures from North Vancouver to Prince George are on Sunday, Wednesday, and Friday. (2 1/2 hours one way to Whistler)*

★★★★ WHISTLER MOUNTAIN

Whistler Resort Guest Services, 604/932-3434
www.tourismwhistler.com

You can quickly orient yourself to the layout of Whistler by taking a ride on the **Whistler Gondola.** Twenty scenic minutes put you at the treeline—the top station is at 6,030 feet—where you'll not only get eye-popping views of Whistler and Blackcomb Villages but you'll also have your choice of more than half a dozen hiking trails to meadows, small lakes, or granite ridges offering even more spectacular wraparound views. Also here is the Roundhouse Lodge, where you can get a bite to eat or a sandwich-style picnic for the slopes. In July, the snows melt, baring Whistler Mountain's rocky bone structure, high alpine trails, and early wildflowers. It's a good time for a hike. Access to the **Harmony Lake Trail and Loop** is not far from the gondola station at the top of the mountain. The route is steep and somewhat challenging, winding down about 400 feet through sparse alpine forest.

SIGHTS

- A B.C. Rail's Cariboo Prospector
- B Blackcomb Mountain
- C Brackendale
- D British Columbia Museum of Mining
- E Shannon Falls Provincial Park

SIGHTS *(continued)*

- F Squamish
- G Whistler Mountain
- H Whistler Village

FOOD

- B Joel's at Nicklaus North

CAMPING

- I Alice Lake Provincial Park
- J Nairn Falls
- K Stawamus Chief Provincial Park
- B Whistler Campground

Note: Items with the same letter are located in the same area.

There are lots of spots along the way to rest or enjoy a sandwich while you take in views of the tiny glacial lake chain. Another very different hike takes you up a moonscape terrain to **Little Whistler Peak,** where you'll have stunning views of Black Tusk Peak and glacial green Cheakamus Lake. A less arduous way to scale this is on horseback.

Details: *Gondola rates are $18 (Canadian) including tax. Kids 13 to 18 and seniors 65 and over ride for $15. Children 12 and under free. Open daily 10 to 5. Inside the Roundhouse Lodge (at the gondola's top station) pick up a trail map or sign up for free guided nature walks, rent snowshoes if the snow has lingered, or get information about horseback trail rides. Be sure to wear sturdy shoes or hiking boots and take a jacket, hat, sunscreen, and water. We encountered mosquitoes around Harmony Lakes; repellant would be handy. It takes about 1½ hours to do the Harmony Lake Trail. Be sure to watch your time; the last gondola goes down the mountain at 5. Advanced hikers can take a full day to walk the Musical Bumps Trail to Singing Pass from the Harmony area. (2–4 hours)*

★★★★ WHISTLER VILLAGE

At the heart of the resort is Whistler Village, a European-style pedestrian enclave with rambling gable-roofed buildings and lanes that meander past lodgings, galleries, shops, restaurants, and ski lifts. At the north end of the village, just steps away, is Whistler Village Center, a complex of shops and restaurants. The Upper Village (Blackcomb lifts) is a five-minute stroll away.

Details: *The Whistler Village Resort Association office in the Conference Center provides information on activities. (1 hour)*

★★★ BLACKCOMB MOUNTAIN

Quiet up top in summer, the mountain has hikes and mountain-biking trails to enjoy. The heaviest wildflower bloom—with heathers, arnica, and Indian paintbrush—comes in August.

Details: *Blackcomb is accessed from lifts in the North Village, near the Chateau Whistler. You can pick up a map at the Wizard Chair, a 10-minute walk from the Whistler Gondola. (1–2 hours)*

★★★ BRACKENDALE

Each winter, from November through February, eagles are drawn to the Squamish Valley because of an abundance of spawning salmon in a

ATTENTION FLYFISHERS!

In the 1950s, Whistler—then known as Alta Lake Fishing Resort—was famous as a summer destination, drawing well-heeled fishers from all over the world. Only in 1966, when the Garibaldi Lift Company opened at the base of snow-laden Whistler and Blackcomb Mountains, did the area begin to draw hoards of skiers. Yet fly-fishing opportunities still abound. Spring and fall are especially good times—fishing is good, and the big crush of visitors has fled. Fish year-round for trout, Dolly Varden, or Kokanee salmon. A half-day (four-hour) trip for one with a guide from Whistler BackCountry (604/932-3474 or www.whistlerback country.com) costs about $119 (U.S. funds); less for two or more people. You'll also need a fishing license (about $12 U.S. for one day).

largely undisturbed habitat. The small village of Brackendale, north of Squamish, is known for the Brackendale Winter Eagles Festival. The Brackendale Art Gallery, a combination restaurant and gallery, is a popular gathering spot for eagle fans. Owner Thor Froslev created the festival in the mid-1980s. In 1997 the government established a 1,300-acre reserve to protect the eagles. In summer, there are outdoor activities and river-running in the area.

Details: *North of Squamish. For details on the festival, call the gallery, 604/898-3333. (½ hour to visit, longer for eagle viewing)*

★★★ BRITISH COLUMBIA MUSEUM OF MINING

Britannia Beach, 604/688-8735 or 604/896-2235
www.bcmuseumofmining.org

In the 1930s, the mines around Britannia Beach, south of Squamish, were the largest producers of copper in the British Empire. Now defunct as a mining community, Britannia Beach is the home of a mining museum where visitors put on hard hats to explore the underground mines on guided tours. The mines are more recently famous as the site where an *X-Files* episode was filmed.

Details: *About 30 miles (45 minutes) from West Vancouver, just off Highway 99. Call for hours. Admission $8 (U.S.). (2 hours)*

★★★ SHANNON FALLS PROVINCIAL PARK

You'll see signs for this park about a mile before you reach the town of Squamish. A viewing platform at the base of Shannon Falls, a short walk from the parking lot, offers a dramatic view of the 1,099-foot waterfall. You can picnic and hike on the grounds as well.

Details: *On Highway 99; watch for signs for this park about a mile before you reach the town of Squamish. (½ hour)*

★★ SQUAMISH

37950 Cleveland Avenue; 604/892-9244 (Visitor Center)

Squamish at the north end of Howe Sound, is a logging town. Huge log booms are assembled here for towing to southern mills. Squamish Loggers Day is an international logging competition held each August. There's plenty of recreation here—rafting trips, sport fishing, golfing, mountain biking. There's the **Railway Heritage Park** to explore, and this is also the destination of the **Royal Hudson Steam Train/M.V. Britannia** tour from North Vancouver. Stop long enough to take a long look at the rock face of **Stawamus Chief Mountain,** referred to as "the Chief." It's a favorite of rock climbers and photographers. There are shops, restaurants, and services in town.

Details: *(1 hour)*

FITNESS AND RECREATION

Whistler is a mecca for fitness, recreation, and special events. First of all, the ski season lasts until the end of April; there's glacier skiing on Blackcomb from May to August. At 5,020 feet, Whistler has the second-highest vertical rise of any North American ski mountain. Between the two mountains there are over 7,000 acres of skiable terrain; Whistler alone has 100 marked trails. The mountains are hosts of the men's World Cup downhill race. Day lift tickets that offer access to both mountains are $57 (Canadian) for adults, $48 for youth and seniors, and $28 for children.

The Whistler/Blackcomb Mountain Ski School offers classes for kids as well as after-ski care. There's a summer trapeze and instruction at the Upper Village near the Blackcomb lifts. The Chateau Whistler has a kids' club with crafts and activities arranged through the health club.

There are three lakes in the main Whistler area: Alta, Green, and Lost. Green Lake has a park at its north end. Alta Lake has trails, boat launches, and picnic park areas. In winter, you can snowshoe or set your own cross-country trails. The Lost Lake trail system, just northwest of the Upper Village, is a favorite for set-track cross-country skiing (day rates are $10 per person; at night it's free and well lit).

There's summer hiking and mountain biking on both mountains. Be aware that you might encounter black bears. Make a lot of noise or wear bear bells.

At village level, there's plenty to do as well. Golf is top-notch—try the Whistler Golf Club, 604/932-4544 or 800/376-1777; Chateau Whistler Golf Club, 604/938-2092; Nicklaus North Golf Course, 604/938-9898; or Sky Golf and Country Club, 604/894-6106 or 800/668-7900. Bicycling trails proliferate. Another way to get away from the ski area into snowy back country is to take a snowmobile ride. Outfitters provide warm snowsuits, protective headgear, and lunch off the beaten path. Sleigh riding, winter fishing, and flightseeing trips can also be arranged through the resort.

The Whistler Activity and Information Centre, 604/932-2394, provides complete information on tour operators, maps, and a list of equipment rental outlets. (Many of the hotels have their own equipment rental shops.) Sleigh riding, dogsledding, winter fishing, and flightseeing trips can also be arranged through the center. The CP Hotel's Chateau Whistler (in the Upper Village) offers comprehensive spa packages. The Delta Mountain Inn (in Whistler Village) has dome-covered tennis courts, and there is a tennis center north of the village. At the Meadow Park Sports Centre, a five-minute drive north of the village, you can ice-skate, swim, work out with weights, or play squash.

FOOD

World-class cuisine and fine dining choices abound in Whistler. **Araxi,** 4222 Village Square, 604/932-4540, in the heart of the village, has a definite European ambience. The **Bear Foot Bistro,** 1121 Village Green, 604/932-1133, also in the village, offers creative food in an Italian country-style setting. **Val d'Isère,** 4314 Main Street, 604/932-4666, serves impressive Alsace-style food. **Chef Bernard's** (Bernard Cassavant, formerly chef of Wildfower at the Chateau Whistler), 4573 Chateau Boulevard, 604/932-7051, offers takeout food and is a good place for breakfast or lunch. **La Rua** (in Le Chamois hotel in the Upper Village), 4557 Blackcomb Way, 604/932-5011, offers high-end Mediterranean food and has a consistent and excellent reputation. Nearby in the Chateau Whistler, **Wildflower,** 4599 Chateau Boulevard, 604/938-2033, serves Northwest produce Canadian Pacific–style in a lively, colorful, and comfortable restaurant that views the slopes. **Quattro at Pinnacle,** 4319 Main Street, 604/905-4844, is an "in" place for skiers to gather for dinner; year-round it serves excellent pasta, and if you can't make up your mind, you can order a sampling of five types. The **Rim Rock Cafe and Oyster Bar,** 2117 Whistler

WHISTLER

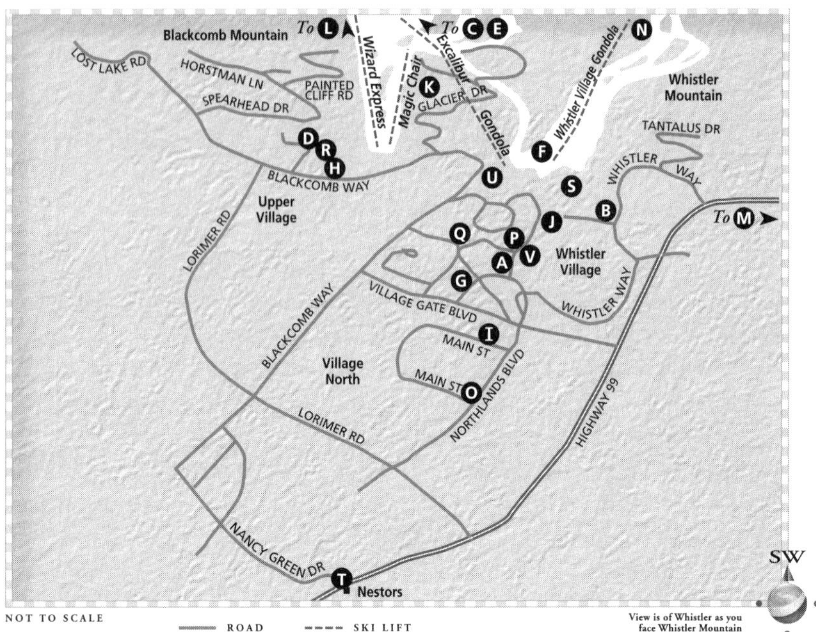

FOOD

- **A** Araxi
- **B** Bear Foot Bistro
- **C** The Bite
- **D** Chef Bernard's
- **E** Christine's Restaurant
- **F** Garibaldi Lift Company Bar and Grill
- **C** Glacier Lodge Restaurant
- **G** Hard Rock Café
- **H** La Rua
- **I** Moe's Deli & Bar

FOOD *(continued)*

- **J** Old Spaghetti Factory
- **K** Quattro at Pinnacle
- **L** Rendezvous
- **M** Rim Rock Cafe and Oyster Bar
- **C** River Rock Grill
- **N** Roundhouse Lodge
- **O** Splitz Grill
- **P** Trattoria de Umberto
- **Q** Val d'Isère
- **R** Wildflower

LODGING

- **R** Chateau Whistler
- **S** Delta Hotel
- **T** Durlacher Hof
- **U** Pan Pacific Lodge Whistler
- **V** Whiski Jack Condos

Note: Items with the same letter are located in the same area.

Road, 604/932-5565, in the Creekside area, is packed with folks craving seafood. **Joel's Restaurant at Nicklaus North,** 8080 Nicklaus Boulevard North, 604/932-1240, overlooks the golf course and is several miles north of Whistler. It's owned by well-known Whistler restaurateur and welcoming host Joel Thibault.

Trattoria de Umberto on Sundial Place, 604/932-5858, has outdoor tables and is a good lunch destination. You'll have fun choosing your special-order hamburger at tiny **Splitz Grill,** 4369 Main Street, 604/938-9300. Good hotel breakfast spots are the Delta and Chateau Whistler. **Moe's Deli & Bar,** 604/905-7772, in the new Delta Village Suites, has a kids' menu—one of the reasons it's a good family spot. The **Hard Rock Café,** 4295 Blackcomb Way, 604/938-9922, and the **Old Spaghetti Factory,** 4154 Village Green, 604/938-1081, are also good family eateries.

And there are plenty of restaurants on the mountains: You can take the high-speed quad chairlift to the **Rendezvous** day lodge complex on Blackcomb to nosh on takeout. Enjoy panoramic views of the village, sip fine wines, and dine off linen at **Christine's Restaurant,** 4545 Blackcomb Way, 604/938-7437; reservations recommended. Blackcomb Mountain's multimillion-dollar **Glacier Lodge Restaurant** can be reached only on skis. It offers ethnic and West Coast cuisine at the **River Rock Grill** and bistro-style counter service at **The Bite.** Atop Whistler, the **Roundhouse Lodge,** 604/932-3434, offers great views down into the village, along with burgers, soups, and sandwiches. Or you can stop for a post-mountain pizza at the **Garibaldi Lift Company Bar and Grill,** 604/905-2220, at the gondola base station at the foot of Whistler Mountain—fairly pricey but fun and lively.

Each November, Whistler Resort hosts the **Cornucopia Food & Wine Celebration,** a three-day event that features tastings, seminars, cooking demonstrations, hands-on workshops, gourmet dining, and special events. Packages start from about $280 U.S. Call 800/944-7853 for details.

LODGING

Accommodations at Whistler range from intimate B&B rooms to suites in grand hotels. For instance, you'll be immersed in an authentic Austrian atmosphere and hospitality at eight-room **Durlacher Hof,** 7055 Nesters Road, 604/932-1924, where you'll doff your shoes and don cozy wool slippers to sit by the *kachelofen* (tile oven) fireplace and be pampered by hosts Erika and Peter Durlacher. At the baronial-style, 558-plus-room **Chateau Whistler Resort,** 4599 Chateau Boulevard, 604/938-8000 or 800/606-8244, you can relax in front of the massive limestone fireplace in the great hall and experience the full services and amenities of a grand hotel resort. With a total of over 4,400 rooms in the Whistler area, you can also pick and choose from anything in between, including a wide variety of condominium rentals through **Whiski Jack Resorts,** 4319 Main Street, 604/932-6500, 800/944-7545, or www.whiskijack.com. Specify whether location adjacent to the lifts is important to you. There's also the impressive new **Pan Pacific Lodge,** 4320 Sundial Crescent, 604/905-2999 or 800/327-8585, and the ever-popular **Delta Whistler Resort,** 4050 Whistler Way, 604/932-1982, 800/515-4050, or www.deltahotels.com, steps from the Whistler gondola. For one-call assistance, contact the resort's central reservations service 800/944-7853 (in the United States and Canada) for brochures, reservations, and information.

CAMPING

Whistler Campground opened in late summer in 1998. It's a private facility just five minutes north of the village on Highway 99. Call the Whistler Activities Center for details. **Nairn Falls** lies 20 minutes north and is closer to Pemberton. **Alice Lake Provincial Park** and **Stawamus Chief Provincial Park** are south of Whistler, near Squamish. For information about these and other parks in the area, call B.C. Parks, Garibaldi-Sunshine District, 604/898-3678.

NIGHTLIFE

Whistler's nightspots are packed Thursday, Friday, and Saturday nights during ski season. In the village center, **Buffalo Bill's,** Village Green, 604/932-6613, below the stairs under the Timberline Lodge, and **Garfinkels,** 604/932-2323, in Town Plaza, often have live bands and a scene that appeals to thirty-somethings. The **Savage Beagle,** 604/938-3337, has a cigar lounge and a downstairs nightclub. **Maxx Fish,** 604/932-1904, with its techno music and trendy interior, and **Tommy Africa's,** 604/932-6090, both cater to a younger crowd.

Scenic Route: Vancouver-Whistler-Lillooet-Fraser River

This route will give you a taste of the best of British Columbia in a few days. It takes you from sophisticated Vancouver northwest to recreation-rich Whistler along Highway 99, the Sea to Sky Highway, which overlooks Howe Sound. On a clear day, it's an absolutely knock-your-socks-off gorgeous drive. Spend time exploring the hiking, biking, golf, and fishing options around Whistler, then continue north to Pemberton, a jumping-off spot into wilderness. Continue northeast on 99, and you'll reach the town of Lillooet, the beginning of the Cariboo Gold Rush Trail, across a road paved only in recent years. (Or with a four-wheel drive and a strong sense of adventure, you can take the Forest Service road northwest of Pemberton and make your way on primitive roads through the wilderness to Gold Bridge. A writer friend and I did this and spent time at Tyax Mountain Lake Resort, 250/238-2221, a destination in the Chilcotin Range wilderness that most folks reach by floatplane.) Continue on 99 to Cache Creek and visit nearby Hat Creek Ranch, a Provincial Heritage site and a living history ranch. A former stagecoach stop, it gives you a feel for life in the late 1800s. Near Cache Creek you can pick up Highway 1 (Trans-Canada Highway). Go north to dude ranch country around Clinton and into the Cariboo and Chilcotin regions. Or take it south along the Thompson and

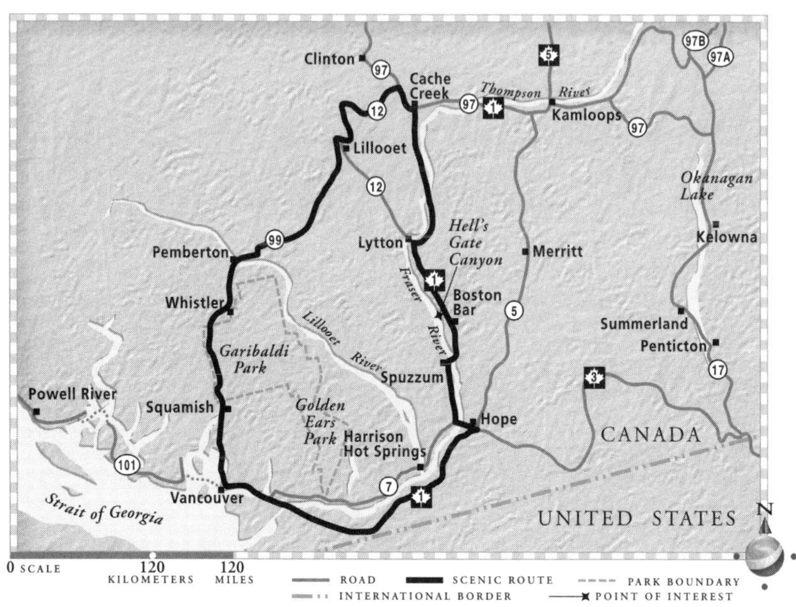

Fraser Rivers and stop at dramatic Hells Gate canyon on the Fraser. The drive is barren and dry until you reach the area around Hope, where the Fraser River valley becomes a verdant farming region en route back to Vancouver.

7
VANCOUVER

Vancouver may be the best example of a Northwest city combining sophisticated elements of urban life—the arts and architecture, culture, entertainment, fine dining—all in the lap of nature. And nature here is at her absolute tip-top, knock-your-socks-off best.

Stroll the perimeter of 1,000-acre Stanley Park, which lies in the heart of the city. Stop somewhere near the dramatic Lion's Gate Bridge and look north across Burrard Inlet to the shore of North Vancouver. You can hike from that shoreline and in less than half an hour be in wilderness. You can drive north and in the same time reach a ski lift at Grouse Mountain. Continue around the park until you reach the skyline view, and you'll see a vibrant cosmopolitan city with a delicious international flavor. Fashion. Business. British heritage. The strong influence of native peoples. An incredibly rich migration (especially of talented chefs) from Hong Kong. There's a large and fabulous Chinatown with the Dr. Sun Yat Sen Chinese Garden (the only Chinese garden ever built outside of China and just one of many very special gardens in this city).

Artist Emily Carr, whose work you will see in the Vancouver Art Gallery, once made an observation about life that also applies to this city: "There is so much to see, so much to bite off and store and chew on."

VANCOUVER

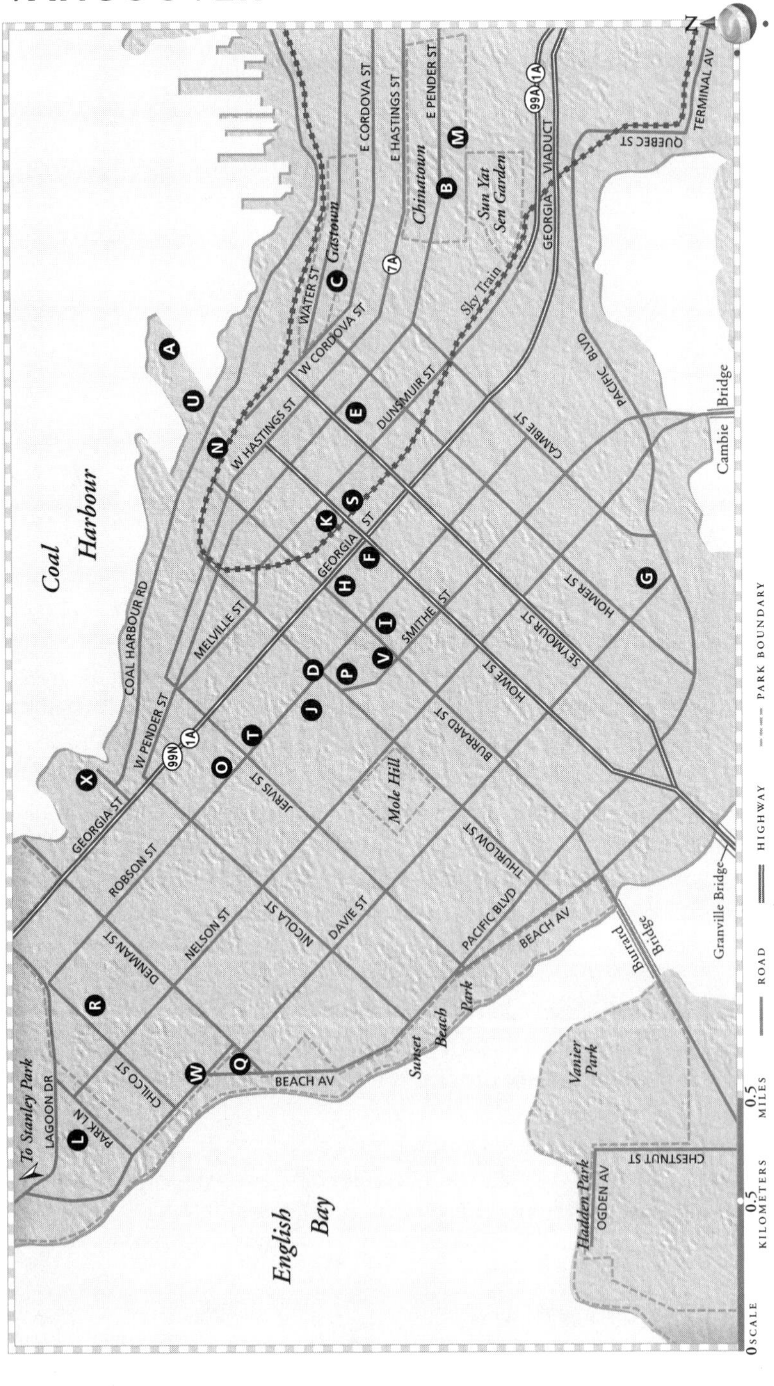

N
Coal Harbour
English Bay
Gastown
Chinatown
Sun Yat Sen Garden
Mole Hill
Sunset Beach Park
Vanier Park
Hadden Park
To Stanley Park
Sky Train
Cambie Bridge
Granville Bridge
Burrard Bridge
WATER ST
E CORDOVA ST
E HASTINGS ST
E PENDER ST
W CORDOVA ST
W HASTINGS ST
W PENDER ST
DUNSMUIR ST
GEORGIA ST
GEORGIA VIADUCT
SMITHE ST
MELVILLE ST
COAL HARBOUR RD
ROBSON ST
NELSON ST
DAVIE ST
PACIFIC BLVD
BEACH AV
CAMBIE ST
HOMER ST
SEYMOUR ST
HOWE ST
BURRARD ST
THURLOW ST
JERVIS ST
NICOLA ST
DENMAN ST
CHILCO ST
LAGOON DR
PARK LN
QUEBEC ST
TERMINAL AV
CHESTNUT ST
OGDEN AV
99A
1A
99N
7A
A
B
C
D
E
F
G
H
I
J
K
L
M
N
O
P
Q
R
S
T
U
V
W
X
ROAD
HIGHWAY
PARK BOUNDARY
0 SCALE
0.5 KILOMETERS
0.5 MILES

A PERFECT DAY IN VANCOUVER

The perfect day in Vancouver is sunny and long. First thing in the morning, hop an Aquabus (one of the small foot ferries that skitter around the city's waterways) at the foot of Hornby Street and take it across False Creek to Granville Island, where things come to life about 9 a.m.; grab some food—coffee or chai (latte-style tea served at JJ Roaster) or a Belgian waffle at the informal Market Grill—and then explore the island's market and art studios. Back downtown, make your way to Robson Street and have lunch at CinCin's (on the balcony, overlooking Robson's shoppers, is perfect). Don't miss the Dr. Sun Yat Sen Classical Chinese Garden (especially in springtime) and the Museum of Anthropolgy. Make dinner reservations for a table with a view at the Teahouse at Stanley Park and relax into your evening as the sun sets on English Bay.

ORIENTATION

Driving north from Seattle on Interstate 5 you'll cross the border at Blaine. (While the primary customs is at the Blaine Peach Arch Park, there is also a truck crossing nearby to the east that is often quicker, albeit less picturesque. Watch for signs as you approach Blaine.) Once you cross the border into Canada, you'll follow Highway 99 to downtown, through Vancouver's suburbs. It's a congested route and can be confusing, but unless you approach from the north (off the Trans-Canada Highway) it's your primary choice. So watch closely for directional signs. Highway 99 will put you on Granville Street, which leads over the Granville Street Bridge, directly into downtown. It's about a

---

SIGHTS

- **A** Canada Place
- **B** Chinatown/Dr. Sun Yat Sen Classical Chinese Garden
- **C** Gastown
- **D** Robson Street
- **E** The Umbrella Shop
- **F** Vancouver Art Gallery
- **G** Yaletown

FOOD

- **H** 900 West at the Hotel Vancouver
- **I** Bacchus
- **J** CinCin
- **K** Diva at the Met
- **L** Fish House at Stanley Park
- **M** Floata
- **N** Herons
- **O** Hon's Wun Tun House
- **P** Piccolo Mondo
- **Q** Raincity Grill

LODGING

- **R** Buchan Hotel
- **S** Four Seasons Hotel
- **H** Hotel Vancouver
- **K** Metropolitan Hotel Vancouver
- **T** Pacific Palisades Hotel
- **U** Pan Pacific Hotel Vancouver
- **V** Sutton Place Hotel
- **W** Sylva Hotel
- **N** Waterfront Hotel
- **I** Wedgewood Hotel
- **X** Westin Bayshore

Note: Items with the same letter are located in the same area.

three hour drive from Seattle to downtown Vancouver under normal border crossing conditions; you can add as much as an hour at peak summer and holiday times.

Downtown Vancouver is located on a peninsula of land that is bordered by several bodies of water—English Bay to the west, Burrard Inlet to the north and east, and False Creek to the South. Highway 99 cuts through downtown and leads north through Stanley Park across the Lion's Gate Bridge to the communities of North Vancouver and West Vancouver. Don't confuse West Vancouver, the community, with the "West End" of Vancouver, the neighborhood north of downtown adjacent to Stanley Park. And, southwest of downtown is the Kitsilano area, referred to as "the West Side."

Paper currency comes in \$5, \$10, \$20, and larger increments. There are \$1 coins referred to as "loonies" (a loon is imprinted on the coin) and \$2 coins called "toonies."

SIGHTSEEING HIGHLIGHTS

★★★★ CHINATOWN/DR. SUN YAT SEN CLASSICAL CHINESE GARDEN

578 Carrall Street; 604/662-3207

www.discovervancouver.com/sun

In the heart of Vancouver's Chinatown—the third largest in North America after San Francisco and New York—the garden is constructed almost entirely of materials from China: carved screens and woodwork, tiles, and stones. The first authentic classical Chinese garden ever built outside of China, it is particularly beautiful when spring cherry blossoms litter the garden.

Details: *Open daily throughout the year; there are tours, tea, and a gift shop. Admission is about \$6. (1–2 hours)*

★★★★ GASTOWN

This historic district of Vancouver, with its cobblestone streets, lies between downtown and Chinatown, mainly around Water Street. Now home to antiques shops, galleries, and restaurants, it was in the late 1800s the thriving center of Vancouver's waterfront commerce. In September Gastown hosts a celebration honoring "Gassy Jack" Deighton, the district's namesake and first saloon keeper.

Details: *For information on current events contact the Gastown Business Improvement Society, 604/683-5650. (2 hours)*

BEAUTIFUL BROLLIES

When it rains in Vancouver, as it often does—57 inches of annual rainfall compared to Seattle's 37 inches—many brightly hued bumbershoots dot the streets. Most come from a Vancouver institution, The Umbrella Store. The owner is in the third generation of his family to operate the store. Many umbrellas are made on site. If it's not too busy, you can get a tour of the workroom and see the ancient Singer sewing machines that are still in use. You can also arrange to have custom-made umbrellas produced, even from your own material.

The store is located at 534 West Pender Street; 604/669-9444, www.theumbrellashop.com

★★★★ **GRANVILLE ISLAND**
604/666-6477
www.granvilleisland.com

Bustling, chic, and colorful, this 20-acre island on False Creek in the heart of Vancouver draws most people to its public market. But the artisans and their work draw visitors again and again. Walk the island's web of small lanes and watch artists and craftsmen at work in their studios, often using Old World tools and techniques to create pottery or tapestries, jewelry, glass sculptures, and more. Some of the best artists in British Columbia can be found here, many since the late '70s and early '80s. To take a circular tour of the artists' studios, a good place to start is the **Crafts Association of B.C.** Crafthouse, 1386 Cartwright Street, 604/687-7270. The nearby **Gallery of B.C. Ceramics** shows the work of members of the **Potter's Guild of B.C.** Another place to start is the **Net Loft,** a complex of studios and shops near the public market. Outside, around its perimeter, you'll find artists' studios. Inside there are shops like **Nancy Lord,** which offers custom-designed coats, clothing, and purses in butter-soft leather. **Maiwa Handprints** has batiks, hand-printed clothing, gifts, artists' supplies, and books. The **Emily Carr College of Art & Design** is on the island.

Details: *The island is small, yet packed with so much it can be con-*

*fusing. Pick up a map at the **Granville Island Information Centre** at the end of Anderson Street near the public market. The island is busiest on weekends. In winter, the public market is closed Mondays, as are many of the studios. Three-hour free parking spaces merely dot the island and are especially hard to find on weekend mornings. You can take a ferry from downtown. The Aquabus, 604/689-5858, runs from the south end of Hornby Street to the Arts Centre on the island. (2–3 hours)*

★★★★ MUSEUM OF ANTHROPOLOGY

6393 NW Marine Drive, 604/822-3825

www.moa.ubc.ca

On a bluff overlooking the ocean, this award-winning building, designed by Arthur Erickson (Canada's leading architect and a local resident), contains open displays of totem poles; potlatch bowls, dishes, and boxes; Bill Reid's massive sculptures *Raven* and *The First Men;* and traditional longhouses. It is a don't-miss destination.

Details: *On the UBC campus. Call for information on special workshops and performances. (2 hours)*

★★★★ QUEEN ELIZABETH PARK

Cambie Street and West 33rd Avenue; 604/257-8570 (conservatory hours), 604/874-8008 (Seasons in the Park reservations)

This 130-acre park claims a hill south of downtown Vancouver and offers one of the best views of the city, particularly from the Seasons in the Park restaurant (Clinton and Yeltsin dined here during the summit) or the overlook nearby. The Plexiglas-encased Bloedel Conservatory is lit at night, filled with tropical plants.

Details: *(1–2 hours)*

★★★★ ROBSON STREET

Downtown Vancouver

This street combines the chic and style of Beverly Hills's Rodeo Drive and the eccentric youthful energy of London's Carnaby Street. It's the fashion heartbeat of the city, where stylish folks of all ages come to explore. You'll find international designers—Ferragamo, Guess, Esprit, and more—Roots, Murchie's Tea, a Virgin Megastore, and plenty of hip coffee shops and restaurants. The counterculture types and conservatives happily mingle, making this area a summertime people-watching feast.

Details: *The main shopping segment is on Robson between Hornby and Cardero Streets. (1–2 hours)*

★★★★ STANLEY PARK

North of downtown, Highway 99
www.parks.vancouver.bc.ca

At 1,000 acres, this is Canada's largest city park, overlooking English Bay and Burrard Inlet. The aquarium is here—be sure to see the fascinating beluga (white) whales—along with rose gardens, restaurants, and hiking and horseback riding trails. The five-mile walk around the park's seawall offers spectacular views.

Details: *Grounds are open 24 hours. There is no admission charge to enter the park, however expect to pay a few dollars for parking at all locations, including the restaurants, so carry change for meters. There is also a park shuttle (about $1.50 U.S.) that stops at 14 locations within the park. (2–3 hours)*

★★★ CANADA PLACE

Imax Theater, 604/682-4629 or 800/582-4629

It's fun to explore this unusual building at the foot of Howe Street. You'll be able to see its design, like a white ship's sail, from all over the city. The Canadian Pavilion of Expo '86, Canada Place houses the Pan Pacific Hotel, restaurants, shops, an IMAX theater, and conference quarters. It's also the cruise ship terminal.

Details: *At the foot of Howe Street. (1–2 hours)*

★★★ CAPILANO SUSPENSION BRIDGE

North Vancouver, 604/985-7474
www.capbridge.com

Soaring 25 stories and covering a 450-foot span over a rushing river, the Capilano Suspension Bridge, Vancouver's oldest commercial tourist attraction, still quickens the heartbeat and steals the breath of visitors as it did over a hundred years ago. Millions have crossed it. A protected outdoor interpretive area on the grounds chronicles the park's growth; you'll also see about 30 totem poles, carved in the 1930s, clustered here in Totem Park. Native Tshimsian and Tlingit carvers work in the Carving Centre near the Trading Post (built in 1911 as a teahouse to honor the queen's birthday). West Coast tribal-style spirit masks, cedar carvings, and other native crafts, and quality clothing, jewelry, and leather goods are for sale here. Cross

STANLEY PARK'S CANNON CALL

If you're near Stanley Park late in the evening, you may hear the unmistakable sound of a cannon shot. It's the Nine O'Clock Gun. Brought to Vancouver from England in the late 1800s, the gun was set up by the Department of Fisheries at Brockton Point. Fired every evening at 9 p.m., it was to remind fishermen of fishing time limits. While today's fishermen wear watches, the gun still fires. In more than a hundred years the only time it was silenced was during World War II.

the bridge and discover a nature exhibit and 15 acres of trails, ponds, and forest to explore.

Details: *The park is about 10 minutes from downtown Vancouver. Go through Stanley Park, over the Lions Gate Bridge, and north one mile on Capilano Road. Admission is $8.25 for adults. The log Bridge House Restaurant on-site is open for lunch and dinner. (2 hours)*

★★★ GRANVILLE ISLAND MUSEUMS

1502 Duranleau St. Granville Island, 604/683-1939
www.granvilleislandmuseums.com

Three unusual museums—or rather private collections gone wild—under one roof are apt to please just about everyone. The **Sport Fishing Museum's** extensive collection includes Hardy reels, extensive fly-fishing gear, salmon fishing history, and much more. The **Model Ships Museum** has an impressive international collection of submarines, battleships, and toy boats and large scale models of warships and other sailing vessels. An extensive working diorama is the star feature of the **Model Train Museum,** and there are shelves and displays of trains including the Royal Hudson, Lionel trains, O gauge, G gauge, standard gauge, steam locomotives and tender, brass locomotives, and many more toy trains.

Details: *Near the entry to Granville Island. Admission is about $5 (U.S.) for adults, $3.50 for students and seniors, $2 for 4 to 12 years, free under 4 years. (1 hour)*

★★★ **UNIVERSITY OF BRITISH COLUMBIA BOTANICAL AND NITOBE MEMORIAL GARDENS**

Botanical Garden at 6804 SW Marine Drive, 604/822-9666
www.hedgerows.com/UBCBotGdn/

The beautiful Nitobe Memorial Gardens combine elements of a tea garden and a landscape garden and are part of the 70-acre Botanical Garden with its natural segments and its medicinal garden and gift shop.

Details: *On the UBC campus. Admission about $4.50. (1 hour for each garden)*

★★★ **VANCOUVER MUSEUM**

1100 Chestnut Street, Vanier Park, Kitsilano
604/736-4431, www.vanmuseum.bc.ca

Founded in 1894, this museum showcases Vancouver's history in a very modern structure. Exhibits and programs focus on the heritage of the lower B.C. mainland, with extensive collections on natural history, archaeology, ethnology, and Asian arts. Children appreciate the antique toy display. The panoramic views of downtown, alone, are worth the stop.

Details: *Combine with a visit to the Museum of Anthropology. Admission charged. (1 to 2 hours)*

★★★ **RICHMOND**

Travel Information Centre, 7888 Alderbridge Way
604/271-8280
www.cityofrichmond.com

A trip to this southern suburb of Vancouver, near Vancouver International Airport, is like going to Hong Kong without the airfare. Chinese families have settled here in droves, and the result has been an explosion of new construction, hotels, and businesses. The Radisson President Hotel has a Buddhist temple. Parker Place shopping center has a food court with an amazing selection of Asian food. If you see "bubble pearl tea" on a menu, try it—you drink it with a wide straw so you can suck up gelatinlike "pearls" at the bottom.

Details: *Take Granville Street south from downtown Vancouver and follow the signs to Vancouver International Airport; near the airport you will see exit signs for Richmond. (2–3 hours)*

★★★ **VANCOUVER ART GALLERY**

750 Hornby Street; 604/662-4719
www.vanartgallery.bc.ca

Designed in 1907 by Francis Rattenbury (Victoria's legendary architect), this gallery is conveniently located on Robson Street. It's well worth a visit for the Emily Carr paintings that are part the gallery's permanent collection. Other Canadian artists are featured as well. Changing special exhibits.

Details: *One block off Robson Street. Admission is $7.50. (1–2 hours)*

★★★ VANDUSEN BOTANICAL GARDEN

5251 Oak Street, Vancouver; 604/878-9274
www.vandusengarden.org

Modern sculptures are a surprise in this 55-acre horticultural showplace made up of numerous specialized gardens. There's a kitchen garden, a fragrance garden, a formal rose garden, and five lakes that attract 65 varieties of birds. Van Dusen features Canada's largest collection of rhododendrons; in spring, vibrant blooms fill Rhododendron Walk. A restaurant and gift shop are on-site.

Details: *At 37th Avenue. Open daily from 10 a.m.; closing at different seasonal hours. (1/2–2 hours)*

★★★ YALETOWN

Vancouver

The streets are packed with cars and delivery trucks, but this warehouse-filled garment district is a fun place to be, day or night. Formerly rundown and forgotten, Yaletown's renewal started with Expo '86. Now a mix of architect and design offices, shops, restaurants, and nightspots, it's livelier than ever. Check out such shops as **Bernstein and Gold** in the 1100 block of Hamilton Street, 604/687-1535, which offers individually designed furniture, much of it down-filled, beautiful European cottons, and beeswax candles. **Don't Show the Elephant** gallery and café serves a refreshing cold coffee and is a chic and unusual stop with Swedish CDs for sale. **Urban Fare,** an upscale market, is a food lover's haven (see Food).

Details: *Located between Pacific Boulevard, Homer Street, and Nelson Street. (1–2 hours)*

FITNESS AND RECREATION

Manfred Scholermann of Rockwood Adventures, 604/926-7705, a former Culinary Olympics chef, has created a series of unique city-to-wilds-type adven-

HOLLYWOOD NORTH

Don't be surprised if you stumble upon filming crews and movie stars when you're exploring Gastown, Robson Street, Chinatown, or many other spots around Vancouver. In 1999, the film and television industry spent over $1 billion here. The province is home to many film and video companies and talent agencies—about 35,000 British Columbians are employed full-time and part-time in the industry. (In fact, the Bridge Studios, located in Burnaby, has one of the largest special effects stages in North America.) *Snow Falling on Cedars, Mission to Mars, Reindeer Games, Double Jeopardy, Final Destination,* and *Romeo Must Die* were all filmed here, as well as, for many years, *The X-Files*. Sign onto the B.C. Film Commission's website—www.bcfilmcommission. You can check the Filmlist under What's New to find the filming schedule for upcoming months.

tures and can lead you walking in town, on the North Shore, to islands, and other spots. Spectacular Adventures, 604/925-8187, in North Vancouver, also offers interesting trips, like picnicking on a glacier.

The Vancouver area offers a great selection of spectator sports. The Canucks hockey games are exciting to watch, and the team is a perennial powerhouse. For a truly memorable experience, take in a Canucks hockey game played at GM Place. Arrive there early and have some food at the Orca Bay Bar and Grill, 604/899-7525; no reservations are accepted on game nights. While at the game, you'll see fireworks and all kinds of entertainment between periods. Maybe the Giant Orca will swoop down on you with a surprise offering!

The B.C. Lions (Canadian Football League) offer up football Canada-style. If basketball is what you want, take in a Grizzlies game. Rounding things out are soccer as played by the 86ers and baseball pitched to you by the Canadians. All individual tickets can be arranged through Ticketmaster; call 604/280-4400.

FOOD

The food scene in Vancouver is dynamic and exciting. Choose from terrific Chinese food, seafood, and a wide variety of restaurants with many different per-

GREATER VANCOUVER

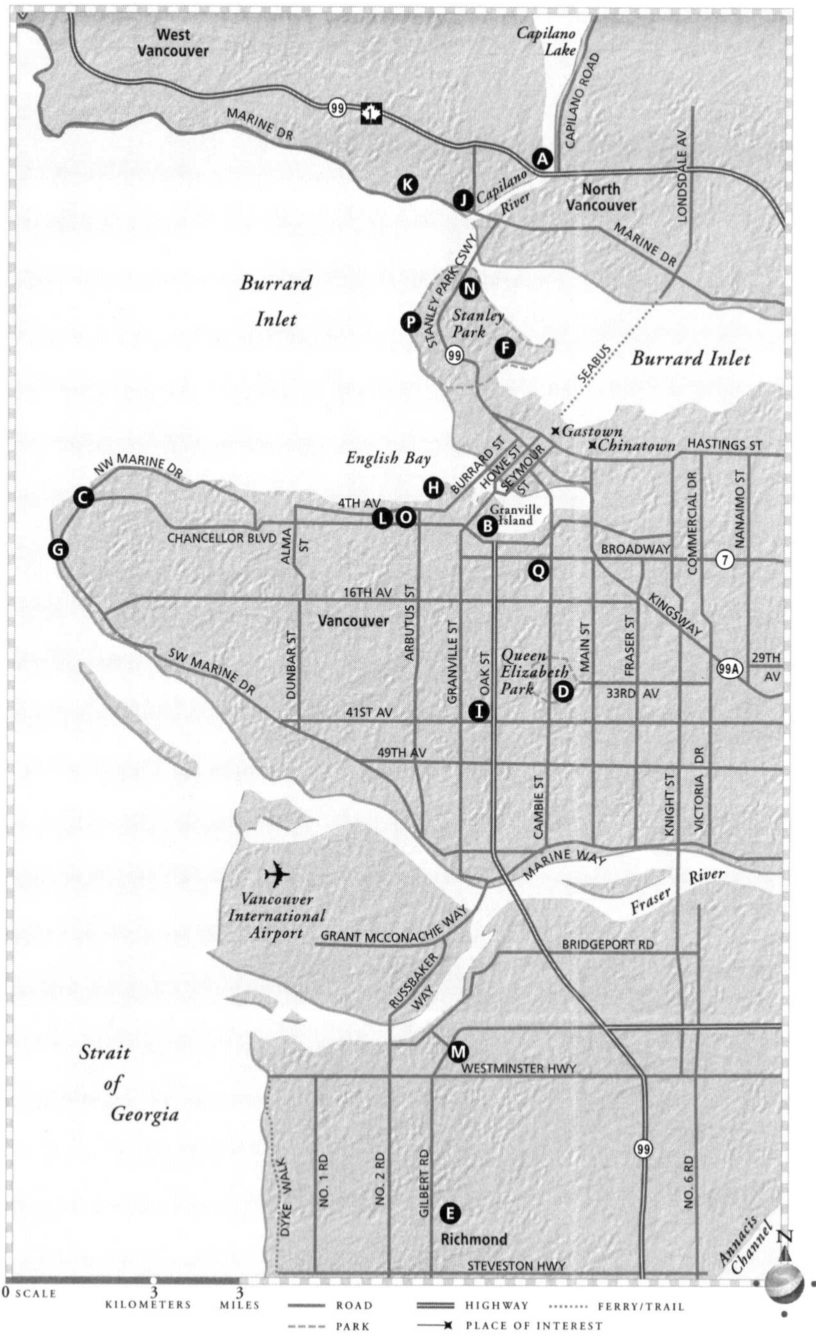

West Vancouver
Capilano Lake
CAPILANO ROAD
99
MARINE DR
LONSDALE AV
A
K
J
Capilano River
North Vancouver
MARINE DR
STANLEY PARK CSWY
Burrard Inlet
N
P
Stanley Park
99
F
SEABUS
Burrard Inlet
Gastown
Chinatown
HASTINGS ST
English Bay
BURRARD ST
HOWE ST
SEYMOUR ST
NW MARINE DR
H
C
4TH AV
L
O
Granville Island
B
CHANCELLOR BLVD
ALMA ST
G
BROADWAY
COMMERCIAL DR
NANAIMO ST
7
Q
16TH AV
ARBUTUS ST
KINGSWAY
Vancouver
GRANVILLE ST
OAK ST
Queen Elizabeth Park
MAIN ST
FRASER ST
29TH AV
99A
SW MARINE DR
DUNBAR ST
D
33RD AV
41ST AV
I
49TH AV
CAMBIE ST
KNIGHT ST
VICTORIA DR
MARINE WAY
Fraser River
Vancouver International Airport
GRANT MCCONACHIE WAY
BRIDGEPORT RD
RUSSBAKER WAY
Strait of Georgia
M
WESTMINSTER HWY
99
DYKE WALK
NO. 1 RD
NO. 2 RD
GILBERT RD
NO. 6 RD
E
Richmond
STEVESTON HWY
Annacis Channel
N
0 SCALE
3 KILOMETERS
3 MILES
ROAD
HIGHWAY
FERRY/TRAIL
PARK
PLACE OF INTEREST

sonalities. Choices range from cheap and cheerful eateries to expensive and elegant ones. And you might as well start where you started this chapter—at Stanley Park: The energetic feel of the **Fish House at Stanley Park,** 604/681-7275, extends to the lively saltwater fish prints that adorn the tomato-red walls of this gray clapboard. For an appetizer try the signature flaming prawns or a sampler of six West Coast oysters from the oyster bar. In summer, a more casual concession below the restaurant serves up take-out food, such as grilled salmon sandwiches. Palms, fig trees, and a conservatory give the **Teahouse at Ferguson Point,** 604/669-3281, on the edge of English Bay, a garden ambience that's especially romantic at sunset. They are noted for their weekend brunch; entrée favorites are the smoked salmon gratin and brioche French toast. Tour buses often crowd the parking lot at **Prospect Point Cafe,** 604/669-2737, because the overlook here has terrific views of the boat traffic on Burrard Inlet and the soaring Lion's Gate Bridge; however, if you're in the park and looking for food on the go, there's a quick-stop kiosk offering hamburgers and hot dogs, espresso drinks, and ice cream; inside, a restaurant with a deck overlooks the inlet.

Stop by **900 West at the Hotel Vancouver,** 604/669-9378, and **Bacchus,** 604/608-5319, in the Wedgewood Hotel for after-shopping drinks or dinner. (At 900 West, try the After the Frost martini, with a frozen grape in the bottom—an award winner from Vancouver and Seattle's International Martini Classic Challenge.) Both of these are a block away from Robson Street. For Chinese vegetarian (you wouldn't know if I hadn't told you) dim sum in a high-energy atmosphere, try **Hon's Wun Tun House,** 604/688-0871, also on Robson—a fun way for shoppers to reenergize. **Piccolo Mondo,** 604/688-1633, is

---

SIGHTS

- Ⓐ Capilano Suspension Bridge
- Ⓑ Granville Island
- Ⓑ Granville Island Museums
- Ⓒ Museum of Anthropology
- Ⓓ Queen Elizabeth Park
- Ⓔ Richmond

SIGHTS *(continued)*

- Ⓕ Stanley Park
- Ⓖ University of British Columbia Botanical and Nitobe Memorial Gardens
- Ⓗ Vancouver Museum
- Ⓘ Van Dusen Botanical Garden

FOOD

- Ⓙ Beach Side Cafe
- Ⓚ Beach House at Dundarave Pier
- Ⓛ Bishop's
- Ⓜ President Chinese Restaurant
- Ⓝ Prospect Point Cafe
- Ⓞ Sophie's Cosmic Cafe
- Ⓟ Teahouse at Ferguson Point
- Ⓠ Tomato Fresh Food Cafe

Note: Items with the same letter are located in the same area.

a quiet, romantic restaurant with an award-winning wine menu, a block off Robson. **CinCin,** 604/688-7338, feels like a rustic Italian villa and serves Mediterranean food on an outdoor terrace overlooking Robson.

For Chinese food, **Hon's,** 604/688-0871, has a location in Chinatown. **Floata,** 604/602-0368, also in Chinatown, has a thousand seats and is another great place to go for dim sum. Out in Richmond, near the airport, **President Chinese Restaurant,** 604/276-8181, in the Radisson President Hotel and Suites, offers great Cantonese food with some Szechuan offerings.

Herons, 604/691-1991, in the Waterfront Hotel, is contemporary and elegant and has water views to go with dinner or cocktails. **Diva at the Met,** 604/602-7788, is a romantic and chic spot for dinner before the theater; weekend brunch is tops, too, and they have a great wine list that includes many outstanding British Columbia wines. **Raincity Grill,** 604/685-7337, on Denman Street with views of English Bay, is known for its long list of Pacific Northwest wines. **Bishop's,** 604/738-2025, just southwest of downtown in the community of Kitsilano, is a magnet for celebrities. Host John Bishop has a reputation not only for serving excellent food (and to-die-for desserts), but also for being a gracious host. Also a celebrity destination is **Lumiere,** known for the creative dishes of chef/owner Rob Feeney.

Funky, casual places for food any time are **Tomato Fresh Food Cafe,** 604/874-6020, at 3305 Cambie Street, where the room sizzles and there's clatter and noise and good food that's not expensive; and **Sophie's Cosmic Cafe,** 604/732-6810, at 2095 West Fourth Avenue, a great kitschy place for a pancake-and-egg breakfast.

Teens and the adventurous of palate will appreciate **Fritz Fry House,** Davie Street, for a decadent hit of french fries with a variety of sauces and the French Canadian favorite poutine—a mix of fries, cheese curds, and gravy.

North across the Lion's Gate Bridge to West Vancouver, you'll find waterview dining in the community of Ambleside with the **Beach Side Cafe,** 604/925-1945. At the **Beach House at Dundarave Pier,** 604/922-1414, the lawn goes right to the beach. This is a great warm-weather place to relax before or after a delicious meal.

A unique way to dine is to take B.C. Rail's **Starlight Dinner** train from North Vancouver to Porteau Cove, along the Sea to Sky Highway and Howe Sound; call for times and details, 800/663-8238.

The **Vancouver Playhouse International Wine Festival** started more than 20 years ago with one founding winery—Robert Mondavi of California. Now each spring it draws over 150 top wine makers from more than 18 countries around the world for a weeklong food and wine extravaganza each spring. It's one of the largest and most popular wine festivals in North America.

You can choose from a variety of events—seminars, tastings, dinners, food pairings. Many take place in top restaurants in the area. For details, call 604/873-3311 or check the website: www.winefest.mybc.com.

For the latest restaurant news, tune in to Vancouver's CFUN 1410 AM on Saturdays from noon to 1 p.m. to hear food expert and author Kasey Wilson and columnist Anthony Gismondi, one of Canada's most respected wine authorities, and their guests as they discuss up-to-the-minute food and wine news on *The Best of Food and Wine.*

LODGING

If you can, stay downtown or near Stanley Park. The Royals—Charles, William, and Harry—stayed at the Canadian Pacific's **Waterfront** hotel during their 1998 visit; the hotel offers tremendous water views at 900 Canada Place Way, 604/691-1991 or 800/441-1414, www.cphotels.com. The best water views are from the **Pan Pacific Hotel Vancouver,** 300–999 Canada Place, 604/662-8111 or 800/937-1515, www. panpac.com—worth a visit to the lobby whether you stay or not. Another waterfront hotel is the **Westin Bayshore,** 1601 Georgia Street, 604/682-3377 or 800/228-3000, www.westin.com; north toward Stanley Park, the Westin is set back from traffic, has been recently renovated, and is a good spot for kids. The **Hotel Vancouver,** 900 West Georgia Street, 604/684-3131 or 800/441-1414, www. cphotels.com, is a Canadian Pacific hotel (now managed by Fairmont Hotels & Resorts) a block away from Robson Street, next to the Vancouver Art Gallery; this is Vancouver's grand old hotel, and it has recently been restored. The **Wedgewood Hotel,** 845 Hornby Street, 604/689-7777 or 800/663-0666, www.travel.bc.ca/w/wedgewood, is an excellent spot with European flair and good jazz in the lounge at Bacchus, its fine restaurant. The **Four Seasons Hotel,** 791 West Georgia Street, 604/689-9333 or 800/332-3442, www.fshr.com, is beautiful and modern with Oriental art and a Four Seasons reputation for service. **Metropolitan Hotel Vancouver,** 645 Howe Street, 604/687-1122 or 800/667-2300, www.metropolitan.com, is contemporary and spacious; Diva restaurant is off the lobby. **Pacific Palisades Hotel,** 1277 Robson Street, 604/688-0461 or 800/663-1815, has a great location in the midst of Robson Street activity. The **Sutton Place Hotel,** 845 Burrard Street, 604/682-5511 or 800/961-7555, www. travelweb.com/sutton.html, has had several names but has always been a luxury property. The **Sylvia Hotel** overlooks English Bay and is the favorite destination of the value-conscious seeking views and old English atmosphere. The **Buchan Hotel,** 1906 Haro Street, 604/685-5354 or 800/668-6654, www.budgethotels.com, is an inexpensive, comfy, no-frills spot in a good location.

B.C.'S SURPRISINGLY POSH WINE COUNTRY

Nicknamed "Palm Springs North," the sunny and temperate Okanagan Valley is still a reasonably well-kept secret. Wineries to visit, over 50 golf courses—including the Okanagan Golf Course's new championship Jack Nicklaus–designed Bear Course—lots of lake recreation, sunny weather, and the growing quality of the facilities are good reasons to go.

In 2000, Mission Hill Winery, south of Vernon, completed a $30 million expansion that created a villalike winery with a bell tower in the Mondavi style. From the grounds you have sweeping views of the valley. Many other wineries such as Tinhorn Creek and Burrowing Owl are also surprisingly posh. VQA (Vinters Quality Assurance) wines from all wineries in the valley are available at the B.C. Wine Information Centre, 888 Westminster Avenue West, Penticton; 250/490-2006; open 9 to 6 daily.

Lodging on the shores of Okanagan Lake is plentiful (but reserve ahead for the best rooms). New in Kelowna is Manteo Resort Waterfront Hotel & Villas, with two- and three-bedroom villas and a 78-room hotel.

You'll need a car to explore, and that means driving (from Vancouver it's a four hour drive), or flying in and renting a car. Improved air access to Kelowna is a plus. Daily direct service from Calgary, Edmonton, Vancouver, and Seattle is currently available on WestJet Airlines, Horizon Air, and Canadian Regional Airlines. Service from the East Coast is improving as well.

A good information contact is the Penticton Chamber of Commerce, 800/663-5052.

SHOPPING

Shopping in Vancouver is a richly varied pleasure, offering a vast array of wares from different niches and cultures. Besides great people-watching, **Robson Street** offers current European, Canadian, and American fashions, bookstores, and specialty boutiques such as **Lush**—offering soaps in deli-style displays and fabulous "bath bombs." **Granville Street,** south of downtown, has classy antiques stores mixed in with fashionable boutiques. **Yaletown** is the place to wander if you're interested in fashion and furnishings. **Granville Island** offers a rare opportunity to buy directly from the artisans who create the work on the premises.

A drive south of downtown along **Main Street,** south of Chinatown, brings you to the **Punjabi District,** with plentiful markets and exotic offerings including numerous sari shops; a good for beautiful materials. **Commercial Street** has Italian specialty shops that include pasta stores, bakeries, and a sausage maker. **Richmond,** south of the airport and a drive from downtown, has the Hong Kong–like Parker Place shopping center.

NIGHTLIFE

Robson Street is always lively. There are restaurants, billiards, and coffee shops. There's good theater in town, too. The dramatic Ford Centre for the Performing Arts, 777 Homer Street, 604/602-0616, and Granville Island feature several theaters. There's a DJ in the pub, and a party atmosphere prevails at the **Yaletown Brewing Co.,** 604/688-0039, 1111 Mainland Street, in the Yaletown area. There are lots of billiards clubs and restaurants here. One of the first to start this trend was **Soho Cafe and Billiards,** 1144 Homer Street, 604/688-1180. Parking in Yaletown day or night is difficult; lots are scarce. A popular Gastown spot is **The Steamworks,** 375 Water Street, 604/689-2739.

8
SAN JUAN ISLANDS

There are about 400 islands in the San Juan archipelago, but when people say "the San Juans" they usually mean Washington's three most popular and populated: Lopez, Orcas, and San Juan. Accessible by ferry, airplane, floatplane, or private and charter boats of all sizes, they form a verdant marine crossroads between the waterfront cities of Seattle, Victoria, Anacortes, and Sidney. Folks come here to see orca whales, explore small coves by boat and beaches by foot, bicycle long country lanes, and wander small villages. Thick with evergreens and interspersed with bucolic farms, meadows, ponds, and wetlands, the islands—particularly San Juan—are becoming more populated. Historic clapboard farmhouses and buildings do still mark the landscape, and you'll see old roses clambering over picket fences. Time seems to slow down here, as if it's measured not digitally but in the graceful swings of an old pendulum clock.

In the best of all worlds you will have time to explore each island. If you must choose, here are some tips: Lopez is the first island reached by ferry from Anacortes and offers lots of flat roads for bicycling, a marina, and Lopez Village, with eateries and shops to explore. It's long been known as the Friendly Island, and Lopez residents give the "Lopez wave" to passing motorists. The island also boasts a winery, berries, salmon, and other fresh and preserved foods. Orcas is the largest island, home to the highest peak (Mt. Constitution), and its irregular saddlebag shape creates East Sound and West Sound. The village of Eastsound is the largest community on the island. Historic Rosario Resort and marina is located here. San Juan Island is the most populous, and Friday Harbor, where the ferry lands, is the largest town in the San Juans. Its snug, east-facing village offers spectacular sunrise views for early risers and a daylong look at ferry and boat activity (with two customs houses here, this is an international crossroads for boaters). You'll see the historical military encampments at San Juan Island's American and English Camps; and there's history and wildlife to learn about at the Whale Museum and other island historical museums. Each May the artists of San Juan Island have an open house, welcoming visitors into their studios.

A PERFECT DAY IN THE SAN JUAN ISLANDS

A perfect day begins with a lazy breakfast and some pleasant conversation at an inn or B&B. After that, bicycling is a perfect way to take in wildflowers, wildlife, and beautiful vistas. Wander the islands' small villages and find an outdoor deck for lunch on a warm day (the Islander Lopez, Christina's on Orcas, or Roche Harbor Resort on San Juan are good bets). Sit outside to take in the crisp scent of salt air, the call of seagulls, and the pleasant hum of the good life.

ORIENTATION

The islands are busy with visitors, and ferry lines are often long in summer. If you are traveling during high season and plan to catch a ferry to the islands from Anacortes, arrive an hour before the ferry departs. A good strategy is to overnight in Anacortes and catch an early ferry. In high season, if you walk on or ride your bicycle, you're almost assured of catching the ferry you aim for. **Washington State Ferries,** 800/843-3779, www.wsdot.wa.gov/ferries/, offers five to seven daily sailings from Anacortes. The ***Victoria Clipper,*** 206/448-5000, www.victoriaclipper.com, offers high-speed passenger-only ferry service from Seattle, 800/888-2535, to Friday Harbor and to Rosario Resort on Orcas Island. **Island Shuttle Express,** 360/671-1137, provides passenger-only service from Bellingham to the San Juan Islands. During the summer months whale-watching cruises are offered. Also from Bellingham, a new catamaran service, **San Juan Island Commuter,** provides access to remote San Juan Islands areas; call 360/734-8180 or 888/734-8180. For daily air service through **West Isle Air** from Anacortes, Bellingham, and Seattle, call 800/874-4434. Floatplane service is available through **Kenmore Air** from Seattle, 800/543-9595, www.kenmoreair.com, and charter service from Seattle is available on **Sound Flight,** 800/825-0722.

Foot passengers have a variety of options on arriving at their island destination. For a cab on Lopez, call 360/468-2227; on San Juan, 360/378-3550 or

SAN JUAN ISLAND

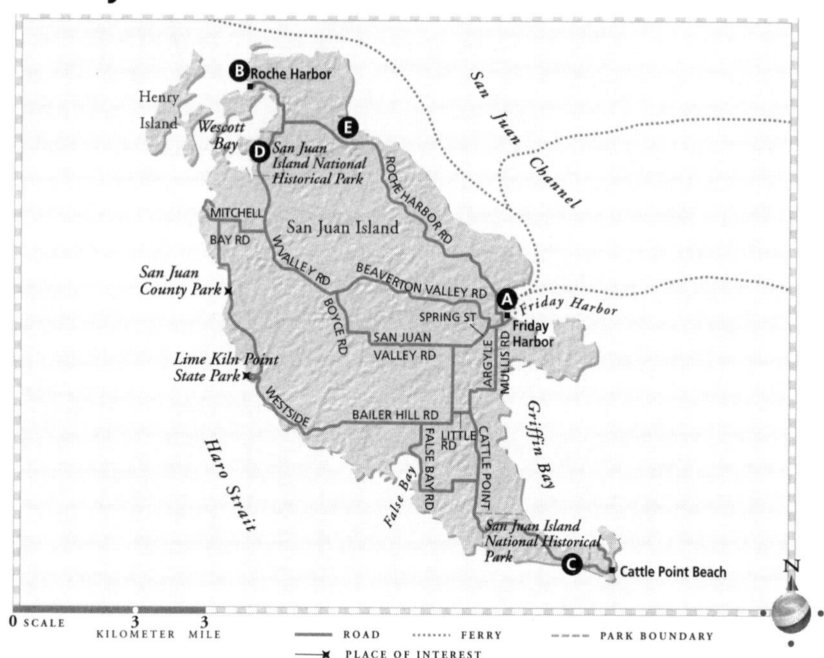

SIGHTS

- Ⓐ Friday Harbor
- Ⓑ Roche Harbor and Hotel de Haro
- Ⓒ San Juan Island National Historical Park (American Camp)
- Ⓓ San Juan Island National Historical Park (English Camp)
- Ⓐ Whale Museum

FOOD

- Ⓔ Duck Soup Inn
- Ⓐ Friday Harbor House
- Ⓑ Lime Kiln Café
- Ⓑ Roche Harbor Resort

LODGING

- Ⓐ Friday Harbor House
- Ⓐ Friday's
- Ⓐ Wharfside B&B

Note: Items with the same letter are located in the same area.

360/378-6777; on Orcas, 360/376-8294. Some inns and B&Bs have pickup service; ask when reserving lodging. For island public transit information, call 360/376-8887 (or plan to rent a bicycle or moped; see Fitness and Recreation).

A couple of local tour operators offer personalized options. To see the island by bicycle on half-day or longer guided tours, call **Cycle San Juans,** 360/468-3251. **Easy Going Outings,** 360/757-0380, offers specialty food day trips and artist visits by van. And for a special, albeit more expensive, vacation, Captain John Colby Stone (of the Captain Whidbey Inn, 800/366-4097 or 360/678-4097) navigates his 52-foot classic ketch, the *Cutty Sark,* through the San Juan Islands on six-day cruises (starting in May and running once a month through September); these include stays in island country inns.

For additional information, contact **San Juan Visitor Information Service,** 360/468-3663 or 888/468-3701, www.sanjuan.com; or contact the San Juan Island Chamber, 360/378-5240.

SIGHTSEEING HIGHLIGHTS

★★★★ EASTSOUND

Orcas

Located at the head of Orcas Island's largest bay, Eastsound is the largest town on the island. Look for historic buildings now housing bookstores, restaurants, and other local commercial enterprises. The Emmanuel Episcopal Church dates back to 1886. When you arrive on Orcas Island, don't forget to set your watch to "Orcas time"—the pace is relaxed.

Details: *The ferry docks at the village of Orcas, at the south end of the island. Follow signs from here to Eastsound (about seven miles). (1–2 hours)*

★★★★ FRIDAY HARBOR

San Juan

This is the largest town in the islands—population about 2,000—and the county seat. The ferry docks here. There are restaurants, a community theater and a movie theater, the Whale Museum, and a marina (the crab shack on the dock sells crab cocktails to go). In May the artists in the community and on the island host an open house; in July there's a jazz festival.

Details: *About 1½ hours by ferry from Anacortes. (2 hours)*

★★★★ LOPEZ VILLAGE

Lopez

You'll see fine glass, jewelry, and artwork at Chimera Gallery, a cooperative of Lopez Island artists; wreaths and accessories at the Lopez Country Store; and fine scents, soaps, and gifts at the Willow Farm

LOPEZ ISLAND

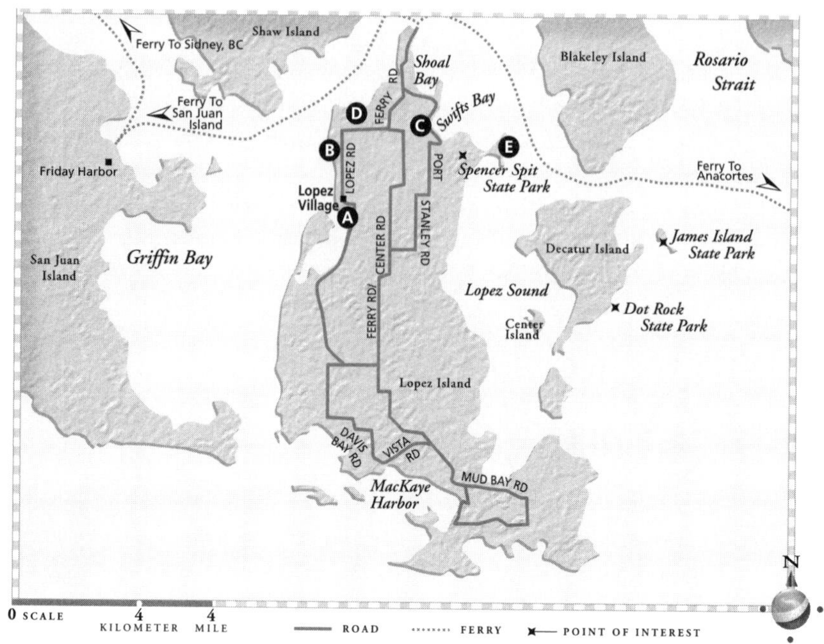

SIGHT

- Ⓐ Lopez Village

FOOD

- Ⓐ The Bay Cafe
- Ⓐ Holly B's Bakery
- Ⓐ Islander Lopez
- Ⓐ Lopez Island Pharmacy
- Ⓑ Lopez Island Vineyards
- Ⓐ Love Dog Cafe

LODGING

- Ⓐ Edenwild Inn
- Ⓒ Inn at Swifts Bay
- Ⓐ Islander Lopez

CAMPING

- Ⓓ Odlin County Park
- Ⓔ Spencer Spit

Note: Items with the same letter are located in the same area.

---

store. Visit the Lopez Historical Museum, 360/468-2049 or 360/468-2049 after hours; donations suggested. Here you will find maritime exhibits, pioneer displays, American Indian art, and what is thought to be the first automobile in San Juan County.

Details: *Go four miles south of the ferry dock on Weeks Road. The museum is open only in the summer; call for hours. (1 hour)*

★★★★ **WHALE MUSEUM**
62 First Street North, Friday Harbor, San Juan Island
360/378-4710, www.whale-museum.org

The museum is located in one of the island's oldest buildings and features exhibits depicting the biology, behavior, and sounds of whales. There are videotapes to watch, an interactive computer, and complete whale skeletons. Other whale-related exhibits include photographs, carvings, and paintings.

Details: *Three blocks northwest of the ferry landing Open daily from Memorial Day weekend through September, 10 to 7; the remainder of the year 10 to 6. Admission is $5, $3.50 for seniors over 62; $2 for students with ID and kids 5 to 12. (1 hour)*

★★★ **MORAN STATE PARK AND MT. CONSTITUTION**
Orcas Island, 360/376-2326
www.orcasisle.com

In 1926 Robert Moran, former mayor of Seattle and shipbuilding tycoon, donated the 5,000-plus-acre park to the state. Drive five miles up 2,409-foot Mt. Constitution for stunning views of the San Juans and the mainland.

Details: *Five miles southeast of Eastsound. Open daily May through September 6:30 to dusk; 8 to dusk the remainder of the year. (1–2 hours)*

★★★ **ROCHE HARBOR AND HOTEL DE HARO**
San Juan Island, 360/378-2155 or 800/451-8910
www.rocheharbor.com

Located on the northwest corner of the island, Roche Harbor is a resort town and a very popular boating destination. Once the site of the largest lime-producing company in the West, it has several historic attractions. The Hotel de Haro, the centerpiece of the Roche Harbor Resort, is on the National Register of Historic Sites and once hosted Teddy Roosevelt. A lovely rose garden lies in front of the inn. A newly expanded marina has doubled the number of boat slips; a marine activities center rents kayaks and small boats in season.

Details: *Northwest of Friday Harbor. (1–2 hours)*

★★★ **SAN JUAN ISLAND NATIONAL HISTORICAL PARK**
(American and English Camps)
125 Spring Street (park office), Friday Harbor
360/378-2240

ORCAS ISLAND

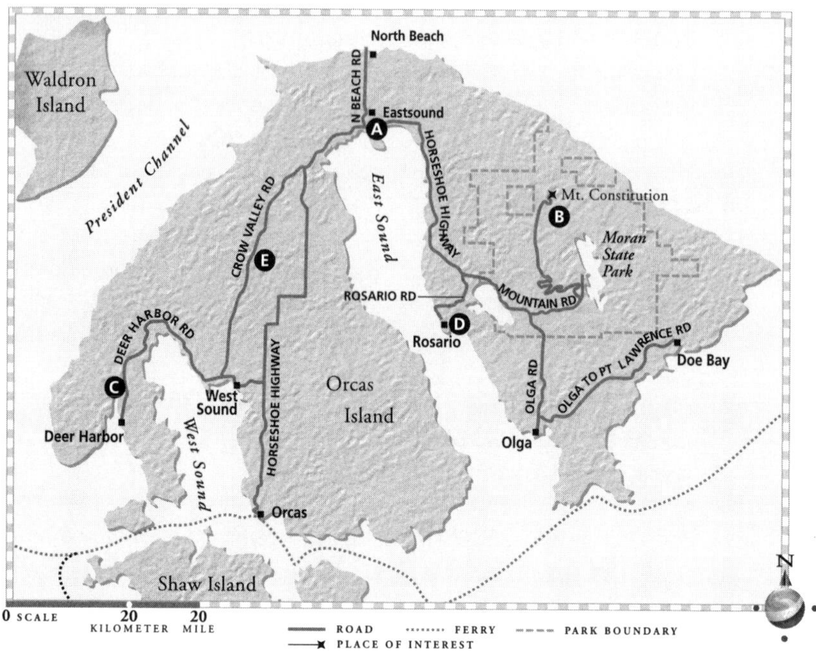

SIGHTS

- Ⓐ Eastsound
- Ⓑ Moran State Park and Mt. Constitution

FOOD

- Ⓐ Christina's
- Ⓒ Deer Harbor Lodge and Inn
- Ⓓ Rosario Resort
- Ⓐ Ship Bay Oyster House

LODGING

- Ⓓ Rosario Resort
- Ⓔ Turtleback Farm Inn

CAMPING

- Ⓑ Moran State Park

Note: Items with the same letter are located in the same area.

This park was created to commemorate the 1872 settlement of the border dispute between the United States and England that began in 1859 with the Pig War. For these years, two encampments were at different ends of the island. The **American Camp,** now a 1,200-acre site at the island's southeastern tip, is about five miles from Friday Harbor. **English Camp,** 520 acres on Garrison Bay, on the northwest side of the island, is not far from Roche Harbor.

Details: *Maps and brochures are available from the park super-*

intendent's office in Friday Harbor. Rangers are at both sites Memorial Day weekend through Labor Day. Picnic sites, beaches, and trails are available; no overnight camping allowed. Visitor centers are on the grounds, hours 8:30–5 daily; grounds are open dawn to 11 p.m. (2 hours at each site)

FITNESS AND RECREATION

Orca-watching season runs May to September, yet July is the peak month in the San Juans. This is a must-do if you visit during these months. Call San Juan Excursions in Friday Harbor, 800/80-WHALE; www.seawhales.com.

The islands are also perfect for summer cycling. Lopez is just a 45-minute ferry ride from Anacortes. Its gently hilly terrain, long popular with cyclists, can easily be explored on a day trip. The other islands are good for cycling as well. Call in advance and you can reserve a bicycle from the Bike Shop, 360/468-3497, or Lopez Bicycle Works, 360/468-2847, on Lopez; on San Juan Island, contact Island Bicycles, 360/378-4941, Susie's Mopeds, 360/378-5244, www.rockisland.com/~sjmoped~/, or Island Scooters and Bike Rentals, 360/378-8811, www.rockisland.com/~sjmoped/.

Several day-use parks make great locations for picnics. On Lopez, the rocky promontory at Shark Reef Day Park has a grassy knoll perfect for a simple sandwich picnic and offers a panoramic view of San Juan Channel (and orcas if you're lucky). Otis Perkins Day Park on Fisherman's Bay has picnic tables and a long beach to stroll.

FOOD

On Lopez, the **Love Dog Cafe,** Village Center, 360/468-2150, is a great stop for breakfast (try waffles from scratch), a lunch of a deli sandwich such as a mouth-watering Reuben, or pasta or seafood for dinner. Cinnamon rolls and sourdough bread are scrumptious picks from **Holly B's Bakery** (closed January to May), Lopez Plaza, 360/468-2133, but you can also get a scone, a slice of pizza, and many other baked goods here. At the **Lopez Island Pharmacy's** real soda fountain, you can try a dish of chocolate raspberry swirl or coffee almond fudge, two favorite island ice creams produced by Lopez Island Creamery. The **Bay Cafe,** in the village, offers adventurous meals. Their menu changes frequently and includes creative items like Dungeness polenta appetizers and chicken satays with curried noodles. The restaurant in the **Islander Lopez,** 360/468-2233, is known for its Sunday brunch with special order omelets and plenty of seafood. At **Lopez Island**

GIANT OCTOPUS?

The San Juan Islands have a rich population of sea life that draws scuba divers. Even the late Jacques Cousteau loved to dive here. One reason is the gentle and intriguing giant octopus, averaging five feet and longer. Even beginners might see one—and can take diving lessons with Island Dive & Water Sports **360/376-7615** or **800/303-8386**, located at Rosario Resort on Orcas Island.

Besides octopuses, divers may see large dogfish (a distant relative to the shark), giant lingcod, shrimp, crab, and much more, including unusual nudibranchs—somewhat like underwater butterflies—of all different colors and sizes.

Vineyards, between the ferry landing and Lopez Village, Siegerrebe and Madeline Angevine grapes are grown on the property and made into wines. Open Wednesdays, Memorial Day to Labor Day, noon to 5. Call 360/468-3644 for a special appointment.

On Orcas, stop by **Christina's,** 360/376-4904, on Main Street in Eastsound, for a glass of Madeline Angevine (or another of the 50 Northwest wines on their list) and a mouthwatering platter of poached oysters, spot prawns, and cracked crab in season. Christina's serves dinner only, but the bar opens at 4 p.m. for appetizers. Just east of Eastsound, **Ship Bay Oyster House,** 360/376-5886, offers baked, fried, and raw oysters and great chowder. On the west side of the island, try a seafood special, a salad, and the homemade bread at the **Deer Harbor Lodge and Inn,** 360/376-4110, www.sanjuanweb.com/ DeerHarborInn/. **Rosario Resort's** dining room, 360/376-2222 or 800/562-8820, in the old Moran Mansion, overlooks the water and is a romantic destination for lunch or dinner.

On San Juan, the dining room at **Friday Harbor House,** 360/378-8455, is open to the public; dinners include fresh local products like island-grown vegetables and Wescott Bay oysters. **Duck Soup Inn,** 360/378-4878, www.ducksoupinn.com, north of Friday Harbor about four miles, is a cozy spot with a stone fireplace and wooden booths that offers homemade breads and fine meals incorporating regional produce. **Roche Harbor Restaurant** at **Roche Harbor Resort,** 360/378-5757, views the marina, and the **Lime Kiln Café** on the dock offers informal meals that are good for families.

LODGING

On Lopez, at the **Inn at Swifts Bay,** 360/468-3636, www.swiftsbay.com, a country hideaway near the ferry landing, guests are pampered with a wide variety of amenities, including slippers to wear to the hot tub and English walking sticks for hiking. Five rooms (adults only) include two upstairs suites with gas fireplaces. **Edenwild Inn,** 360/468-3238, www.edenwildinn.com, in Lopez village, looks like a vintage country farmhouse, yet it was built in 1990. Its sophisticated decor, antiques, and paintings provide a serene setting—though on warm nights you might hear the frogs in nearby ponds. The **Islander Lopez,** 360/468-2233, sports a totally rebuilt marina with a dock store offering provisions and supplies for boaters. Its great location on Fisherman's Bay (lodging is across the road from the bay), along with a swimming pool, hot tub, and wide grassy play areas, makes it a great choice for families. This is a family-oriented resort with plenty of activities; 50 slips in the marina offer guest moorage. You can reserve fishing or sailing charters from the marina.

On Orcas, **Rosario Resort,** 800/562-8820, www.rosario-resort.com, centers around the historic 1909 Moran Mansion, and in the lobby are some original Moran furnishings, like the Arts and Crafts–style conversation chairs. You'll have outstanding water views from 127 rooms (located not in the mansion but on the hillside nearby). There's a dock for visiting boats. A spa offers exercise and yoga classes, a weight room, a swimming pool, and massage facilities. Tennis courts are nearby. And you don't have to be a guest to experience organist Christopher Peacock's recital and history presentation; check with the resort for dates. **Turtleback Farm Inn,** 360/376-4914, is a restored turn-of-the century farmhouse located on 80 acres of farm and forest land, with views of farm meadows where sheep graze and geese wander. One peek inside the inn's very own cookbook and you know you're in for a breakfast treat.

On San Juan, perched on the hillside above the marina, **Friday Harbor House,** 360/378-8455, www.karuna.com/fhhouse, a 20-room Mediterranean-style inn, claims the best of the views. Rooms are elegant—all have fireplaces and Jacuzzis, most have views of the harbor. The dining room, where you can enjoy a continental breakfast of fruit and flaky scones, views the harbor too. If lodging aboard a boat appeals to you, the **Wharfside B&B,** 360/378-5661, www.rockisland.com/~pcshop/wharfside.html, an older 60-foot boat with two staterooms, right in the midst of the action at the marina in Friday Harbor, is a perfect choice. A stay at **Friday's** historic inn, 360/378-5848 or 800/352-2632, www.friday-harbor.com, in downtown also puts you in the center of the action; deluxe rooms have water views.

CAMPING

Where Salish Indians used to camp on Lopez Island's **Spencer Spit,** today you'll see the colorful tents of bicyclists, kayakers, and campers. A homesteader's abode for picnicking, eye-popping views of the islands, mountains, boat traffic, and shorefront and walk-in camping make this 129-acre state park a great destination for day-trippers as well as overnighters. **Odlin County Park** offers overnight camping on a first-come, first-served basis (check the sign at the Anacortes ferry for availability); for best luck in getting a spot, arrive before noon. **Moran State Park,** on Orcas (see page 143) has over a hundred developed sites for tents or motor homes. Call 360/376-2326; reservations are strongly suggested. Call the Washington State Parks reservation line, 800/452-5687, www.parks.wa.gov/rnw.htm. There are also numerous small island state parks, accessible only by boat.

9 BELLINGHAM AND NORTHWEST WASHINGTON

A waterfront university town, Bellingham is the historic and cultural hub of Whatcom County, the fertile and forested northwestern region of Washington. Although it's 90 miles north of Seattle and 50 miles south of Vancouver, Bellingham is a logical halfway point between the two cities because of the slowdown before the Canadian border. Stop and sample the lifestyle that has earned Bellingham a spot as one of the nation's most livable cities.

Its history includes a brief flurry with gold rush fever, a period of coal mining, and a constant relationship with logging. If the city (population over 60,000) feels spread out and disjointed, that's because it's a combination of four Bellingham Bay communities—Bellingham, Whatcom, Sehome, and Fairhaven—settled starting in the 1850s. Before that the Lummi, Nooksack, and Semiahmoo Indians occupied the coast along the bay.

Two spectacular old highway routes are connected to the city: Chuckanut Drive, a historic cliff-hugging road along the coast from the Skagit River delta in the south (which offers breathtaking views of the San Juan Islands en route to Fairhaven), and the Mt. Baker Highway, a winding, ever-climbing route that cuts through the Nooksack Valley to the east and winds through the foothills of Mt. Baker, ending at Artist Point, a spectacular vantage for views of the mountain.

Western Washington University, located in Bellingham, is a popular state university; its campus has a notable outdoor sculpture collection. The Alaska Marine Highway System's southern terminus is at Fairhaven, and there is pas-

NORTHWEST WASHINGTON

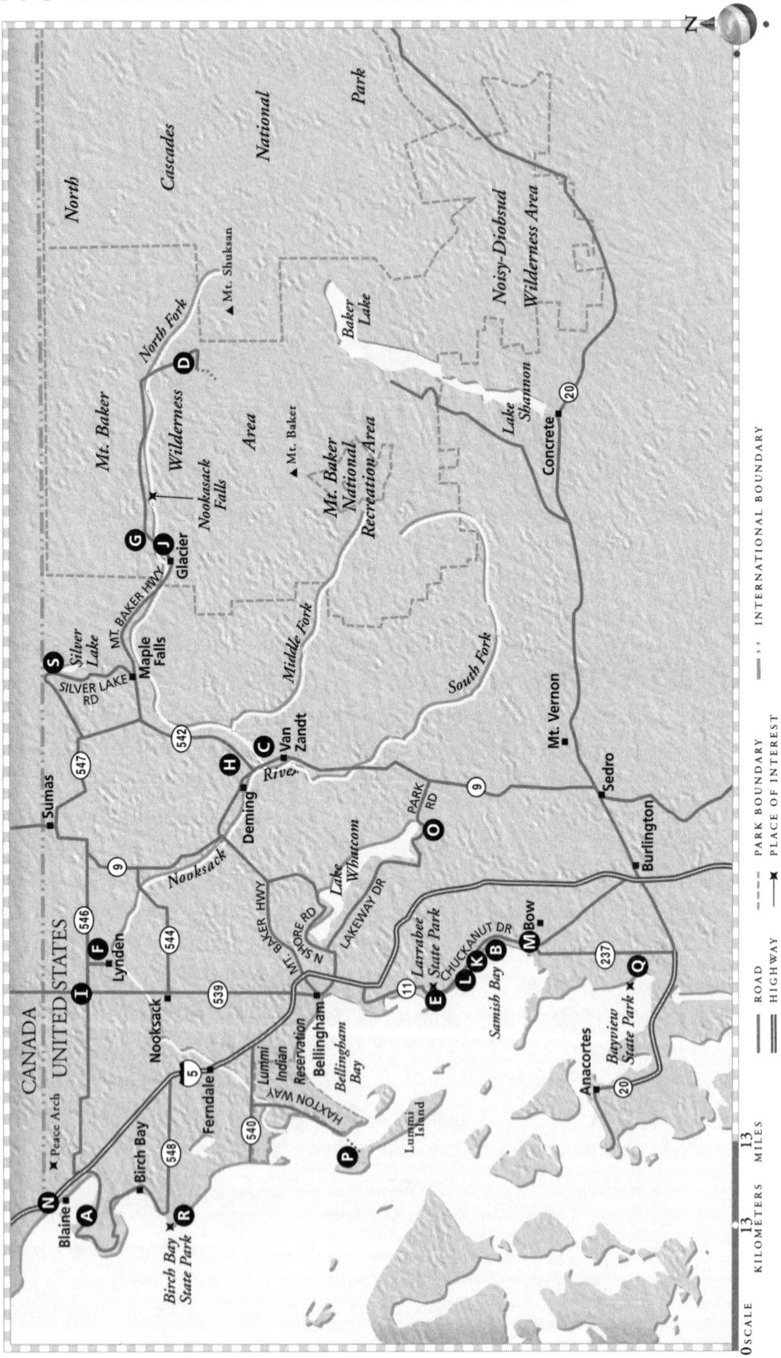

CANADA
UNITED STATES
North Cascades National Park
Mt. Baker Wilderness Area
Mt. Shuksan
Mt. Baker
Mt. Baker National Recreation Area
Noisy-Diobsud Wilderness Area
Baker Lake
Lake Shannon
Concrete
North Fork
Nooksack Falls
Glacier
MT. BAKER HWY
Silver Lake
SILVER LAKE RD
Maple Falls
Middle Fork
South Fork
Nooksack River
Van Zandt
Deming
Sumas
Mt. Vernon
Sedro
Burlington
PARK RD
Lake Whatcom
LAKEWAY DR
N SHORE RD
MT. BAKER HWY
Lynden
Nooksack
Bellingham
Lummi Indian Reservation
Bellingham Bay
HAXTON WAY
Lummi Island
Larrabee State Park
CHUCKANUT DR
Samish Bay
Bow
Anacortes
Bayview State Park
Ferndale
Birch Bay
Birch Bay State Park
Blaine
Peace Arch
5 9 11 20 237 539 540 542 544 546 547 548
A B C D E F G H I J K L M N O P Q R S

ROAD — HIGHWAY — PARK BOUNDARY — PLACE OF INTEREST — INTERNATIONAL BOUNDARY

0 SCALE 13 KILOMETERS 13 MILES

N

senger ferry service to the San Juans and Victoria, British Columbia, from here, as well as an Amtrak station.

A PERFECT DAY IN NORTHWEST WASHINGTON

Start early, after breakfast, and explore Old Fairhaven (if you haven't had breakfast, stop at the Colophon Cafe). A visit to the Whatcom Museum offers both a great feel for the past and a look at more modern-day artists. A half-day kayak exploration on Bellingham Bay is an exhilarating way to see the town from the water. In the evening, I suggest a splurge on dinner at the Oyster Bar and a retreat back to town to a B&B—Schnauzer Crossing would be one of my favorite picks. Farm country and mountain wilderness lovers should plan a different approach and drive the Mt. Baker Highway, which takes you through the pastoral Nooksack Valley. Pick up a sandwich at Everybody's Store, a short detour from your route, and continue on to Picture Lake for a picnic lunch. Stop and marvel at the overlook at Heather Meadows and again at the end of the road at Artist Point. If the day is sunny and clear you'll feel as if you've been beamed up into the land of enchantment.

ORIENTATION

Bellingham is a city of over 60,000 people, 90 miles north of Seattle via Interstate 5. Downtown is easy to spot by the conspicuous presence of the historic

---

SIGHTS

- Ⓐ Blaine
- Ⓑ Chuckanut Drive
- Ⓒ Everybody's Store
- Ⓓ Heather Meadows Interpretive Center
- Ⓔ Larabee State Park
- Ⓕ Lynden
- Ⓖ Mt. Baker Highway and Scenic Byway
- Ⓗ Nooksack Valley

FOOD

- Ⓕ Dutch Mothers Restaurant
- Ⓘ Edaleen Dairy
- Ⓙ Milano's Market and Deli
- Ⓚ Oyster Bar
- Ⓛ Oyster Creek Inn
- Ⓜ Rhododendron Café

LODGING

- Ⓓ Glacier Creek Lodge & Cabins
- Ⓝ Inn at Semiahmoo

LODGING *(continued)*

- Ⓞ South Bay B&B
- Ⓟ The Willows
- Ⓟ West Shore Farm Bed and Breakfast

CAMPING

- Ⓠ Bayview State Park
- Ⓡ Birch Bay State Park
- Ⓔ Larabee State Park
- Ⓢ Silver Lake Park

Note: Items with the same letter are located in the same area.

Whatcom Museum of History and Art building. Bellingham Bay and Squalicum Harbor lie to the west. Farmlands, forestlands, and Mount Baker lie east. Western Washington University and the historic Fairhaven District (with train and cruise terminals) are south of the city.

Bellingham International Airport, served by United Express, Horizon, and charter airlines, is located north off I-5 exit 258; for airport information call the administration office at 360/676-2500. Whatcom Transportation Authority (WTA) provides over 20 routes linking Whatcom County communities; for information, call 360/676-7433.

Shuttle bus services are available from Sea-Tac Airport and from Vancouver; for details contact Bellingham/Whatcom County Convention & Visitors Bureau at 360/671-3990 or www.bellingham.org.

SIGHTSEEING HIGHLIGHTS

★★★★ CHUCKANUT DRIVE

Take this route from I-5 if you're driving north from Seattle, as a slower way to Bellingham, particularly if it's lunch or dinnertime. Several restaurants on the drive feature oysters; some started as oyster shacks decades ago. Taylor United, Inc.'s Samish Bay Oyster Farm has a retail outlet with shucked or in-the-shell oysters, clams, and other shellfish, as well as a video, recipes, and other information on the oyster.

Details: *Going north, take Exit 231 off I-5. This is SR 11, which runs through the community of Bow and along the shores of Samish Bay, winding north to Fairhaven. An access road to Taylor United is next to the Oyster Creek Inn. Follow the signs. There is plenty of parking at Taylor United and great views of the bay. It's open daily 8 to 5. (45 minutes)*

★★★★ HEATHER MEADOWS INTERPRETIVE CENTER

Mt. Baker/U.S. Forest Service office, Glacier, 360/599-2714

Nothing is quite as exhilarating as an alpine meadow on a hot, dry day with a crisp, blue sky overhead, wraparound views of mountain peaks and shimmering glacial lakes, and the sweet smell of mountain blueberries rising all around. Heather Meadows is such a setting and offers views of and trails to Bagley Lakes, mountain ridges dotted with bonsailike silver fir, 500-year-old mountain hemlock, and glacially carved basalt formations bared to the sun. Challenging trails take off from here. (Note: If you do hike, keep in mind that you are in high-altitude terrain and the weather can change very quickly. Check with the

CRUISING NEARBY OR FAR AWAY

From Bellingham, you can head up the Inside Passage to Alaska on Alaska Marine Highway System ships; their port facility at Fairhaven is the southern terminus; call 800/642-0066 or 360/676-8445. Island Shuttle Express, 360/671-1137, provides passenger-only service to and from the San Juan Islands. During the summer months, whale-watching cruises are offered. A new catamaran service, the San Juan Island Commuter, provides access to remote state parks such as Sucia, Matia, Jones, and Stuart Islands and is perfect transportation for hikers, campers, and kayakers; call 360/734-8180 or 888/734-8180. It departs from the Bellingham Cruise Terminal in Fairhaven. Also from the terminal, mid-May through early October, Victoria/San Juan Cruises offers passenger-only service to Victoria, leaving at 9 a.m. and returning at 8 p.m.; fare includes a salmon dinner. Call 800/443-4552 for information.

For more information, contact the Bellingham Whatcom County Convention and Visitors Bureau, 800/487-2032 (recorded message) or 360/671-3990. The main office is at 904 Potter Street just off I-5.

ranger about conditions; take water, food, warm clothing, a map, and other hiking essentials.) The visitors center has interpretive displays about the natural and historical information of the area. Built as a warming hut by the Civil Conservation Corps in 1940, the center was renovated in 1994. Just steps from the center you'll find a self-guided trail.

Details: *Near the top of Mt. Baker at the end of SR 542. The center is open daily through mid-October, 10 to 4:30; a ranger is on hand to answer questions. There are plenty of picnic tables nearby. (1 hour–full day)*

★★★★ MT. BAKER HIGHWAY AND SCENIC BYWAY

Mt. Baker, in North Cascades National Park, dominates the horizon east of Bellingham and delights winter skiers (and snowboarders) and summer hikers. Along the 55-mile route to the mountain you'll meander through farmland and forest as you follow the north fork of the

Nooksack River. The drive offers plenty to see and do. **Nooksack Falls,** about seven miles east of Glacier, drops 170 vertical feet; its proximity to the highway makes for an easy stop. From here, the route is designated the Mt. Baker Scenic Byway. About 11 miles from Glacier, watch for a grove of towering Douglas firs, hundreds of years old. Several miles past here you will see a sign for Heather Meadows (see page 152). First you'll come upon the flower-filled meadows surrounding **Picture Lake,** which often reflects nearby **Mt. Shuksan** on its surface. Trails around the lake lead through wildflowers that include lupines and fireweed. Follow the road to its very end and you'll pass Heather Meadows, a must stop before you reach **Artist Point** viewpoint with its stunning views of Mt. Baker and Shuksan. Trails take off from here and from Heather Meadows.

Details: *Stop at the U.S. Forest Service/Glacier Public Service Center, 360/599-2714, about a mile east of the town of Glacier. Here you can get brochures, maps, and advice on the scores of hikes in the area available for all skill levels; many are wheelchair accessible. (3–5 hours)*

★★★★ WESTERN WASHINGTON UNIVERSITY

Bellingham, 360/650-3963

Expansive views of the San Juan Islands and an extensive outdoor sculpture collection draw visitors to this campus on Sehome Hill, overlooking Bellingham Bay. The first large-scale sculpture, *Rain Forest,* a bronze fountain by artist James Fitzgerald, was installed in 1960. Now there are over 22 large-scale pieces on campus, including the work of Isamu Noguchi, Mark di Suvero, and Robert Morris.

Details: *Take I-5, Exit 252 to Bill McDonald Parkway; audio phone tour and/or brochure available at the Western Gallery and Visitors Information Center while the university is in session. (2 hours)*

★★★★ WHATCOM MUSEUM OF HISTORY AND ART

121 Prospect Street, Bellingham, 360/676-6981

You will notice the unusual main building immediately, since it dominates the city's skyline. Built in 1892, the former city hall displays permanent exhibits of regional history and hosts ever-changing shows of contemporary art. Additional buildings include Syre Education Center (201 Prospect), with exhibits on Northwest birds, Northwest Coast First Nations, and Inuit (Eskimo) peoples. The Arco Exhibit Gallery (206 Prospect) features contemporary art. The Whatcom Children's Museum (227 Prospect) has plenty of hands-on activities.

Details: *All buildings are open noon to 5 Tuesday through Sunday. Children's museum opens at 10 Thursday, Friday, and Saturday; admission $2. Admission to other galleries by donation. (1–2 hours)*

★★★ BLAINE

Visitor center, 215 Marine Drive
360/332-4544 or 800/624-3555

This is the northwesternmost town in the continental United States, perhaps best known as home to the **Peace Arch,** a 67-foot classical Doric monument, reminding us with its inscription that the United States and Canada are "Children of a Common Mother." In 40-acre Peace Arch State Park, you can walk freely between the two borders. Semiahmoo Resort is at the tip of Blaine's Semiahmoo Spit, across the bay from downtown.

Details: *(1/2–1 hour)*

★★★ FAIRHAVEN

Considered the historic old town of Bellingham, Fairhaven has its own colorful history as a boomtown of the 1880s that never really quite exploded. Today, its historic brick buildings are home to shops, eateries, and galleries and are great for casual exploring. Don't miss Artwood, a fine woodworking gallery. The Alaska Ferry terminal and Amtrak depot are just west of the district.

Details: *From I-5, take Exit 250 south of downtown. (1 hour)*

★★★ LARABEE STATE PARK

245 Chuckanut Drive, 360/676-2093

This was the first state park in Washington; it covers almost 2,000 acres of forest and park, with frontage on Samish Bay. Enjoy the tidepools, swim, hike, camp, and picnic. The park provides the southern access to six-mile Interurban Trail, a nonmotorized path for hikers, bikers, and horses that parallels Chuckanut Drive through the forest.

Details: *87 campsites, 26 full hookups; reservations, 800/452-5687. (2 hours)*

★★★ LYNDEN

Chamber of Commerce, 360/354-5995

Founded by Dutch settlers, this farming community keeps its heritage alive with a working windmill, a pioneer museum, and a spring Holland Days festival. The **Dutch Village Mall** on the town's main street

(655 Front Street) is accentuated by a 72-foot-tall working windmill. The interior simulates a Dutch street scene with tulips, a flowing canal, and cobblestone streets. Inside is access to Dutch Village Inn, 360/354-4440, a motel in the windmill. In December there is a holiday lights festival.

Details: *Exit 256 off I-5 and north on Highway 539; follow signs. Mall open Monday through Saturday 10 to 9. Most of town is closed Sunday. (2 hours)*

★★★ MT. BAKER THEATER

106 N. Commercial, 360/734-6080

Opened in 1927, this 1,500-seat vaudeville movie palace features elaborate Moorish-Spanish–style architecture and is on the National Historic Register. A $1.6 million renovation project in the mid-1990s returned it to its former glory. Live musical and theater performances, as well as movies and special events, are held here.

Details: *Call 360/734-4950 for movie information. (15 minutes or more)*

★★★ NOOKSACK VALLEY

Small farming communities dot the verdant Nooksack Valley east of Bellingham, including Everson, Deming, Nooksack, Nugents Corner, Van Zandt, and Lynden (see above). There are berry farms and an increasing number of apple orchards. The apples grown here differ from those grown in the state's hotter eastern region. You won't find Red Delicious or Granny Smiths, but tasty alternatives. The full-flavored Jonagold is the prominent apple. Two farms about 15 miles east of Bellingham, not far from Everson near Highway 9, are open in the fall for harvest festivities. Also visit **Cloud Mountain Farm & Nursery,** 360/966-5859, and **Stoney Ridge Farm,** 360/966-3919—don't miss their caramel apple pie à la mode. **Mount Baker Winery,** 360/592-2309, offers wine tasting.

Details: *To reach the Nooksack Valley from I-5 in Bellingham, take Exit 255 (to the Mt. Baker Highway). Call for directions to the farms. Mt. Baker Winery's tasting room is open daily, except Monday, 11 to 5. You'll see the sign a mile before Deming on the Mt. Baker Highway. (4–6 hours)*

★★ BIG ROCK GARDEN

2900 Sylvan Street, Bellingham, 360/676-6985

Formerly a private nursery, Big Rock Garden has a fine collection of

SIDE TRIP: LUMMI ISLAND

Lummi Island is a quiet residential island that lies about 15 miles northwest of Bellingham. It's less than two miles wide and nine miles long, has about 600 residents, has no real town—just a store, library, and restaurant—and has 20 miles or so of country road for driving, cycling, or strolling. A private ferry provides island access from Gooseberry Point on the Lummi Indian Reservation (the island is not part of the reservation). On the island, a pocket park and deck just north of the ferry terminal offer the only public beach access. Three times a year, artists host open houses, and several studios can be visited year-round. To reach the island take Exit 260 from Interstate 5 and follow the signs west. The Whatcom Chief *ferry holds about 20 cars and a handful of passengers and leaves the mainland at 10 minutes past the hour (round-trip $4). The* ***Beach Store Cafe,*** *360/758-2233, lies near the ferry landing and serves local seafood and island-grown produce—including fruits and greens fresh from the orchard and garden. Open 8 a.m. to 9:30 p.m. daily in summer; closed some days in winter.*

Lodging on the island can be had at ***The Willows,*** *2579 West Shore Drive, 360/758-2620, with two guest houses in a restful and country cottage setting across the road from the beach. Nearby is the* ***West Shore Farm Bed and Breakfast,*** *2781 West Shore Drive, 360/758-2600, an octagonal contemporary built in the 1970s by the owners, with a wood cookstove in the kitchen and a view deck.*

rhododendrons and Japanese maples and views overlooking Lake Whatcom.

Details: *Open April 1 through October. Admission is free. (45 minutes)*

★ EVERYBODY'S STORE
Highway 9, Van Zandt, 360/592-2297

This is a small roadside store with everything from medicinal herbs to wine and wool socks. It's a fun detour en route to Mt. Baker from Bellingham—and a good place to get a made-to-order sandwich.

Details: *There are picnic tables on the lawn out back. (15 minutes)*

BELLINGHAM

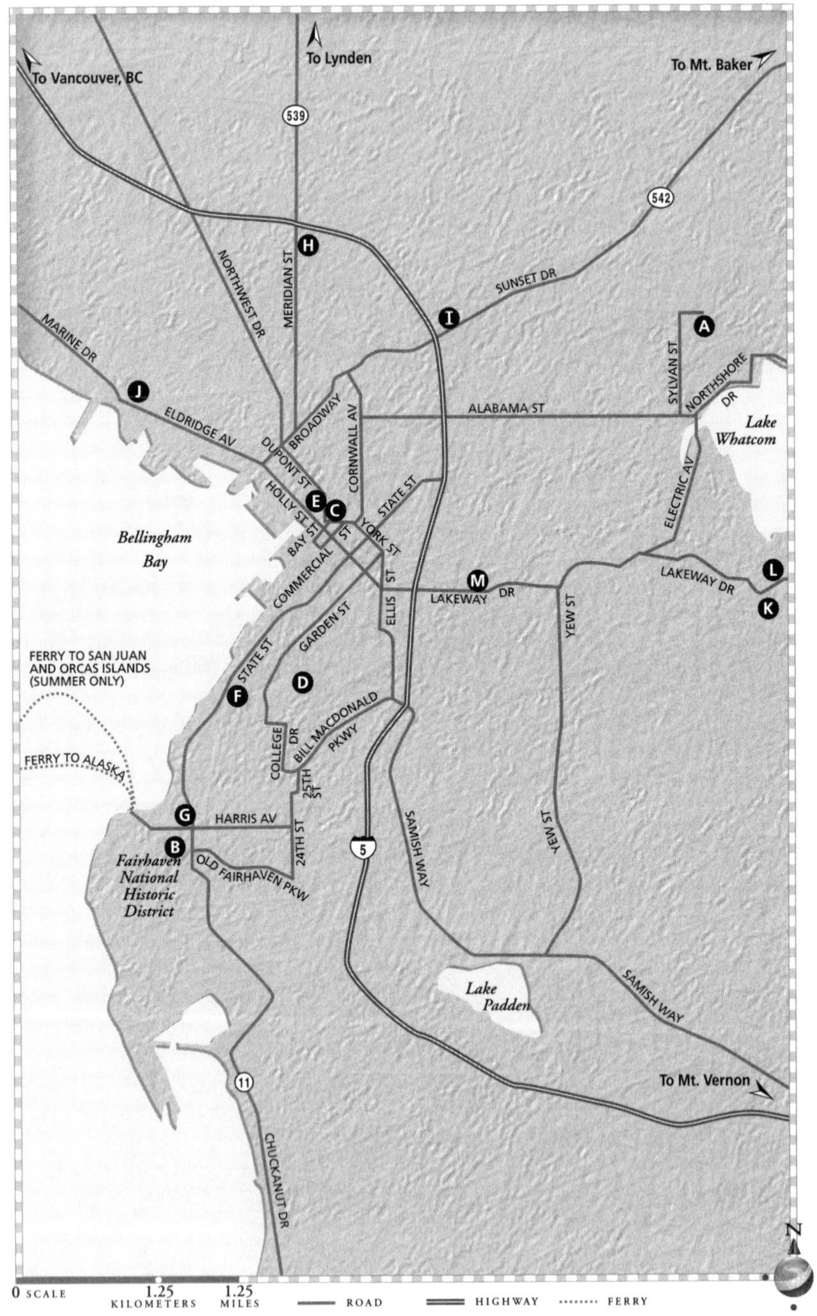

To Vancouver, BC
To Lynden
To Mt. Baker
539
542
NORTHWEST DR
MERIDIAN ST
SUNSET DR
MARINE DR
ELDRIDGE AV
BROADWAY
DUPONT ST
CORNWALL AV
ALABAMA ST
SYLVAN ST
NORTHSHORE DR
Lake Whatcom
ELECTRIC AV
HOLLY ST
STATE ST
BAY ST
YORK ST
Bellingham Bay
COMMERCIAL ST
ELLIS ST
LAKEWAY DR
YEW ST
GARDEN ST
FERRY TO SAN JUAN AND ORCAS ISLANDS (SUMMER ONLY)
COLLEGE DR
BILL MACDONALD PKWY
25TH ST
FERRY TO ALASKA
HARRIS AV
24TH ST
5
SAMISH WAY
Fairhaven National Historic District
OLD FAIRHAVEN PKW
Lake Padden
To Mt. Vernon
11
CHUCKANUT DR
N
0 SCALE
1.25 KILOMETERS
1.25 MILES
ROAD
HIGHWAY
FERRY

FITNESS AND RECREATION

Bellingham is known for the Ski-to-Sea Race & Festival, held each year on Memorial Day weekend. It's an 85-mile relay that includes seven events, parades, and a carnival. The six-mile Interurban Trail, a path for hikers, bikers, and horses that parallels Chuckanut Drive through the forest, is south of Bellingham.

Whale-watching cruises can be taken through Island Mariner in Bellingham, 360/734-8866 or 888/373-8522, and through San Juan Island Shuttle Express, 360/671-1137. Viking Cruises out of La Conner, 360/466-2639, also offers whale-watching and sight-seeing.

Whatcom Falls Park, 1401 Electric Avenue, located on 241 acres on Whatcom Creek, has hiking trails, waterfalls, picnic shelters, barbecue pits, tennis courts, a juvenile fishing pond, and more. A highlight is the fish hatchery; for hours or information call 360/676-2138. Lake Padden Park, 4882 Samish Way, on over 1,000 acres, has hiking and bridle trails around the lake and an 18-hole municipal golf course. For fishing, swimming, windsurfing, and seasonal kayak rentals, call 360/676-6985.

FOOD

The **Orchard Street Brewery,** 360/647-1614, is tucked away in an industrial strip north of downtown (call for directions), but well worth finding for yummy pizzas, salads, baked soups, and microbrews. The **Colophon Cafe,** 1208 11th Street, 360/647-0092, a bookstore café (located in Village Books) in Old Fairhaven, features homemade soups, sandwiches, quiches, and wonderful desserts. **Pastazza,** 360/714-1168, in Barkley Village (a Bellingham residential community east of I-5 at Exit 255), offers homemade pastas and sauces. Their sweet potato ravioli with tomato fennel sauce is a favorite. Next door, the **Pastazza Presto** retail store sells pastas, sauces, and ice cream. The **Cliff House,** 331 N. State Street, 360/734-8660, offers a wide seafood selection (dinner only, served 5 to 10 daily). The whisky crab soup is reason enough to stop. Seating on their wraparound deck offers views of Bellingham Bay.

SIGHTS

- Ⓐ Big Rock Garden
- Ⓑ Fairhaven
- Ⓒ Mt. Baker Theater
- Ⓓ Western Washington University
- Ⓔ Whatcom Museum of History and Art

FOOD

- Ⓕ Cliff House
- Ⓖ Colophon Cafe
- Ⓗ Orchard Street Brewery
- Ⓘ Pastazza/Pastazza Presto

LODGING

- Ⓙ DeCann House
- Ⓚ Big Trees B&B
- Ⓛ Schnauzer Crossing
- Ⓜ A Secret Garden

Along the Chuckanut Drive route (going south to north), the **Rhododendron Cafe,** 553 Chuckanut Drive, 360/766-6667, in Bow is small and casual, with fresh local ingredients. Perhaps the oldest oyster eatery, the **Oyster Bar,** 240 Chuckanut Drive, 360/766-6185, has a casual name and a rustic exterior, yet it's an elegant restaurant with fine linens, premium wines, waiters in black ties, and knockout sunset views of Samish Bay. A classic entrée preparation features oysters crispy fried with an herbed parmesan crust and a lightly tart apple aioli. The restaurant is open for dinner only. Bowls of oyster crackers and bottles of Tabasco sauce lend a casual touch to the **Oyster Creek Inn,** 360/766-6179, an old favorite, newly renovated, nearby. Menu choices include oysters raw on the half shell, a baked sampler, and a stew that is a delicate mix of extra small Samish Bay oysters, cream, milk, and herbs.

North of Lynden, stop at **Edaleen Dairy,** 9593 Guide Meridian Road (SR539), 360/354-3425, open 8 to 7:30 daily except Sundays, for fabulous ice-cream cones. In Lynden, the **Dutch Mothers Restaurant,** 405 Front Street, 360/354-2174, is known for its Dutch cuisine. **Milano's Market and Deli,** 360/599-2863, in Glacier, offers hearty pastas and sandwiches and is a good stop for families.

LODGING

Many of Bellingham's B&Bs are in historic homes. **DeCann House,** 2610 Eldridge Avenue, 360/734-9172, is affordable and is set in a Victorian home in a historic neighborhood. Set on a wooded lot on the east side of town, **Big Trees,** 4840 Fremont Street, 360/647-2850, is a post-Victorian, Craftsman-style home nestled among old-growth cedars and firs with views of Lake Whatcom. **A Secret Garden,** 1807 Lakeway Drive, 360/671-5327, is a turn-of-the-century Victorian-style home. A little more expensive, **Schnauzer Crossing,** 4421 Lakeway Drive, 360/733-0055 or 800/562-2808, is a stylish enclave with two guest rooms and a separate modern cottage, with great views of Lake Whatcom and a meditation garden and teahouse. **South Bay B&B,** 4095 South Bay Drive, Sedro Wooley, 360/595-2086, overlooking Lake Whatcom, is another wonderful retreat, so high in the trees you'll feel as if you are a bird.

Mt. Baker Lodging and Travel, 360/599-2453, and Mt. Baker Chalet, 360/599-2405, are two reservation services that represent homes and cabins in the Mt. Baker area (specify whether you're looking for a rustic cabin experience or a "house" experience). The **Glacier Creek Lodge & Cabins,** 360/599-2991, with rooms and small cabins with kitchenettes, is just off Mt. Baker Highway—perfect for skiers or hikers.

The **Inn at Semiahmoo,** 800/770-7992, is a full-service resort near

Blaine and the Canadian border. Nature lovers can explore the gently sloping beach along two sides of the mile-long spit or go whale-watching; golfers can escape to the Arnold Palmer–designed course. The inn offers 198 rooms (16 are suites). Spa packages for two include accommodations.

CAMPING

Larabee State Park, on Chuckanut Drive, has 51 standard campsites, 25 full hookups, 8 walk-in campsites, and a great location. Near Anacortes are two other waterfront parks that offer camping: **Bayview State Park** (near the Padilla Bay Interpretive Center) between Mt. Vernon and Anacortes, with about the same number of campsites; and **Birch Bay State Park,** southwest of Blaine. Reservations are needed May 15 through September 15; call 800/452-5687 to reserve at most state parks. Reservations can be made 11 months in advance of your arrival date. West of Glacier, **Silver Lake Park** is a 411-acre Whatcom County Park that encompasses a former private resort and early homestead. There are 73 campsites; seven cabins are available for rental year-round. For cabin rentals, call 360/599-2776 well in advance. You can also rent a stall in the outdoor stable for your horse.

10 LEAVENWORTH

In little more than 30 years, Leavenworth has gone from ugly duckling to beautiful swan, from a dismal highway town to a Bavarian-style village that is one of the state's favorite visitor destinations and recreation areas. Located in the foothills of the Cascades, flanked by soaring, snowcapped mountains, Leavenworth started the 1900s with prosperity and high hopes as a hub for the Great Northern Railroad. But in the 1920s, the railroad moved to Wenatchee, 30 miles farther east. Leavenworth floundered for decades, depending on the timber and fruit industries for its survival. Finally, in the 1960s, it reinvented itself as an alpine village, to fit its awe-inspiring geography. Since then visitors have come in ever growing numbers.

It can be a jam-packed tourist destination—there are more than 15 festivals every year, including favorites like Maifest, Autumn Leaf, and Christmas Lighting. It can also offer the serenity of a quiet small town, and a growing number of special lodgings are convenient to town but seem worlds away.

More and more, Leavenworth is becoming an arts town as well. The Icicle Creek Music Center offers chamber and other musical events year-round. The Leavenworth Summer Theater performs *The Sound of Music* outdoors. A summer festival features an accordion music competition and folk dancing. In the works for a spring event are artist and artisan workshops and shows.

A PERFECT DAY IN AND AROUND LEAVENWORTH

On a perfect summer day around Leavenworth, you'll wake early in a cozy room, go for a hike in the woods and listen to the bird calls, and picnic by the river or on a promontory with views of the Cascades. Then you could play golf or go fishing. But be sure to save time for exploring Leavenworth and Cashmere. On a perfect winter day, you may awaken to a new snowfall, then strap on cross-country skis to explore the very Bavarian landscape.

ORIENTATION

Leavenworth, with a year-round population of 2,300 (it can increase a dozen times during a festival), lies 120 miles east of and about two hours from Seattle. It is easily accessed via two major routes (combining them offers a good circle route—see the Cascade Loop route at the end of this chapter). You can follow Interstate 90 east; past Cle Elum (at milepost 85), take the Wenatchee exit, following signs to U.S. 97. This carries you north over Blewett Pass to the junction of Highway 2. Leavenworth lies four miles west. Or, from the Seattle/Bellevue area, you can drive north on Interstate 405 to Bothell, take Highway 522 east to Monroe, and connect to Highway 2, which takes you over Stevens Pass to Leavenworth.

While you'll more than likely drive here, you can also arrive on a plane or train. Horizon Airlines, 800/547-9308 or www.horizonair.com, provides eight direct flights from Seattle and two direct flights from Portland per day to Pangborn Memorial Airport in East Wenatchee, 30 miles east of Leavenworth. Amtrak, 800/872-7245, provides train service to downtown Wenatchee, 25 miles from Leavenworth. Alki Tours of Seattle, 800/895-2554, offers train-trip packages for some Leavenworth festivals.

Free public transportation for the area is provided by Link Bus Service of Chelan County, 509/662-5919 or 800/851-5465 (Washington only).

SIGHTSEEING HIGHLIGHTS

★★★★ ICICLE CREEK MUSIC CENTER

800/574-2123 or 509/548-6347

www.cascade.net/~icicle

Founded in 1995, the center features the music of the Kairos Quartet—the resident chamber musicians—and special performances by musicians from all over the country. Performances are in the Chapel

LEAVENWORTH AREA

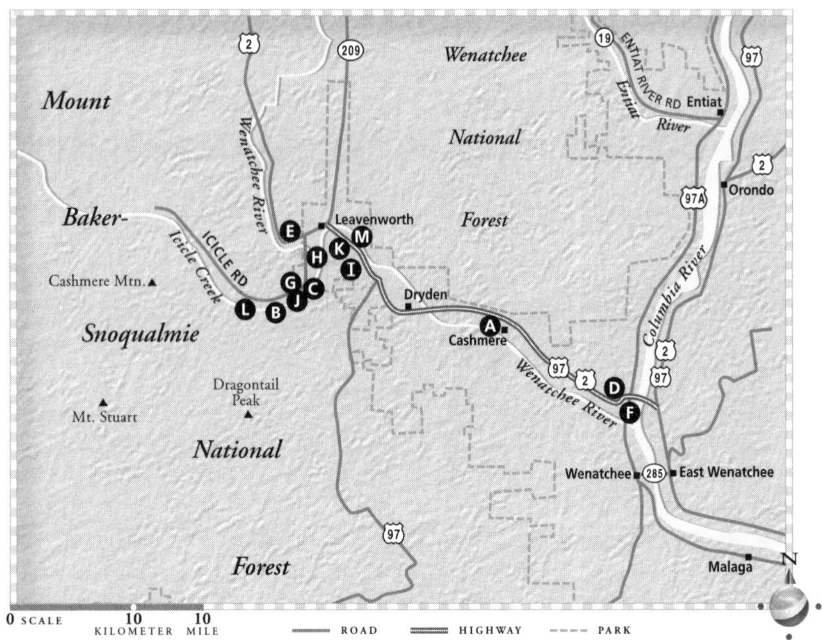

SIGHTS

- **A** Chelan County Historical Museum and Pioneer Village
- **B** Icicle Creek Music Center
- **C** Leavenworth National Fish Hatchery
- **A** Liberty Orchards
- **D** Ohme Gardens

SIGHTS *(continued)*

- **E** Tumwater Canyon
- **F** Washington Apple Commission Visitors Center

FOOD

- **A** Bob's Apple Barrel
- **G** Homefires Bakery

LODGING

- **H** All Seasons River Inn
- **I** Mountain Home Lodge
- **J** Sleeping Lady

CAMPING

- **K** Chalet Trailer Park
- **L** Icicle River RV Park
- **M** Pine Village Resort

Note: Items with the same letter are located in the same area.

Theater on the grounds of the Sleeping Lady Conference Center west of Leavenworth. Lodging is also available at the conference center on Icicle Road west of Leavenworth. Don't miss the glass icicle sculpture by Dale Chihuly at the entrance to the conference center dining room.

Details: *Tickets are $14 general admission, $12 senior, $7 for stu-*

dents and kids under 12. Call for information on performances as well as weekend music retreat packages (including lodging and fine food at the Sleeping Lady). (3–4 hours for dinner and performance)

★★★★ OHME GARDENS

Wenatchee, 509/662-5785
www.ohmegardens.com

The view alone from here is worth the stop. The gardens, nine acres that overlook Wenatchee and the confluence of the Wenatchee and Columbia Rivers, are well known for their over 120 varieties of plants and flowers, the native stone path winding through the grounds, and many pools with waterfalls. Sit and contemplate the beauty from one of over 50 stone benches on the site.

Details: *Just north of Wenatchee at the junction of Highways 2 and 97. Admission $5 for adults and $3 for kids 7 to 17; Open 9 to 6 daily April 15 through October 15. (2 hours)*

★★★★ TUMWATER CANYON

Near Leavenworth

In autumn, this canyon west of Leavenworth is brilliant with fall color. Several turnouts provide unhurried views of the Wenatchee River—from tranquil pools to raging rapids. Look closely and you will see evidence of the devastating forest fires that raged out of control here in the mid-1990s.

Details: *A nine-mile stretch along Highway 2 just west of Leavenworth. (10 minutes)*

★★★ CHELAN COUNTY HISTORICAL MUSEUM AND PIONEER VILLAGE

600 Cottage Avenue, Cashmere

A stop here offers an entertaining respite for travelers crossing Stevens Pass and a quick history lesson on the settlement of central Washington. Besides a schoolhouse, blacksmith's shop, and railroad office, the village includes a hotel, saddle and print shops, a jailhouse, a saloon, and an assay office—most built by pioneers before 1892.

Details: *About 12 miles east of Leavenworth on busy U.S. Route 2; take the second Cashmere exit. Located less than a block from Route 2, the museum is open from April 1 to October 31, Monday through Saturday 9:30 to 5, Sunday noon to 5. Suggested donation $5 per family, $3 per person, $2 seniors and students, $1 kids 5 to 12. (1 hour)*

LEAVENWORTH

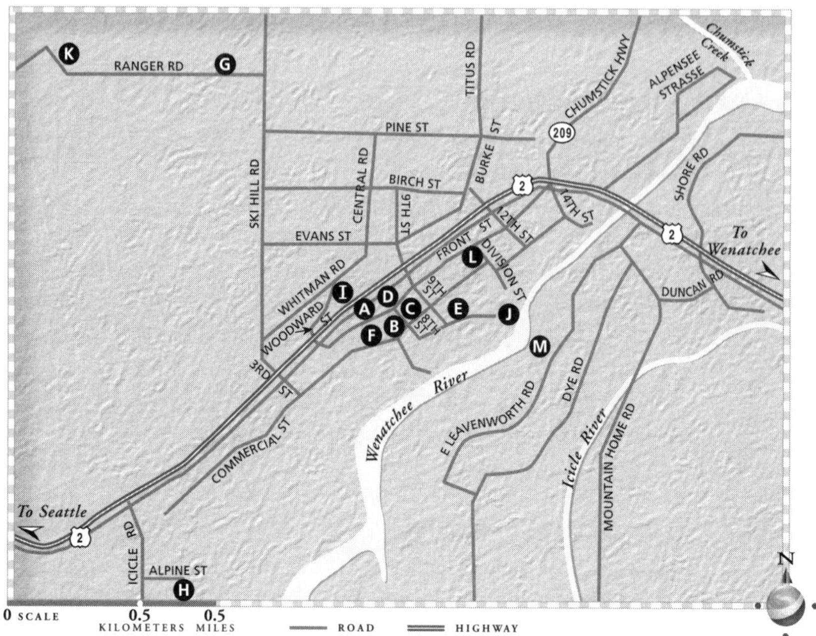

SIGHTS

- **A** Enzian Falls Championship Putting Course
- **B** Nutcracker Museum

FOOD

- **C** Best of the Wurst
- **D** Leavenworth Brewery
- **E** Lorraine's Edel House
- **F** Restaurant Osterreich
- **D** Visconti's

LODGING

- **G** Abendblume Pension
- **H** Alpen Rose Inn
- **I** Enzian Motor Inn
- **J** Haus Lorelei
- **K** Haus Rohrbach Pension
- **L** Hotel Pension Anna
- **M** Run of the River Inn

Note: Items with the same letter are located in the same area.

★★★ LIBERTY ORCHARDS

117 Mission Street, Cashmere, 509/782-4088
www.libertyorchards.com

You can visit the home of Aplets & Cotlets, founded by two young Armenians who fled the unrest in Turkey in the early 1900s. In the gift store, you'll find generous samples of Aplets—inspired by a Turkish confection and first produced in 1918—and other kinds of fruit gelatin candies.

Details: *Open Monday through Friday 8 to 5:30, weekends 9 to 5. Visit weekdays and take a 20-minute guided kitchen tour. The store offers a wide variety of gifts. (30 minutes)*

★★★ NUTCRACKER MUSEUM

735 Front Street, Leavenworth
509/548-4708 or 800/892-3989
www.nussnackerhaus.com

There are more than 3,000 different kinds of nutcrackers in this small museum, upstairs one level from Leavenworth's main street. They range from thumbnail-size to larger than life. A 15-minute video offers a look at the history of nutcrackers.

Details: *Open daily May through October from 2 to 5. Admission is charged. (45 minutes)*

★★ ENZIAN FALLS CHAMPIONSHIP PUTTING COURSE

590 Highway 2, Leavenworth, 509/548-5269

This 18-hole championship putting course in downtown Leavenworth provides a challenge for the pros and fun for the beginners; the pro shop is an authentic alpine meadow cabin. Fun just to stop and look at.

Details: *Open 4 p.m. to dusk on weekdays, 9 a.m to dusk on Saturday, and noon to dusk on Sunday. There is a per person fee for 18 holes. (1½–2 hours)*

★ LEAVENWORTH NATIONAL FISH HATCHERY

Icicle Road, Leavenworth, 509/548-7641

Self-guided tours can be taken almost every day from 7:30 to 4. Kids love to watch the huge schools of fingerlings. During late spring and early summer, you may see spawning fish.

Details: *Just west of town on Icicle Road; look for signs. Admission is free. (1 hour)*

★ WASHINGTON APPLE COMMISSION VISITORS CENTER

2900 Euclid Avenue, Wenatchee
509/663-9600 weekdays, 509/662-3090 weekends

Located near Ohme Gardens, the center offers much information on the state's apple business. There are displays, free samples, and an informative video on the apple industry.

Details: *Monday through Saturday 9 to 5, Sunday 10 to 4. Admission is free. (1 hour)*

FITNESS AND RECREATION

Hiking, whitewater rafting, fishing, and boating are some favorite summer activities here. There are numerous outfitters; call the chamber at 509/548-8807. Leavenworth may be best known for its winter activities. The family Ski Hill just east of town invites sledders and beginning skiers. For cross-country ski lessons and rentals, check out the Leavenworth Nordic Center, 509/548-7864. The hills around Leavenworth are alive with fun snow activities. Snowmobiling tours are offered by Mountain Springs Lodge, 509/763-2713. You'll find sleigh rides at Red-Tail Canyon Farm, 509/548-4512, or Eagle Creek Ranch, 509/548-4566, up Valley Road northeast of town.

Icicle Junction (on the corner of Highway 2 and Icicle Road, 888/462-4242) offers family entertainment with bumper boat rides during summer months, an 18-hole miniature golf course, and an arcade filled with games.

FOOD

For gourmet Austrian food that's lighter than traditional German food (though you'll still find full-flavored entrées like savory lamb shanks), try **Restaurant Osterreich** on Front Street, below the Tyrolean Ritz Hotel, 509/548-4031. The menu changes frequently at **Lorraine's Edel House,** 320 Ninth Street, 509/548-4412, but you can expect piquant salads and fresh seafood dishes. In summer, there's outdoor seating on the torch-lit patio of this comfortable 1920s house close to the heart of downtown. The pub, beer hall, and dining levels of **Visconti's** pasta and pizza restaurant overlook the **Leavenworth Brewery,** 636 Front Street, 509/548-4545. Their Whistling Pig Wheat beer, known as "the Pig," is a local favorite. The **Best of the Wurst** is an outdoor stand at 220 Eighth Street that offers grilled hamburgers and knockwurst sandwiches. Great on a cold day, **Homefires Bakery,** 509/548-7362, is on the west side of town; take the Icicle Road two miles and watch for signs. Open Thursday through Monday.

East from Leavenworth to Wenatchee is a major apple-growing area. Fruit stands are open from May to October, where you'll find classics such as Red and Golden Delicious, Granny Smiths, Jonathans, and newer apples like Fuji and Gala. Watch for **Smallwood Harvest,** 509/548-4196, dealing in antiques,

DELICIOUS APPLES

Washington state grows more than half of the fresh eating apples consumed in the United States (between 80 and 135 million boxes a year)—far more than any other state or region. Over a third of those are Red Delicious apples, the nation's favorite apple. Of the growing areas in the state, most are in Eastern Washington. The two best-known areas are the Wenatchee Valley—with an apple information center—and the Yakima Valley—with an fruit information center.

The Washington Apple Commission offers recipes and an excellent description of the various types of apples and their best uses: Visit its website at www.bestapples.com.

fruits, and ice cream, one mile east of Leavenworth on Highway 2, and **Prey's Fruit** nearby. In Cashmere, **Bob's Apple Barrel** fruit stand marks the main entrance to town off Highway 2. You'll find large bins of apples, apple cider, butters, vinegars—even apple milkshakes. Streusel-topped apple pies, rustic Normandy Farm bread—a light rye made with apple cider—macaroons and fudgy chocolate cookies are well worth a stop at **Anjou Bakery** 509/782-4360, one mile east of Cashmere.

LODGING

There are over 1,000 rooms within 20 miles of Leavenworth, and your choices range from a wide variety of in-town B&Bs to rustic cabins or elegant mountain retreats. Call the chamber at 509/548-5807. **All Seasons River Inn,** 8751 Icicle Road, about 1.5 miles (a 20-minute walk) out of Leavenworth, 509/548-1425 or 800/254-0555, is an adults-only, nonsmoking bed-and-breakfast. Email them at allriver@rightathome.com. Affordable **Alpen Rose Inn,** about five blocks from downtown Leavenworth, 509/548-3000 or 800/582-2474, www.alpenroseinn.com, is an adults-only, nonsmoking inn with full complimentary breakfast and desserts in the evening and a swimming pool. **Hotel Pension Anna,** in downtown Leavenworth, 509/548-6273 or 800/509-ANNA, www.pensionanna.com, is an authentic Bavarian-style inn; a former church adjacent to it contains a large suite. **Abendblume Pension,** 509/548-4059 or

A PYGMALION STORY

The story of the amazing rebirth of Leavenworth is told in *Miracle Town: Creating America's Bavarian Village in Leavenworth, Washington,* by Ted Price, published by Price & Rodgers (Vancouver, Washington), 1997. It chronicles the struggles and triumphs of the community and gives you a sense of the people who pulled together to create the delightful theme town. It's available through the Leavenworth Chamber of Commerce; 509/548-5807.

800/669-7634, email: abendblm@ rightathome.com, is an Austrian-style country home about a mile from downtown Leavenworth in the midst of a meadow with mountain views all around. It's an adult retreat with luxury amenities. Breakfast often includes tasty Aebleskivers, a unique Danish pancake. The amazingly reasonable **Haus Lorelei,** 347 Division Street, 509/548-5726 or 800/514-8868; www.hauslorelei.com, is just a short walk from downtown on a promontory over the Wenatchee River. All 10 guest rooms are individually decorated with antiques; two riverside rooms have four-poster canopy beds with lace hangings. **Haus Rohrbach Pension,** 509/548-7024 or 800/548-4477, is a comfortable chalet-style home (and separate suites) on the outskirts of Leavenworth. It has terrific valley views, Tumwater Mountain at its back door, a swimming pool in the front yard, and rates to meet every budget. **Mountain Home Lodge,** 509/548-7077 or 800/414-2378, in a comfortable contemporary building, lies three miles from the outskirts of Leavenworth, up a primitive winding road to an alpine meadow with stunning views of the mountains. A massive stone fireplace is the focal point of the dining room. There are miles of hiking trails; in winter this is a cross-country ski destination. It has a main inn and two new separate classy cabins. Call for rates, which vary with the season. A surprisingly good value for all its chic atmosphere and attention to detail, **Run of the River Inn,** 800/288-6491, is less than two miles from Leavenworth on the Icicle River. This comfortable country-style log inn overlooks wetlands and is situated between two bird refuges, so it seems worlds away from everything. Hiking brochures and information await you, but you may be tempted in laze in your porch swing. The **Enzian Motor Inn,** 509/548-5269 or 800/223-8511, www.enzianinn.com, is right on Highway 2. With two pools, including a covered pool, it's a favorite with families. A complimentary buffet breakfast is served.

CAMPING

There are three campgrounds around Leavenworth offering easy access to town and plenty of amenities: **Pine Village Resort,** 509/548-7709 or 800/562-5709, **Icicle River RV Park,** 509/548-5420, and **Chalet Trailer Park,** 800/477-2697. The cost for each is about $25 per night.

Scenic Route: Cascade Loop

This is a Washington classic, best planned for warmer months—from May to October—when the snows blocking the North Cascades Highway have melted. The loop offers a tour of the most beautiful mountain scenery and many of the best recreation options in the state and is a sure bet for sunshine. From Interstate 5, head east across Highway 2 to Leavenworth. Spend some time touring, hiking, or overnighting here. The apple town of Cashmere is about 10 miles east of Leavenworth and worth a detour for a look at the Chelan County Historical Museum and Pioneer Village, 509/782-3230, or a tour of Liberty Orchards, 509/782-2191, makers of Aplets and Cotlets. Traveling on, you'll reach the city of Wenatchee at the confluence of the Wenatchee and Columbia Rivers, in the heart of one of the state's largest apple producing areas. You can visit the Washington State Apple Commission Visitors Center, 509/663-9600, for free apple samples and juice. Also take time to visit Ohme Gardens (you'll see signs from the freeway), overlooking the rivers and city.

Then take Highway 97 or 97A north along either side of the Columbia River. Highway 97 on the east side passes several state parks with riverfront access and the popular Desert Canyon golf course, 509/784-1111. Highway 97A passes Rocky Reach Dam, 509/663-7522, with guided tours available. Both highways lead to Lake Chelan

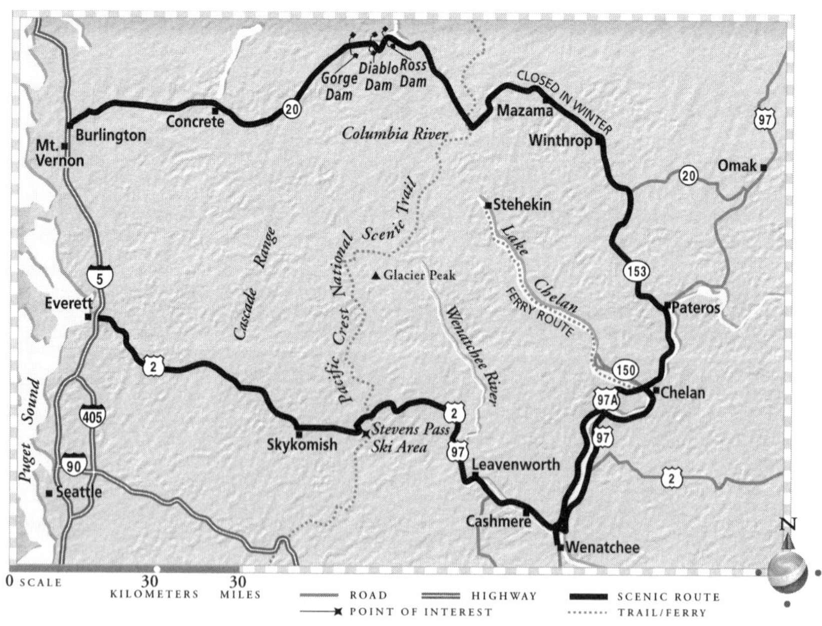

and the community of Chelan, 800/424-3526, www.lakechelan.com. This is a resort town destination for scores of sun and fun seekers. All summer long the lake is abuzz with boats, skiers, and jet skis. There are many beachfront resorts and condominiums, but the best known is Campbell's Lodge, 800/553-8225. Popular with families since 1901, it's right on the lake in the heart of Chelan, a Norman Rockwell–style small town. Wapato Point, 509/687-9511, about seven miles northwest of Chelan in the small town of Manson, is a popular condominium resort destination. From Chelan, you can take an unusual detour to Stehekin, a remote village of about 70 year-round residents, 50 miles from Chelan at the northwest end of the lake in Chelan National Recreation Area. The Lake Chelan Boat Company, 509/682-2224 or www.ladyofthe lake.com, runs boat and catamaran service here several times a day. You can also go by floatplane with Chelan Airways, 509/682-5555. Either way, you feel like you're journeying over a fjord. You can make it a day trip or an overnight. Stehekin Lodge is right at the landing. It offers motel-like rooms in the small main building and individual cabins nearby that have a more rustic flavor. A more luxurious lodging is Silver Bay Inn, 509/682-2212 or 800/555-7781, with house and cabin rentals in a more private setting; a rolling lawn goes down to the water. Stehekin Valley Ranch, 509/682-4677 or 800/536-0745, offers cabins, fishing, horseback riding, and more. In summer, there's plenty of hiking—trailheads leading into North Cascades National Park begin here—and a nearby waterfall to visit.

From Chelan, go north (first along Highway 97, then Highway 153) to the Western-style town of Winthrop in the Methow Valley. In winter, this is a cross-country skiing mecca. In summer it's a great place to fish, mountain bike, and ride horses. Spend some time exploring the main street here, or stop for lunch at the Winthrop Brew Pub, 155 Riverside Avenue, 509/996-3183, in a quirky red schoolhouse-style structure along the river. There are numerous lodgings in the valley (call central reservations at 800/422-3048), however, Sun Mountain Lodge, a top-ranked destination resort 10 miles from town, 509/996-2211 or 800/572-0493, is a must-visit if just for the view or a meal. From the dining room you'll have sweeping, eagle-perch views of the valley—enhancing the fine food. Continuing northwest of Winthrop on Highway 20 you'll come to Mazama, with Mazama Country Inn, 509/996-2681 or 800/843-7951, a secluded lodge in the woods. Nearby is the newly built Freestone Inn, 800/639-3809, with rooms and cabin rentals. Then, heading west, you'll take the mountain route. Do this in early morning if possible or you'll face the sun while you're driving and lose some of the views. Stop at the 5,447-foot Washington Pass Overlook for a spectacular view of the North Cascades. About 35 miles from the overlook you'll encounter Ross, Diablo, and Gorge Dams. All offer tours. The most unique is the four-hour guided tour of Diablo

Lake by Seattle City Light. It includes lunch, a boat cruise, a powerhouse tour, and a vertical railway ride; this runs mid-June through September. Reservations are required, call 206/684-3030. Continue west through the lush and green Skagit Valley. You'll encounter I-5 access at Sedro Wooley.

For more information on the route, contact the Cascade Loop Association, 509/662-3888 or www.cascadeloop.com.

11 SPOKANE

Isolated by geography and situated far from other cities of its size, Spokane is the prosperous and historical hub of the Inland Empire, which skirts the thriving bread basket of Washington's great Columbia Basin. The city of 200,000 is known for hot summers, cold winters, and spring lilacs. The Lilac Festival in May kicks off with the annual 12K Bloomsday Race, which attracts more than 50,000 participants.

The Spokane natives who fished for salmon were the primary residents until 1810, when the Northwest Fur Company built the first non-native trading post in the Northwest at Spokane House. In the 1870s, grain and lumber replaced fur trading as a commercial focus. The town moved to Spokane Falls, 10 miles southeast of the post, where mills were built to harness the water power. This impressive falls is now the heart of Riverfront Park, the site of Expo '74. In the late 1800s, Spokane experienced an "Age of Elegance," spurred by the wealth from silver mines in nearby Coeur d'Alene, Idaho. You'll see how the silver barons spent their money—on the Victorian-style homes and mansions in Browne's Addition. A recent flurry of historic renovation in buildings and hotels around town may signal a new age of elegance for the city.

Spokane makes a great stopover if you're driving to the Northwest from eastern regions or traveling east to the prime resort areas of northern Idaho at Coeur d'Alene (a half-hour away) or Priest Lake (two hours northeast). It also works well to combine visits to Pullman, in the Palouse region to the south; to Lake Roosevelt and Grand Coulee Dam to the west; or to the interior of British Columbia.

A PERFECT DAY IN SPOKANE

Exploring downtown's Riverfront Park is a must. Take the gondola ride above Spokane Falls. Picnic on the grounds or grab lunch at one of several restaurants nearby. Then head south of town to explore the Cheney Cowles Museum and tour Campbell House, which echoes the wealth of Spokane's early boom days. To end the day with some exercise, stroll through Manito Park or head to the Little Spokane River for a hike or a little canoeing.

ORIENTATION

Interstate 90 leads like a lax string from Seattle across state to Spokane, about 280 miles. While it takes about 5 to 5 ½ hours, it's an elegant drive under normal conditions as the route shows off some of the most beautiful scenery in the state, carrying you through the Cascade Mountains and over the dramatic Columbia River Gorge at Vantage, then through wheat and farming country to Spokane. The freeway cuts through the middle of Spokane on an east-west line. It parallels Sprague Avenue (about three blocks north of the freeway), which divides the city into North and South designations. Division Street is the major thoroughfare running north and south, and it divides the city into East and West.

A walking map is available for self-guided tours of historic downtown or Browne's Addition buildings. The Spokane Area Convention and Visitors Bureau Visitor Information Center at 201 West Main Avenue, 888/SPOKANE (888/776-5263), www.visitspokane.com, will provide maps and answer any questions you might have. The Spokane International Airport is seven miles southwest of town.

SIGHTSEEING HIGHLIGHTS

★★★★ CHENEY COWLES MEMORIAL MUSEUM

2316 West First Avenue, 509/363-5315 or 456-3931
www.cheneycowles.org

Spokane's best museum is ensconced amidst the elegant homes of Browne's Addition. (Note: Until fall 2001, the museum is under construction and exhibits and programs have been relocated. Call for information and locations.) It focuses on the pioneer history of the

SPOKANE

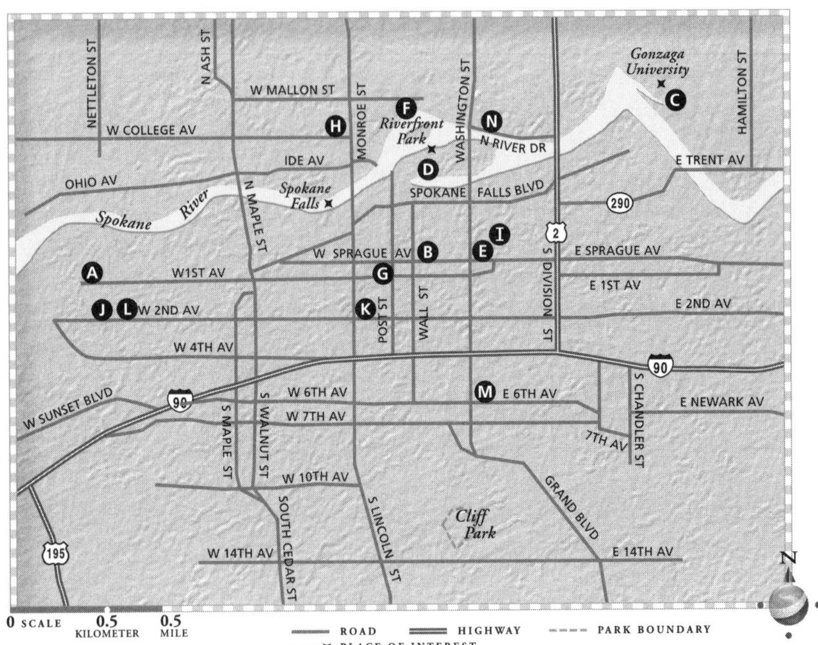

SIGHTS

- **A** Cheney Cowles Memorial Museum
- **B** Douglas Gallery
- **C** Jundt Art Museum and Bing Crosby Collection at Gonzaga University
- **D** Riverfront Park

FOOD

- **E** Ankeny's
- **F** Clinkerdagger
- **G** Fugazzi Dining Room
- **H** Milford's Fish House and Oyster Bar
- **I** The Onion
- **J** Patsy Clark's Mansion
- **K** Steam Plant Grill

LODGING

- **L** Fotheringham House
- **M** Kempis Suites
- **G** Lusso Hotel
- **E** The Ridpath Hotel
- **N** West Coast Grand Hotel at the Park

Note: Items with the same letter are located in the same area.

Inland Empire and includes an exhibit of Plateau Indian arts and an art gallery. Campbell House is a restored turn-of-the-century home located on the museum's grounds.

Details: *Open Tuesday through Saturday 10 to 5, Wednesday until 9, and Sunday 1 to 5. Admission $4; a tour of Campbell house included. (2 hours)*

★★★★ JUNDT ART MUSEUM AND BING CROSBY COLLECTION AT GONZAGA UNIVERSITY

Pearl Avenue, 509/323-6611 (museum)
Standard Steet at Boone Avenue, 509/323-4097 (Crosby Collection)

On the grounds of Spokane's well-known Jesuit university, you'll find a dramatic Dale Chihuly work, the *Gonzaga Red Chandelier,* and several other of his glass pieces and drawings at the Jundt Art Museum. Constantly rotating exhibits include local, regional, national, and international works, by contemporary artists and old masters; selections from the museum's Rodin collection are always on exhibit. Crosby Center, a student enclave, has pictures and memorabilia concerning Bing Crosby, who attended Gonzaga, on display in the Crosbyana Room. His childhood home, with more displays, is on campus.

Details: *The museum is on the west corner of Gonzaga's campus. Going north on Division Street, take a right on DesSmet and a right on Pearl; go south and you'll see the museum, a brick building with copper roof; summer hours Tuesday through Friday 10 to 4, Saturday noon to 4. Open Monday during the school year. Crosby summer hours 8:30 to 4:30; open later during the school year. Admission is free. (1–2 hours)*

★★★★ RIVERFRONT PARK

Downtown Spokane, 509/456-4386
www.spokaneriverfrontpark.com

The site of Expo '74 has been transformed into a lively 100-acre park that lies at the heart of the downtown, built around the Spokane River and Spokane Falls. The gondola ride leaves from the west edge of the park and carries riders over the Spokane River, with a spectacular view of the falls and of Canada Island, the site of Canada's Expo exhibit. In addition to the outdoor art, including an intriguing series of joggers, visitors can enjoy a tour train, an amusement park, ice-skating in winter, and an IMAX theater on the grounds. The Spokane River Centennial Trail is an easy paved walkway that parallels the river.

Details: *Call for hours of operation, season pass rates, and special events. Call 509/625-6604 for IMAX show information. Admission to attractions varies. (2 hours or more)*

★★★ CAT TALES ZOOLOGICAL PARK

17020 North Newport Highway, 509/238-4126
www.cattales.org

KIRTLAND CUTTER— SPOKANE'S FAMOUS ARCHITECT

Many of the grand historic homes around Spokane, particularly those in Browne's Addition southwest of downtown, are the work of famous American architect Kirtland Kelsey Cutter. Cutter came to the city in the late 1800s. Although he had studied art in Europe and wanted to be an architect, when he arrived in Spokane, he first went to work for his uncle as a bank clerk. When the railroads expanded and boom times hit nearby Coeur d'Alene silver mines, Cutter's skills blossomed as he began to design elaborate homes for the wealthy, with no expense spared. For silver baron, Patsy Clark, Cutter designed an unusual mansion with Moorish overtones. It is now a popular restaurant (see page 183).

Cutter's work wasn't restricted to residental properties. One of the town's most interesting historic renovations in recent years, the highly visible twin-towered Washington Water Power Central Steam Plant was the heating plant for downtown during most of the 1900s. It, too, was designed by Cutter. It now houses a retail complex called Steamplant Square (see Steamplant Grill, page 185). His work is on the Web as well. Access the city park website: debut.net/south-hill/brownes_addition.html.

There are 30 species of rare and endangered big cats including lions, pumas, lynx, tigers, and leopards in this zoological park and training center. Animals can be viewed up close (from about eight feet away).

Details: *Open summers Tuesday through Sunday 10 to 6; otherwise Wednesday through Sunday 10 to 4. Admission $6 adults, $5 seniors (free on Sunday), $4 kids under 12. Guided tours are available. (2 hours)*

★★★ MANITO PARK

Grand Avenue (south of downtown), 509/625-6622

There's a lilac garden here, of course, as well as rose, Japanese, perennial, and formal gardens; a conservatory with tropical foliage and seasonal flowers; and a duck pond. The park is best May through October; it offers a cool, green respite from high summer temperatures.

***Details:** Located between 17th and 25th Avenues. The conservatory and Japanese garden are open 8 to dusk. Admission free. (1–2 hours)*

★★★ SILVERWOOD THEME PARK

26225 North Highway 95, Athol, Idaho, 208/683-3400
www.silverwood4fun.com

A Victorian-era theme park with food, shows, and games of skill. Thrilling rides like Skydiver, the Thunder Canyon river raft ride, and a 55-mile-per-hour wooden roller coaster called the Timber Terror—the names speak for themselves—attract teenagers and excitement seekers. Ferris wheels, carousels, and shows such as performances by international skaters round out the entertainment. Tinywood is a section for toddlers, complete with a roller coaster, pump cars, and tree climbs. There's pizza and casual food at High Moon Saloon and all-you-can-eat family meals with chicken, mashed potatoes, and biscuits at Lindy's Country Restaurant.

***Details:** Fifty miles northeast of Spokane via Interstate 90; take Highway 95 north from Coeur d'Alene and go 15 miles. Open May through September; call for hours. Admission about $25 for ages 8 to 64, about $17 for ages 3 to 7 and 65 and over. (full day)*

★★★ SPOKANE HOUSE INTERPRETIVE CENTER

Nine Mile Falls, 509/466-4747
www.riversidestatepark.org

In 1810, Jaco Finlay was commissioned by the Pacific Fur company to set up a trading post where the Spokane and Little Spokane Rivers meet. It was the Northwest's first non-native trading post. Markers outline the site, and artifacts excavated in 1953 are on display in the interpretive center. An exhibit also traces the history of Northwest fur companies, including Pacific and Hudson Bay.

***Details:** Located in Riverside State Park, nine miles northwest of downtown and less than a mile north of the community of Nine Mile Falls. Open mid-May to early September, Wednesday through Sunday 9 to 6. Admission $1. You can picnic on the grounds. (1 hour)*

★★ DOUGLAS GALLERY

120 North Wall Street, 509/624-4179

Bronze sculptures, hand-blown glass art, and fine paintings are a specialty of this 5,000-square-foot art gallery. A lower level "vault" showcases the works of many Northwest artists.

Details: *Open Monday through Thursday 10 to 6, Friday and Saturday 10 to 7. Admission free. (30 minutes)*

★★ JOHN A. FINCH ARBORETUM
3404 Woodland Boulevard, 509/624-4832

There are more than 2,000 labeled ornamental trees, shrubs, and flowers on this 65-acre park, somewhat hidden away in the north part of town but worth a visit, especially in May when over 70 varieties of crab apples bloom.

Details: *Open dawn to dusk daily. Admission free. (2 hours)*

★★ RED SHED FARM MUSEUM
North of Spokane, 509/466-2744

This family-owned museum on a working wheat farm north of Spokane gives you a feel for farm life in the 1920s, 1940s, and 1950s, with re-created kitchens and a bedroom suite. There are over 500 farm implements and tools that have been passed down in the family. And the farm may have the largest collection of ironstone dishes in the Northwest.

Details: *The farm lies 13 miles north of the city. Call for directions and to confirm visiting hours. At the farm, ring the bell to summon the owners. (1–2 hours)*

FITNESS AND RECREATION

It's becoming less and less a well-kept secret that Spokane is a golfer's paradise; there are over 30 courses within an hour of the city. Municipal golf courses offer attractively landscaped grounds, great play, and great value. Tops are Downriver, 509/327-5269, Esmeralda, 509/487-6291, Indian Canyon, 509/747-5353, and the Creek at Qualchan, 509/448-9317; you can also call the City of Spokane, 509/625-6453, for details and tee times. County courses are equally fine and include Hangman Valley, 509/448-1212; Liberty Lake, 509/255-6233; and Meadow Wood, 509/255-9539. A golf map is available from the visitors center.

Runners come here in May for the annual 12K Bloomsday run. The Spokane River Centennial Trail is a 39-mile trail for walkers, runners, and bicyclists that runs from downtown east to the Idaho border. Hiking and canoeing trails around the Little Spokane River west of the city put you in a wetlands area reminiscent of a Lewis and Clark exploration. Mt. Spokane (at 6,000 feet), a 30-minute drive north, offers summertime hiking and mountain

SIDE TRIP: PULLMAN TO COEUR D'ALENE

About 75 miles southeast of Spokane is **Pullman,** *the site of Washington State University and home to the Cougars. This is a picturesque college town set against the rolling wheat fields for which the Palouse region of Washington is known. On campus, you can get an ice-cream cone or view cheese makers at work at* **The Creamery,** *known for producing Cougar Gold, a nutty white cheddar that claims diehard fans. It comes packed in a can, as it did during World War II.*

About 50 miles south of Spokane, just off SR 195, is **Steptoe Butte State Park.** *Take a winding road to the top of the 3,612-foot butte, and on a clear day you can see into Montana.*

Palouse Falls, *about 100 miles southwest of Spokane (take SR 261 south off I-90 near Ritzville), is in an area called the Channeled Scablands, sculpted by the floods of the Ice Age. The falls drop almost 200 feet and offer an impressive contrast to the surrounding dry canyon.*

Traveling west of Spokane along U.S. 2 leads you into bare, arid country, which is beautiful if you have the inclination to appreciate it. Take SR 25 north to see **Roosevelt Lake,** *stretching about 150 miles from Grand Coulee Dam to the Canadian border; houseboat rentals are available. About 90 miles west along U.S. 2, then SR 174, is* **Grand Coulee Dam,** *perhaps the most famous of many Northwest dams and truly a spectacle to see, especially after dark when a laser light show showcases the spillway.*

To the east is Idaho. Just over the border, **Coeur d'Alene Resort** *is a prime destination for avid golfers anxious to try their hand—or club—on its renowned floating green. For area information, contact the visitors bureau at 800/286-5544.*

biking and wintertime cross-country and downhill skiing—a great low-key ski destination for families.

The Spokane Indians, 509/535-2922 or www.spokaneindiansbaseball.com, play minor-league baseball in Avista Stadium, a classic outdoor baseball field. In winter, the Spokane Chiefs hockey team, 509/535-7825, www.spokanechiefs.com, plays in the Arena, often against Canadian teams. The Spokane Shadow, 509/326-4625 or www.spokane shadow.com, plays soccer in Joe Albi Stadium.

FOOD

Ankeny's, 515 West Sprague Avenue, 509/838-2711, on the top floor of the Ridpath Hotel downtown, offers expansive views of the city and river, beef and seafood meals, and late evening entertainment. Their entrées are moderately priced. The **Calgary Steak House,** 3040 East Sprague Avenue, 509/535-7502, is a good place for family dinners and has a children's menu, but expect to pay a hefty price for a New York steak. A lively place to go for a good hamburger and family dining is **The Onion,** 302 West Riverside Avenue (downtown), 509/747-3852; and 7522 North Davidson, 509/482-6100. **Clinkerdagger,** 621 West Mallon Street, 509/328-5965, has some views of the river and tasty pasta dishes, but the draw here is the desserts. **Patsy Clark's Mansion,** 2208 Second Avenue, 509/838-8300, in Browne's Addition, is dark and romantic—a dressy spot to go for a special evening. The **Fugazzi Dining Room** at Hotel Lusso, 1 North Post Street, 509/624-1133, has an international menu with such offerings as wild mushroom ravioli and Moroccan chicken. **Luna,** 5620 South Perry, 509/448-2383, a European bistro-style restaurant tucked away in the pretty residential neighborhood of Southhill, is a little pricey, but the innovative food, using seasonal produce, is wonderful. **Milford's Fish House and Oyster Bar,** 719 North Monroe Street, 509/326-7251, is miles from the saltwater, but the fish is fresh from Puget Sound and simply and deliciously prepared. For budget-friendly options in fun settings, try **Knight's Diner,** 2909 North Market, 509/484-0015, located in an old Pullman train car (breakfast and lunch only); or the **Milk Bottle Restaurant,** 802 West Garland Avenue, 509/325-1772, located in a former dairy. Homemade ice cream is a great reason to go to the Milk Bottle.

There are a number of brewpubs around town, many with live entertainment on weekends. A popular spot is the **Bayou Brewery,** 1003 E. Trent, 509/484-4818, with a New Orleans Mardi Gras theme, great Cajun food, bands, and comedy groups on weekends. Its good for families on weeknights. **The Ram** brewpub and restaurant, 509/326-3745, is a lively watering hole with music and entertainment near the Arena. The **Cavallino Lounge** in the **Lusso Hotel,** with its blown-glass chandeliers from Italy and purple drapes, is a busy nighttime gathering spot; it's a nonsmoking establishment, and folks come for the unique martinis.

You can nosh on a burger, chicken wrap, grilled salmon, and more in the

GREATER SPOKANE

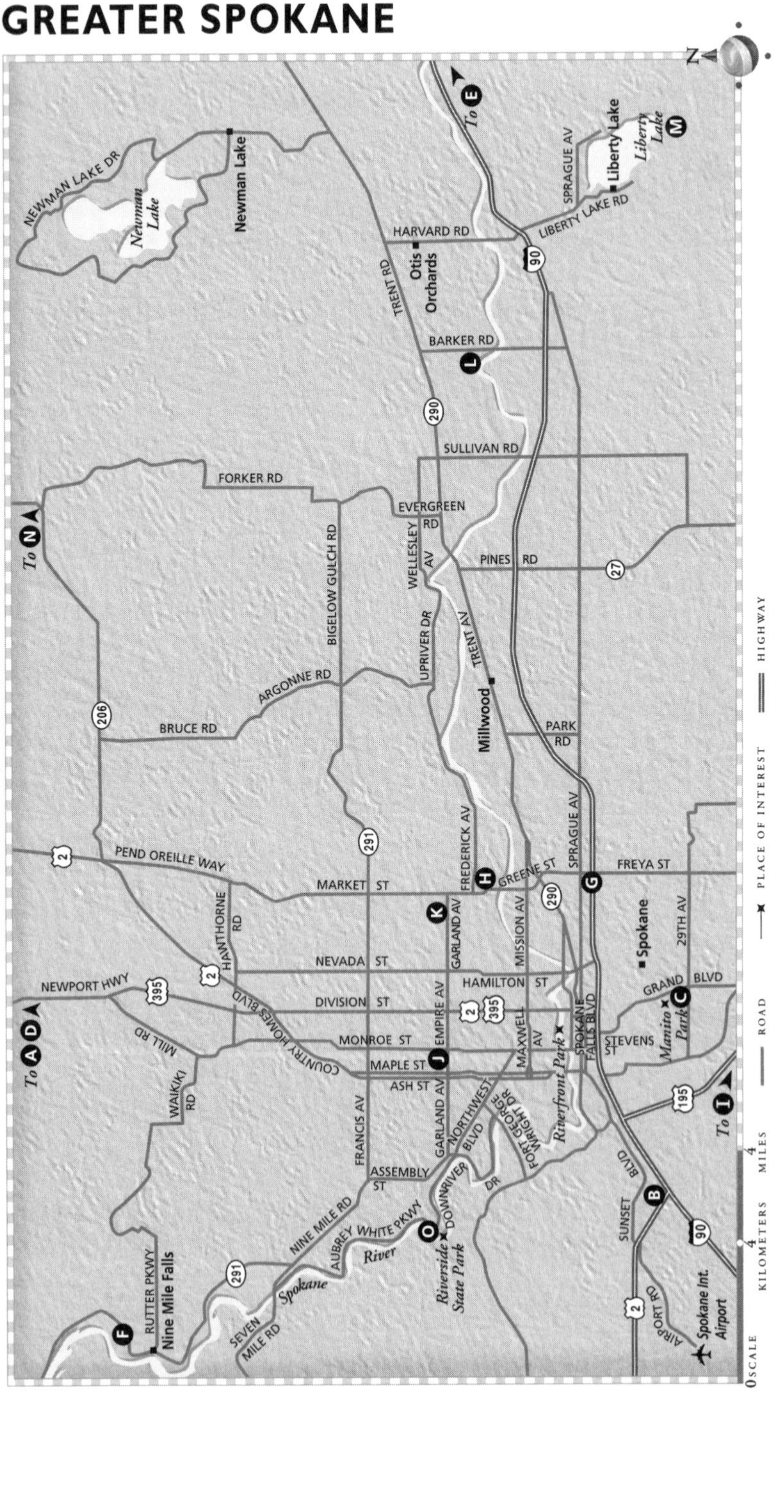

To E
Newman Lake
Newman Lake
NEWMAN LAKE DR
SPRAGUE AV
Liberty Lake
Liberty Lake
M
LIBERTY LAKE RD
HARVARD RD
90
Otis Orchards
TRENT RD
BARKER RD
L
290
SULLIVAN RD
FORKER RD
To N
EVERGREEN RD
WELLESLEY AV
BIGELOW GULCH RD
PINES RD
27
UPRIVER DR
TRENT AV
ARGONNE RD
Millwood
206
BRUCE RD
PARK RD
SPRAGUE AV
291
FREDERICK AV
2
PEND OREILLE WAY
H
GREENE ST
G
FREYA ST
MARKET ST
HANTHORNE RD
K
GARLAND AV
MISSION AV
290
Spokane
29TH AV
NEVADA ST
HAMILTON ST
GRAND BLVD
NEWPORT HWY
395
DIVISION ST
C
Manito Park
COUNTRY HOMES BLVD
EMPIRE AV
SPOKANE FALLS BLVD
To A D
MILL RD
MONROE ST
MAXWELL AV
Riverfront Park
STEVENS ST
MAPLE ST
J
ASH ST
WAIKIKI RD
NORTHWEST BLVD
FORT GEORGE WRIGHT DR
195
To I
FRANCIS AV
GARLAND AV
ASSEMBLY ST
DOWNRIVER DR
SUNSET BLVD
B
NINE MILE RD
AUBREY WHITE PKWY
O
90
Riverside State Park
Spokane River
291
RUTTER PKWY
Nine Mile Falls
F
SEVEN MILE RD
2
AIRPORT RD
Spokane Int. Airport

SCALE 0 4 KILOMETERS 4 MILES
ROAD
PLACE OF INTEREST
HIGHWAY

Steamplant Grill, 159 S. Lincoln, 509/777-3900 or www.steamplant square.com, a fun eatery in Steamplant Square.

LODGING

The most exciting news in recent years centers on historic renovation. Examples are two luxury boutique hotels new in the late 1990s. West Coast Hotels' **Lusso Hotel,** 1 North Post Street, 509/747-9750 or 800/426-0670, combines two centennial buildings with an amazing renovation; the interior includes Italian marble archways and a five-story, hand-sanded cherry staircase. The **Kempis Suites,** 326 West Sixth Avenue, 509/747-4321, in the building that department store mogul Charles Kemp built in 1906, houses 15 apartment-size units with antique furnishings, kitchens, and dining rooms or offices. **West Coast Grand Hotel at the Park** (formerly Cavanaugh's), 303 West North River Drive across from Riverfront Park, 509/326-8000 or 800/325-4000, has over 400 rooms, seven floors, and a terrific location. Some rooms have fireplaces (the suites), whirlpool tubs, and river views. There are two pools (one indoors). West Coast also owns the **Ridpath Hotel,** 515 West Sprague Avenue, 509/838-2711 or 800/325-4000. For years the classic hotel in the city, it has an outdoor pool and over 300 rooms. **Fotheringham House,** 2128 West Second Avenue in Browne's Addition, 509/838-1891, was home to Spokane's first mayor, David B. Fotheringham. Now it's a historic B&B with four rooms. It has no phones or TVs but has plenty of Victorian character. Another B&B is **Waverly Place,** 709 West Waverly Place, 509/328-1856, a 1902 Victorian home located in Corbin Park, an elegant older neighborhood north of the river. It offers central air-conditioning and a pool. There are also a number of national chain hotel and motels convenient to downtown.

SIGHTS

- Ⓐ Cat Tales Zoological Park
- Ⓑ John A. Finch Arboretum
- Ⓒ Manito Park
- Ⓓ Red Shed Farm Museum
- Ⓔ Silverwood Theme Park
- Ⓕ Spokane House Interpretive Center

FOOD

- Ⓖ Calgary Steak House
- Ⓗ Knights Diner
- Ⓘ Luna
- Ⓙ Milk Bottle Restaurant

LODGING

- Ⓚ Waverly Place

CAMPING

- Ⓛ KOA of Spokane
- Ⓜ Liberty Lake Park
- Ⓝ Mt. Spokane State Park
- Ⓞ Riverside State Park

CAMPING

Mt. Spokane State Park, 509/238-4258, about 30 miles northeast of Spokane, offers a dozen or so sites for tents or self-contained RVs and a few primitive sites. **Riverside State Park,** 509/456-3964, is about six miles northwest of downtown. **KOA of Spokane,** 3025 North Barker Road, 509/924-4722, has over 150 sites for trailers and tents. It's located in Otis Orchards about 13 miles east of Spokane (take Exit 293 off Interstate 90). **Liberty Lake Park,** 3707 South Zephyr Road, Liberty Lake, 509/456-4730 for group reservations or 509/255-6861, offers swimming beaches with lifeguards and tent and RV camping; there is a fee for park admittance.

12 WASHINGTON'S WINE COUNTRY

How do you get to Washington's wine country? Go east from Seattle on I-90 to Ellensburg. In the middle of the state, hang a right on I-82 and follow it almost to the Oregon border. You've just followed the Yakima River, the wine country's main artery and a rich agricultural path through former desert. Home to more than 40 wineries, Washington's wine region is the second largest in the country. At the Tri-Cities—Richland, Kennewick, and Pasco—the Yakima meets the Columbia and Snake Rivers, and the wine appellations fan out along these waterways.

In all, the route is about 250 miles. That's a bit of a drive on an ordinary day, but special winery events, warm weather, summer and fall produce, and some pretty interesting Western towns, museums, the Yakama Reservation (the tribe uses the original spelling of the word), and a special excursion up the Columbia River to Hanford Reach offer further reasons to go. Yakima and the Tri-Cities are the region's population centers.

Not far from Yakima, the town of Toppenish is the valley's "mural town." It's home to over 50 historical murals done by well-known Western artists. Prosser, 50 miles southeast of Yakima, is the birthplace of the state's modern wine industry; wine grape varieties were developed and tested at Washington State University's Extension Center north of town by Dr. Walter Clore, who's considered the father of Washington's wine industry.

Come to the valley in summer when the more than 400 crops raised here,

WASHINGTON'S WINE COUNTRY

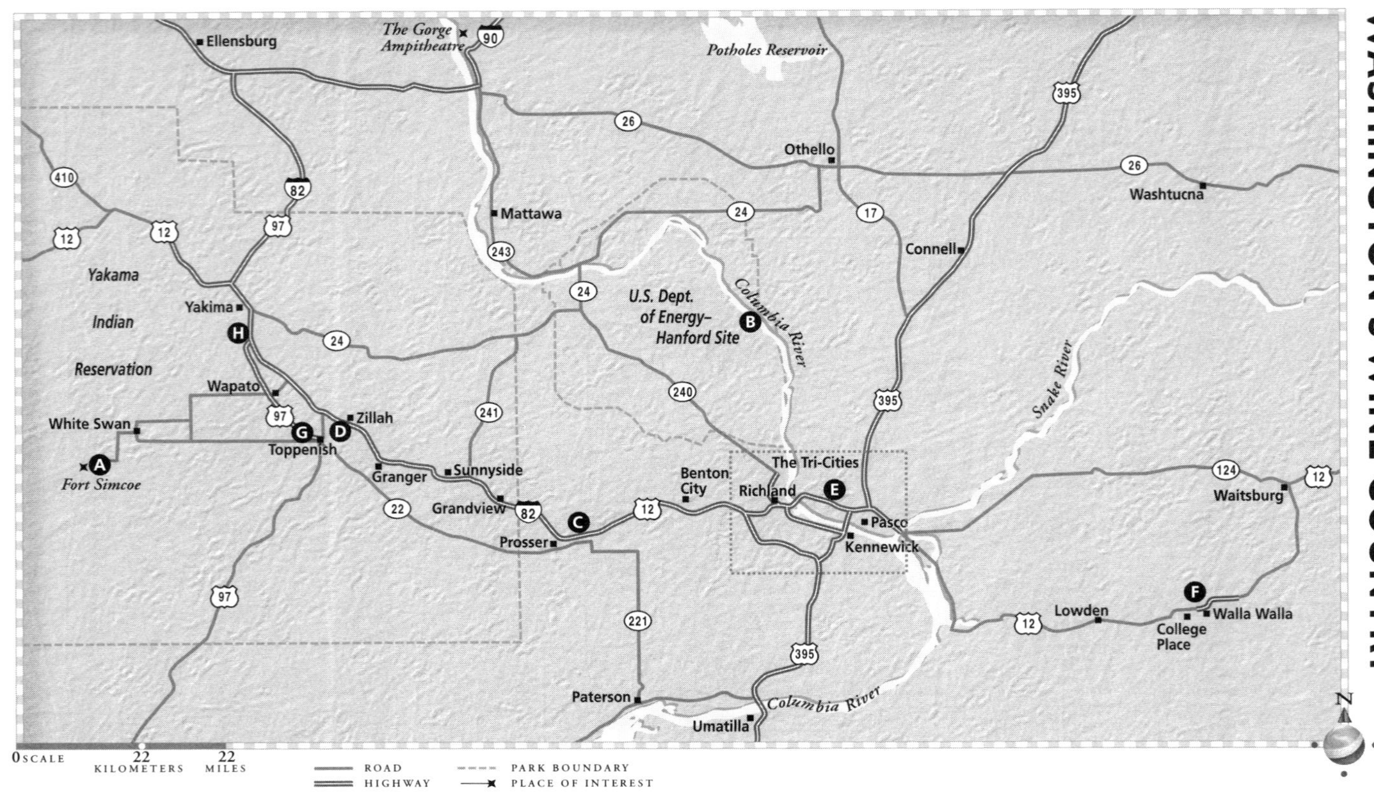

such as apricots, Rainier cherries, Bing cherries, peaches, and corn are plentiful. Apples are harvested August through October—this valley vies with the Wenatchee area as the state's apple capital—and wine grapes shortly thereafter in time for Octoberfest celebrations.

A PERFECT DAY IN THE WINE COUNTRY

Prosser (my hometown) would be the starting point. Take a stroll in the early morning (near sunrise, before it gets hot) through a vineyard, or bike along a country road. If it's a summer Saturday, head to the city park and have a cup of coffee at the informal farmers' market (there are also great farmers' markets in Yakima and Pasco).

Later in the day, stop at a grocery for bread and cheese. Visit Hogue Vineyards (just off I-82 east of town), with its fancy tasting room, to sample wines and pick up pickled asparagus or other Hogue specialties to add to the picnic supplies. Cross the road to Chinook's white clapboard cottage tasting room and sample their merlot. Then picnic on the grounds of either winery, preferably in a shady spot. For ambitious wine-tasting, I'd head for Benton City's Sunset Road, which lies in the midst of a prized microclimate, and visit several wineries there that include Kiona Vineyards and Hedges Cellars (Call Hedges in advance for a tasting appointment, 800/859-9463). In the heat of summer, book lodging with a swimming pool nearby or head to a community pool to cool off.

ORIENTATION

The wine region embraces the Yakima Valley, the Tri-Cities area (where the Yakima, Columbia, and Snake Rivers meet), and the area around Walla Walla. Interstate 82 provides the backbone for the region.

You can reach Toppenish in the Yakima Valley from the Columbia Gorge and Portland. Highway 97 leads from the gorge through the small town of

---

SIGHTS

- **A** Fort Simcoe
- **B** Hanford and Hanford Reach
- **C** Prosser
- **D** Toppenish
- **E** Tri-Cities (Kennewick, Richland, Pasco)
- **F** Walla Walla
- **G** Yakama Nation Reservation
- **H** Yakima
- **H** Yakima Valley Museum

Note: Items with the same letter are located in the same area.

Goldendale (there's an observatory here); the road passes Maryhill Museum (see the Portland chapter).

For lodging and event infomation call the **Yakima Valley Visitors & Convention Bureau,** 800/221-0751, or the **Tri-Cities Visitor and Convention Bureau in Kennewick,** 800/254-5824 or 509/735-8486.

SIGHTSEEING HIGHLIGHTS

★★★★ HANFORD AND HANFORD REACH

Columbia River Journeys, 509/943-0231

In the mid-1940s Hanford, near the Tri-Cities town of Richland, was designated as one of the sites involved in development of materials for the atomic bomb. Because of the project's secrecy, the segment of the Columbia River where the first reactors were built was closed to the public. Reopened only in the 1970s, this free-flowing segment of the Columbia—particularly the area called the Hanford Reach—can be visited on jetboat excursion with **Columbia River Journeys.** This is a special trip that sends shivers down your spine, revealing a beautiful and historic wildlife-rich area, with the defunct reactors rising eerily in the background.

Details: *Cost is $42 for adults, $32 for ages 4 to 11, under 4 free. (4 hours)*

★★★★ TOPPENISH

Chamber and Mural Society, 5A South Toppenish Avenue 509/865-3262

The murals on Toppenish's Old Timers Plaza show the Yakama natives picking hops and getting them to market. Other murals portray the life of the tribes and the settlement of the region. One mural depicts the signing of an 1855 treaty with territorial governor Issac Stevens, that's still in effect today. In all the town has over 50 murals that show the area's history and enliven the buildings (most by noted Western artists). The project restored the town and gives a visually stimulating look at the history of the valley. Toppenish is also home to the **Yakima Valley Rail and Steam Museum,** 509/865-1911, with summer train excursions, and the **American Hop Museum,** 509/865-4677. **Kraff's** clothing store has a wide selection of Western-style Pendleton pillows and blankets.

Details: *20 miles southeast of Yakima between I-82 and Highway 97. (1–2 hours)*

WINE GRAPES IN THE YAKIMA VALLEY

Yakima Valley CVB

★★★★ **WALLA WALLA**

Chamber of Commerce, 509/525-0850

This gracious old college town—home to Whitman College—owns a goodly share of Northwest history. Lewis and Clark stopped here in 1805, then fur trappers arrived and set up a fort. West of town, Marcus Whitman built a mission in the 1830s. The Whitman Massacre in 1847 occurred when the Cayeuse tribe attacked the missionaries, blaming them for a deadly attack of measles. You can visit the **Whitman Mission National Historic Site** interpretive center. The exhibits at **Fort Walla Walla Museum** look at pioneer life. Walla Walla has a festival to celebrate its famous sweet onion. And several of the state's highly regarded wineries are here. Downtown is experiencing increasing historic renovation, and several winery tasting rooms are located here.

Details: *The Whitman Mission is seven miles west of town. (4–6 hours)*

★★★★ **YAKIMA**

Visitors bureau, 509/575-3030 or 800/221-0751

Email: yvvcb@televar.com

TRACTORS AND COMBINES AND BUGGIES, OH MY

Farmers spruce up tractors, combines, and grape harvesters with lights for the Sunnyside Farm Implement Parade early in December. It's a unique valley celebration that has drawn national media attention and a growing number of fans. Winter is not the best time to visit the valley (it can be cold and dismal), but if you're here, check out the parade. For information, call 509/837-5939. Also, the town of Toppenish has added a lighted Western parade with two dozen horse- and mule-drawn wagons, Conestogas, buggies, and stagecoaches in early December.

This city of 60,000 is the major commercial gateway to the Yakima Valley's rich agricultural region. Irrigation in the early part of the century turned the desert of mixed volcanic sediment into richly fertile land. Stop at **Washington's Fruit Place** for a closer look at this agricultural story. **Historic Front Street** downtown offers a look at the city's past, as does the **Yakima Electric Railway Museum,** which offers rides on its antique trolleys.

Details: *Request a brochure from Washington's Fruit Place, 105 South 18th Street, 509/576-3090, less than a mile from I-82 at Exit 33. (4 hours to explore the town, 45 minutes at the fruit interpretive center)*

★★★ PROSSER

Washington's modern-day wine industry started at Washington State University's Extension Center outside this classic small town with its tree-shaded streets, old brick courthouse, and the Yakima River ambling by. The museum in the city park is a worthy and shady stop. Each August, the town draws thousands of folks to the outdoor wine and food festival. In September a hot-air balloon rally fills the skies with color.

Details: *About 50 miles southeast of Yakima on I-82. (2–3 hours)*

★★★ TRI-CITIES (KENNEWICK, RICHLAND, PASCO)

Visitors Bureau, 509/735-8486 or 800/254-5824

Richland, Kennewick, and Pasco spread out broadly around the Columbia River. Hanford Atomic Works is located near Richland. There are shopping centers, business districts, colleges, wineries, and more. The Atomic Cup hydroplane races are held here each summer. In early September Pasco hosts a unique salsa festival.

Details: *(A day or longer)*

★★★ YAKAMA NATION RESERVATION

Highway 97 and Buster Road, Toppenish, 509/865-2800

The reservation blankets nearly 1.5 million acres in southeastern Washington. A cultural center, state park, tepee camping, powwows, and murals convey the history and way of life of the 14 tribes that make up the Yakamas and the role they play in the Yakima Valley. (Note that the tribe and town spellings are different.) The Indian Nation Cultural Center includes a museum, theater, library, gift shop, restaurant, and camping facilities. Browse the 12,000-square-foot museum's dioramas, artifacts, rock art, tule shelters, and clothing. At the museum store, you can find small dream-catchers, some wrapped in white buckskin; check out the moccasins and baskets, too. Many items are made locally by members of the Yakama Nation. Sample frybread and other native foods in the museum restaurant. There is also a large casino complex nearby.

Details: *For visitor information, call 509/865-5121, ext. #436, or write Odessa Johnson, Yakama Nation, P.O. Box 151, Toppenish, WA 98948. Call 509/865-2000 for information on camping, tepees, and RV hookups. Open daily 8 to 10. Admission is charged. (2 hours)*

★★★ YAKIMA VALLEY MUSEUM

2105 Tieton Drive, Yakima, 509/248-0747

This is a really fine museum (and getting better all the time) with a large carriage display, changing exhibits, and a display on apple industry label art. One of the best exhibits here is the working soda fountain on the lower level that re-creates one of Yakima's popular 1950s-era drugstore fountains. Go for a Green River Soda or a big, fat hot fudge sundae.

Details: *In Franklin Park. (1–2 hours)*

★★ FORT SIMCOE

White Swan

This was home to the infantry who watched over the area in the mid-1800s. Restored officers quarters are open to the public. Plan to picnic on the old parade ground. The annual Treaty Day Pow Wow in White

WASHINGTON'S WINE COUNTRY

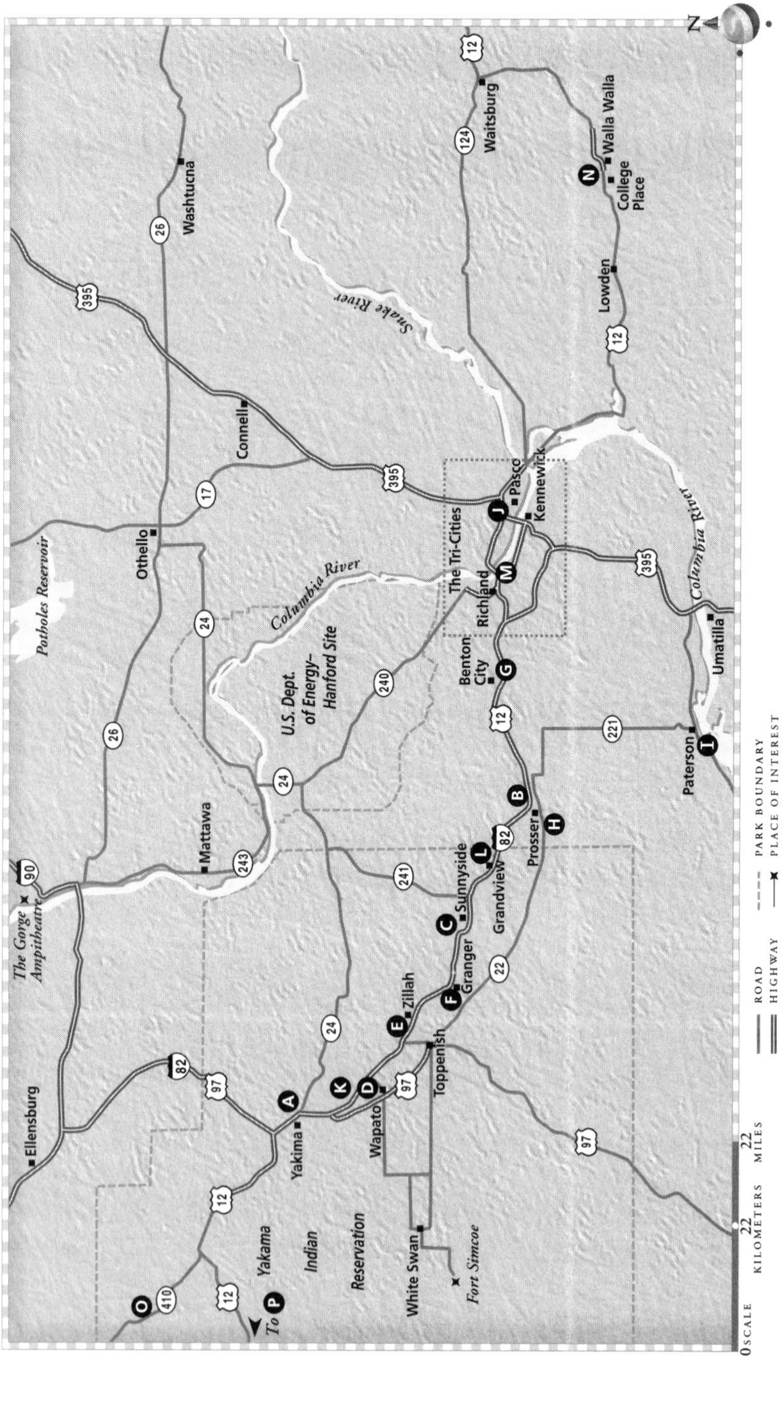

Ellensburg
Yakima
Wapato
Toppenish
White Swan
Fort Simcoe
Yakama Indian Reservation
To P
Zillah
Granger
Grandview
Sunnyside
Prosser
Paterson
Benton City
Richland
The Tri-Cities
Kennewick
Pasco
Umatilla
Columbia River
Snake River
Walla Walla
College Place
Lowden
Waitsburg
Washtucna
Connell
Othello
Mattawa
Potholes Reservoir
The Gorge Ampitheatre
U.S. Dept. of Energy–Hanford Site

ROAD
HIGHWAY
PARK BOUNDARY
PLACE OF INTEREST

0 SCALE 22 KILOMETERS
22 MILES

Swan the first week of June includes arts displays and dancing demonstrations, as does Toppenish's Fourth of July Pow Wow and Rodeo.

Details: *Near the town of White Swan 30 miles west of Toppenish. (2 hours)*

FITNESS AND RECREATION

Floating the Yakima River, especially along the Ellensburg Canyon route, is a favorite summertime activity. Fly-fishing on the Yakima is also a prime activity; The Evening Hatch guide service, 509/962-5959 or www.theeveninghatch.com, offers day and overnight fishing tours.

You can bicycle or jog the Yakima River Greenway. The Apple Tree Golf Course and Restaurant, 509/966-5877 (pro shop), in Yakima is a fun course to play and worth a stop, just to see its signature 17th hole, Apple Island. Other golf courses dot the valley.

The jetboat trip up to Hanford Reach offers not only a look at the original nuclear reactors and the site of White Bluffs—the town that was removed when Hanford was built—but also a look at the rich wildlife of the river, including beaver and white pelicans.

FOOD

In Yakima, **Deli di Pasta,** 509/453-0571, in the historic district on Front Street, is a great choice for fine Italian meals. Nearby in the restored train station is

---

FOOD

- Ⓐ Birchfield Manor
- Ⓑ Chukar Cherries
- Ⓒ Darigold Dairy Fair
- Ⓐ Deli di Pasta
- Ⓓ Donald Mercantile
- Ⓔ El Ranchito Restaurant and Bakery
- Ⓕ Granger Berry Patch
- Ⓐ Grant's Brewery Pub
- Ⓖ Rocky Mountain Chocolate Factory
- Ⓗ Snipes Mountain Brewery

WINERIES

- Ⓑ Chinook Winery
- Ⓘ Columbia Crest Winery
- Ⓙ Gordon Brothers Cellars
- Ⓖ Hedges
- Ⓗ Hinzerling Winery
- Ⓑ Hogue Cellars
- Ⓙ Preston Winery
- Ⓚ Sagelands Vineyard
- Ⓛ Tucker Cellars

LODGING

- Ⓐ Birchfield Manor
- Ⓜ DoubleTree/Hanford House
- Ⓝ Green Gables Inn
- Ⓜ Shilo Inn
- Ⓒ Sunnyside Inn

CAMPING

- Ⓞ American River
- Ⓟ Packwood
- Ⓟ Rimrock Lake

Note: Items with the same letter are located in the same area.

the state's first brewpub, **Grant's Brewery Pub,** 509/575-2922, where you'll find tasty local microbrews. Birchfield Manor (page 197), 509/452-1960, a short drive east of town, offers weekend gourmet dinners worth planning around. **Snipes Mountain Brewery,** 509/837-2739, is a brewpub in Sunnyside in an unexpectedly grand building. It makes a good lunch stop. You can watch cheese making at the **Darigold Dairy Fair** in Sunnyside, 509/837-4321, a fun stop for the whole family with sandwiches, ice cream, and cheeses, including soft curds, to sample and buy.

Donald Mercantile, at Donald off I-82 near Wapato, 509/877-3115, is a fun stop for old-time atmosphere and fresh produce; but if you love fresh peaches, you *must* stop in July for their fresh peach sundaes. The **Rocky Mountain Chocolate Factory,** 509/829-3330, carries chocolate raspberry fudge (among a dozen delicious varieties) for about $8 per pound and offers samples of its daily specials. Frozen red and golden raspberries, boysenberries, loganberries, and huckleberries are sold in gallon containers (about $35 a gallon). Outside Granger at the **Granger Berry Patch,** 509/854-1413, you can pick up raspberry, blackberry, or other preserves. Just outside Prosser, don't miss the free tastings of dried Bing, Rainier, and tart cherries, plus blueberries and cranberries, at **Chukar Cherries,** 320 Wine Country Road, 509/786-2055. The Truffle Chocolate Cherries (dried sweet cherries coated in milk chocolate) make great gifts, if you can bear to give them away.

WINERIES

There are more than 50 wineries in this region, many with tasting rooms and picnic spots located at vineyards or in small towns. You'll need at least three days to seriously explore as there are roughly four areas: the Yakima Valley, Benton City, Tri-Cities area, and Walla Walla wineries. Below are just a few of the wineries you can visit. Call ahead for tasting hours and tour information.

Traveling southeast from Yakima, the first winery sign you'll likely see is for **Sagelands Vineyard** (formerly Staton Hills), 509/877-2112, east of Yakima, in an attractive building with a great valley view. **Tucker Cellars,** 509/837-8701, between Sunnyside and Grandview, offers free tastes of its fresh popcorn daily and sells bags of popped corn and small jars and gallon jugs of unpopped corn, as well as Tucker's honey-pickled asparagus and other food products. **Hinzerling Winery,** 509/786-2163, in Prosser, is the Yakima Valley's oldest family-owned and -operated winery, and wine maker Mike Wallace is a highly visible member of the valley wine-making community. At the **Hogue Cellars,** 509/786-4557, east of Prosser, you'll find jars of pickled asparagus, snap peas, carrots, and spicy beans, as well as other gift items in their newly redone tasting room. Nearby, in a charming clapboard farmhouse, is **Chinook Winery,** 509/786-2725, known especially for its excellent merlot. The biggest, most impressive wine facility in the region is **Columbia Crest Winery,** 509/875-2061, at Paterson, about 30 miles east of Prosser near the Columbia River.

Near Benton City is the Red Mountain area (with its own unique microclimate), along Sunset Road, and a number of wineries worth a detour, including the elegant new **Hedges** château.

Gordon Brothers Cellars tasting room is in Pasco, off I-182 at Exit 9. The **Preston Winery,** 509/545-1990, is one of the pioneer grape growers in the state and a delightful country winery with expansive vineyard vistas.

And there are special events like **Spring Barrel Tasting** on the last weekend of April, coinciding with asparagus season. The **Tri-Cities Northwest Wine Festival** is held in mid-November in Pasco. And each year Yakima Valley wine producers host an open house right after Thanksgiving, offering samplings of varietal wines along with foods prepared to match; recipe cards of the dishes are also available. For a brochure and map to all the wineries, call the **Yakima Valley Wine Growers Association** at 800/258-7270 or pick up ***The Grape Vine,*** a free seasonal guide to valley activities, available in many restaurants, stores, and area lodgings. Or for touring information contact the **Washington Wine Center** in Seattle, 206/667-9463; www.washingtonwine.org.

LODGING

Birchfield Manor, 509/452-1960 or 800/375-3420, a Victorian-style B&B in the country just outside Yakima, offers gourmet meals and a pool. Down the valley, try the pleasant, surprisingly affordable **Sunnyside Inn,** 509/839-5557 or 800/221-4195, a 12-room (eight with Jacuzzis, two with fireplaces) inn. There are a number of convenient **Best Western** motor inns along the route, 800/528-1234. The **DoubleTree/Hanford House** in Richland is right on the Columbia, as is a nearby **Shilo Inn,** 509/946-4661 or 800/222-2244. In Walla Walla, the **Green Gables Inn** B&B, 509/525-5501 or 888/525-5501, www.greengablesinn.com, is a grand home on a quiet street close to Whitman College.

CAMPING

Although there are some campgrounds scattered around Yakima and the Tri-Cities, it can get so hot here in the summer that the best option for campers is to tour the valley, then head west of Yakima along U.S. 12—the White Pass

Highway—to **Rimrock Lake** or **Packwood** (this puts you close to Paradise on Mt. Rainier). Or take SR 410 over Chinook Pass (closed in winter) from U.S. 12 to the campgrounds along the **American River.** These are in the William O. Douglas and Goat Rocks wilderness areas, where the Wenatchee National Forest, 509/653-2205, and the Gifford Pinchot National Forest meet.

13
CENTRAL OREGON

When Sunriver Resort south of Bend, Oregon, was built in the late 1960s, it changed the whole destiny of central Oregon. It was a new concept then—a planned community of residences, bicycle trails, a small airport, restaurants, and a village, set around lakes, rivers, and two beautiful golf courses. And that was just the beginning of this high-desert region's modern-day resort wonders. Now this area is a haven for summer recreation and private residential communities.

There are golf courses galore—more than 24 around Bend alone—and a slew of resorts. Mix that with hot, dry summers, a wildlife-rich landscape, rivers to float, caves to explore, dramatic geologic formations, some wonderful museums, plenty of art, music festivals—and you've got a destination that's a delight for the whole family.

Bend is the epicenter of this resort wonderland. The Western-style town of Sisters, northwest of Bend, and nearby Black Butte Ranch, combine small-town charms with major recreational opportunities. When the snow falls, this is one of the Northwest's most popular winter resort areas, famous for the skiing opportunities on Mt. Bachelor.

There are spectacular geologic features in the area, such as Newberry National Volcanic Monument south of Bend, which includes Lava Butte and Lava Lands, and the John Day Fossil Beds National Monument northeast of Bend. The High Desert Museum between Sunriver and Bend and the Museum at Warm Springs are attractions that offer plenty of exploring on less glorious days.

CENTRAL OREGON

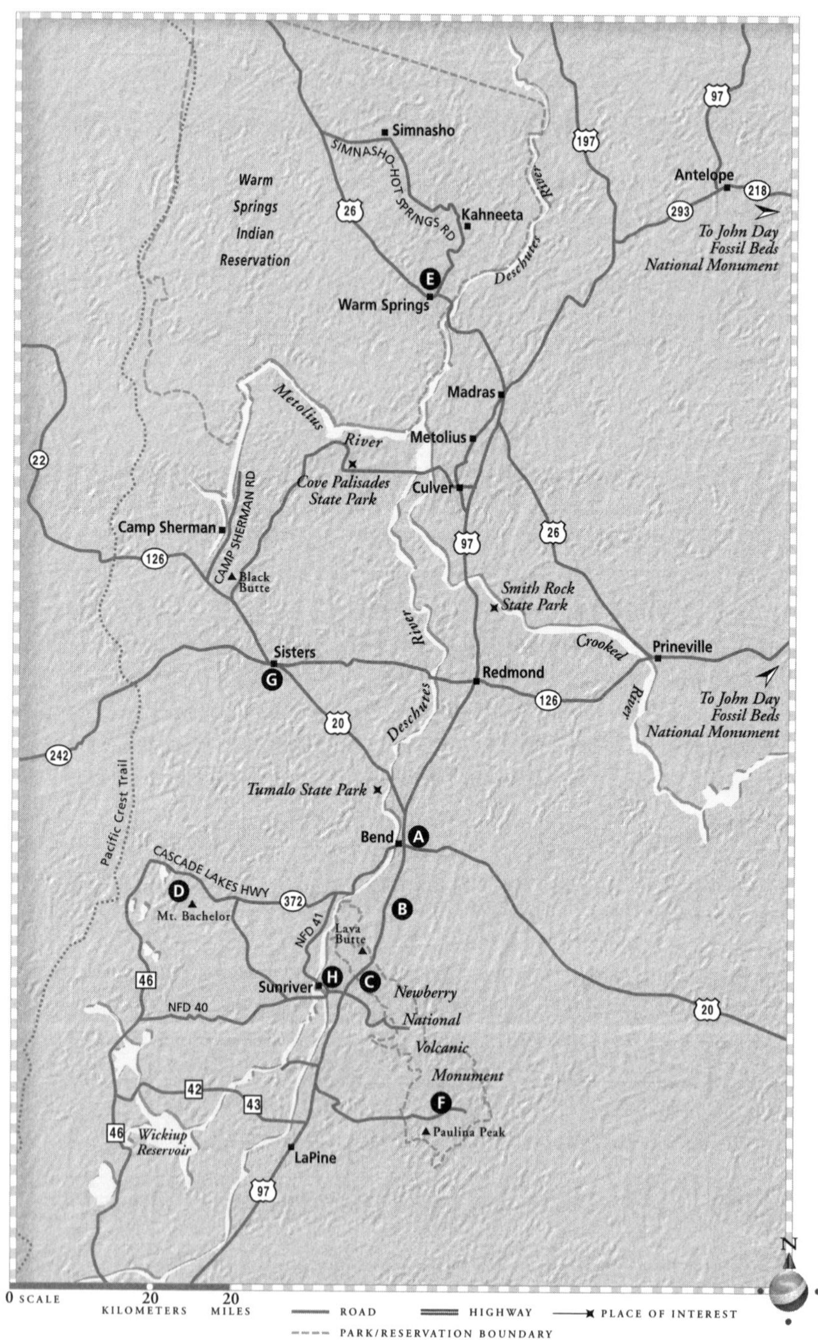

Simnasho
SIMNASHO-HOT SPRINGS RD
Kahneeta
Warm Springs Indian Reservation
Warm Springs
Deschutes River
Antelope
To John Day Fossil Beds National Monument
Madras
Metolius River
Metolius
Cove Palisades State Park
Culver
Camp Sherman
CAMP SHERMAN RD
Black Butte
Smith Rock State Park
Crooked River
Prineville
Sisters
Redmond
Deschutes River
To John Day Fossil Beds National Monument
Tumalo State Park
Pacific Crest Trail
Bend
CASCADE LAKES HWY
Mt. Bachelor
NFD 41
Lava Butte
Sunriver
Newberry National Volcanic Monument
NFD 40
Paulina Peak
Wickiup Reservoir
LaPine
0 SCALE 20 KILOMETERS 20 MILES
ROAD
HIGHWAY
PLACE OF INTEREST
PARK/RESERVATION BOUNDARY
N

A PERFECT DAY IN CENTRAL OREGON

For a perfect warm-weather day, rise early with the sun so you can capture the fresh, dewy sensation left by a cool night before temperatures rise. You can bicycle, play golf (set up a tee time well in advance), or fish, depending on your preference. As the day heats up, float the Deschutes River (use lots of sunscreen) or hang out by a pool. To get out of the sun, spend time inside the High Desert Museum, the Museum at Warm Springs, or in the galleries in Bend or Sisters.

ORIENTATION

Bend—synonymous with central Oregon—is a three-hour drive from Portland along Highway 26 and Highway 97. You can also reach central Oregon from Salem via Santiam Pass (Highways 22 and 20), a prettier yet more winding route that takes about three hours as well. Perhaps the most beautiful drive is from Roseberg in the southern part of the state. From Interstate 5, this route follows Highway 138 along the Umpqua River and takes you by Diamond Lake and Crater Lake; the driving time is about four hours.

A city of 50,000, Bend sits in the midst of high desert country, bordered by the Deschutes National Forest and the Cascade Mountains. Highway 97 cuts through the city center (becoming Division Street within city limits). Sunriver lies about 15 miles south of Bend. The Redmond Municipal Airport (north of Bend) offers flight connections to the area. There is also a small-plane airport at Sunriver.

For a packet of information on lodging and recreation, stop by the spacious visitor center north of town; or contact the Central Oregon Visitors Association, 63085 North Highway 97, Suite 107, Bend, Oregon 97701, 800/800-8334, or the Bend Chamber Visitor and Convention Bureau, 800/905-2363.

If you find yourself short of breath, remember this is high desert country. You're at 3,600 feet altitude and higher in Bend; 4,200 feet at Sunriver. There can be dramatic changes in temperature; 90-degree summer days can cool to the mid-30s at night.

SIGHTS

- **A** Bend
- **B** High Desert Museum
- **C** Lava Butte and Lava Lands Visitor Center
- **D** Mt. Bachelor
- **E** Museum at Warm Springs
- **F** Newberry National Volcanic Monument
- **G** Sisters
- **H** Sunriver Resort

SIGHTSEEING HIGHLIGHTS

★★★★ HIGH DESERT MUSEUM

59800 S. Highway 97, 541/382-4754
www.highdesert.org

This museum combines historical artifacts, living history presentations, and wildlife with indoor and outdoor exhibits. It also features Western and Native American artifacts; new in 1999 is a Native American wing with more than 7,000 items on display. You can also stroll through time in the Earle A. Chiles Center, which re-creates the sounds and sights of historical events in central Oregon. There are wildlife demonstrations and interpretive talks throughout the day. Outside, view live demonstrations in the sawmill and a settlers' cabin.

Details: *Located six miles south of Bend. Open 9 to 5 daily, except major holidays. Admission $7.75, $6.75 for seniors and youths between 13 and 18, $3.75 for ages 5 to 12, ages 4 and under free. (3 hours)*

★★★★ MT. BACHELOR

This 9,065-foot mountain draws skiers and snowboarders from mid-November through the Fourth of July for its 300-plus inches of dry powder, 70 runs, and seven express chairs. In summer, rides to the summit showcase views of the high desert and the Cascades. The route to the mountain from Bend is the Cascades Lake Highway.

Details: *About 22 miles and less than 30 minutes west of Bend. (2 hours–full day)*

★★★★ MUSEUM AT WARM SPRINGS

541/553-3331
www.tmaws.org

Over 7,500 square feet of exhibits include more than 600 items—photographs, rare documents, artifacts, and displays—detailing the history of the Warm Springs, Wasco, and Paiute tribes. Outside, an amphitheater features living history, storytelling, crafts, and dance demonstrations.

Details: *On the Warm Springs Indian Reservation, off Highway 26, an hour north of Bend. Open daily 9 to 5. Admission $6. For more information write: Confederated Tribes of Warm Springs, P.O. Box C, Warm Springs, OR 97761. (3 hours)*

★★★★ NEWBERRY NATIONAL VOLCANIC MONUMENT

www.fsfed@us/rb/deschutes

ART AND MUSIC

Bend is an art rich community, and there are plenty of galleries to explore. Be sure to stop by the Mirror Pond Gallery (Central Oregon Arts Association), 875 N.W. Brooks Street, 541/317-9324, at Riverfront Plaza, in a restored historic house overlooking Mirror Pond. Over 150 artists, most from central Oregon, show here. You can pick up a gallery guide map. Mockingbird Gallery, 869 N.W. Wall Street, 541/388-2107, shows paintings, bronze sculptures, and art glass of Western artists, and Ballantyne & Douglas, 869 N.W. Wall, Suite 104, 541/617-9516, has fine art of regional and national artists of distinction. The Blue Spruce Gallery, south of town, specializes in the pottery of Oregon artists, including richly textured raku items. First Friday Gallery Walks are held monthly (except January) from 5 to 9 p.m.

The summertime Cascade Festival of Music in Bend showcases jazz, pop, rock, blues, and the classics and draws plenty of music fans to riverside Drake Park for picnics and good sound. There's also the Sunriver Music Festival each August. Sisters is a great destination for shopping; quilts are a specialty—each summer the town hosts a popular outdoor quilt show.

Just east of LaPine is a five-mile-wide caldera containing Paulina and East Lakes—two of Oregon's best fishing areas—lava formations, a large obsidian field, and waterfalls. The view from Paulina Peak is breathtaking.

Details: *Naturalist walks are offered in spring and summer through the Deschutes National Forest. The information center on County Road 21 has information, maps, and displays. (4–6 hours)*

★★★★ SUNRIVER RESORT
541/593-1000 or 800/547-3922
www.sunriverresort.com

This is one of the Northwest's best year-round resort destinations. The 35,000-square-foot main lodge reopened in 1998 after $5.5 million was spent renovating the Cascadian-style structure. This is worth a visit, as it overlooks beautiful meadows and mountain scenery typical of central Oregon. The resort includes three 18-hole championship courses, 35 miles of paved bike paths, 28 tennis courts, an indoor racquet club, a marina for canoeing and whitewater rafting, a shopping village, and more.

Details: *15 miles south of Bend; call for information and reservations. (2–4 hours)*

★★★ BEND

800/905-2363 (chamber of commerce)
www.bendchamber.org

This city bustles but retains a small-town feel with Mirror Pond, flanked by Drake Park, at the heart of downtown. There are shops, restaurants, and galleries. The best view of the city is from Pilot Butte State Park, a 500-foot cinder cone. You'll spot nine Cascade peaks as well.

Details: *The visitors center is on U.S. 20, a mile northwest of Bend. (2 hours)*

★★★ LAVA BUTTE AND LAVA LANDS VISITOR CENTER

Highway 97, 541/593-2421 (April through October) or 541/388-5664.

Lava Butte, part of Newberry National Volcanic Monument, is one of about 300 cinder cones that erupted on the flanks of 500-square-mile Newberry Volcano (the Newberry caldera is the site of the eruption). One trail goes over molten land created from lava flow; another leads to native plants. Displays include touch tables and videos that teach about the geology and attractions of the area.

Details: *12 miles south of Bend. Guided tours include panoramic views. Operated by the U.S. Forest Service. Visitor center open daily 9:30 to 5 in summer. Admission charge per car; small charge for shuttle bus to the top of the butte. (1–2 hours)*

★★★ SISTERS

541/549-0251 (chamber of commerce)
www.sisterschamber.com

This Old West–style town west of Bend was established in 1885 as an outpost for Company A of the First Oregon Volunteers. The town hosts a stunning quilt show each summer, when quilts are displayed on the main street of town. They've held a rodeo each June for almost 60 years. Near Sisters is the largest llama breeding ranch in the world.

SIDE TRIP: JOHN DAY FOSSIL BEDS NATIONAL MONUMENT

Fifty million years ago, the 14,000-acre site of John Day Fossil Beds National Monument, northeast of Bend, was almost a tropical forest. Today it contains one of the world's most complete records of natural history. Bones, leaves, wood, nuts, and seeds have been preserved in deposits of volcanic ash. They tell a more fascinating story than Jurassic Park*—of camels, rhinoceroses, three-toed horses, and huge animals that have no modern-day counterparts. Three separate units make up the national monument. Each has unique landscapes, attractions, and scientific importance. It's best to start your exploration at the main visitor center at the Sheep Rock unit. It's open daily from March through October. Here you'll get dramatic views of Picture Gorge and can explore the Cant Ranch House visitors center with its displays of prehistoric animal fossils, including the skull of a saber-toothed cat. The ranch house was built in the early 1900s and is on the National Historic Register. The stunning red and yellow accents to the cone-shaped Painted Hills were created by volcanic ash. This unit is located 10 miles north of the town of Mitchell. The dramatic pinnacles of the Clarno Unit were created from mudflows. All three units are located north of U.S. 26; Clarno lies east of U.S. 97. For more information, contact John Day Fossil Beds National Monument, HCR 82, Box 126, Kimberly, OR 97848; 541/987-2333.*

The ***Kam Wah Chung Museum,*** *on Ing Hay Way in the community of John Day (call City Hall for information, 541/575-0028), celebrates the herbal medicine practices of Chinese mine and railroad workers in the area.*

Details: *Sisters lies on Highway 20 about 22 miles northwest of Bend. (2 hours)*

FITNESS AND RECREATION

For much of the year this is the golf resort capital of the Northwest. Acclaimed resorts like Sunriver, Black Butte, Eagle Crest, and Kah-Nee-Ta focus on the

CENTRAL OREGON

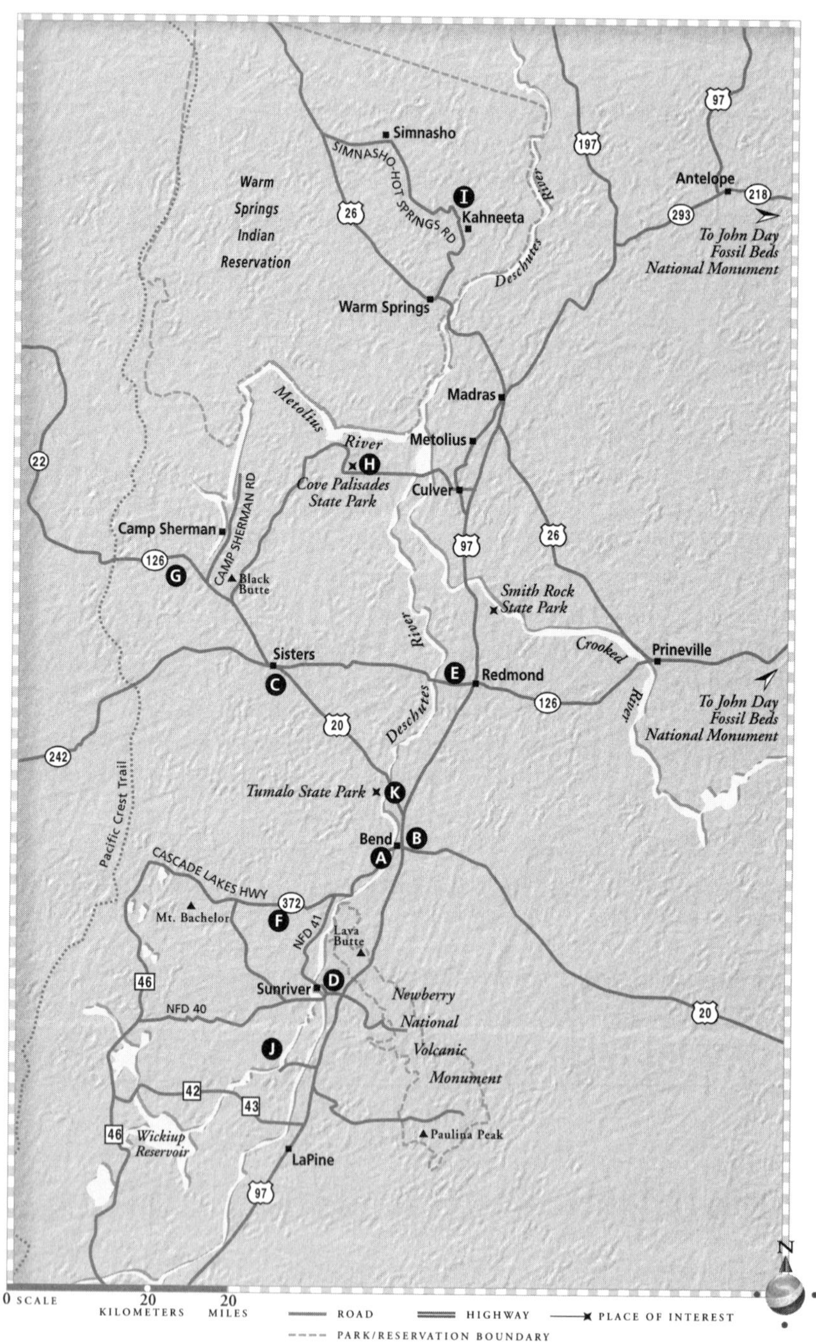

Simnasho
SIMNASHO-HOT SPRINGS RD
Warm Springs Indian Reservation
26
I
Kahneeta
Deschutes River
197
97
Antelope
218
293
To John Day Fossil Beds National Monument
Warm Springs
Madras
Metolius River
Metolius
H
Cove Palisades State Park
Culver
22
Camp Sherman
CAMP SHERMAN RD
126
G
Black Butte
97
26
Smith Rock State Park
River
Crooked River
Prineville
Sisters
C
E
Redmond
126
To John Day Fossil Beds National Monument
20
Deschutes
242
Pacific Crest Trail
Tumalo State Park
K
Bend
B
A
CASCADE LAKES HWY
372
Mt. Bachelor
F
NFD 41
Lava Butte
46
Sunriver
D
Newberry National Volcanic Monument
NFD 40
20
J
42
43
46
Wickiup Reservoir
Paulina Peak
LaPine
97
N
0 SCALE
20 KILOMETERS
20 MILES
ROAD
HIGHWAY
PLACE OF INTEREST
PARK/RESERVATION BOUNDARY

sport. However, a wide variety of other activities and facilities make these great destinations for families. There are 24 courses—public and private—around Bend for all levels of expertise; most offer stunning scenic views that please whether or not your game does. Golfers can request a copy of the Oregon Golf Guide from the state tourism department.

The Metolius River northwest of Bend is a National Wild and Scenic River, and the area around it offers fly-fishing, horseback and llama riding, mountain lodges, mountain biking, and more. Lakes here offer water sports such as water-skiing and windsurfing. The Metolius Recreation Area encompasses Black Butte Ranch; call 541/595-6117 for more information or access their website: www.ohwy.com/or/m/metolrec.htm. The Deschutes River has Class I to Class V river-rafting options.

Mt. Bachelor, southwest of Bend, has six-day lodges, runs of up to two miles in length, and a vertical drop of 3,100 feet. Mountain bikers will find hundreds of miles of single-track trails and plenty of high country areas to explore. With stunning rock spires that tower above Crooked River Canyon, Smith Rock State Park is one of the state's most popular destinations for rock climbers. There are also more doable hiking trails and picnic spots. The park is located nine miles northeast of Redmond.

FOOD

Bend offers more restaurants than any other town in the area. Choices include the historic **Pine Tavern Restaurant,** 967 Northwest Brooks Street, 541/382-5581, with its outdoor terrace and river view, featuring a salad bar and other healthy choices for lunch and dinner. The remarkable **Cafe Rosemary,**

FOOD

- Ⓐ Broken Top Club
- Ⓑ Cafe Rosemary
- Ⓑ Goody's Soda Fountain
- Ⓒ Hotel Sisters and Bronco Billy's Saloon
- Ⓑ Jake's Diner and Truck Stop
- Ⓓ Meadows
- Ⓑ Pine Tavern Restaurant
- Ⓑ Scanlon's
- Ⓓ Sunriver Village

LODGING

- Ⓔ Eagle Crest Resort
- Ⓕ Inn of the Seventh Mountain
- Ⓖ The Lodge at Black Butte Ranch
- Ⓑ River House
- Ⓓ Sunriver Resort

CAMPING

- Ⓗ Cove Palisades State Park
- Ⓘ Kah-Nee-Ta Resort
- Ⓙ LaPine State Park
- Ⓚ Tumalo State Park

Note: Items with the same letter are located in the same area.

222 N.W. Irving, 541/317-0276, is a true gourmet restaurant in an old brick building on a side street in Bend; dinners are pricey (but worth it), while lunch is easier on the budget and still lets you experience the special Cafe Rosemary salad—with fresh greens, fresh fruits, and nuts—that's served at dinner. The **Broken Top Club** restaurant, 61999 Broken Top Drive, 541/383-8210, in the sparkling clubhouse outside Bend, offers mountain views and fine dining options like grilled salmon with a sauce of red peppers. **Scanlon's,** 61615 Mt. Bachelor Drive (just off Century Drive), also offers fine dining and yummy savories like focaccia bread with olive oil for dipping. And for a great ice-cream cone, get in line at **Goody's Soda Fountain,** 957 N.W. Wall Street, 541/389-5185. **Jake's Diner & Truck Stop,** 6120 South Highway 97, 541/382-1041, is popular with locals for its huge portions at regular prices; breakfast is served 24 hours. Folks gather at the **Deschutes Brewery & Public House,** 1044 N.W. Bond Street, 541/382-9242, Bend's first brewpub, for light midday meals, but the place comes alive at night. Or try the **Bend Brewing Co.,** 1019 Brooks Street, 541/383-1599.

The place for special meals at Sunriver Lodge is **Meadows** restaurant, 541/593-1000, with its fabulous views—a good Sunday brunch destination. Take-out or sit-down Chinese and pizza meals can be had in **Sunriver Village.**

In Sisters, the **Hotel Sisters and Bronco Billy's Saloon** at 105 Cascade Street, 541/549-7427, re-creates the atmosphere of a Western town in the early 1900s; seafood and lighter choices are available, but Western-style food, like the lip-smackin' ribs, is the specialty here.

LODGING

The most famous lodging destination in the area is **Sunriver Resort** (see page 204), 541/593-1000 or 800/547-3922. Sunriver Vacations, 800/874-7644, can arrange private condominium, cabin, or home rentals. **Black Butte Ranch,** located on the high meadows of the mid-Cascades on 1,800 forested acres near the Deschutes National Forest, is a residential community, like Sunriver, with two golf courses, tennis courts, swimming pools, and bicycle and jogging trails. It offers views of seven mountain peaks and is quieter and more low-key than Sunriver. A restaurant and accommodations can be found at the **Lodge at Black Butte Ranch,** 800/452-7455, www.blackbutteranch.com. The **River House,** 3075 N. Highway 97 in Bend, 800/547-3928, is near the River's Edge Golf Course, has indoor and outdoor pools and a convenient main thoroughfare location, and offers good value. **Eagle Crest Resort,** 800/682-4786, is set on 700 acres of high desert just west of Redmond on Highway

126 and offers hotel-style rooms or two- to three-bedroom townhome rentals. The **Inn of the Seventh Mountain,** 18575 S.W. Century Drive, Bend, 800/452-6810, puts you up close to Mt. Bachelor and offers all-inclusive vacation packages. There are more economical motels, some bed-and-breakfast inns, and a hostel. Contact the Central Oregon Visitors Association for more information, 800/800-8334.

CAMPING

One of the special camping features of the area is the collection of tepees at **Kah-Nee-Ta Resort** on the Warm Springs Reservation located in dry, rugged country 11 miles north of Warm Springs, off Highway 26. Accommodations range from the village RV park, camping sites, and tepees to lodge rooms. Try their Bird-in-Clay dinner (a specialty) and their special salmon bake. For reservations, call 800/554-4786. Southwest of Madras, the Deschutes, Metolius, and Crooked Rivers merge at Lake Billy Chinook, which is the recreational hub of **Cove Palisades State Park,** named after the basalt formations (palisades) that tower over the lake. For reservations, call 800/452-5687. Just five miles northwest of Bend is **Tumalo State Park,** 541/388-6055, reservations 800/452-5687. It offers more than 80 sites and good fishing and lies along the Deschutes River. The river also runs along the outskirts of the campsites at **LaPine State Park,** 30 miles southwest of Bend. It's open year-round and has more than 140 sites, three yurts, and five cabins; call 800/452-5687 for reservations. A day-use cabin on picnic grounds accommodates group gatherings and is centrally located to Cascade Lakes Highway, half an hour from Newberry Crater. For more information, call the ranger at 541/536-2428.

Scenic Route: Oregon Trail Towns

This is perhaps the oldest scenic trail in the Northwest. It was the final approach to the Willamette Valley ("the land of milk and honey") for thousands of settlers who made their way west in the huge 2,000-mile migration that began in 1847. More than 300,000 settlers crossed this wagon route in what is called the biggest overland migration ever. In 1998, the Tamustalik Cultural Center, near Pendleton, was completed. It's the last of five major centers marking significant aspects of the journey. Some of the centers are building restorations; most are impressive new facilities.

This drive primarily follows Interstate 84 from the Idaho border to Portland and leads through rolling dry hills, along the dramatic Columbia Gorge to the forests and valleys of western Oregon. As you drive, remember all those weary pioneers who crept along the trail in wagons into a mysterious wilderness and a new life. Thank your automobile and the highway gods. And keep your gas tank full.

Our route begins 50 miles northwest of Boise, Idaho, at Ontario, Oregon, where the Malheur, Payette, Owyhee, and Snake Rivers converge. Here you'll find Four Rivers Cultural Center, 676 S.W. Fourth Avenue, Ontario, 888/211-1222 or 541/889-8191, email: frcc@micron.net, nestled in Treasure Valley beneath the Elkhorn Mountains. Exhibits in the 10,000-square-foot museum reflect the mix of cultures residing in this area—the

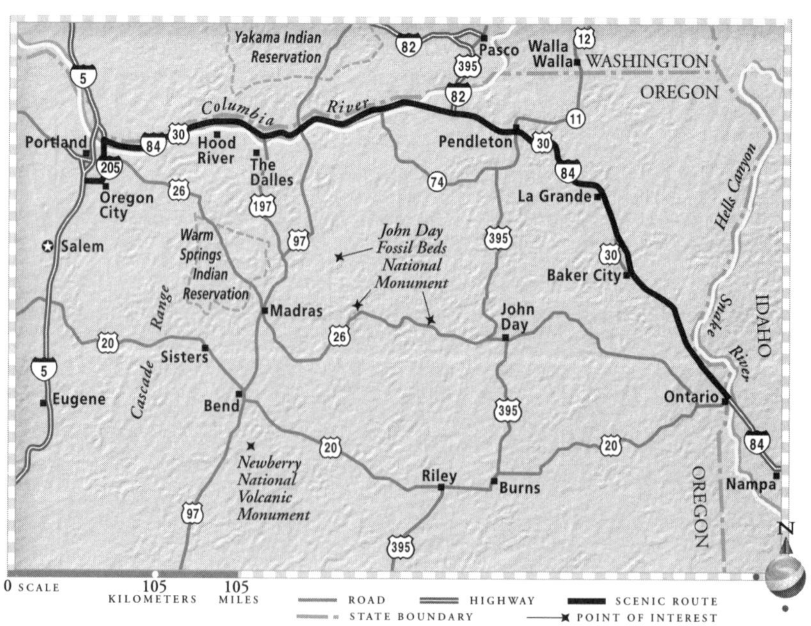

Paiute Indians, the Basque descendants of early settlers (many raised sheep), and Japanese Americans released from WWII internment camps to work in the growing farming industry along with the Hispanics who migrated north from Mexico. Outside the center is a Japanese garden designed by internationally renowned landscape artist Hoichi Kurisu.

The next stop is at the National Historic Oregon Trail Center at Flagstaff Hill, six miles east of I-84, just north of Baker City, 541/523-1843 or 800/523-1235. This is where the pioneers caught their first real glimpse of the promised land, a sweeping vista that is much the same as it was 150 years ago. The museum tells the pioneers' story through exhibits and living history presentations. Nearby are nearly five miles of interpretive trails where you can see actual ruts left by the wagon wheels.

Built in 1998, the Tamustalik Cultural Institute, east of Pendleton at the base of the Blue Mountains, 541/276-3873, chronicles the history and culture of the confederated Umatilla tribes and looks at the impact the thousands of settlers had on their cultures up through the mid-1900s. The museum store features native arts and crafts.

Continuing northwest on I-84, the next stop is at the Columbia Gorge Discovery Center/Wasco County Historical Museum, one mile west of the Dalles off I-84, 541/296-8600; watch for signs. This facility opened in 1997 and features special exhibits and programs chronicling the geologic story that began more than 40 million years ago when the Columbia Gorge was born of volcanoes, earthquakes, and raging floods. It looks, too, at the 10,000 years or so of known history of the Native Americans along the river.

And finally you'll come to the End of the Oregon Trail Interpretive Center in Oregon City, 10 miles south of I-84 just west of Portland (off Interstate 205 at Exit 10). Here, three 50-foot-tall covered wagon–shaped buildings dominate Abernethy Green, the main arrival area for the emigrants. The center is a living history exhibit with eight performances daily in the summer (call in advance for times, 503/657-9336). Each year, mid-July through early August, the Oregon Trail Pageant (a separate group) presents an outdoor historical drama. For ticket reservations, call 503/657-0988 or check out www.teleport.com/~norrisa/otp_home.shtml.

14
MEDFORD AREA

The mesmerizing blue depths of Crater Lake, the magic of Shakespeare, and the seductive thrill of riding the Rogue River are what draw many to this southwestern corner of Oregon. Gold, discovered in the Rogue Valley in 1852, is what originally drew the white settlers. Until then, the residents were the Rogue Indians.

Once the bustling center of gold fever, Jacksonville, a National Historic Landmark town, lost out in a business disagreement with the Oregon & California Railroad when the railroad reached southern Oregon in 1883. The railroad built its station five miles east of Jacksonville in what's now known as Medford. Jacksonville is home to the Peter Britt Music Festival, during which outdoor performances fill summer nights with melody. Medford, a city of about 50,000, is the commercial hub of the region's fruit growing industry and the home of mail-order fruit marketer Harry & David and rose purveyor Jackson & Perkins. Nearby in Ashland, the Oregon Shakespeare Festival delights theater and non-theater buffs alike, who enjoy classic and contemporary productions in this picturesque village setting.

The sleeping giant is the amazing Siskiyou mountain range that stretches west to the ocean. Millions of years ago, it was an island in the Pacific that eventually folded up and reconnected to the continent. There are misty crumpled valleys, forebidding rivers (the Illinois River has even more challenging rapids than the Rogue), torrentially wet winters, blistering summers, and unusual flora such as the insect-eating pitcher plant. The Rogue River, protected by the Wild and Scenic Rivers Act, winds its way through here. It's no wonder that a 30-mile stretch of it is one of the remotest in the country.

A PERFECT DAY IN THE ROGUE VALLEY

A perfect day would dawn clear and warm, and almost the whole of it would be spent out-of-doors. After a night in a cozy B&B in or near Ashland, head to Lithia Park for an early morning walk along Ashland Creek to breathe in the warm summer scent of the forest and stop to see the swans on its lake. Then drive to Crater Lake, stopping at Beth's for lunch or a piece of pie, but eating light. Back in Ashland, splurge on an early dinner at Primavera. End your day with a performance at the Oregon Shakespeare Festival's outdoor Elizabethan Theater (take a cushion along, or plan to rent one, for the hard outdoor seats).

ORIENTATION

Medford is about five hours and 273 miles south of Portland. This city of about 60,000 is the commerical hub of southwesternern Oregon. While there is a regional bus service, it's not geared to tourists, and this is an area best explored by car. United and Horizon fly into the Rogue Valley International Medford Airport, the air hub for this part of Oregon. Ashland lies to the south, Crater Lake to the east, and the Rogue River and surrounding national forest to the west.

The **Medford Visitor and Convention Bureau's** visitors center is located just off Interstate 5 at Exit 27 and is open during the summer; its office downtown, at 304 S. Central Avenue, is open year-round. For information, contact 541/779-4847 or 800/448-4856, www.medfordchamber.com. Contact the **Ashland Chamber of Commerce** at 541/482-3486 or www.ashlandchamber.com.

SIGHTSEEING HIGHLIGHTS

★★★★ ASHLAND

Oregon Shakespeare Festival, 541/482-4331
www.orshakes.org

Nestled in the forest-rich foothills of the Siskiyou Mountains, Ashland is a charming village filled with historic homes and many top-notch restaurants. The **Oregon Shakespeare Festival** draws visitors from all over the world (and has done so for more than 50 years).

MEDFORD AREA

N

Klamath National Wildlife Refuge
Winema National Forest
Collier Memorial State Park
Chiloquin
Klamath Falls
Lower Klamath National Wildlife Refuge
97
Upper Klamath Lake
Agency Lake
62
Fort Klamath
K
Kimball State Park
B
Crater Lake
H
Crater Lake National Park
Pacific Crest Trail
Rogue River National Forest
Cascade Range
230
Prospect
140
66
Umpqua National Forest
Eagle Point
Rogue River
J
A
I
E
Mt. Ashland
Ashland
Talent
Medford
C
D
Jacksonville
238
MT ASHLAND SKI RD
Applegate River
Valley of the Rogue State Park
Myrtle Creek
5
Grants Pass
99
Murphy
Oregon Caves National Monument
F
Rogue River National Forest
46
G
199
Cave Junction
42
Siskiyou National Forest
OREGON
CALIFORNIA

ROAD
HIGHWAY
PARK/AREA BOUNDARY
PLACE OF INTEREST
STATE BORDER
TRAIL

0 SCALE 20 KILOMETERS
20 MILES

Most theater buffs make their reservations a year in advance (see page 218). **Lithia Park,** a beautiful 100-acre area, provides a perfect accent for the festival's theater complex that rises above it. A small historic plaza downtown is a gathering spot. Ashland's intimate atmosphere makes you want to park the car and explore. Southern Oregon State University is here. Small galleries, shops, and interesting bookstores beckon for browsing. Nearby, jetboats and river rafts ply the wild and scenic Rogue and Klamath Rivers.

Details: *12 miles south of Medford off I-5. (2–4 hours, or overnight for a theater visit)*

★★★★ CRATER LAKE NATIONAL PARK

541/594-2211 (current road and weather information)
www.nps.gov/crla

Oregon's only national park is a humdinger. Crater Lake, the deepest lake in the United States, is a caldera formed thousands of years ago when Mt. Mazama collapsed in explosive volcanic eruptions. It lies on the crest of the Cascade Range, 80 miles northeast of Medford. Built in 1915, the impressive Crater Lake Lodge was completely renovated and reopened in 1995. Activities here include hiking and bus tours of Rim Drive, narrated boat trips to Wizard Island (in the middle of the lake), launch trips to the lodge and exhibit building at Rim Village, nature hikes, and naturalist programs. **The Pinnacles** are surrealistic spires of eroded volcanic rock near the lake.

SIGHTS

- **A** Ashland
- **B** Crater Lake National Park
- **C** Harry & David's Country Village
- **C** Jackson & Perkins
- **D** Jacksonville
- **E** Mt. Ashland Ski Area
- **F** Oregon Caves National Monument
- **C** Southern Oregon History Center

FOOD

- **G** Caves Fountain
- **H** Crater Lake Lodge
- **I** New Sammy's Cowboy Bistro
- **F** Oregon Caves Lodge

LODGING

- **H** Crater Lake Lodge
- **C** DoubleTree Hotel
- **F** Oregon Caves Lodge
- **C** Under the Greenwood Tree

CAMPING

- **J** KOA Glenyan
- **K** Mazama Village

Note: Items with the same letter are located in the same area.

Details: 72 miles east of Medford on SR 62. Pets are not allowed in public buildings or on trails. Admission is $5 per private vehicle per day; $2 per bicycle. (half day minimum)

★★★★ OREGON CAVES NATIONAL MONUMENT

541/592-3400 (lodge)

www.oregoncaves.com

These 480 acres of marble caves with columns and curtains of calcite form a series of beautiful underground galleries and rooms; just be prepared to climb a lot of steps. Above ground, the historic **Oregon Caves Lodge** is a classic, offering rustic rooms.

***Details:** 80 miles southwest of Medford. Guided tours conducted daily. Admission charged; children under 6 not admitted. Open year-round. (2 hours)*

★★★ JACKSONVILLE

541/899-8118

www.jacksonvilleoregon.org

There are more than 80 historic homes and buildings in this National Historic Landmark town, five miles west of Medford, that boomed in the mid-1800s as a gold town. It's a charming, out-of-the-way detour and perhaps best known as home to the Peter Britt summer music festival, mostly held in outdoor venues.

***Details:** Take State Route 238 west off I-5. For information on self-guided tours, go to the Rogue River Valley Railway Depot at Oregon and C Streets. Open from June to August daily 10 to 4; Saturday to Monday 10 to 4 the rest of the year. (1 hour)*

★★ HARRY & DAVID'S COUNTRY VILLAGE

1314 Center Drive, Medford, 541/776-2277

www.harryanddavid.com

Probably you or someone you know has received a fruit basket filled with juicy pears and more from this leading mail-order fruit and gift company. You can tour their plant and visit their Country Store, packed with fruits, gourmet foods, and samples. Jackson & Perkins flowers (owned by the same company) are available here.

***Details:** South Gateway Center (off I-5 at Exit 27), Medford. Call for reservations for free tours of the plant and bakery. (1 hour)*

★★ JACKSON & PERKINS

2518 South Pacific Highway, Medford, 800/872-7673

www.jacksonandperkins.com

A WINNING COMBO: OREGON BLUE CHEESE AND PEARS

Medford's Harry & David's fruit baskets have made Oregon pears justly famous. Nearby in Central Point, about four miles north of Medford, is a much more low-key and less well-known company that produces another famous regional food. Since the 1950s Oregon Blue Cheese has been made at the Rogue River Valley Creamery by the Vella family. You can visit the creamery, 311 North Front Street, Central Point, 541/664-2233, and get an informal tour, taste samples, and buy cheese. They make the cheese twice a week, often on Mondays and Wednesdays, but call ahead as their schedule can change.

Gardeners will recognize this mail-order company as the world's largest private rose grower. Their test and display gardens near Medford are worth a visit.

Details: *The gardens can be seen any time of day (just down the road from the Country Village); May through September are prime bloom months. You may picnic on the grounds. (15 minutes–1 hour)*

★★ MT. ASHLAND SKI AREA

541/482-2897

www.mtashland.com

This 7,500-plus-foot mountain showcased within the Siskiyous is a smaller, low-key family skiing and snowboarding destination, with beginner to advanced slopes; four chairlifts provide access to more than 23 runs.

Details: *18 miles south of Ashland. (Full day)*

★★ SOUTHERN OREGON HISTORY CENTER

106 N. Central Avenue, Medford, 541/773-6536

www.sohs.org

Historical and cultural exhibits of the Southern Oregon Historical Society are on display at this center in downtown Medford.

Details: (1 hour)

FITNESS AND RECREATION

Theater is big recreation in this region, and outdoor evening theater performances at the Oregon Shakespeare Festival run from mid-February through October. There are 11 plays presented each season. For tickets or information, contact the box office, 541/482-4331, www.orshakes.org. For music under the stars, try the Peter Britt Music Festival, which runs June to September, for schedule and information, contact 800/882-7488 or www.brittfest.org.

Movies have immortalized the Rogue—think Meryl Streep in *The River Wild* and John Wayne in *Rooster Cogburn.* Outfitters offering river trips are plentiful. Raft Trips Adventure Center in Ashland, 541/488-2819 or 800/444-2819, www.raftingtours.com, schedules adventure tours for white-water rafting and biking; they also rent bikes.

The Southern Oregon Reservation Center, 800/547-8052, www.sorc.com, offers one-call information on theater reservations, river trip reservations, lodging, and more.

FOOD

In Ashland, **Primavera,** 241 Hargadine, 541/488-1994, has great appetizers, pasta, seafood, and vegetarian dishes, and a consistent and well-deserved reputation as a must-go—as does the **Chateaulin,** 50 East Main Street, 541/482-2264, fun for hors d'oeuvres and wine before the theater. For yummy Italian food, try **Il Giardino,** 5 Granite Street, 541/488-0816. Many restaurants have café or bistro menus, lighter choices for before-theater meals. For a quick lunch downtown, try **Pangea,** 272 East Main, 541/552-1630, which offers delightful grilled or wrap sandwiches. The **Standing Stone Brewing Company,** 101 Oak Street, 541/482-2448, is a light, airy brewpub and a reasonable stop for lunch or dinner.

Halfway between Ashland and Talent on Highway 99, **New Sammy's Cowboy Bistro,** 541/535-2779, serves dinners only Thursday through Sunday (fewer days in winter), seats only a handful of people, and has no sign (call for directions and reservations), but plenty of gourmets know about it; it's funky, tiny, and booked months ahead.

Crater Lake Lodge offers great views with dinner, whether you're staying there or not. Sample regional fare in the dining room at **Oregon Caves Lodge** or try an ice-cream cone from the **Caves Fountain,** a 1930s-style soda fountain at 20000 Caves Highway, Cave Junction, 541/592-3400.

LODGING

Ashland is known for its many bed-and-breakfast lodgings. Most homes are

ASHLAND

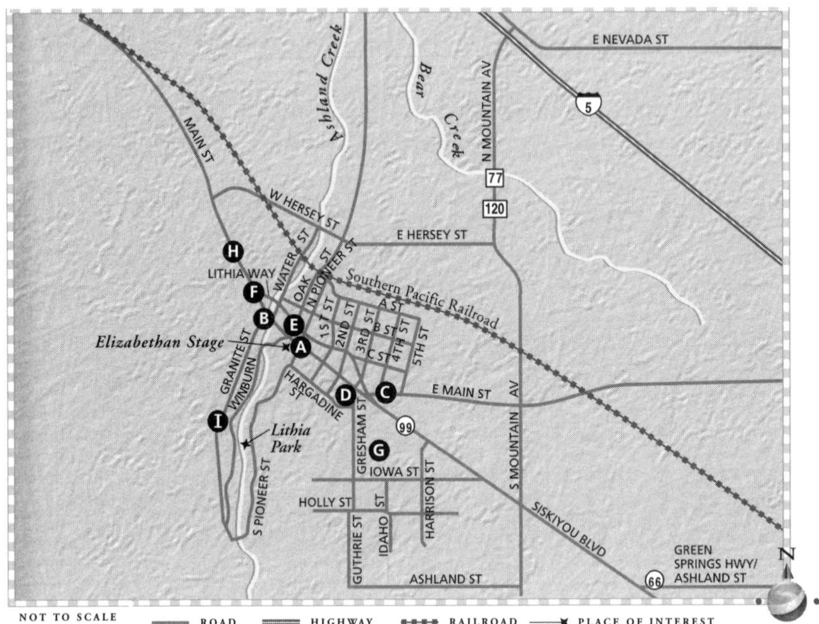

FOOD

- Ⓐ Chateaulin
- Ⓑ Il Giardino
- Ⓒ Pangea
- Ⓓ Primavera
- Ⓔ Standing Stone Brewing Company

LODGING

- Ⓕ The Bard's Inn
- Ⓖ Chanticleer Inn
- Ⓗ Iris Inn Bed and Breakfast
- Ⓘ Lithia Rose Lodging-on-the-Park

older, and sometimes the rooms are small. However, it's fun to be within walking distance of the theater. The **Lithia Rose Lodging-on-the-Park,** 163 Granite Street, 541/482-1882 or 800/354-9914, across from Lithia Park, boasts a well-deserved reputation for great breakfasts and a charming back garden. The bungalow-style **Chanticleer Inn,** 120 Gresham Street, 541/482-1919 or 800/898-1950, a longtime lodging that's comfortable and quiet, and the Victorian-style **Iris Inn Bed and Breakfast,** 800/460-7650, are a bit further away but also popular. Most B&Bs have a two-night minimum. **The Bard's Inn,** 132 Main Street, 800/528-1234, is a Best Western lodging that has a swimming pool—very inviting in the heat of summer.

BOOKS FOR THE ROAD

If you're on a long road trip, stop by Blackstone Audiobooks on the south edge of Ashland. They offer an unexpectedly convenient service for travelers—you can rent books for 10 to 45 days and return them in mailers provided by Blackstone. Call for directions, 541/482-9239, www.blackstoneaudio.com.

Out of town toward Jacksonville, **Under the Greenwood Tree,** 3045 Bellinger Lane, Medford, 541/776-0000, is a 125-year-old historic country B&B with huge trees, a beautiful garden, and the feel of a plantation; breakfasts are the creation of owner Renate Ellam, a Cordon Bleu–trained chef.

These are only a few suggestions; there are hundreds of rooms in Ashland and Jacksonville inns, and two services can provide more information. The Ashland Area Association of Oregon Bed & Breakfast Guild offers reservations, information, and brochures, 800/983-4667; the Ashland B&B Clearinghouse, 541/488-0338, lists not only B&Bs but also old hotels, motels, and new inns. The Southern Oregon Reservation Center, 800/547-8052, offers ticket and lodging package combinations—great for visitors who haven't planned ahead for theater tickets, which can be hard to come by spontaneously.

The **Oregon Caves Lodge,** 20000 Caves Highway, Cave Junction, 541/592-3400, is a classic, offering rustic rooms; it's fun to stay here even if the guest rooms have paper-thin walls. The patio of **Crater Lake Lodge,** 541/830-8700, offers one of the best views in the whole state; a stay at this refurbished national park lodge is a real treat.

Located centrally in Medford, the **DoubleTree Hotel** at 200 North Riverside Avenue, 800/222-8733 or 541/779-5811, has 180-plus rooms and two outdoor swimming pools.

CAMPING

To camp near Ashland, contact **Glenyan Campground,** which offers more than 60 sites near Emigrant Lake about six and a half miles southeast of Ashland on Highway 66; call 541/488-1785 for reservations. **Mazama Village,** 541/594-2255, ext. 3705, at Crater Lake's south entrance, offers almost 200 campsites on a first-come, first-served basis.

Scenic Route: Southwest Oregon

This route takes you from high mountain views at Crater Lake to where the Rogue River meets the Pacific. On Interstate 5, halfway between Medford and Grants Pass, take Exit 40 at Gold Hill and head north on Highway 234, then east on Highway 62 to Crater Lake, where you can drive the rim loop in summer. Tour boats visit Wizard Island, in the center of the caldera (a crater with a diameter many times that of the original volcanic vent). Historic Crater Lake Lodge, restored and reopened in 1995, sits on the rim.

From here go north to Diamond Lake Resort on Highway 138. Continue west to Roseburg, along the Umpqua River. Visit wineries or fish or raft here. From Roseburg go north on I-5 and take Exit 136 and Highway 138 to Elkton. West of Elkton you reach the ocean and the wildlife-rich area around Reedsport. Explore the Dean Creek Elk Viewing Area east of Reedsport, or whale-watch in Winchester Bay.

Highway 101 takes you through coastal forests and along beaches and dunes through Coos Bay, Bandon, Port Orford, and Brookings. The route dips into California, then follows the Smith River northeast along Highway 199 to Cave Junction; visit Oregon Caves National Monument.

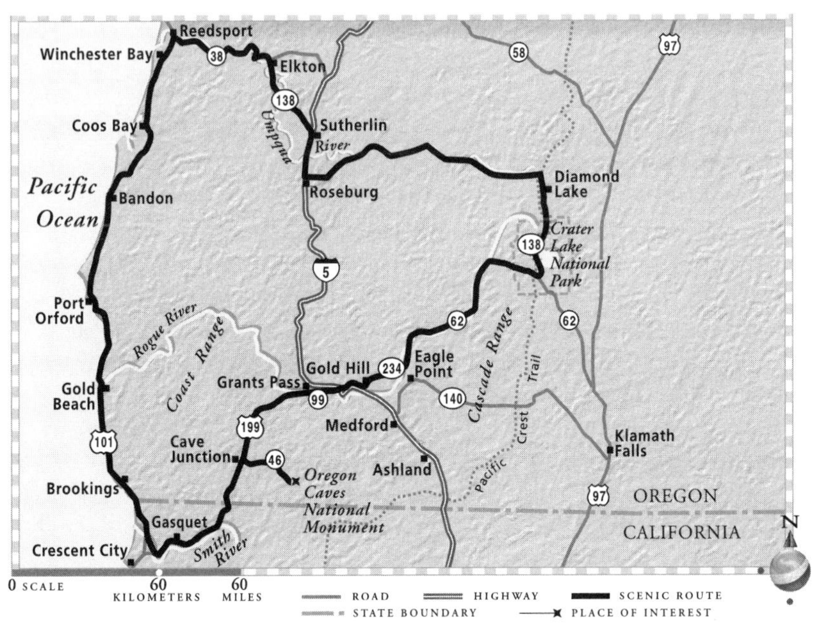

15 WILLAMETTE VALLEY

After crossing the endless midwestern flatlands and battling the uncompromising Rockies, the pioneers of the 1840s surely must have thought they had reached the Promised Land when their dusty Conestoga wagons rolled into the Willamette Valley—the fabled Oregon Territory. Before them was a vision that could have been brushed by an eighteenth-century landscape artist. Grasslands stretched 100 miles north and south in fertile elegance, mixed generously with majestic fir trees. Here and there, commanding Oregon oaks lent dignity to the pastoral scene.

A century and a half later, this elegant, bucolic valley, cradle of much of Oregon's history, nurtures a different influx of pioneers: wine makers. Along with the wineries, a good crop of bed-and-breakfast and a growing number of restaurants have developed.

Summer is the most rewarding time to visit. Wildflowers are out, fruits and produce are at their peak, and the wineries have new releases and longer tasting-room hours. Produce stands, historic small towns, charming inns, picturesque covered bridges, and college towns (there are three universities here) offer plenty to explore.

Many travelers take I-5 for speed and miss the real beauty of the Willamette Valley. A loop drive, beginning at Portland, Eugene, or Springfield, exploring 99E and 99W (which parallel Interstate 5), gives you the feel of the region at a slower pace. It's definitely worth the side trip, and it's even more rewarding if you stay overnight.

A PERFECT DAY IN THE WILLAMETTE VALLEY

Stay in the country at a B&B. And whether it has a great view or you drive to a high viewpoint or take a hot-air balloon ride, make sure you get a panorama of the green, green valley with Mt. Hood looming to the east. A perfect summer day will include exploring produce stands and wineries, many of which offer great views of the valley and picnic spots. Explore the small towns and try an out-of-the-way excursion to the Briggatine Monastery to buy fudge or to Mt. Angel for a look at the beautiful church. End your perfect day by finding a country restaurant for dinner and then retire to your cozy B&B.

ORIENTATION

Interstate 5 cuts through the Willamette Valley on a north/south line from Portland 115 miles to Eugene. However, that's the least pretty way to see the valley. Two slower but better touring routes are Highways 99E and 99W. The latter is the valley's classic wine touring trail, leading you from southwest Portland (a congested area for driving) and Newberg through the valley's north, central, and southern wine regions to Eugene. The university town of Corvallis is the midway point to break up a two-day wine touring trip. For quieter, off-the-beaten path lodgings, choose B&Bs away from towns.

Highway 18, southwest of McMinnville, leads to Lincoln City; U.S. 20, west of Corvallis, cuts west to Newport. Both central Oregon coast destinations combine well with Willamette wine country touring.

The Willamette Valley Visitors Association (associated with the Albany Convention and Visitors Association) provides general touring maps and valley information; call 541/928-0911 or 800/526-2256, or check the website: www.albanyorvisit@proaxis.com.

SIGHTSEEING HIGHLIGHTS

★★★★ ALBANY

Visitors Center, 300 Second Avenue SW, 541/928-0911 or 800/526-2256, www.albanyvisitors.com

This town boasts about 700 buildings on the National Historic Register; self-guided walking tour brochures help you locate them. Several areas feature construction from the 1840s onward. A half-dozen covered bridges lie near town.

Details: *(2–4 hours)*

WILLAMETTE VALLEY

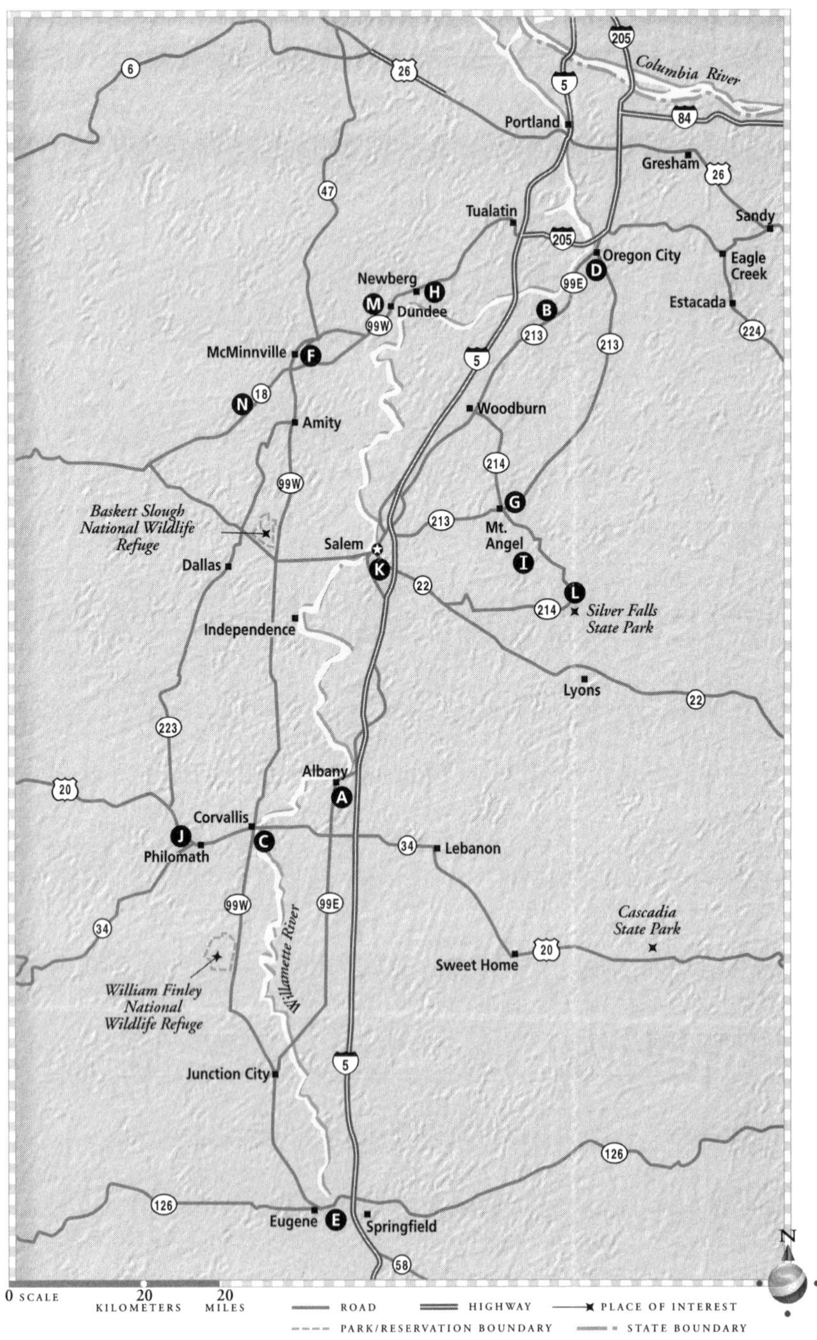

★★★★ CHAMPOEG STATE PARK

General information, 503/678-1251

Camping reservations, 800/452-5687

On the banks of the Willamette River, Champoeg State Park offers hiking and biking trails, a garden with native plants, a visitors center and museum with historic exhibits, and a museum store. Picnic sites and overnight camping are available.

Details: *Halfway between Portland and Newberg, off Interstate 5 at Exit 278. Day-use admission fee about $3. (2–4 hours)*

★★★★ COVERED BRIDGES

Lane County Visitors Association, 800/547-5445

www.visitlanecounty.org

About 50 covered bridges of the more than 400 built in Oregon still exist, and most are in the Willamette Valley. More than 20 bridges are in Lane County, and several lie around Albany and Eugene. Specific bridge information is on the county's bridge website: www.viser.net/~draft/bridges/bridges.shtml.

SIGHTS

- Ⓐ Albany
- Ⓑ Champoeg State Park
- Ⓒ Corvallis
- Ⓓ End of the Oregon Trail Interpretive Center
- Ⓔ Eugene
- Ⓕ McMinnville
- Ⓖ Mt. Angel
- Ⓗ Newberg
- Ⓘ Oregon Garden
- Ⓙ Philomath
- Ⓚ Salem
- Ⓛ Silver Falls State Park

FOOD

- Ⓜ Firestone Farms
- Ⓕ Golden Valley Brewery & Pub
- Ⓒ Nearly Normal's
- Ⓕ Nick's Italian Cafe
- Ⓜ Red Hills Provincial Dining
- Ⓔ Sweetwaters Restaurant and Lounge
- Ⓜ Tina's
- Ⓜ Your Northwest

WINERIES

- Ⓗ Duck Pond Cellars
- Ⓝ Oregon Wine Tasting Room
- Ⓗ Rex Hill Vineyards and Winery

LODGING

- Ⓒ Hanson Country Inn
- Ⓕ Orchard View Inn
- Ⓗ Partridge Farm
- Ⓗ Spring Creek Llama Ranch
- Ⓗ Springbrook Hazelnut Farm
- Ⓕ Steiger Haus
- Ⓔ Valley River Inn
- Ⓕ Youngberg Hill Ranch

CAMPING

- Ⓑ Champoeg State Park
- Ⓛ Silver Falls State Park

Note: Items with the same letter are located in the same area.

Details: *Touring maps are available from the Lane County Visitor Association. (Time varies)*

★★★★ END OF THE OREGON TRAIL INTERPRETIVE CENTER

Oregon City, 503/657-9336

www.endoftheoregontrail.org

Three 50-foot-tall covered wagon–shaped buildings dominate Abernethy Green, the main arrival area for the emigrants reaching the Willamette Valley. The center is a living history exhibit with eight performances daily in summer (call in advance for times).

Details: *20 minutes southeast of Portland, off Interstate 205 at Exit 10. (1–2 hours)*

★★★★ SALEM

Visitors Center, 1313 Mill Street SE

503/581-4325 or 800/874-7012

The state capital and second largest city in Oregon, Salem is also home to Willamette University. The art-deco style **State Capitol Building,** built in 1938, is on the National Register of Historic Places and has free tours available (hours vary) and grounds to explore. The **Mission Mill Village,** 1313 Mill Street S.E., 503/585-7012 or 800/874-7012, is a five-acre park, home to a historic woolen mill, a museum, and several historic houses; it's open daily, admission is charged. **Made in Salem** gallery, an artists' cooperative, 189 Liberty Street NE, 503/399-8197, in the Reed Opera House shopping mall, is well worth a stop. **Deepwood Estate** is a historic home on several acres with gardens to tour. **Schreiner's Iris Gardens,** 3671 Quinaby Road N.E., is only open during bloom season, May through June; however, a catalog is available by calling 800/419-4747, ext. 71. The **Wheatland Ferry** north of town gives you an old-fashioned way to cross the Willamette River.

Details: *The Salem Visitors Center is at the Mission Mill Museum. (4–6 hours)*

★★★ CORVALLIS

Visitors Center, 420 NW Second Street, 541/757-1544 or 800/334-8118, www.visitcorvallis.com

Life in this quintessential college town centers on Oregon State University; guided campus tours are offered Monday through Friday, 541/737-2626 or 800/291-4192. Downtown is a thriving area of

HAZELNUT HEAVEN—LIVING HISTORY

When you tour the Willamette Valley, you'll understand why so many regional restaurants offer dishes featuring the small nugget-like hazelnut (known as filberts to some of us). Hazelnut orchards abound in the valley. You'll see some of them as you drive along 99W. You can take an even closer look at the history of this nut at the 200-plus-acre Dorris Park Ranch, a working filbert farm and Oregon's first living history farm. It's located not far from Eugene, near Springfield. Originally settled by George and Lulu Dorris in 1892, the property lies along the Willamette River with 75 acres of orchards and picturesque pastures, forests, and wetlands. Walking tours are available and there are special events. Contact the Willamalane Park and Recreation District, 541/736-4044 or www.willamalane.org, for more information.

shops and restaurants. The **Benton County History Center,** 110 N.W. Third Street, 541/758-3550, offers a look at this farming region's history. Da Vinci Days, a stimulating festival of art, science, and technology, is held here each July.

Details: *(2–3 hours)*

★★★ EUGENE

Visitor Center, 115 W. Eighth, Suite 190, 541/484-5307 or 800/547-5445, www.visitlanecounty.org

This city, at the southern end of the valley, is the seat of scenic Lane County and the cultural hub of Willamette Valley. This is home to the **University of Oregon,** 541/346-3027, http://uoma.uoregon.edu, where you can visit the university's famed Asian art collection in the Museum of Art Wednesday through Sunday. Downtown, the **Hult Center for the Performing Arts,** 541/682-5000, is a striking modern building with a permanent collection of local fine art; it also features guest performers, musical theater, and dance. **Fifth Street Public Market,** 541/484-0383, is lively and filled with galleries and restaurants. **Sawmill Ballroom Lavender Farm,** 29251 Hamm Road, 541/686-9999 or 888/686-8169, specializes in Tuscan lavender.

Details: *Information is available through the Convention and Visitors Association of Lane County. (4–6 hours)*

★★★ MCMINNVILLE
503/472-6196 (chamber of commerce)

Located in the north end of the Willamette Valley, McMinnville is home to Linfield College, site of the annual International Pinot Noir Festival. In the historic downtown, a six-block section between Third and Fourth Streets, there are shops and galleries and a handful of restaurants and wineries.

Details: *The chamber of commerce, at the corner of Adams (southbound 99W) and Fourth Streets, has a free walking guide of the district and a map detailing Yamhill County's major towns. (1–2 hours)*

★★★ MT. ANGEL
503/845-6882 (chamber of commerce)
www.octoberfest.org

This east Willamette town is a German community founded in the late 1800s. It is unusual and special and worth a detour if you're in the area. Each fall, it hosts a boisterous Oktoberfest, but the reason to come is to visit Mt. Angel Abbey, built by Benedictine monks on a hilltop overlooking the town. The three-day Bach Festival is held here in late July (inquire early if interested). The library designed by Alvar Aalto is worth a visit for its unique architecture and its view.

Details: *On SR 14, east of Salem. (2 hours)*

★★★ NEWBERG
115 N. Washington Street; 503/538-2014 (chamber of commerce)
www.newberg.org

At the north end of the valley, this area has more than 30 wineries and is the gateway to Willamette Valley wine touring. Rex Hill, Duck Pond Cellars, Amity, Ponzi, Sokol Blosser, Champoeg, Oak Knoll, and Adelsheim wineries are here.

Details: *From I-5 in Portland, go west 20 miles on State Route 99W. (2 hours to half day)*

★★★ OREGON GARDEN
Silverton, 503/874-8100 or 877/674-2733
www.oregongarden.org

The 60-acre first phase of the 240-acre Oregon Garden destined to be the state's most impressive display garden, opened to the public in May 2000. Visitors can tour the rose, conifer, and children's gardens, as well as attend concerts and special events. While the garden will mature with time, there are many water features and massive plantings of annuals. A project of the Oregon Association of Nurserymen, the garden celebrates the state's thriving nursery industry.

Details: *About 15 miles southeast of Salem, off Interstate 5, exits 263 and 260. Admission charged. Open 10 to 6 daily in summer. (1 hour)*

★★★ PHILOMATH

541/929-6230 (historical museum)
www.peak.org/~lewisb/museum.html

This small town west of Corvallis is in tree-farming country. Home to the Benton County Historical Museum, Philomath is a good stop en route from Corvallis to ocean beaches. The town hosts the Shrewsbury Renaissance Fair the second weekend in September.

Details: *About six miles west of Corvallis on SR 34. (1 hour)*

★★★ SILVER FALLS STATE PARK

Park information, 503/873-8681, reservations, 800/452-5687

Oregon's largest state park, located near Salem, has 10 waterfalls and hiking in Silver Creek Canyon. Swimming, guided horseback riding, and camping facilities are also available (see page 233).

Details: *Five miles east of Salem on Highway 22. (2 hours to overnight stay)*

FITNESS AND RECREATION

This is bicycling country, and good maps of routes are available. Bicyclists will appreciate the path that parallels 99W. The free Willamette Valley bicycle loop guide covers a 195-mile cycling and driving route; call 800/526-2256 for information. There are two large wildlife refuges here. Baskett Slough National Wildlife Preserve is a 2,500-acre wintering ground for the dusky Canada goose. The preserve lies just west of 99W on Highway 22; it's a great place to stretch your legs, but there are no tables or restrooms. William L. Finley National Wildlife Refuge is a 5,000-acre-plus habitat for geese, elk, and other animals; the entrance is about eight miles south of Corvallis. There are plenty of trails to hike.

FOOD

Summer is berry time in the valley, and there are all kinds: strawberries, loganberries, gooseberries, blueberries, red and black raspberries, Marion and boysenberries. You'll see roadside stands, but be sure to watch for **Firestone Farms,** just south of Dundee, 503/864-2672, www.firestonefarms.com. They sell a wide selection of berries and other produce, plus a vast array of Northwest gourmet foods (sample some at the tasting bar). Their peach or berry milkshakes alone are worth the stop. Newly opened in Dundee, **Your Northwest,** 110 S.W. Seventh Street, 503/554-8101, is a retail store featuring the Northwest's finest foods and artisan products. Two restaurants in the north end of the valley are worth remembering: **Tina's,** in Dundee at 760 Highway 99W, 503/538-8880; and **Red Hills Provincial Dining,** 276 S.W. Highway 99W, 503/538-8224, where the setting is elegant. Reservations are suggested at restaurants; many do not take credit cards. **Nick's Italian Cafe,** 521 East Third Street, in McMinnville, 503/434-4471, is a perennial favorite and has an extensive wine list with many Oregon vintages. À la carte and five-course price-fixed menus include favorites like homemade pastas and grilled salmon. **Golden Valley Brewery & Pub,** 980 East Fourth Street, also in McMinville, 503/472-2739, offers British-style brews (you can view production), homemade sausages, and jazz and blues on weekend evenings. **Nearly Normal's,** in Corvallis, 541/753-0791, serves up vegan and vegetarian fare in a fun, rustic setting. Fresh seasonal produce and a creative chef make **Sweetwaters Restaurant and Lounge,** at Eugene's Valley River Inn, 1000 Valley River Way, 541/687-0123; a good destination. Locally caught salmon is a specialty.

WINERIES

Tasting facilities at the wineries range from elegant to rustic. Many offer free samples; a few charge a small fee, often good toward a purchase. Most wineries are friendly and family-owned, making a few thousand cases per year—primarily consumed in-state. While many wineries are clustered in towns right on 99W, some of the best are tucked away in the hills, down long, winding, and often rutted roads. Along 99W, watch for the blue signs that point the way to most wineries. A map is a necessity. Pick up a copy of the Oregon Wine Advisory Board's free brochure, "Discover Oregon Wineries," with details on nearly all locations, plus comprehensive maps. Call the advisory board at 800/242-2363. Or check out the Oregon Wine Commission's website at www.oregonwine.org—maps and complete descriptions of the different areas of the valley are found here.

The **Oregon Wine Tasting Room,** southwest of McMinnville on SR 18,

503/843-3787, has a changing sampling from many Oregon wineries (including those without tasting rooms of their own). The adjoining Lawrence Gallery, featuring northwestern art and a restaurant, makes this a great stop.

If you can make only a short visit to the wine country, you'll find many fine wineries to visit in Yamhill County. From Portland, one of the first you'll encounter is **Rex Hill Vineyards and Winery,** a great facility with picnic grounds at 30835 Highway 99W, 503/538-0666; www.rexhill.com. Call for a schedule of the hot air balloon rides that embark from here. South of here, **Duck Pond Cellars** is just off the highway (their T-shirts make great souvenirs). Memorial Day weekend, wineries kick off peak season with open houses, live music, food, and new wine releases. Admission prices and hours vary, but most of the wineries, including some not generally open to the public, welcome visitors Friday to Sunday from at least 11 to 4. Wineries are also open for tours Thanksgiving weekend. The *Oregon Wine* newspaper, available free at wineries, publishes complete details.

LODGING

Accommodations here are plentiful and diverse. The Willamette Valley offers more than two dozen bed-and-breakfast options. Near McMinnville, you can stay in an 1892 Queen Anne Victorian, set in 10 acres of vineyard, at **Mattey House B&B,** 10221 N.E. Mattey Lane, 503/434-5058 or www.matteyhouse.com.

Alpine-style **Steiger Haus,** 503/472-0821 or 800/445-7744, is a contemporary home with five rooms in McMinnville near Linfield College. **Youngberg Hill Ranch,** 503/472-2727, has a panoramic valley view. It's a contemporary home with period styling.

Near Newberg and McMinnville, you can pet the llamas at the **Partridge Farm,** 503/538-2050. Learn about hazelnuts at **Springbrook Hazelnut Farm,** 503/538-2050 or 800/793-8528, a historic home with a lap pool. Near Dayton, you'll see Arabian horses and have a territorial view from **Wine Country Farm,** 800/261-3446 or 503/864-3446 or www.winecountryfarm.com.

Near Corvallis, **Hanson Country Inn,** 503/752-2919, is a historic estate home with a real country feel. Most inns have restrictions regarding children, smoking, and pets. Some require two-night stays over weekends. For a complete list of B&Bs and other lodging call the Willamette Valley Visitors Association, 800/526-2256.

The **Valley River Inn,** in Eugene, 1000 Valley River Way, 541/687-0123 or 800/543-8266, overlooks the Willamette River. You can check out bicycles at the front desk or arrange to go fishing for salmon or winter steelhead (catch a fish and the hotel chef will cook or smoke it for you).

CAMPING

Champoeg State Park, between Portland and Newberg (Exit 278 off Interstate 5), offers year-round camping in a variety of facilities: tent, walk-in, group, and RV campsites. Yurts are also available. Scenic **Silver Falls State Park,** near Salem, is Oregon's largest state park, covering about 8,000 acres. There are 51 tent sites and 53 electrical and water sites. For fees and reservations for both parks call Reservations Northwest, 800/452-5687.

16 OREGON COAST

Dunes resembling sugar. Dramatic Haystack Rock. Depot Bay's signature bridge. Salishan Lodge. Great seafood and some of the finest public beaches in the country. These are just a few of the attractions of the Oregon coast. No wonder the nearly 400 miles of Highway 101, from Brookings in the south to Astoria in the north, is a world-renowned vacation destination. Most of the coast highway, officially designated as a Scenic Byway in 1998, misses very little shoreline (cutting inland primarily south of Tillamook and at Coos Bay). You have spectacular views much of the way.

The drawbacks? Highway 101 can slow to a crawl in the height of summer, when crowds descend. Set aside at least five days if you plan to explore the whole coastline. Still, you'll spend a lot of time on the road. Most folks pick a spot and stay for a while—a good idea if relaxing is your goal. Accommodations vary widely from posh and luxurious resorts to simple and spartan vacation rentals.

One suggestion that's purely a taste issue: Consider the "personality" of your beach town destination and accommodation. What's your preference? A quintessential gray-shingled beach and arts community? You'll probably most enjoy Cannon Beach. A classic saltwater taffy, walk-the-promenade-and-ride-the-carousel community? Try Seaside. A lively and busy spot—perhaps one that hosts the largest seafood festival on the coast? You're looking for Newport.

Good advice no matter what your destination: Reserve accommodations well in advance.

OREGON COAST

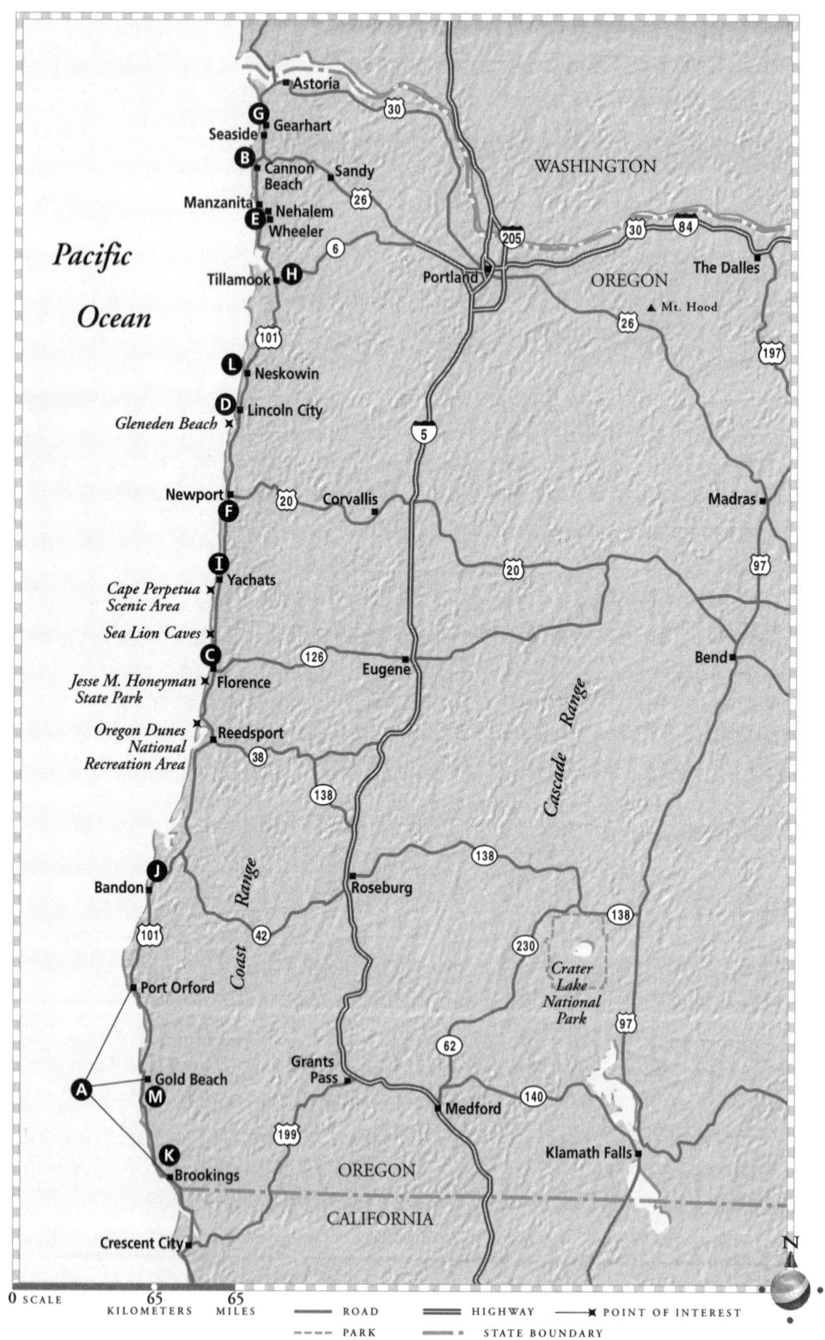
Astoria
Gearhart
Seaside
Cannon Beach
Sandy
Manzanita
Nehalem
Wheeler
Pacific
Ocean
Tillamook
Portland
WASHINGTON
OREGON
The Dalles
Mt. Hood
Neskowin
Lincoln City
Gleneden Beach
Newport
Corvallis
Madras
Yachats
Cape Perpetua Scenic Area
Sea Lion Caves
Eugene
Bend
Jesse M. Honeyman State Park
Florence
Oregon Dunes National Recreation Area
Reedsport
Cascade Range
Bandon
Coast Range
Roseburg
Crater Lake National Park
Port Orford
Gold Beach
Grants Pass
Medford
Klamath Falls
Brookings
OREGON
CALIFORNIA
Crescent City
N
0 SCALE
65 KILOMETERS
65 MILES
ROAD
HIGHWAY
POINT OF INTEREST
PARK
STATE BOUNDARY

A PERFECT DAY ON THE OREGON COAST

A perfect day is lazy and beautiful. Have breakfast in your room overlooking the beach, then find a long stretch of sand and go barefoot. Play in the surf. Or sunbathe. Pick a seaside town—Cannon Beach is a good one—and explore. Look for glass art, crafts, pottery, and other artisan-created specialty items. For lunch, crab anything or clam chowder are both good options. And, if regulations permit, build a beach fire at night and gather around it with your loved ones.

ORIENTATION

The Oregon coast breaks into three areas—north, central, and south. Highway 101 connects to Interstate 5 via more than half a dozen routes that on a map look like rungs of a rope ladder. The southern coast is the most remote area—it's about 240 miles from Portland to Bandon, via Highway 42 west of Roseburg. A visit here requires the biggest time committment if you are starting out from the Portland area.

The central coast includes Newport (about 115 miles from Portland and reached from Corvallis on Highway 20), with its aquarium, and Florence (accessed from Eugene via Highway 126), with the nearby dunes; a long weekend gives you time to explore both areas. Lincoln City is also on the central coast, about 90 miles from Portland. Looking at a map you may be tempted to take 99W from

---

SIGHTS

- Ⓐ Brookings/Gold Beach/Port Orford
- Ⓑ Cannon Beach
- Ⓒ Florence
- Ⓓ Lincoln City
- Ⓔ Manzanita/Nehalem/Wheeler
- Ⓕ Newport
- Ⓖ Seaside
- Ⓗ Tillamook
- Ⓘ Yachats

FOOD

- Ⓙ Bandon's Cheddar Cheese
- Ⓒ Blue Heron Bistro
- Ⓗ Blue Heron French Cheese Co.
- Ⓔ Blue Sky Cafe
- Ⓓ Chez Jeanette
- Ⓚ Chives
- Ⓔ Newhalem Bay Winery
- Ⓖ Pacific Way Cafe & Bakery
- Ⓓ Salishan Lodge
- Ⓕ Tables of Content
- Ⓗ Tillamook Cheese Factory

LODGING

- Ⓛ The Chelan
- Ⓕ Hallmark Resort
- Ⓓ Salishan Lodge
- Ⓐ Shilo Oceanfront Resorts
- Ⓕ Shilo Oceanfront Resorts
- Ⓑ Stephanie Inn
- Ⓕ Sylvia Beach Hotel
- Ⓜ Tu Tu Tun Lodge

CAMPING

- Ⓒ Jessie Honeyman State Park

Note: Items with the same letter are located in the same area.

Portland. That's a great choice if you want to mix in a tour of the wine country around Newberg and McMinnville, but it's slow and the roads are often congested—sources of frustration for the beach-bound visitor. The best route timewise is to go south on I-5 to Salem on then west on highways 22 and 28.

Cannon Beach and Seaside are on the north coast, about 80 miles from Portland via U.S. 26. (an efficient drive, with few small towns to slow you). An overnight gives you a relaxing getaway. And, if you are really short on time, you can start early and spend a day exploring one of the communities.

SIGHTSEEING HIGHLIGHTS

★★★★ CANNON BEACH

503/436-2623 (chamber of commerce)
www.cannonbeach.org

Known for its impressive sand-sculpting contest and Haystack Rock, one of the world's largest monoliths, this is a quirky, with-it arts village. It's also popular, so expect to find crowds. There are over 20 galleries here, most along Hemlock Street, interesting shops to browse, and eateries. Stephanie Inn is here. **Haystack Rock** is about a mile's hike down the beach south from town. Nearby, **Ecola State Park** is a day-use park whose scenic cliff trail is well worth the stop. They also have a Storm Festival in November; and December weekend holiday events for families.

Details: *Ecola State Park is two miles north of town off the coast highway. Admission $3 per vehicle; pedestrians free. (2 hours)*

★★★★ FLORENCE

541/997-3128 or 800/524-4864 (chamber of commerce)
www.florencechamber.com

About 5,000 people live in this gateway to the **Oregon Dunes National Recreation Area.** Nearly half of this 30,000-acre area is open sand dunes, some reaching up to 400 feet high and about a mile in length. It's stunning. A few miles south of Florence is **Jessie Honeyman State Park** (see Camping). Nearby **Heceta Head Lighthouse** is perhaps the most photographed spot on the Oregon coast. About 11 miles north of town are the **Sea Lion Caves,** 541/547-3111, www.sealioncaves.com; take an elevator to a huge, impressive cave to see huge and impressive (and stinky—be prepared) sea lions.

Details: *(2–4 hours)*

★★★★ NEWPORT

541/265-8801 or 800/262-7844 (chamber of commerce)
www.newportchamber.org

This historic community is the largest port on the central coast and known for its annual seafood festival. It's home to the **Oregon Coast Aquarium,** 541/867-3474, www.aquarium.org, which in turn is home to seals, sea lions, otters, and other large sea animals like a giant Pacific octopus. You can see the dozens of smaller critters that hang out in tidepools. The **Mark O. Hatfield Marine Science Center,** 541/867-0100, www.hmsc.orst.edu, is a major center for marine studies. The new public wing here is part of a recent $5 million renovation. There are displays and tidepool animals to touch. **Rogue Ales,** 2320 OSU Drive, 541/867-3660, www.rogue.com, with tours and tastings, is located on the historic bayfront.

Details: *(4–6 hours)*

★★★ BROOKINGS/GOLD BEACH/PORT ORFORD

Gold Beach Chamber of Commerce, 800/525-2334
www.goldbeach.org
Brookings-Harbor Chamber of Commerce, 800/535-9469
www.brookings-harbor.com

This southern part of the Oregon coast, sometimes referred to as Curry County, backs up to the Siskiyou Forest. Beaches are smaller, and there's more of a Big Sur feel. You can hike here any time of year and have wide chunks of beach all to yourself. Jetboat trips from Gold Beach up the Rogue River are a famous way to explore this area (Rogue River Mail Boat Trips have been operating since 1895). Increased ecotourism offerings also make it a prime destination for beach adventures. Take a self-guided forest and beach hike or for insider's expertise, hire a guide. Port Orford is the site of a battle between Native Americans and the first whites attempting to settle the area. Brookings is referred to as Oregon's "banana belt," as temperatures are warmer here than anywhere else on the coast.

Details: *Rogue River Mail Boat Trips, 800/458-3511, www.mailboat.com. (2–4 hours minimum)*

★★★ LINCOLN CITY

541/994-8378 or 800/452-2151 (visitors bureau)
www.oregoncoast.org

This is the closest coastal city to Portland. Conditions are great for

THE OREGON COAST WELCOMES YOU

As you drive along the coast, you'll see distinctive Oregon Welcomes You signs with a yellow sun, green trees, and blue water. These direct you to visitors centers located in almost every community. They are open daily with maps and brochures available, whether or not a host is on duty. For more information, contact the Oregon Coast Visitors Association, 541/574-2679 or 888/628-2101 (toll free), www.oregon-coast.org.

kite flying, and you'll see these colorful wisps all over town. It boasts 2,500 ocean-view rooms and is a prime location to watch storms or sunsets. It's also busy and commercial, with a large factory store outlet and Chinook Winds Casino. **Salishan Lodge,** 888/725-4742, www.salishan.com, the coast's most famous resort, is a few miles south at Gleneden Beach.

Details: *(2–4 hours)*

★★★ MANZANITA/NEHALEM/WHEELER

This three-town area, spread around Nehalem Bay, is only a dozen or so miles south of Cannon Beach. It offers ocean beaches, a warm water lake to swim in, river recreation, and lots of rustic vacation rentals, and it's relatively undiscovered. Manzanita is a secluded beachside area with an 18-hole golf course. There's an antiques mall to explore in Nehalem, right on 101. **Nehalem Bay Winery** has wine tasting in a historic cheese factory. Resident elk can be seen around the Nehalem River estuary. **Nehalem Bay State Park** extends to the tip of the spit enclosing the bay and offers over 200 campsites and yurt camping. Wheeler is south of the bay and offers fishing and boating.

Details: *Contact the Nehalem Bay Chamber of Commerce, 503/368-5100. For state parks reservations, contact 800/452-5687 or www.prd.state.or.us. (3–4 hours)*

★★★ SEASIDE

888/306-2326 (visitors bureau)
www.seasideor.com

RESTAURANTS COOK YOUR CATCH

There's a longtime tradition with many Oregon coast restaurants that the chef will cook your catch of the day—and serve it to you at dinnertime. Check in advance with the restaurant of your choice to see whether it accommodates fishers' bounty and expect to pay for meal preparation. Still, it's a delightful way to experience your very own fresh seafood.

Lewis and Clark's party came here in 1806 to take salt from the sea by erecting a salt cairn, and you can see a replica of it at the south end of the **Promenade,** which fronts the wide beach. Feed the seals at **Seaside Aquarium** on "the Prom." There's a museum in town as well. **Gearhart,** a quiet community of residential homes and a couple golf courses north of Seaside, is a favorite of well-to-do Portlanders.

Details: *(1–2 hours)*

★★★ TILLAMOOK

You'll see pastureland and dairies and cattle all around Tillamook. Most of the county's milk goes into the production of cheese, particularly at the **Tillamook Cheese** factory. Kids love the ice cream sold on-site, and it's fun for the whole family to watch the cheese makers at work. You can also visit **Blue Heron French Cheese Co.** for cheese and wine tasting. The **Naval Air Station Museum,** housed in a rare WWII blimp hangar that is the largest wooden structure in the world, displays a collection of warplanes and a jet simulator you can climb into.

Details: *Tillamook Cheese is at 4175 Highway 101 N.; 800/542-7290, www.tillamookcheese.com. Summer hours are daily 8 to 8; winter daily 8 to 6. Blue Heron is one mile south of the Tillamook Cheese factory; 800/275-0639, www.blueheronoregon.com. Open summer 8 to 8; winter 9 to 5. The Naval Air Station Museum, 503/842-1130, www.tillamookair.com, is open during the summer 9 to 6. Admission is $5. (1 hour for each)*

★★★ YACHATS

541/547-3530 (chamber of commerce)
www.pioneer.net

This is a small, low-key village at the mouth of the Yachats River. Between June and September smelt come ashore to spawn. A July Smelt Fry Festival celebrates the event. Several thousand acres of rain forest make up **Cape Perpetua Scenic Area,** and the visitors center south of town displays exhibits on the natural forces that shaped the Oregon coast. It also offers Saturday environmental programs, such as tidepool explorations—great for families. **Cape Perpetua Overlook** is the highest point on the Oregon coast and has great views.

Details: *The Cape Perpetua Visitors Center is three miles south of Yachats and two miles off U.S. 101; 541/547-3289. Summer hours daily 9 to 5. Admission is $3 per vehicle. (1–2 hours)*

FITNESS AND RECREATION

The beaches are rich with recreational opportunities such as hiking, horseback riding, golfing, dune buggy riding, and lighthouse exploring. Kite flying is popular—particularly in Lincoln City. Wildlife-watching is good all along the coast. Anywhere the forests meet the rocky headlands, you may see deer or sometimes elk. In Newport, a visit to the Oregon Coast Aquarium lets you touch sea stars and other tidepool animals. Also in Newport, you can learn more about the many lighthouses on the coast at the new interpretive center at Yaquina Head Lighthouse, 750 Lighthouse Drive, 541/574-3100. On the south coast, in Reedsport, there's a Marine Discovery area on the bayfront.

Fishing and boating excursions abound. Charters are available for halibut fishing in May and June, chinook salmon through the summer, and lingcod, sea bass, and other rockfish all year. Major ports are at Garibaldi, Depoe Bay, Newport, Winchester, Charleston, Gold Beach, and Brookings. Prices range from $40 to over $150 for half- to full-day trips. And you don't have to join a charter to fish. You can throw in a line or crab year-round anywhere there's a bay. Marinas and bait shops sell bait and rent crabbing rings (about $4) and boats (prices vary).

Depoe Bay, known as having the world's smallest harbor, is a whalewatching destination, as a number of whales make the central coast their year-round home. Guided Zodiak boat ecotours give visitors a look at nearby secluded coves and beaches.

FOOD

There are 20 food festivals on the Oregon coast, and seafood is plentiful. Depoe Bay is famous for its salmon bakes, Yachats hosts an annual smelt festival, and the Newport Seafood Festival is the biggest on the coast. So, not surpris-

CANNON BEACH

John Elk III

ingly, casual meals are a breeze. Every town has cafés or little hole-in-the-wall eateries where you can buy fish and chips made with fish caught fresh that morning. With the exception of the **Pacific Way Cafe & Bakery,** (closed Tuesday and Wednesday) in Gearhart north of Seaside, 503/738-0245, which makes great basic fare such as sandwiches, soups, and seafood pizzas, the following are some special places to watch for along the coast. The **Blue Sky Cafe,** in Manzanita, 503/368-5712, offers a creatively diverse menu—both a Thai chicken entrée and bread pudding can be found on the menu—that draws plenty of fans. The dining room at **Salishan Lodge,** in Gleneden Beach, 541/764-2371, offers a soothing decor and a view of Siletz Bay. Menu selections emphasize locally harvested seafood and produce. **Chez Jeanette,** also in Gleneden Beach, 541/764-3434, serves French food in an intimate atmosphere. Try dinner (set menu by reservation) at the **Tables of Content** at the Sylvia Beach Hotel, 541/265-5428, if you're in Newport. The **Blue Heron Bistro,** 100 Commercial Street, 541/267-3993, in Coos Bay is a good dinner choice as well. In Brookings, **Chives,** 541/469-4121, is a surprisingly sophisticated eatery—linen tablecloths, art on the walls—with excellent service and a big city menu that might include items like roast pheasant and polenta.

If you catch a fish or crab during the day, yet want to dine out that night, check in advance with your restaurant of choice. Many restaurants along the coast will prepare your own fish or crab and serve it to you.

BEACH SAFETY AND TIDEPOOLS

Winter storm watching is a favorite activity of Northwest beach-goers. The waves can grow to 30 feet or more as they crash to shore, and it's best to watch them from a safe distance. Keep safety in mind at all times at the beach. But be especially careful in the spring, and make sure that children stay safely away from logs or other debris in the surf.

When exploring tidepools, it's fine to touch starfish and anemones, but consider the health of these critters and leave them in their habitat.

Oregon's beaches belong to the public, so you can explore any of them. And, unless otherwise advised, beach fires are permitted.

In Tillamook (see page 240), visit the **Tillamook Cheese Factory** for tasting and **Blue Heron French Cheese Co.** for cheese and wine tasting. In Nehalem, the **Nehalem Bay Winery**—the only winery on the coast—has wine tasting in a historic cheese factory. On the southern coast, you can also visit **Bandon's Cheddar Cheese** outlet, 800/548-8961, for samples and to see cheese being made.

LODGING

The beachfront **Stephanie Inn,** in Cannon Beach, 800/633-3466, www.stephanieinn.com, a modern 46-room inn with fireplaces in all the rooms and great views, is a favorite coast getaway destination for romantic couples. There's a restaurant with two dinner seatings by reservation only. The best suites are pricier, so check on package offerings. The funky and comfortable **Sylvia Beach Hotel,** 541/265-5428, is a renovated clapboard inn in Newport, named after the owner of a famous Paris bookstore in the 1920s. Each of the 20 rooms is named after a well-known writer. It sits on a small bluff overlooking the beach. The Colette, Mark Twain, and Agatha Christie rooms have fireplaces and are wheelchair accessible. **Salishan Inn,** at Gleneden Beach, 541/764-3600 or 888/725-4742, is across the street and up the road from the waterfront, but that doesn't deter the legions who love this golf and tennis resort with a well-deserved reputation for comfort and fine dining.

Good choices for families, with direct beach access and indoor swimming pools, are The **Shilo Oceanfront Resorts,** 800/222-2244 or www.shiloinns.com, in Lincoln City and Newport. On-site restaurants offer a kids menu, and video arcades are nearby. The **Hallmark Resort** in Newport, 888/448-4449 or www.hallmarkinns.com, also offers an indoor swimming pool and direct beach access. It is nearby to Yaquina Bay State Park and the Yaquina Bay overview and lighthouse museum. **The Chelan,** 503/392-3270, a small older condominium unit at Neskowin and a family favorite, is an off-the-beaten path hideaway in a low-key beach community. Rooms have fireplaces and views of the beach. **Tu Tu Tun Lodge,** on the Rogue River near Gold Beach, 541/247-6664, www.tututun.com, offers fishing and rafting, yet is a romantic destination.

CAMPING

There are 19 state park campgrounds, with options like yurt and cabin rentals, and 72 day-use properties that provide a special way to experience the natural beauty of the coast. **Jessie Honeyman State Park,** 541/997-3641 or 800/452-5687, www.prd.state.or.us, three miles south of Florence in the Oregon Dunes National Recreation Area, is the largest beachside state park. It also has a lake that provides warm swimming waters and paddleboat recreation. Camping spots are plentiful all along the coast and include yurts and rentals. The only caveat here, worth repeating: Reserve well in advance.

17 ASTORIA

Fans of Lewis and Clark, history buffs, sailors, hikers, kayakers—in short, explorers of all breeds—will have a field day roaming the history-rich seaport town of Astoria and the Columbia River estuary. As you drive into town, the unremarkable 1920s-era buildings lining Commercial Street give no clue that this is the oldest white settlement west of the Mississippi. John Jacob Astor sent fur traders here to set up shop in 1811. The town thrived as a coastal port from the mid-1800s to the early 1900s. But in 1922, a fire leveled the downtown, at the time built on wooden pilings over the Columbia River. Fortunately, the Victorian homes that popped up in the boom days of the 1800s and at the turn of the last century were spared. You'll easily spot the most imposing one—the red-roofed mansion built in 1885 by Captain George Flavel, pioneer Columbia River bar pilot and colorful entrepreneur. From the three-story octagonal turret, Captain Flavel watched his ships ply the waters of the Columbia. Nearby at Fort Clatsop, Lewis and Clark reached the end of their journey years earlier.

It rains a lot in Astoria, and it doesn't have the "beach town" feel of other spots on the coast. Yet a walking tour along Franklin Avenue's historic homes takes you back in time, and exploring the huge Columbia River Maritime Museum will fill your mind with high seas fantasies, as well as keep you dry in a drizzle or downpour. And when the sun shines, ahh, it's glorious. Meanwhile, think of Astoria as a mystical seaport—a dream-catcher snagging men's visions at the mouth of the West's mightiest river.

SEAFOOD, ANYONE ?

The Astoria-Warrenton Crab and Seafood Festival, a three-day food, wine, and arts and crafts celebration, packs the town at the end of April. The festival is held at the Hammond Mooring Basin (where Keiko the whale was filmed in the making of *Free Willy*), with river tours and water taxis to Astoria's West Mooring Basin. For more information, contact the Astoria-Warrenton Area Chamber of Commerce at 800/875-6807.

A PERFECT DAY AROUND ASTORIA

Spend the night in a historic B&B. After breakfast, drive to the Astoria Column to climb 166 steps to the top of the 125-foot-tall monolith for a bird's-eye view of the town and the Columbia estuary. Visit the Captain George Flavel House, then head to the Columbia River Maritime Museum. Drive to Fort Clatsop to watch historical reenactments of Lewis and Clark's winter there. A map will lead you to this and other historic forts (such as Fort Stevens State Park), viewpoints, and beachfront communities. Back in Astoria, choose a waterfront spot to dine and watch boats ply the river as the sun sets.

ORIENTATION

Astoria is a hilly town of about 10,000. Its companion community of Warrenton, across Youngs Bay to the west, has about 4,000 residents. There are three basic ways to approach by car: on State Highway 26 from Portland; going north on the Oregon coast on 101; and coming south from Washington.

For details, contact the Astoria–Warrenton Area Chamber of Commerce at 800/875-6807 or www.oldoregon.com.

SIGHTSEEING HIGHLIGHTS

★★★★ CAPTAIN GEORGE FLAVEL HOUSE

Eighth and Duane Streets, 503/325-2203

Considered by many to be the finest example of the Queen Anne style of architecture in Oregon, the house was a gift to the town in 1934 by

ASTORIA AREA

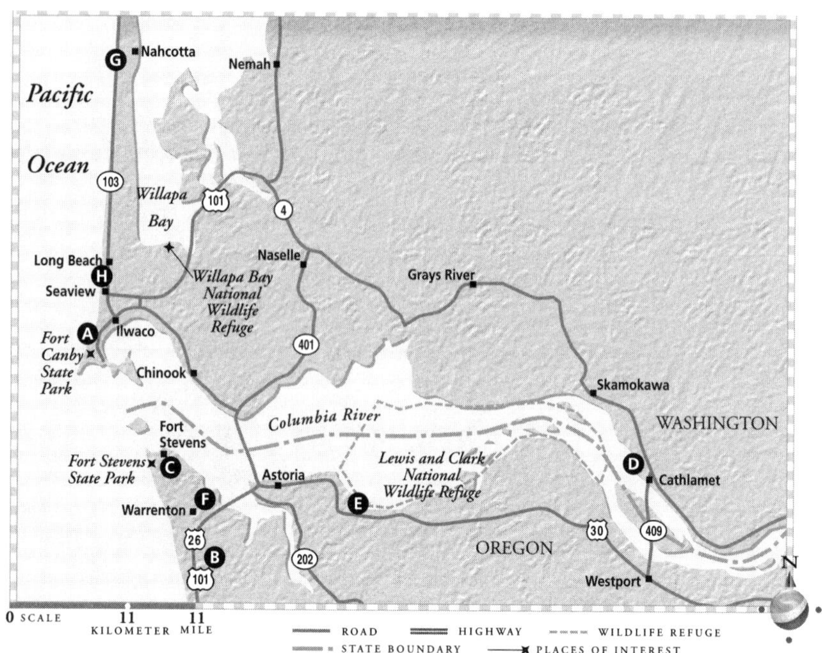

SIGHTS

- **A** Fort Canby State Park
- **B** Fort Clatsop National Memorial
- **C** Fort Stevens and Fort Stevens State Park
- **D** Julia Butler Hansen Columbia White-tailed Deer Refuge

SIGHTS *(continued)*

- **E** Twilight Eagle Sanctuary and Burnside Area
- **F** Warrenton

FOOD

- **G** The Ark
- **H** The Shoalwater

LODGING

- **F** The Shilo Inn

CAMPING

- **A** Fort Canby State Park
- **C** Fort Stevens State Park

Note: Items with the same letter are located in the same area.

Flavel's great-granddaughter and is now a museum. The Clatsop Historical Society has refurbished it to look as it did during Captain Flavel's time. Inside, the woodwork and much of the furniture is in the Eastlake style. There are six different fireplaces with hand-carved mantels in varying woods and tile from different countries. There are also paintings by maritime artist Cleveland Rockwell and Astoria native John H. Trullinger.

ASTORIA

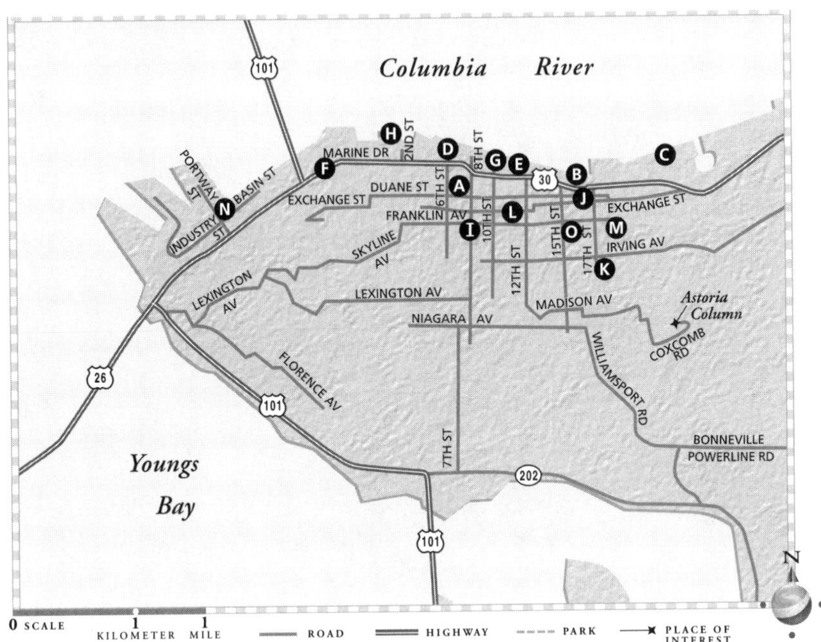

SIGHTS

- **A** Captain George Flavel House
- **B** Columbia River Maritime Museum
- **C** Heritage Museum

FOOD

- **D** Cannery Cafe
- **E** Columbian Cafe
- **F** Josephsons Smokehouse & Specialty Seafood
- **G** Pacific Rim Gallery
- **H** Ship Inn Restaurant & Pub

LODGING

- **I** Clementine's
- **J** Captain's Inn
- **K** Columbia River Inn
- **L** Franklin Street Station
- **M** Martin & Lilli Foard House
- **N** Red Lion Inn
- **O** Rosebriar Hotel

Details: *The home is open daily 10 to 5; $5 admission includes entry to the Heritage Museum. (1 hour)*

★★★★ COLUMBIA RIVER MARITIME MUSEUM

1792 Marine Drive, 503/325-2323

www.crmm.org

24,000 square feet of maritime exhibits take you from the time of dugout canoes to submarine technology. Displays focus on Chinook Indian artifacts, navigation, marine safety, and whaling. Another exhibit looks at the period when Astoria was considered the "Salmon Capital of the World." The museum has a waterfront location with great views. Tour a lightship, the *Columbia,* that once guided ships to safety at the mouth of the river.

Details: *Open daily 9:30 to 5. Admission $5. (1½ hours)*

★★★★ FORT CLATSOP NATIONAL MEMORIAL

Highway 101, 503/861-2471

www.nps.gov/focl

This is the westernmost point reached by the Lewis and Clark expedition undertaken to expand knowledge of the Louisiana Purchase and open the West. The fort, basically two log cabins with seven small rooms, is a re-creation of the site where Meriwether Lewis and William Clark made camp during the winter of 1805–06. It was built in 1955 from a drawing on the cover of Clark's field book. Historical reenactments, a visitors center, and plenty of hiking trails make this a great stop for the whole family.

COLUMBIA RIVER CRUISIN'

In summer 2000 the new *Columbia Queen* steamboat, sister ship to the *Mississippi Delta Queen* operated by the Delta Steamboat Co., 800/297-3960 or www.columbiaqueen.com, began regular trips cruising the Columbia River from Portland. It joins other cruise lines and offers another way to experience Astoria. Extensive cruise trips are offered by companies like Alaska Sightseeing/Cruise West, 800/888-9378, www.cruisewest.com; American West Steamboat Company, 800/434-1232, www.columbiarivercruise.com; and Special Expeditions, 800/397-3348, wwwexpeditions.com. Or contact the Astoria-Warrenton Area Chamber of Commerce, 503/325-6311, for more information.

Cruise routes often go east along the Columbia as well, some as far as Hell's Canyon, and offer excursions including Maryhill Museum, Hood River, and the Dalles.

SIDE TRIP: LONG BEACH PENINSULA AND WILLAPA BAY

*The southern coast of Washington—***Long Beach and Willapa Bay***—has long been a destination for Portlanders. Long Beach is the state's oldest coastal resort. It has a restored downtown, a new boardwalk, and 26 miles of sandy beach. And as home to the* **World Kite Museum and Hall of Fame,** *Third Street Northwest and Pacific Highway, 360/642-4020, it's obviously one of the world's best places to fly kites. Two hundred thousand high-flyers gather here the third week in August to celebrate the kite. The small museum's special exhibit of fighter kites—ranging from huge Japanese models used in team fighting to small ones from Java, decorated with ground glass for a competitive edge—shows a tiny portion of its 1,200-kite collection. Admission is $1 for adults. Open through August daily 11 to 5.* **Willapa Bay** *is a large saltwater inlet created by Long Beach peninsula. Preserved as Willapa National Wildlife Refuge, it is also home to well-known oyster farms. There are canoe and kayak put-ins here.*

Details: *Six miles southwest of Astoria. Open mid-June through Labor Day 8 to 6, the rest of the year 8 to 5. Re-enactments are held during the summer. Admission $2 for adults 17 and up, $4 per carload. (2 hours or more)*

★★★★ FORT STEVENS AND FORT STEVENS STATE PARK

Highway 101, 503/861-3170 or 503/861-2000 (museum)
www.ohwy.com/or/f/ftsteven.htm

Commissioned as a Civil War fortification in 1863, the fort guarded the entrance to the Columbia until shortly after World War II. Gun emplacements still exist. A museum, gift shop, and Chinook longhouse are on the grounds. The *Peter Iredale,* shipwrecked in 1906, can be seen at all times but accessed only at low tide. The park's attractions include the fort, South Jetty Overlook, located where the ocean and river meet, a wildlife viewing platform, and 8.5 miles of paved bike and hiking trails (bicycle rentals from Memorial Day through Labor Day).

Details: *Five miles northwest of Astoria. Park admission $3. (2–3 hours)*

★★★ FORT CANBY STATE PARK

Ilwaco, Washington, 360/642-3078

www.parks.wa.gov

On the Washington side, this park overlooks the mouth of the Columbia River. The **Lewis and Clark Interpretive Center** tells the story of the 1804–1806 expedition; **Cape Disappointment Lighthouse,** built in 1856, is the oldest in Washington and open for tours. The park has many trails that pass through forest on the way to isolated coves and sandy beaches.

Details: *Three miles southwest of U.S. 101 at Ilwaco. Admission is free. (2 hours)*

★★★ JULIA BUTLER HANSEN COLUMBIA WHITE-TAILED DEER REFUGE

This reserve on the Washington side of the river is home to the endangered Columbia white-tailed deer and also provides habitat for bald eagles, other raptors, river otters, and waterfowl.

Details: *Northwest of Cathlamet on SR 4 in Washington. (1 hour)*

★★★ TWILIGHT EAGLE SANCTUARY AND BURNSIDE AREA

An observation platform overlooks protected eagle habitat and Cathlamet Bay. And there's kayaking on the John Day and Columbia Rivers.

Details: *Just east of Astoria, off Highway 30. (1–2 hours)*

★★★ WARRENTON

A waterfront community with two mooring basins, charters, pleasure-boat facilities, and a waterfront trail makes for a fun detour and exploration.

Details: *West of Astoria on Highway 30, across Youngs Bay. (1 hour)*

★★ HERITAGE MUSEUM

1618 Exchange Street, 503/325-2203

This museum looks at maritime culture and the salmon canning industry. Others exhibits focus on the Chinese who lived here early in this century and worked in the fishing industry.

Details: *Open daily 11 to 4. Admission $5, includes entry to Flavel House. (1 hour)*

FITNESS AND RECREATION

Twilight Eagle Sanctuary and Burnside Area, just east of Astoria, offers water trails for canoeing or kayaking and spots for eagle viewing. You can also see wildlife at the Julia Butler Hansen Columbia White-Tailed Deer Refuge, across the river in Washington. Forts on both sides of the river offer plenty to explore.

A block south of the Flavel House, you'll find Franklin Avenue, the town's primary residential street in earlier times. Over 20 historical homes lie in the eight blocks that stretch east to Exchange Street. You can pick up a walking tour booklet and audiotape at Flavel House, the Heritage Museum, or the Chamber of Commerce Information Center.

FOOD

The reputation of the **Columbian Cafe,** 1114 Marine Drive, 503/325-2233, for great vegetarian dishes, seafood stews, and creative surprises, is so great that folks come to Astoria just to eat here. It's quirky and often packed. The café at the **Pacific Rim Gallery,** 108 10th Street, 503/325-5450, serves coffee, ice cream, and light fare to enjoy while you take in the work of regional artists. The **Cannery Cafe,** Sixth Street at the river, 503/325-8642, in a historic salmon cannery, is the best place to go for Sunday brunch. The **Ship Inn Restaurant & Pub,** 1 Second Street, 503/325-0033, is known for fish and chips and river views. For a quick bowl or picnic container of clam chowder, stop by the small food bar at **Josephsons Smokehouse & Specialty Seafood,** 106 Marine Dr., 503/325-2190 or 800/772-FISH; the big draw here is the variety of smoked seafood (which you can order online at www.josephsons.com) that's made the family-owned business, in Astoria for over 75 years, famous.

Two renowned restaurants on the Long Beach Peninsula (on the southwestern Washington coast) offer fancier fare—**The Ark,** in Nahcotta, 360/665-4133, and **The Shoalwater,** at the Shelburne Inn in Seaview, 360/642-2142.

The **Wet Dog Cafe,** 144 11th Street, 503/325-6975, is a riverfront brewpub featuring music and dancing Thursday, Friday, and Saturday nights until 1:30 a.m. The menu—steaks, pastas, and an awesome soft taco grande—also includes burgers such as the Blues Burger and the Hip Hop Burger (bacon or ham with choice of cheese). Four different beers are brewed on site. The other popular spot for music and dancing is the **Red Lion,** 400 Industry

WET NORTHWEST WELCOME FOR LEWIS & CLARK

In November of 1805, when legendary explorers William Clark and Meriwether Lewis reached the broad mouth of the Columbia River near present-day Astoria, they thought they had arrived at their destination—the Pacific Ocean. Further west, they soon discovered the ocean itself, abroil with crashing waves and winter storms. The reception it offered was anything but peaceful, and the weather served up a dismal and stormy December and Christmastime. They built Fort Clatsop, just west of Astoria, and took refuge, working on their maps and journals and stocking up for the return journey. According to Clark they had traveled 4,132 miles in 554 days. The reenactment of their time, at Fort Clatsop (see page 249) takes you back to those days. As the bicentennial of their trip approaches, other special events and celebrations will unfold chronicling this journey of discovery. Contact the Astoria Chamber of Commerce for information on the latest plans; 800/875-6807 or www.oldoregon.com.

You can also learn much more about Lewis and Clark's adventures at www.lewis-clark.org.

Street, 503/325-7373 or 800/547-8010, featuring nightly entertainment in the Seafare Lounge.

LODGING

Astoria's historic-home B&Bs offer good value and are close to town. Many are on Franklin Avenue. Some rooms offer great views of the river. The very affordable **Rosebriar Hotel,** 636 14th Street, 503/325-7427 or 800/487-0224, once a convent, was Astoria's first B&B. In the next block is slightly more expensive **Franklin Street Station,** 1140 Franklin Street, 503/325-4314 or 800/448-1098, a popular and homey inn. Also a good value, **Clementine's,** 847 Exchange Street, 503/325-2005 or 800/521-6801, is a two-house complex near Flauel House. Try other historic and easy-on-the-wallet B&Bs like **Captain's Inn,** 1546 Franklin Street, 503/325-1387 or 800/876-1387; **Columbia River Inn,** 1681 Franklin Street, 503/325-5044 or 800/953-5044; and **Martin & Lilli Foard House,** 690 17th Street, 503/325-1892.

Motel lodging includes the **Red Lion Inn,** 400 Industry Street, 503/325-7373 or 800/547-8010, with stunning views of the river, and the **Shilo Inn** in Warrenton, west on Harbor Drive off Highway 101, 800/222-2244, an all-mini-suites motel with covered pool.

CAMPING

Camping at local state parks offers wonderful options, particularly if you make friends with the rain. Some Oregon and Washington state parks offer yurts, a convenient camping option for those who don't want to carry a lot of gear. **Fort Stevens State Park** is one of the most popular state parks in Oregon and one of the largest (3,500 acres). It has 596 campsites, five group camps, and nine yurts, with prices from $14 to $20. Reservations are advised; 800/452-5687. It's off U.S. Highway 101 near Hammond and Warrenton junction. **Fort Canby State Park** (see page 251) has about 250 campsites with prices from $11 to $16. For information, call 360/642-3078; for reservations, 800/452-5687.

18 PORTLAND

Portland, like Paris and New Orleans, has a river running through it. And like those famous cities, it has both a bustling business side and a "village within a city" personality—an intimacy of scale and experience that draws you in and makes you feel very much at home. Half a million people live within the city limits, and well over a million and a half live in the metro area. But unless you're here during a big event or caught in a traffic jam, it doesn't feel like a big city. Short city blocks have something to do with this feeling, as do the South Park Blocks and Pioneer Courthouse Square, spots resembling village greens where Portlanders go to gather and be entertained or relax.

An active arts and theater scene, vibrant restaurant offerings, a reputation as the microbrew capital of the Northwest (and perhaps the country), wonderful parks and public gardens—such as the Japanese Garden and Portland's International Rose Garden (Portland is known for its June Rose Festival)—and lots of recreation options add to the rich and delectable fabric of life here. With Portland State University near the heart of downtown you have a mix of business folks and students producing an offbeat creative energy that makes Portland so appealing.

The Columbia River defines Portland's (and the state's) northern limits and adds a vagabond seaport dimension to this city. Ships and boats leaving here have access to the Pacific Ocean and the world to the west, and to the Snake River and Hell's Canyon to the east.

A PERFECT DAY IN PORTLAND

Portland is a breakfast town, so start with a huge glass of fresh-squeezed orange juice at the Heathman Restaurant. Then stroll through the South Park Blocks and visit the Portland Art Museum and the Oregon History Center. Or, if you're in the mood to buy, buy, buy, indulge in tax-free shopping at favorite stops like Nordstrom, Nike Town, and Pioneer Place. To get a panoramic view of the city, drive to Pittock Mansion or the Japanese Garden. A perfect day in Portland ends with a warm summer stroll along the riverfront, stopping in for a drink or dinner at a riverfront restaurant. But take note: You shouldn't leave the Portland area without seeing the Columbia Gorge—so cut the above day short if you have to and take an easy half-day driving tour of the amazing waterfalls and views east of the city along the Columbia River.

ORIENTATION

Portland's numerous one-way streets and its bricked transit mall (parts of which are blocked to drivers) running along S.W. Fifth and Sixth Avenues make for some confusion in getting around. Walking is a good option, as is Portland's well-planned public transportation. Tri-Met transit is convenient and inexpensive; and MAX (Metropolitan Areas Express) light rail runs from downtown 15 miles east across the Willamette to the Lloyd District and Gresham. New in 1998 is a westside route that services the zoo, World Forestry Center, Washington Park, and Hillsboro. Both services are wheelchair accessible and free in "Fareless Square," a 300-block downtown area bordered on the west and south by Interstate 405, on the east by the Willamette River, and on the north by Irving Street. Gray Line offers guided bus tours of the city and to Mt. St. Helens, the gorge, and Mt. Hood; call 800/422-7042 for schedule information.

SIGHTSEEING HIGHLIGHTS

★★★★ JAPANESE GARDEN
611 SW Kingston, 503/223-1321
www.japanesegarden.com

Five gardens make up almost six acres of serenely beautiful gardens overlooking Portland. They are particularly awe-inspiring in spring when the cherry trees are in bloom. Adjacent you'll find the International Rose Test Garden. The Japanese Garden is also near Hoyt Arboretum.

Details: *In Washington Park. Open June through August 9 to 8; April,*

DOWNTOWN PORTLAND

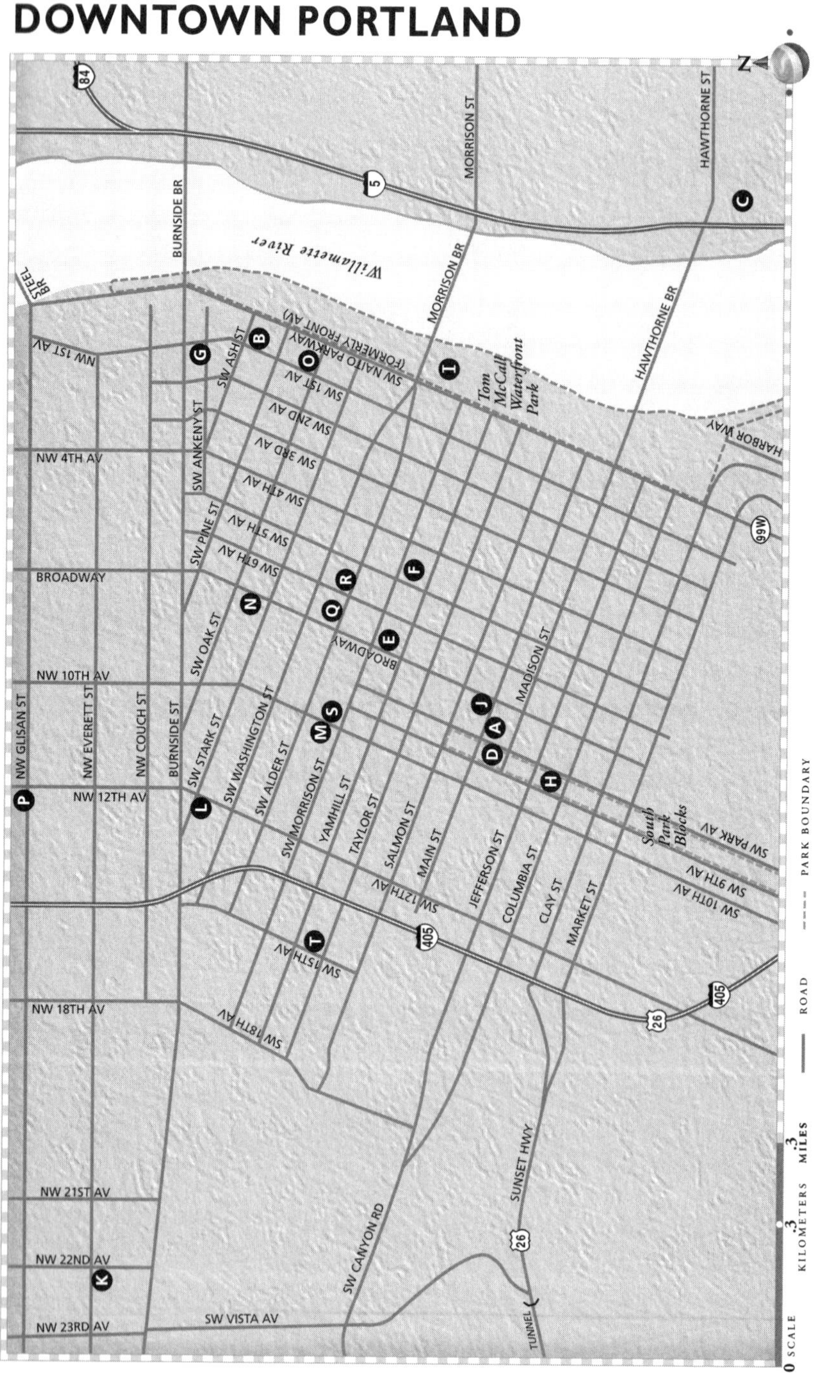

May, and September 10 to 7; and the remainder of year 10 to 4. Admission $6; seniors and students $4. (1–2 hours)

★★★★ OREGON HISTORY CENTER

1200 SW Park Avenue, 503/222-1741

www.ohs.org

The three-dimensional mural on the outside of this building catches your eye first; inside, explore the history of Oregon and the Northwest. There are changing exhibits. A special souvenir suggestion—you can order copies from the large collection of archival photographs that are suitable for framing.

Details: *Admission $6. (1–2 hours)*

★★★★ OREGON MARITIME CENTER AND MUSEUM

113 SW Naito Parkway, 503/224-7724

Stop by this museum in the historic iron-fronted Smith Building in the Skidmore/Old Town district. View ship models and exhibits, or tour the steamer *Portland*, moored at the seawall across waterfront park.

Details: *Call for hours. Admission is $4. Handicapped access is available. (1–2 hours)*

★★★★ OREGON MUSEUM OF SCIENCE AND INDUSTRY (OMSI)

1945 SE Water Avenue, 503/797-4000

www.omsi.edu

SIGHTS

- **A** Oregon History Center
- **B** Oregon Maritime Center and Museum
- **C** Oregon Museum of Science and Industry
- **D** Portland Art Museum
- **E** Pioneer Courthouse Square
- **F** Pioneer Place
- **G** Saturday Market
- **H** South Park Blocks
- **I** Tom McCall Waterfront Park

FOOD

- **J** Heathman Restaurant and Bar
- **K** Il Fornio
- **L** Jake's Famous Crawfish
- **M** Jake's Grill
- **N** London Grill
- **O** McCormick & Schmick's Seafood Restaurant
- **P** Oba
- **Q** Pazzo Ristorante
- **R** Red Star Tavern and Roast House

LODGING

- **N** Benson Hotel
- **R** Fifth Avenue Suites Hotel
- **S** Governor Hotel
- **J** Heathman Hotel
- **Q** Hotel Vintage Plaza
- **T** The Mallory

Note: Items with the same letter are located in the same area.

SIDE TRIP: COLUMBIA RIVER GORGE LOOP

Both a fabulous day trip from Portland and a destination in itself, the **Columbia River Gorge National Scenic Area** *is a don't-miss sight, particularly the view from* **Crown Point Vista House,** *a truly top-of-the-world experience on the Historic Columbia River Highway. You reach it off Interstate 84. Exit east of Troutdale or increase your speed and follow Interstate 84 east of Portland. Dozens of waterfalls enrich your drive. The most stunning is* **Multnomah Falls,** *which drops 620 feet to the historic lodge below. Hood River is the windsurfing capital of the world. Go up the* **Hood River Valley** *in spring as it transforms into a blanket of apple and pear blooms set against Mt. Hood, or in summer to sample the berries and other fruit here.*

Skamania Lodge, *west of Stevenson on SR 14, 509/427-7700, offers panoramic views of the Columbia from its inn and golf course.*

Maryhill Museum of Art, *509/773-3733, is 100 miles east of Portland on SR 14 on the Washington side of the river. It was built by eccentric railroad tycoon James Hill early in the century and is now home to an amazing collection of small Rodin sculptures and many personal possessions of Queen Marie of Romania. It's open daily 9 to 5. Admission is charged. Be sure to look at the replica of Stonehenge that Hill had built nearby.*

Several cruise lines operate trips up the Columbia, most embarking from Portland. New in 2000 is the **Columbia Queen** *(sister ship of the* **Delta River Queen,** *which sails the Mississippi), operated by the Delta Steamboat Co., 800/297-3960 or www.columbiaqueen.com, making regular trips cruising the Columbia River from Portland. More than a relaxing cruise, more than a great getaway, a trip up the Columbia River offers you a journey through incredible geology. Witness the moody, misty beauty of the Columbia Gorge and the dry hills near Maryhill, the moonscapelike basalt flats along the Snake River, and the deep cut of Hell's Canyon, where you can take a thrilling jetboat ride.*

MOUNT HOOD

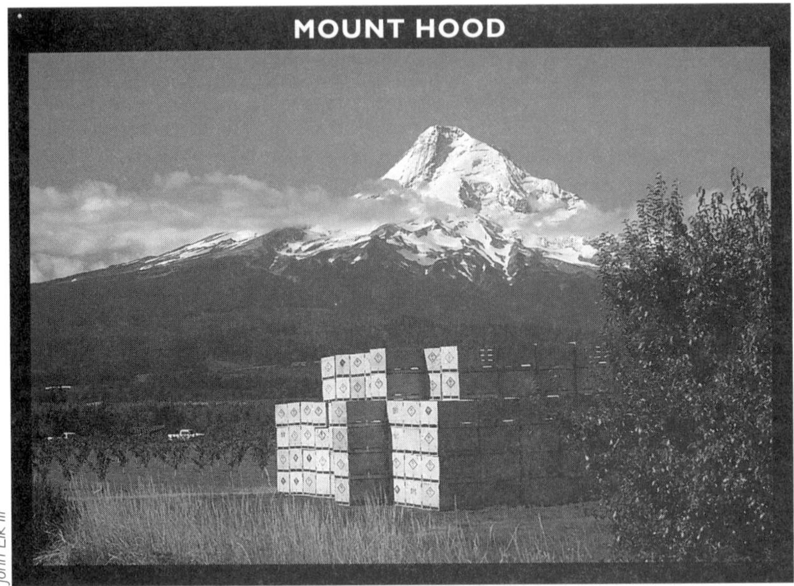

John Elk III

With six exhibit halls, an Omnimax theater, and the Murdock Sky Theater, OMSI, on the east bank of the Willamette River, is one of the largest science museums in the country. Visitors can tour the USS *Blueback* submarine (which appeared in *The Hunt for Red October*) and even beam a message into space. A great place for kids.

Details: *Call for hours and admission prices. (2 hours)*

★★★★ THE OREGON ZOO

www.oregonzoo.org

This wonderful zoo has major exhibits that simulate the animals' natural environments, such as the African Rain Forest, which features forest rainstorms for authenticity. The zoo lies against the hills, with the Rose Test Gardens and Japanese Gardens nearby (a visit to all three would be a full day's outing). A train offers excursions through the zoo and park. In December, the ZooLights Festival draws visitors with over 300,000 lights.

Details: *West of downtown on U.S. 26 about three miles; 503/226-1561. Open daily at 9; closing varies. Admission $6.50. (2–3 hours)*

★★★★ PORTLAND ART MUSEUM

1219 SW Park at Jefferson, 503/226-2811

www.portlandartmuseum.org

This hundred-year-old museum on the South Park Blocks has an impressive painting collection that includes works of masters like Monet and Renoir. Enjoy the permanent collections of Asian, European, and American works, and special exhibits.

Details: *Open Tuesday through Sunday 10 to 5, and until 9 on Wednesday and the first Thursday of the month. (1–2 hours)*

★★★★ TOM MCCALL WATERFRONT PARK

Sweeping lawns and jogging paths along this downtown waterfront make it a particularly wonderful spot on a warm summer night. Stroll by the Waterfront Story Garden, a granite and cobblestone tribute to storytellers in the midst of Japanese American Historical Plaza, where 100 cherry trees commemorate the Japanese American internments of World War II.

Details: *This three-mile-long downtown riverfront runs between the Willamette River and Naito Parkway (formerly Front Street). The sternwheeler* Cascade Queen *departs from River Place Marina and tours the Portland harbor area. Contact 503/223-3928 or www.sternwheeler.com. The* Portland Spirit *offers sight-seeing and meal cruises on the Willamette; call 503/224-3900 or 800/224-3901, www.portlandspirit.com.*

★★★ THE GROTTO

Sandy Boulevard (Highway 30) at Northeast 85th Avenue
503/254-7371, www.thegrotto.org

Portland's forested, gladelike Grotto was established as a Catholic sanctuary in 1924. It's named for the rock cave hewn from the base of a 110-foot cliff rising over the central plaza. Explore the 62-acre grounds enjoying reflection ponds and sculptures. The 550-seat chapel has cathedral-like acoustics; nearby is the natural stone grotto. In December, a Festival of Lights at the Grotto with choral performances, runs nightly except for Christmas day.

Details: *Located a mile south of the Portland airport. Admission is free. Small charge to ride the elevator to the upper garden. (1½ hours).*

★★★ PIONEER COURTHOUSE SQUARE

This is Portland's outdoor living room, an open brick courtyard where people gather to take in the sun and to lunch from brown bags, and where special events, including floral displays, are often featured. It's a great spot to people-watch.

Details: *S.W. Broadway Avenue and S.W. Morrison Street. (10 minutes to 1 hour)*

★★★ SATURDAY MARKET

SW First Avenue, 503/222-6072

www.saturdaymarket.org

From March to Christmas Eve, several hundred craftspeople and food purveyors gather each weekend to sell handmade goods, including woodcrafts, leather items, and clothing.

Details: *Beneath the Burnside Bridge. (1–2 hours)*

★★★ SOUTH PARK BLOCKS

This is a beautiful tree-studded strip of green space in the heart of downtown, surrounded by the city's cultural stalwarts like the Portland Art Museum and the Oregon History Center, and with Portland State University at one end. People gather here to talk, play chess, or watch the world go by.

Details: *Between Park Avenue and Ninth Avenue. (20 minutes)*

★★ PIONEER PLACE

700 SW Fifth Avenue, 503/228-5800

In the heart of downtown, this fashionable four-level shopping mall, adjacent to Saks Fifth Avenue, contains Williams-Sonoma, Anne Taylor, and many other shops and eateries. An underground tunnel connects to parking.

Details: *Open Monday through Friday 9:30 to 9, Saturday 9:30 to 7, Sunday 11 to 6. (2 hours)*

★★ PITTOCK MANSION

3229 NW Pittock Drive, 503/823-3624

This restored French Renaissance house was built by Henry Pittock, the founder of the *Daily Oregonian,* in the early 1900s. It's filled with antiques and is a beautiful house to tour, but just as wonderful—and as good a reason to come here—is the incredible view of the city. This is a good spot to have a sandwich picnic.

Details: *Off Burnside. The house is open daily noon to 4. Admission is $4.50. It's free to tour the grounds; open daily from 7 to 9. (1 hour)*

★★ WORLD FORESTRY CENTER

4033 SW Canyon Road, 503/228-1367

www.worldforest.org

This museum in Washington Park contains exhibits on the old-growth forests of the Pacific Northwest, firefighting, and tropical rain forests. A

GREATER PORTLAND

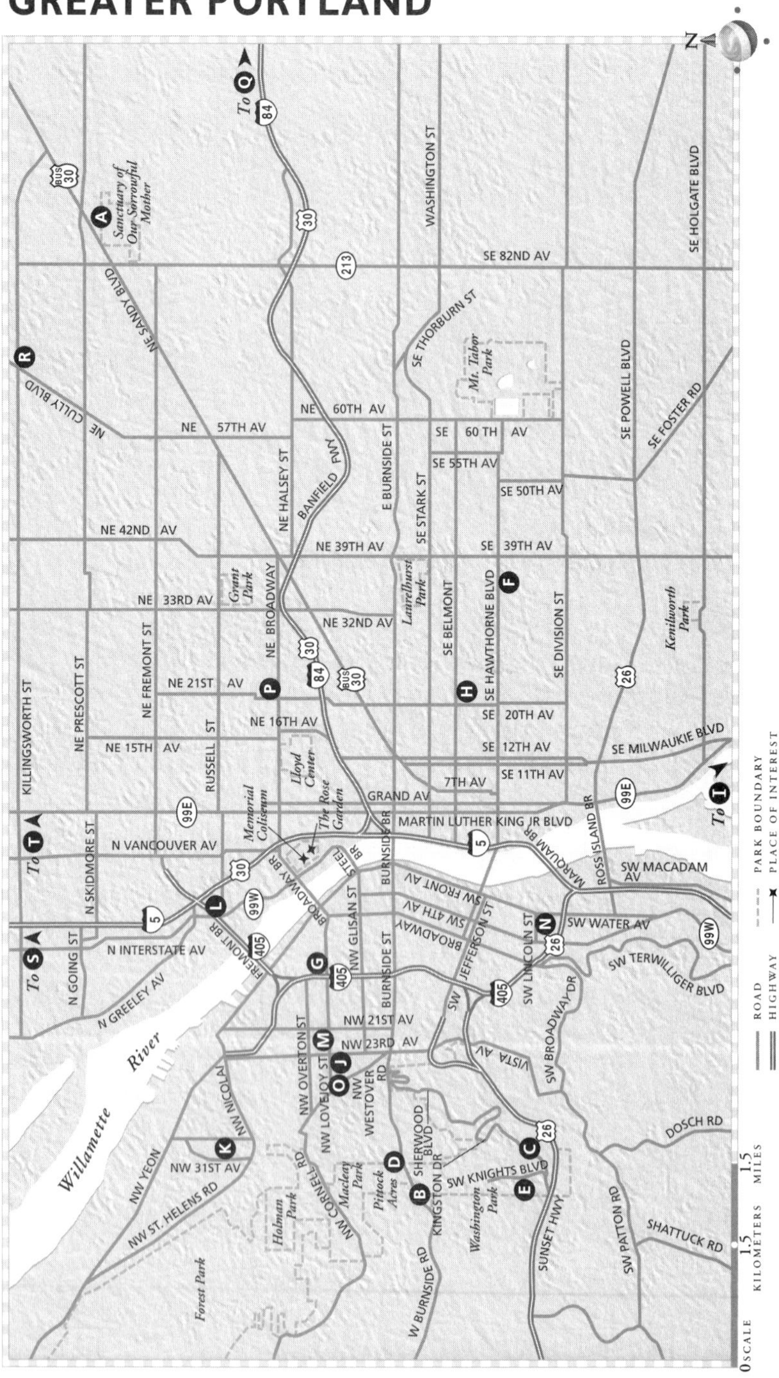

N

To Q
84
30
BUS 30
A Sanctuary of Our Sorrowful Mother
213
WASHINGTON ST
SE 82ND AV
SE HOLGATE BLVD
NE SANDY BLVD
R
NE CULLY BLVD
SE THORBURN ST
Mt. Tabor Park
NE 60TH AV
NE 57TH AV
SE 60TH AV
SE 55TH AV
SE 50TH AV
SE POWELL BLVD
SE FOSTER RD
NE HALSEY ST
BANFIELD FWY
E BURNSIDE ST
SE STARK ST
NE 42ND AV
NE 39TH AV
SE 39TH AV
F
Grant Park
NE BROADWAY
NE 33RD AV
NE 32ND AV
Laurelhurst Park
SE BELMONT
SE HAWTHORNE BLVD
SE DIVISION ST
Kenilworth Park
KILLINGSWORTH ST
NE PRESCOTT ST
NE FREMONT ST
NE 21ST AV
P
H
26
NE 16TH AV
SE 20TH AV
NE 15TH AV
RUSSELL ST
Lloyd Center
SE 12TH AV
SE MILWAUKIE BLVD
SE 11TH AV
7TH AV
GRAND AV
99E
Memorial Coliseum
The Rose Garden
MARTIN LUTHER KING JR BLVD
ROSS ISLAND BR
To I
To T
N SKIDMORE ST
N VANCOUVER AV
STEEL BR
BURNSIDE BR
5
MARQUAM BR
SW MACADAM AV
30
L
99W
BROADWAY BR
NW GLISAN ST
BURNSIDE ST
SW FRONT AV
SW 4TH AV
BROADWAY
SW JEFFERSON ST
N
SW WATER AV
To S
N GOING ST
N INTERSTATE AV
FREMONT BR
405
G
SW LINCOLN ST
SW TERWILLIGER BLVD
N GREELEY AV
SW
NW 21ST AV
SW BROADWAY DR
Willamette River
M
NW 23RD AV
NW OVERTON ST
J
VISTA AV
NW NICOLAI
O
NW LOVEJOY ST
NW WESTOVER RD
K
SHERWOOD BLVD
DOSCH RD
NW YEON
NW 31ST AV
NW CORNELL RD
D
C
Macleay Park
Pittock Acres
SW KNIGHTS BLVD
NW ST. HELENS RD
Holman Park
B
KINGSTON DR
E
Washington Park
SUNSET HWY
SW PATTON RD
SHATTUCK RD
Forest Park
W BURNSIDE RD

ROAD
HIGHWAY
PARK BOUNDARY
PLACE OF INTEREST

0 SCALE 1.5 KILOMETERS 1.5 MILES

tall "talking tree" at the entry captures the attention of children. Outside exhibits also included.

Details: *Open 9 to 5 daily. Admission $4.50; $3.50 for seniors and students. (1–2 hours)*

FITNESS AND RECREATION

The Portland area boasts 37,000 acres of public parkland. The Willamette River Trail offers walkers, joggers, bicyclists, and in-line skaters miles of scenic riverfront to explore. A double-decker trolley serves this area as well. Indoor ice-skating is available at Clackamas Town Center and Lloyd Center.

The best sporting event in Portland is a Trailblazers game. NBA action is hard to beat. Go early to the Rose Quarter arena and choose from numerous eating venues that include a sports grill. The people-watching is as much fun as the game itself! Halftime at the games features the very athletic Blazer Dancers. In the mood for some arena football? The Forest Dragons will serve up just what you're looking for. If soccer is your game, you should give the Portland Pythons a try. And if you crave the excitement of hockey, the Winter Hawks will have you on your feet. Don't overlook some great minor-league baseball played by the Rockies. Individual tickets can be purchased through Ticketmaster, 503/224-4400

SIGHTS

- Ⓐ The Grotto
- Ⓑ Japanese Garden
- Ⓒ The Oregon Zoo
- Ⓓ Pittock Mansion
- Ⓔ World Forestry Center

FOOD

- Ⓕ Bread and Ink Cafe
- Ⓖ BridgePort Brewing Company
- Ⓗ Genoa
- Ⓘ Papa Haydn East
- Ⓙ Papa Haydn West

FOOD *(continued)*

- Ⓚ Portland Brewing Company Taproom & Grill
- Ⓛ Widmer Brothers Gasthaus
- Ⓜ Wildwood

LODGING

- Ⓝ DoubleTree
- Ⓞ Heron Haus B&B
- Ⓟ White House

CAMPING

- Ⓠ Ainsworth State Park
- Ⓠ Cascade Locks Marine Park
- Ⓠ Crown Point RV Park
- Ⓡ Fir Grove RV and Trail Park
- Ⓢ Jantzen Beach RV Park
- Ⓣ Portland Meadows RV Park

Note: Items with the same letter are located in the same area.

A CITY OF BRIDGES

It's hard to visit Portland without noticing the many varied bridges that cross the Willamette River. Ten bridges, in fact, most built in the early 1900s, connect the west and east portions of the city. The oldest, built in 1910, is the Hawthorne Bridge. The Steel Bridge, built in 1912, has two levels and handles Amtrak trains on the lower level and Max light rail and automobiles on the top. You'll perhaps become most familiar with the Burnside Bridge as Burnside is in the center of town, dividing Portland into north and south districts, and you'll find yourself frequently crossing this bridge. Each bridge has it's own unique characteristics; and you can learn more about them in a fine exhibit at the Oregon Museum of Science and Industry.

FOOD

The Bijou Cafe, 132 S.W. Third Avenue, 503/222-3187, is a funky gathering spot and a great breakfast start. Even simple scrambled eggs are great here. Near N.W. 23rd, **Il Fornio** offers Italian countryside charm and great French toast. **McCormick & Schmick's Seafood Restaurant,** First and Oak Streets, 503/224-7522, offers an updated version of traditional seafood. At **Dan and Louis' Oyster Bar Restaurant and Museum,** 208 S.W. Ankeny Street, 503/227-5906, oyster and crab stews, clam and salmon chowders, and oysters on the half shell have kept folks coming back since 1907. To sample Portland's "brew madness," visit one of several brewpubs for a tour and a meal. **BridgePort Brewing Company,** 1313 N.W. Marshall Street, 503/241-7179, has brewery tours daily at 2 and 5. **Portland Brewing Company Taproom & Grill,** 2730 N.W. 31st, 503/228-5269, has tours on Saturday by appointment. **Widmer Brothers Gasthaus,** 929 North Russell, 503/281-3333, has tours Fridays at 2 and 3, and Saturdays at 1 and 2. Several Portland-based tour companies offer microbrewery tours or transportation to and from pubs; these include Custom Tailored Tours, 360/245-0536 or 800/391-5761; EcoTours of Oregon, 503/245-1428 or 888/868-7733; and Van-Go Tours, 503/292-2085.

Genoa, 2832 S.E. Belmont Street, 503/238-1464, while expensive, has served top-rated classic Italian food for more than a quarter of a century. Its seven-course fixed-price dinner has seatings on the hour and half-hour from

A BOOK EMPIRE

Book lovers get "that look" in their eyes at the mention of Powell's. It is perhaps the Northwest's most famous bookstore. The main store, Powell's City of Books, 503/228-4651 or 800/878-7323, fills three-plus stories for a whole city block and has a coffee shop.

And there are other neighborhood and specialized branches. The Travel Store at Pioneer Square, 800/546-5025, Powell's Books on Hawthorne, 800/603-3876; Powell's Books for Cooks and Gardeners on S.E. Hawthorne, 800/354-5957; Powell's Technical Books, N.W. Park and Couch, 800/225-6911. Powell's Books in Beaverton, Highway 217, exit at Progress, 800/466-7323, and Powells at PDX (the airport) for a book hit on your way out of town, 800/229-3664. You can also book-look till you drop on the Web at www.powells.com.

5:30 to 9:30 p.m. Four-course dinners are an option Monday through Thursday. Reservations are a must.

Bread and Ink Cafe, 3610 S.E. Hawthorne, 503/239-4756, is a friendly neighborhood hangout in the Hawthorne district. Breads baked fresh daily are a specialty, as is the eclectic menu of American classics and Mediterranean and Mexican specialties. This is a good spot for a late-night dessert. Around since 1892, **Jake's Famous Crawfish,** 401 S.W. 12th Avenue, 503/226-1419, is Portland's best-known seafood restaurant. Nearby, **Jake's Grill,** 611 S.W. 10th Avenue, 503/220-1850, at the corner of S.W. 10th and Alder in downtown Portland, does for steaks what the original Jake's does for seafood in an old-fashioned dark wood and tile-floored saloon atmosphere.

The **Heathman Restaurant and Bar,** on Broadway at Salmon, 503/241-4100, is a great spot to dine before or after attending a performance nearby at Portland Center for the Performing Arts. Breakfast here is great and brunch on Sunday is tops. The **London Grill,** Benson Hotel, 309 S.W. Broadway, 503/295-4110, is a legendary Portland gathering spot. **Macheezmo Mouse** (several outlets) serves healthy Mexican food, so you'll have no guilt when you nosh on the cheesy, black bean tortillas drizzled with fresh salsa in a high-tech, high-energy environment. Great for kids. **Oba,** in the heart of the Pearl District at 12th and Hoyt, 503/228-6161, is a richly colorful restaurant serving up tasty Brazilian-style food to match its energetic interior—the cheese dip, coconut prawns, and volcano cake are worth the trip. The chef uses lots of lime and different flavors. **Papa Haydn East,** 5829 S.E. Milwaukie, 503/232-9440, is known for fresh local foods—Hood River pears, Oregon raspberries, Dungeness crab. **Papa Haydn West,** at 701 N.W. 23rd Avenue, 503/228-7317, is best known for its desserts. **Pazzo Ristorante,** at Hotel Vintage Plaza, 627 S.W. Washington Street, 503/228-1515, has both a soothing and energizing feel and is open daily for breakfast, lunch, and dinner. Like the **Red Star Tavern and Roast House,** 503/222-0005, on the premises of another Kimpton Hotel, Fifth Avenue Suites, it mixes menu items that comfort or challenge. **Wildwood,** 1221 N.W. 21st Avenue, 503/248-9663, is known for the trendsetting talents of chef/owner Corey Schreiber.

LODGING

The **Benson Hotel,** 309 S.W. Broadway, 503/228-2000, is a distinguished and historic luxury hotel in downtown Portland offering 286 rooms. The **Governor Hotel,** 611 S.W. 10th at Alder, 503/224-3400 or 800/554-3456, is another historic Portland hotel in the heart of downtown. The **Heathman Hotel,** 1001 S.W. Broadway, 503/241-4100, has direct access to the Arlene Schnitzer Concert Hall. The **Hotel Vintage Plaza,** 422 S.W. Broadway, 503/228-1212, is a Kimpton Hotel with a small-inn feel. Rooms are named after Oregon wineries, and wine is offered to guests late in the afternoon. **Fifth Avenue Suites Hotel,** 506 S.W. Washington at Fifth Avenue, 503/222-0001 or 800/711-2971, is another Kimpton boutique-style hotel, with cheery and sophisticated one-bedroom suites, an on-site Aveda Spa, Red Star Tavern, and Roast House restaurant. The **Embassy Suites,** in the historic Multnomah Hotel, 319 S.W. Pine Street, 503/279-9000 or www.embassy-suites.com, includes breakfast with your room and offers good value, particularly in the off-season. **The Mallory,** 729 S.W. 15th (at Yamhill), 503/223-6311 or 800/228-8657, offers well-kept, old-style rooms at reasonable rates, just a few blocks' walk from the heart of downtown.

Several **DoubleTree** hotels are in good locations—downtown, at the airport, and at Jantzen Beach along the Columbia River; the Jantzen Beach DoubleTree is at 909 North Hayden Island Drive, 503/283-4466.

There are numerous B&Bs in Portland. **Heron Haus B&B,** 503/274-1846 or www.heronhaus.com, is in a large home in a residential area near lively N.W. 23rd. East of the river, **The White House,** 503/287-7131, is in a historic mansion on N.E. 22nd. For a brochure from Portland Metro InnKeepers Association, call 800/955-1647.

SIDE TRIP: MOUNT ST. HELENS NATIONAL VOLCANIC MONUMENT

This Washington mountain blew 1,300 feet of its top off in May 1980, spewing volcanic ash for hundreds of miles, changing lives, and reconfiguring the mountain and surrounding area. Though much of the landscape within the blast zone is haunting and stark, there's regrowth, with wildflowers and wildlife evident. Over 70 miles of trails have been constructed for viewing the volcanic destruction and regrowth.

Exits to a number of visitors centers are only about an hour's drive north of Portland on I-5. A free (donations accepted) visitor center in the city of Castle Rock (off I-5, Exit 49, west into town) features exhibits by survivors and residents of the area. This is a good place to start to understand the human impact of the eruption.

Then head to the first visitor center established by the Forest Service, the ***Mount St. Helens National Volcanic Monument Visitor Center,*** *360/274-2100, at Silver Lake. (Take Exit 49 from I-5 and go east on SR 504 about five miles.) This center has exhibits on seismology and current conditions. Admission (about $8) is charged here, but it provides access to all other forest service centers for the day, including* ***Coldwater Ridge,*** *at milepost 43, 360/274-2131, which features exhibits on the post-eruption recovery of the blast area and future views of what the mountain will likely look like a hundred years from now.* ***Johnston Ridge Observatory,*** *at milepost 53.8, is the end of the road and offers the most impressive view of the crater, up close. Be sure to stay for the video presentation of what happened during the eruption.*

If you are short on time, two centers—the ***Mount St. Helens National Volcanic Monument*** *and the* ***Johnston Ridge Observatory****—are the ones to head for.*

For trip planning help and information, contact the Mount St. Helens Information Resource Center, 360/274-3406, 360/274-3231, or www.mountsthelens.com.

CAMPING

Three camping parks near the Columbia River, about four miles north of downtown, offer convenience to sights and recreation: **Fir Grove RV and Trail Park,** 503/252-9993; **Jantzen Beach RV Park,** 503/289-7626, with shady spots and a golf course nearby; and **Portland Meadows RV Park,** 503/285-1617, close to the Portland Meadows racetrack that operates October through April. Rates are about $20 per night. Other camping options take you east along the Columbia River Gorge: **Crown Point RV Park,** 503/695-5207, near the historical Vista House (see page 259); **Ainsworth State Park** 503/695-2261; or **Cascade Locks Marine Park,** 541/374-8619, on 200 acres of waterfront park.

SHOPPING

In 1960 the Lloyd Center was the "world's largest shopping center." Although there've been a lot of bigger shopping centers built since then, there are still 200 stores here, including Meier & Frank and Nordstrom. The center's skating rink was recently redeveloped into a state-of-the-art facility.

There are numerous neighborhoods to explore for fun shopping and people-watching. There's **23rd Avenue** in Northwest Portland. South of here is the **Pearl District,** a lively mix of restaurants, galleries, and antiques shops in a former warehouse area. **Old Sellwood Antique Row,** further south still, was settled in the 1850s and named for the Reverend James Sellwood. This unique neighborhood has become a top antiques district; it's along S.E. 13th Avenue, six blocks east of the Sellwood Bridge. The hip, '60s-style **Hawthorne District,** in Southeast Portland, is another area popular with shoppers.

APPENDIX

Consider this appendix your travel toolbox. Use it along with the material in the Planning Your Trip chapter to craft the trip you want. Here are the tools you'll find inside:

1. Planning Map. Make copies of this map and plot out various trip possibilities. Once you've decided on your route, you can write it on the original map and refer to it as you're traveling.

2. Mileage Chart. This chart shows the driving distances (in miles) between various destinations throughout the region. Use it in conjunction with the Planning Map.

3. Special Interest Tours. If you'd like to plan a trip around a certain theme—such as nature, sports, or art—one of these tours may work for you.

4. Calendar of Events. Here you'll find a month-by-month listing of major area events.

5. Resource Guide. This guide lists various regional chambers of commerce and visitors bureaus, state offices, bed-and-breakfast registries, and other useful sources of information.

6. Metric Conversion Chart. This chart will help you convert U.S. measures and weights when in Canada.

PLANNING MAP: Pacific Northwest

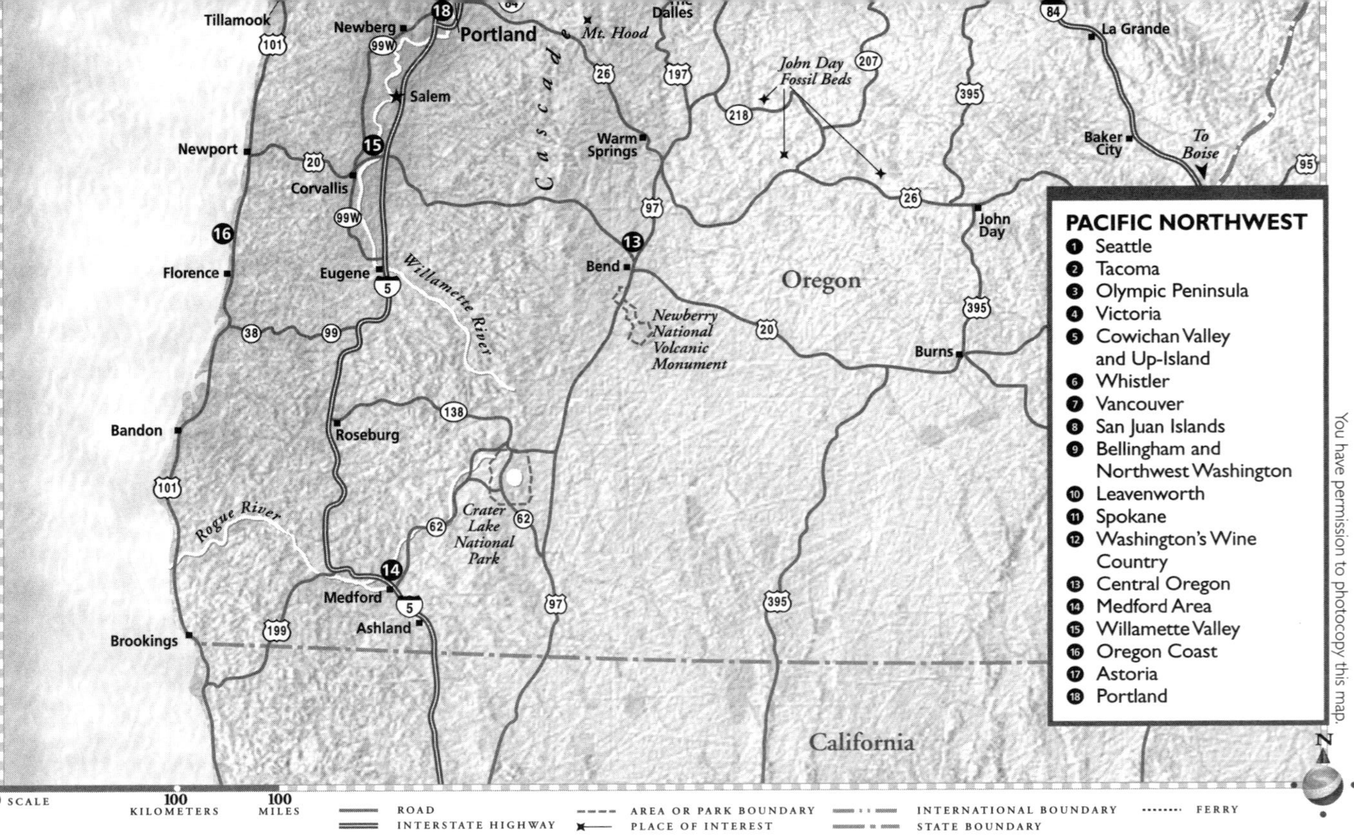

PACIFIC NORTHWEST
1 Seattle
2 Tacoma
3 Olympic Peninsula
4 Victoria
5 Cowichan Valley and Up-Island
6 Whistler
7 Vancouver
8 San Juan Islands
9 Bellingham and Northwest Washington
10 Leavenworth
11 Spokane
12 Washington's Wine Country
13 Central Oregon
14 Medford Area
15 Willamette Valley
16 Oregon Coast
17 Astoria
18 Portland
Oregon
California
Portland
Tillamook
Newberg
Salem
Newport
Corvallis
Florence
Eugene
Bandon
Roseburg
Brookings
Medford
Ashland
Bend
Warm Springs
Mt. Hood
Cascade
Willamette River
Rogue River
Crater Lake National Park
Newberry National Volcanic Monument
John Day Fossil Beds
John Day
Burns
Baker City
La Grande
To Boise
101
99W
20
38
99
5
138
62
199
97
26
197
218
207
395
84
95
N
0 SCALE
100 KILOMETERS
100 MILES
ROAD
INTERSTATE HIGHWAY
AREA OR PARK BOUNDARY
PLACE OF INTEREST
INTERNATIONAL BOUNDARY
STATE BOUNDARY
FERRY

You have permission to photocopy this map.

PACIFIC NORTHWEST MILEAGE CHART

	Seattle	Port Townsend	Vancouver, B.C.	Whistler, B.C.	Tacoma	Bellingham	Yakima	Spokane	Bend	John Day	Ashland	Crater Lake	Eugene	Brookings	Portland
Port Townsend	60														
Vancouver, B.C.	140	130													
Whistler, B.C.	210	200	70												
Tacoma	31	87	174	244											
Bellingham	88	78	52	122	122										
Yakima	142	194	273	343	166	223									
Spokane	278	331	412	482	303	360	205								
Bend	325	364	468	538	296	416	219	384							
John Day	408	461	541	611	433	490	267	329	153						
Ashland	466	504	609	679	437	557	478	644	196	349					
Crater Lake	424	463	567	637	395	515	325	489	104	257	104				
Eugene	289	328	432	502	261	380	301	467	115	250	182	140			
Brookings	525	564	668	738	497	616	537	703	297	486	147	205	241		
Portland	170	208	313	383	141	261	185	351	158	285	289	247	112	348	
Astoria	174	188	317	386	145	265	222	445	252	379	393	351	216	340	97

SPECIAL INTEREST TOURS

With the *Travel Smart: Pacific Northwest* guidebook you can plan a trip of any length—a one-day excursion, a getaway weekend, or a three-week vacation—around any special interest. To get you started, the following pages contain six suggested itineraries geared toward a variety of interests. For more information, refer to the chapters listed—chapter names are bolded and chapter numbers appear inside black bullets. You can follow a suggested itinerary in its entirety, or shorten, lengthen, or combine parts of each, depending on your starting and ending points.

Discuss alternative routes and schedules with your travel companions—it's a great way to have fun, even before you leave home. And remember: Don't hesitate to change your itinerary once you're on the road. Careful study and planning ahead of time will help you make informed decisions as you go, but spontaneity is the extra ingredient that will make your trip memorable.

BEST OF THE REGION TOUR

It would take three weeks to spin through this itinerary. But if a driving tour is what you're after, this trip gives you the best of sights and scenery.

- ❼ **Vancouver** (Stanley Park, Robson Street, Granville Island, Museum of Anthropology)
- ❹ **Victoria** (Butchart Gardens, Royal British Columbia Museum, the Empress Hotel, Government Street)
- ❽ **San Juan Islands**
- ❾ **Bellingham and Northwest Washington** (North Cascades National Park)
- ❿ **Leavenworth** (Cascade Loop Drive: Lake Chelan, Winthrop)
- ❶ **Seattle** (Pike Place Market, Seattle Art Museum, Ballard Locks, Museum of Flight)
- ❷ **Olympic Peninsula** (Hurricane Ridge, Port Townsend, Hoh Rain Forest, Cape Flattery)
- ⓰ **Oregon Coast** (Oregon Dunes National Monument, seaside towns)
- ⓲ **Portland** (Oregon Zoo, Japanese Garden, Oregon History Museum, Portland Art Museum, Columbia River Gorge Loop, Maryhill Museum)

Time needed: 3 weeks

NATURE LOVER'S TOUR

Nature lovers can be happy just about anywhere in the Northwest. Here are some high-interest destinations.

❻ **Whistler** (Brackendale Eagle Tours)
❺ **Cowichan Valley and Up-Island** (Pacific Rim National Park)
❾ **Bellingham and Northwest Washington** (Whale-watching tours or kayaking from Bellingham, La Connor, Anacortes, or the San Juan Islands)
❶ **Seattle** (Seattle Aquarium, whale-watching boat tours from Everett)
❸ **Tacoma and Mt. Rainier** (Nisqually Delta)
⓰ **Oregon Coast** (Oregon Coast Aquarium in Newport, Oregon Dunes National Recreation Area in Florence)
⓭ **Central Oregon** (John Day Fossil Beds)

Time needed: 2 weeks

ARTS AND CULTURE TOUR

Opportunities to enjoy arts and culture are concentrated in the larger cities; out-of-the-way exceptions are noted here as well.

- ❼ **Vancouver** (Granville Islands artisan studios, Vancouver Art Gallery, Museum of Anthropology)
- ❺ **Cowichan Valley and Up-Island** (Chemainus Island history in murals)
- ❹ **Victoria** (Royal British Columbia Museum)
- ❶ **Seattle** (Seattle Art Museum, Seattle Asian Art Museum, Henry Art Gallery, Museum of Flight)
- ❸ **Tacoma and Mt. Rainier** (Tacoma Art Museum, Washington State History Museum, Broadway Performing Arts Center)
- ⓲ **Portland** (Portland Art Museum, Maryhill Museum on the Columbia Gorge)
- ⓯ **Willamette Valley** (End of the Oregon Trail Interpretive Center)
- ⓭ **Central Oregon** (High Desert Museum, the Museum at Warm Springs)
- ⓬ **Washington's Wine Country** (Yakama Reservation Museum, Toppenish history in murals)

Time needed: 2 weeks

FAMILY FUN TOUR

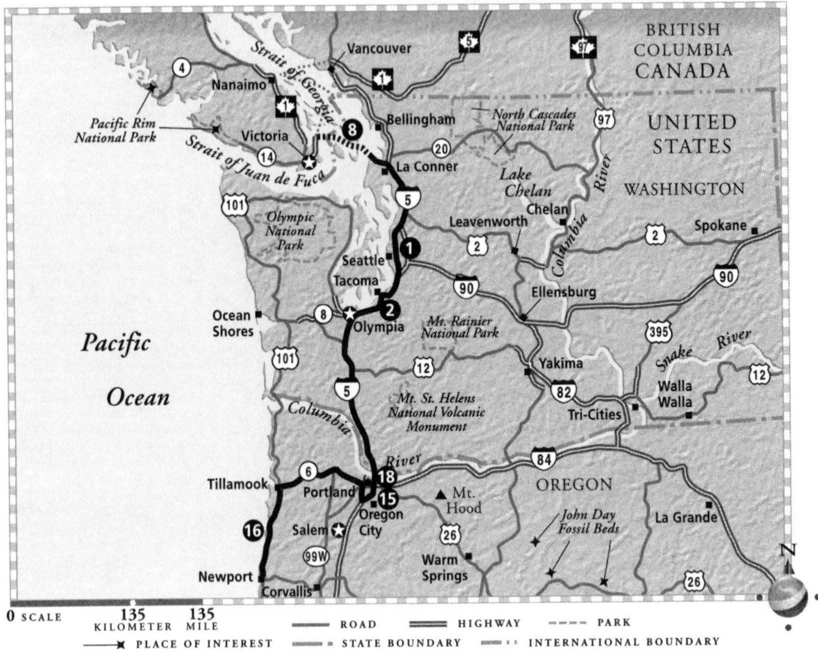

Many of the Northwest's outdoor activities—boating, hiking, beach exploring—are fun for the whole family. Here are some special stops that will please folks in all age groups.

8 **San Juan Islands** (ferry rides, whale-watching, kayaking, and canoeing)
1 **Seattle** (Seattle Center, Hiram M. Chittenden Locks, Museum of Flight, Woodland Park Zoo)
2 **Tacoma and Mt. Rainier** (Point Defiance Zoo and Aquarium, Northwest Trek Wildlife Park, Children's Museum of Tacoma)
18 **Portland** (Oregon Zoo, Oregon Museum of Science and Industry)
15 **Willamette Valley** (End of the Oregon Trail Interpretive Center in Oregon City)
16 **Oregon Coast** (Oregon Coast Aquarium, Tillamook cheese factory)

Time needed: 10 days

WINE REGIONS TOUR

The wine regions of Oregon, Washington, and British Columbia are magnets for good living. The balmy-to-hot summer weather in the Willamette, Yakima, Columbia, and Okanagan Valleys, as well as the recreation and food choices you'll find here, make for richly varied destinations.

❾ **Bellingham and Northwest Washington** (Nooksack Valley)
❼ **Vancouver** (International Wine Festival, wineries)
❺ **Cowichan Bay and Up-Island** (small wineries with tasting rooms)
❹ **Victoria** (wine festival)
❽ **San Juan Islands** (winery on Lopez Island)
❶ **Seattle** (wineries on Whidbey Island and around Seattle)
⓬ **Washington's Wine Country** (Yakima Valley, Columbia Valley/Tri-Cities area, Walla-Walla tours and wine festivals)
⓯ **Willamette Valley** (valley wineries, Oregon Wine Tasting Room)
⓮ **Medford Area** (wineries in Roseburg)

Time needed: 10 days

SUMMERTIME MOUNTAINTOP TOUR

Touring the mountaintops of the Northwest in summer offers great views and a different way to look at the mountains. It's also a treat for non-skiers. Atop many mountains, you'll still find patches of snow, even at the height of summer. The roads down many of these slopes are favorites with mountain bikers.

- 6 **Whistler** (horseback riding and hikes to Harmony Lake on Whistler Mountain, hikes through wildflowers on nearby Blackbob Mountain)
- 9 **Bellingham and Northwest Washington** (Mt. Baker's Artist Point, hikes and interpretive center at Heather Meadows)
- 3 **Tacoma and Mt. Rainier** (Mt. Rainier's classic Paradise Lodge with restaurant and lodging)
- 18 **Portland** (Mt. Hood, with classic Timberline Lodge restaurant and lodging, Mt. St. Helens Volcanic Monument and Interpretive Center)
- 13 **Central Oregon** (bicycling or in-line skating down Mt. Bachelor)
- 14 **Medford Area** (boat tours of Crater Lake, Crater Lake Lodge)

Time needed: 2 weeks

CALENDAR OF EVENTS

January

Snow Lunacy Festival (Ashford, WA)

A family-oriented day of events and amateur cross-country ski competitions on trails adjacent to Mt. Rainier National Park. The Mt. Tahoma Trails Association. raises funds to maintain 75 miles of trails in the park, the largest no-fee ski area in North America; 360/569-2724

Brackendale Eagles (Brackendale, BC)

Record gathering of eagles in this small community between Vancouver and Whistler; volunteers can participate in a bird count or arrange for river float trips. Contact the Brackendale Art Gallery, 604/898-3333 or www.mountain-inter.net/~gallery/

Boxing Day Sales (Victoria, Vancouver Island, BC)

The traditional English holiday is the time to shop Victoria's Government Street shops for buys on sweaters and china.

February

Chinese New Year (Seattle, WA, and Vancouver, BC)

The Northwest's two largest Chinese communities celebrate the new year with parades and festivities.

Newport Seafood and Wine Festival (Newport, OR)

The Northwest's first seafood and wine festival, started in 1976; thousands attend the last full weekend in February, to indulge in seafood and taste offerings of wineries from the West Coast. Call 541/265-8801 or 800/262-7844; www.newportchamber.org

Smelt Derby (LaConner, WA)

This arts village was once famous for its huge February run of smelt. The run is now much smaller, but you can still catch this herringlike fish here from waterfront docks. A fun family event with a 10K Smelt Run, a fishing contest for kids, fish painting, and a kayaking race. 888/642-9284

Northwest Flower and Garden Show (Seattle, WA)

The Northwest's largest flower and garden show features elaborate garden exhibits, demonstrations, and vendors, and draws thousands from all over the country; 206/789-5333

Wintergrass Bluegrass Festival (Tacoma, WA)

A large and popular music festival held in various places throughout Pierce County; 253/926-4164

Oregon Shakespeare Festival (Ashland, OR)

One of the most famous Shakespeare festivals around, held annually in picturesque Ashland. Performances begin in February and run through October; 541/482-4331 or www.orshakes.org/

Pacific Northwest Wine Festival (Victoria, BC)

Hosted by the Victoria Symphony Society, this event takes place at the Empress and features wines of the whole Northwest region, seminars and tastings. 250/385-9771 or www.victoriasymphony.bc.ca

March

Annual Oyster Olympics (Seattle, WA)

Oyster growers and lovers slurp and compare bivalves from bays all over the Northwest. A celebrity slurp, competitions, wine and microbrew tastings. Tickets (about $70) must be purchased in advance. This bash regularly sells out. Anthony's HomePort on Shilshole Bay, 206/283-7566

Beachcomber's Fun Fair (Ocean Shores, WA)

Beach finds—glass floats, bottles, shells, driftwood, and less expected items—compete for awards, and scientists and naturalists present information on a variety of beach-related subjects, such as ocean tides, coastal birds, and much more, during this resort community's celebration. 360/289-2451 or 800/76-BEACH

Whale Watch Week (Oregon coast)

During gray whale migration in March and December, volunteers are on hand at more than two dozen spots along the Oregon coast to assist visitors viewing the whales. For a list of the sites, contact 541/563-2002 or www.whalespoken.org

April

Wenatchee Apple Blossom Festival (Wenatchee, WA)

One of the state's oldest festivals. Events run over a two-week period and coincide with peak apple and pear bloom from the end of April into May, 509/662-3616 or www.appleblossom.org

Spring Barrel Tastings

(Yakima Valley, WA; Willamette Valley, OR; Okanagan Valley, BC)
Wine touring during spring barrel tastings is a fun way to explore these agricultural regions. For Oregon contact 800/242-2363 or www.oregonwine.org. For Washington 800/258-7270 or www.washingtonwine. Note: The British Columbia spring wine fest is in May. Check the Okanagan Wine Festival Society website: www.owfs.com

Vancouver Playhouse International Wine Festival (Vancouver, BC)

Considered by many to be the best wine festival in North America, this event draws principals of wineries from around the world for a week of tastings, seminars, and dinners. Call Ticketmaster, 604/280-4444 or 604/873-3311; www.winefest.mybc.com

Astoria-Warrenton Crab and Seafood Festival (Astoria, OR)

A popular three-day food, wine, and arts and crafts celebration held at the Hammond Mooring Basin; contact 800/875-6807 or www.oldoregon.com

May

Lilac Festival and Bloomsday Run (Spokane, WA)

The Lilac Festival kicks off with the Bloomsday Run. One of the biggest 12K events in the Northwest, it draws over 50,000 participants to Spokane streets for a running celebration of spring; 800/248-3230 or www.visitspokane.com for festival information; www.bloomsdayrun.org for race information.

Ste. Michelle Summer Concerts (Woodinville, WA)

A diverse lineup of well-known national and international artists are featured every summer in outdoor performances on Chateau Ste. Michelle's grounds northeast of Seattle. 800/267-6793 or www.stemichelle.com

Western Art Auction (Ellensburg, WA)

Western art fans gather to see and bid on some of the best work of noted Western artists. Contact the Western Art Association, 509/962-2934.

Northwest Folklife Festival (Seattle, WA)

A celebration of the Northwest's diverse heritage, Northwest Folklife Festival is one of the nation's largest free events. Thousands of regional and international artists are featured in music and dance performances, exhibits, demonstrations, and workshops. Always held on Memorial Day weekend; www.nwfolklife.org

Cinco de Mayo Celebration (Pasco, WA)

Held the first week in May, this festival includes dancing horses, salsa bands, and more Hispanic sights, sounds, and tastes. Bands and other Hispanic musicians from eastern Washington perform. 509/545-0738

Victoria Harbour Festival/Swiftsure Race (Victoria, BC)

Celebrates Victoria Day weekend and Memorial Day with a parade, the Swiftsure International Yacht Race, and four nights of free headliner music. On Victoria Harbour; 250/953-2033 or www.harbour.city. victoria.bc.ca

June

Dragon Boat Festival (Vancouver, BC)

Over 2,000 paddlers aboard highly colorful and exotic dragon boats ply waters of False Creek; the festival includes family events and entertainment; 604/688-2382

Rose Festival (Portland, OR)

This monthlong festival of over two dozen events, including two parades, an air show, and a waterfront festival, is one of the oldest and most popular in the Northwest; 503/227-2681 or www.rosefestival.org

Sandcastle Contest (Cannon Beach, OR)

Every year in June sand fans gather to build and sculpt beach creations; the event draws 15,000 to 30,000 folks; 503/436-2623, or www.cannon beach.org

Van Dusen Flower and Garden Show (Vancouver, BC)

The first weekend in June, Van Dusen Botanical Garden hosts a show built around an annual theme. It includes garden displays, speakers, crafts and artisans, and entertainment; 604/878-9274 or 604/257-8671.

Peter Britt Music Festival (Jacksonville, OR)

The festival runs June to September, mostly in outdoor venues—offering music under the stars. For schedule and information, contact 800/882-7488, or www.brittfest.org

Sisters Rodeo (Sisters, OR)

This Old West event, into its sixth decade, is held every year the second weekend in June. Grounds are about six miles east of Sisters on Highway 20. Call 800/827-7522.

Mural in a Day (Toppenish/Yakima Valley, WA)

Western artists add a historically accurate mural to this Western-style town. Festivities include a breakfast, food fair, and wagon tours. Coincides with the Yakama Nation's Pow Wow and Parade; 800/569-3982

International Accordion Festival (Leavenworth, WA)

Festival highlights include a unique accordion parade through the center of town, plus workshops, performances, and competition for all ages. 509/548-5807 or www.leavenworth.org

Bard on the Beach Shakespeare Festival (Vancouver, BC)

From June to September, some of Shakespeare's best-loved plays are performed in open-ended tents on the beach at Vanier Park. Call the box office for reservations, 604/739-0559, or visit www.faximum.com/bard

July

Sisters Quilt Show (Sisters, OR)

Quilts from around the world are displayed; many hang from the street railings of this Western town. Held the second Saturday in July; classes (sign up in advance) organized by the Stitchin' Post, 541/549 6061. Or call the chamber of commerce at 541/549-0251

Symphony of Fire (Vancouver, BC)

A grand display of fireworks matched with music lights the skies over Vancouver. Watch from the land or from a cruise boat. Contact the Vancouver Fireworks Society, 604/738-4304 or 738-4307; for harbor tours contact 604/688-7246 or www.boatcruises.com

International Pinot Noir Celebration (McMinnville, OR)

This three-day event on the grounds of Linfield College, with tastings and elegant meals, is pricey and sells out months in advance (call in February if you want to attend). One of the country's premiere wine festivals; 503/472-8964 or 800/775-4762.

DaVinci Festival (Corvallis/Willamette Valley, OR)

A fun and stimulating festival of art, science, and technology. Contact 541/757-1544 or 800/334-8118 or www.visitcorvallis.com

AT&T Family Fourth at Lake Union (Seattle, WA)

An impressive evening show over Lake Union. Fireworks are digitally choreographed to a special program of American music broadcast over several local radio stations. Daylong events in Gas Works Park at the north end of Lake Union; www.familyfourth.org

Jazz in the Valley (Ellensburg, WA)

Ellensberg's jazz festival features blues, mainstream jazz, and more and takes place in the historic heart of this central Washington university town. 509/925-2002 or 888/925-2204.

Seattle SeaFair (Greater Seattle, WA)

The Northwest's largest summer festival includes the Torchlight parade in downtown Seattle, neighborhood parades and events, hydroplane races, fleet tours, an air show, and more. Held throughout the month. 206/728-0123 or www.seafair.com

Nanaimo Marine Festival and World Championship Bathtub Race (Nanaimo, BC)

This four-day festival ends with a famous bathtub race across the Strait of Georgia from Nanaimo to Kitsilano Beach in Vancouver. 250/753-7223, www.bathtub.island.net

August

Abbotsford International Airshow (Abbotsford, BC)

A weeklong show includes the latest in aircraft technology and stunt aerobatics; it draws over 300,000 attendees each year to Abbotsford Airport. 604/852-8511 or www.abbotsfordairshow.com

Sunriver Music Festival (near Bend, OR)

For over two decades this classically focused festival has drawn crowds to Sunriver. Pop musicians also perform. 541/593-1084 or www.sunrivermusic.org

International Kite Festival (Long Beach, WA)

The beautiful long stretch of beach is thick with kites from all over the world during this week of festivities; www.kitefestival.com or contact the chamber of commerce at 800/451-2542 or www.funbeach.com

Bellingham Festival of Music (Bellingham, WA)

A two-week-long classical musical festival with national headliners and symphony performances, held at Western Washington University and Semiahmoo Resort. Contact 800/335-5550 or 360/676-5997, or www.bellinghamfestival.org

Prosser Wine and Food Fair (Prosser, WA)

Thirty of the state's leading wineries pour samples at what's been called the grand daddy of Washington's outdoor wine festivals. 800/408-1517 or 509/786-4545

Symphony Splash (Victoria, BC)

Members of the Victoria Symphony perform a blend of classics and popular favorites from a barge anchored in Victoria's Inner Harbour. 250/385-6515 or 888/717-6121

September

Bumbershoot Arts Festival (Seattle, WA)

One of the Northwest's largest and favorite festivals, with music, theater, dance, comedy, and visual arts. Held over Labor Day weekend. 206/281-7799 or www.bumbershoot.org

Puyallup Fair (near Tacoma, WA)

The Northwest's largest state fair, operating for a hundred years, offers rides, displays, food, and top headliner entertainment. 253/841-5045 or www.thefair.com

Feast of Fields (Victoria, WA)

A celebration of the bounty of foodstuffs grown on the island

Fiery Food Festival (Pasco, WA)

A food festival that includes a parade of salsa bands, folk dancers, and dancing horses. Street vendors sell many varieties of sweet and hot peppers, as well as onions and garlics; and there's a salsa food competition. 509/545-0738

Washington State Autumn Leaf Festival (Leavenworth, WA)

This celebration of the fall color in the central Cascades includes a grand parade, entertainment, Bavarian wagons, and Tyrolean Haflinger horses. 509/548-5807 or www.leavenworth.org

Mount Angel Annual Oktoberfest (Mt. Angel, OR)

The unique German community celebrates a traditional and boisterous Oktoberfest with continuous live music on four stages and a traditional Biergarten, Weingarten, and Microgarten. www.oktoberfest.org

Shrewsbury Renaissance Faire (Philomath, OR)

Games, contests, food, and music of Renaissance times. Held the second weekend in September. 541/929-2454 or www.peak.org/shrewsbury

Wooden Boat Festival (Port Townsend, WA)

A festival that highlights the maritime history of this busy seaport with a gathering of wooden boats of all types and sizes. Sponsored by the Wooden Boat Foundation. 360/385-3628 or www.olympus.net/wbf/

October

Okanagan Valley Wine Festival (Okanagan Valley, BC)

A ten-day event at wineries and different venues throughout the Okanagan Valley, includes tours, seminars, and entertainment. 250/860-5999

Remlinger Farms Harvest Festival (Carnation, WA)

A family harvest-time extravaganza with rides, exhibits, good food, and fields filled with pumpkins for jack-o'-lanterns. 425/451-4135 or www.remlingerfarms.com

November

Arts Alive (La Conner, WA)

Art shows and demonstrations in a picturesque waterfront town. First weekend in November; 888/642-9284

Thanksgiving in the Wine Country (Yakima Valley, WA)

This holiday open house on the weekend following Thanksgiving features wine tasting and food to sample at each winery, with recipe cards to collect. 800/258-7270 or www.winesnw.com

Stormy Weather Festival (Cannon Beach, OR)

The first weekend in November. Live music, art, and Quick Draw—six Northwest artists each produce a piece of art in one hour and mat and frame it. It's auctioned off on the spot. 503/436-2623 or www.cannon beach.org

Whatcom Artists' Studio Tour (Bellingham, WA)

Two weekends in early November. About 20 studios and galleries are open to the public; artisans include glassblowers, metalsmiths, painters, potters, and woodworkers. 360/733-3432

Cornucopia (Whistler, BC)

Wineries gather for a harvest celebration in Whistler Village that includes gourmet dinners, wine tastings, food and wine seminars, cooking demonstrations, and special events. Weekend event and lodging packages are available. Contact 800/WHISTLER or 604/932-2394; www.tourismwhistler.com

International Martini Challenge (Seattle and Vancouver, BC)

Celebrity judging, competition, and martini madness are highlights of this friendly rivalry between Seattle and Vancouver. Contact the Mayflower Park Hotel, 206/623-8700 or 800/426/5100, in Seattle for more information.

December

Lighted Boat Parades (Seattle, Portland, Vancouver, and Victoria, BC)

In December these waterfront cities (as well as smaller Northwest waterfront communities) often have boat parades and caroling.

Farm Implement Parade (Sunnyside, WA)

One of the Northwest's most unusual parades—tractors, combines, and grape harvesters covered with lights gather the first Saturday in December and parade down the main street of this small Yakima Valley town. 800/457-8089

Winterstart Festival (Whistler, BC)

This ski resort's season begins with a celebration of mountain sports and lifestyle with a freestyle skiing event, World Cup competitions, snowboarding, great live music, and other festivities. 604/932-2394

Lynden Christmas Festival (Lynden, WA)

The holiday lighting display in the town of Lynden includes an impressive thirteen-piece Nativity scene, a carousel, skaters, and tulips; a parade celebrates Sinterklaas—the Dutch Santa. 360/354-5995

ZooLights Festival (Portland, OR)

The Oregon Zoo celebrates the holidays with the ZooLights Festival, featuring over 300,000 lights. 503/226-1561

ChristmasTime! at the Butchart Gardens (Victoria, BC)

Hundreds of thousands of twinkling lights, outlining trees, flower beds, and landcape features transform 50-acre Butchart Gardens into a holiday wonderland. Music daily starting in late afternoon. Afternoon tea is especially festive (reservations recommended). 250/652-4422 or www.butchartgardens.com

RESOURCES

Tourism Agencies

Oregon: Call Portland, Oregon, Visitors Association (POVA), 800/345-3214, for a free visitors guide. For an *Oregon Travel Guide and Accommodations Guide,* call 800/547-7842; or visit www.pova.com or www.traveloregon.com.

Washington: For a *Washington State Lodging & Travel Guide,* or to talk to a travel counselor, call 800/544-1800; or visit www.experiencewashington.com.

British Columbia: Call 800/663-6000 for province information and lodging reservations. Visit Tourism Vancouver's website at www.tourismvancouver.org.

Parks

National Parks: Call National Parks and Forest Information, 800/280-2267 or 800/365-2267, for information and reservations.

State Parks Reservations: Reservations can be made up to 11 months in advance for Washington and Oregon state parks by calling 800/452-5687.

Ferries and Tours

Washington State Ferries: The ferry system operates 10 routes in the state, 206/464-6400 or 800/843-3779 (in Washington only), www.wsdot.wa.gov/ferries. Vehicle reservations, for international travel only, must be made at least 24 hours prior to sailing.

British Columbia Ferries: Call 604/444-2890 for information; call toll free in Canada, 888/724-5223, or visit at www.bcferries.bc.ca.

Grayline Tours: Call 800/426-7532, or visit www.sightseeing.com.

Culture and Entertainment

Native American information: Affiliated Tribes of Northwest Indians, 222 N.W. Davis, Suite 403, Portland, OR 97209; 503/241-0070, fax 503/241-0072.

Oregon microbreweries: For a booklet listing many Oregon microbreweries, contact Oregon Brewers Guild, 510 N.W. Third Avenue, Portland, OR 97209; 503/295-1862, 800/440-2537; www.oregonbeer.org/~beer.

RESOURCES

Wineries

Oregon—Oregon Wine Advisory Board, 1200 N.W. Naito Parkway, Suite 400, Portland 97209; 503/228-8336 or 800/242-2363 for free winery brochures; www.oregonwine.org.

Washington—For the Yakima Valley, call 800/258-7270; for the Washington State Wine Center, call 206/667-9463, or visit www.washingtonwine.org

British Columbia—For winery touring information and map from Okanagan-Kelowna Info Centre, call 250/861-1515.

Bed-and-Breakfasts

Border to Border Bed and Breakfast Directory, a 64-page brochure, lists 350 B&Bs (most in Oregon, some in Washington); published by Moria Mountain Publishing, P.O. Box 1283, Grants Pass, OR 97528; 800/841-5448; www.moriah.com/inns.

B.C. Bed and Breakfast Directory, published by Monday Publications, 1609 Blanshard Street, Victoria, B.C. V8W 2J5; for information call 250/382-6188; www.monday.com/tourism.

METRIC CONVERSION CHART

1 U.S. gallon = approximately 4 liters
1 liter = about 1 quart
1 Canadian gallon = approximately 4.5 liters

1 pound = approximately 1/2 kilogram
1 kilogram = about 2 pounds

1 foot = approximately 1/3 meter
1 meter = about 1 yard
1 yard = a little less than a meter
1 mile = approximately 1.6 kilometers
1 kilometer = about 2/3 mile

90°F = about 30°C
20°C = approximately 70°F

INDEX

MAP INDEX

Jim MacPherson

ABOUT THE AUTHOR

Jena MacPherson's roots run deep in the Pacific Northwest. Her ancestors were pioneers on Orcas Island in the San Juan Islands and homesteaders near Kamloops, B.C., and Prosser in the Yakima Valley in Washington, where she was born and raised on the family mint farm. Her grandfather collected automobiles and loved to drive, and her British mother wouldn't fly, so Jena's earliest memories are of travel—along the backroads of the Northwest and on cross-country trains and trans-Atlantic cruise ships; it was an experience that whetted her appetite for adventure, and cultivated her interest in foods and fine cuisine. For more than 10 years Jena has reported on the Northwest for Sunset Magazine. She has also contributed to Odyssey and Journey magazines and to a book on the West by Sunset Books. Jena loves to hike, golf, kayak, and cross-country ski and follows the work of Northwest artists and artisans. She lives in Seattle, on the shores of Puget Sound, with her husband, Jim, and their dog, Molly the Magnificent.

ACKNOWLEDGMENTS

Many thanks to my editor, Suzanne Samuel, for her guidance and hard work, and to countless Northwest travel and information specialists who've assisted me over time. Special thanks to food and wine professionals Jerry DiVecchio, Sinclair Philip, Jon Rowley, Kasey Wilson, and Anthony Gismondi for teaching me to appreciate this region's special bounty. Thanks to Liz Osborne, Joanne and Leah Otness, Megan Chance, Elizabeth DeMatteo, Melinda McRae, and Sharon Thomas for easing the process. And my special gratitude to Jim and Molly for their love, help, and support.

For Travelers With Special Interests

Guides

The 100 Best Small Art Towns in America • Asia in New York City
The Big Book of Adventure Travel • Cities to Go
Cross-Country Ski Vacations • Gene Kilgore's Ranch Vacations
Great American Motorcycle Tours • Healing Centers and Retreats
Indian America • Into the Heart of Jerusalem
The People's Guide to Mexico • The Practical Nomad
Saddle Up! • Staying Healthy in Asia, Africa, and Latin America
Steppin' Out • Travel Unlimited • Understanding Europeans
Watch It Made in the U.S.A. • The Way of the Traveler
Work Worldwide • The World Awaits
The Top Retirement Havens • Yoga Vacations

Series

Adventures in Nature
The Dog Lover's Companion
Kidding Around
Live Well

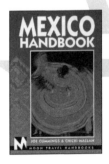